from GUTENBERG *to* BERNERS-LEE

HOW THE INVENTION OF THE MEDIA CHANGED THE WORLD

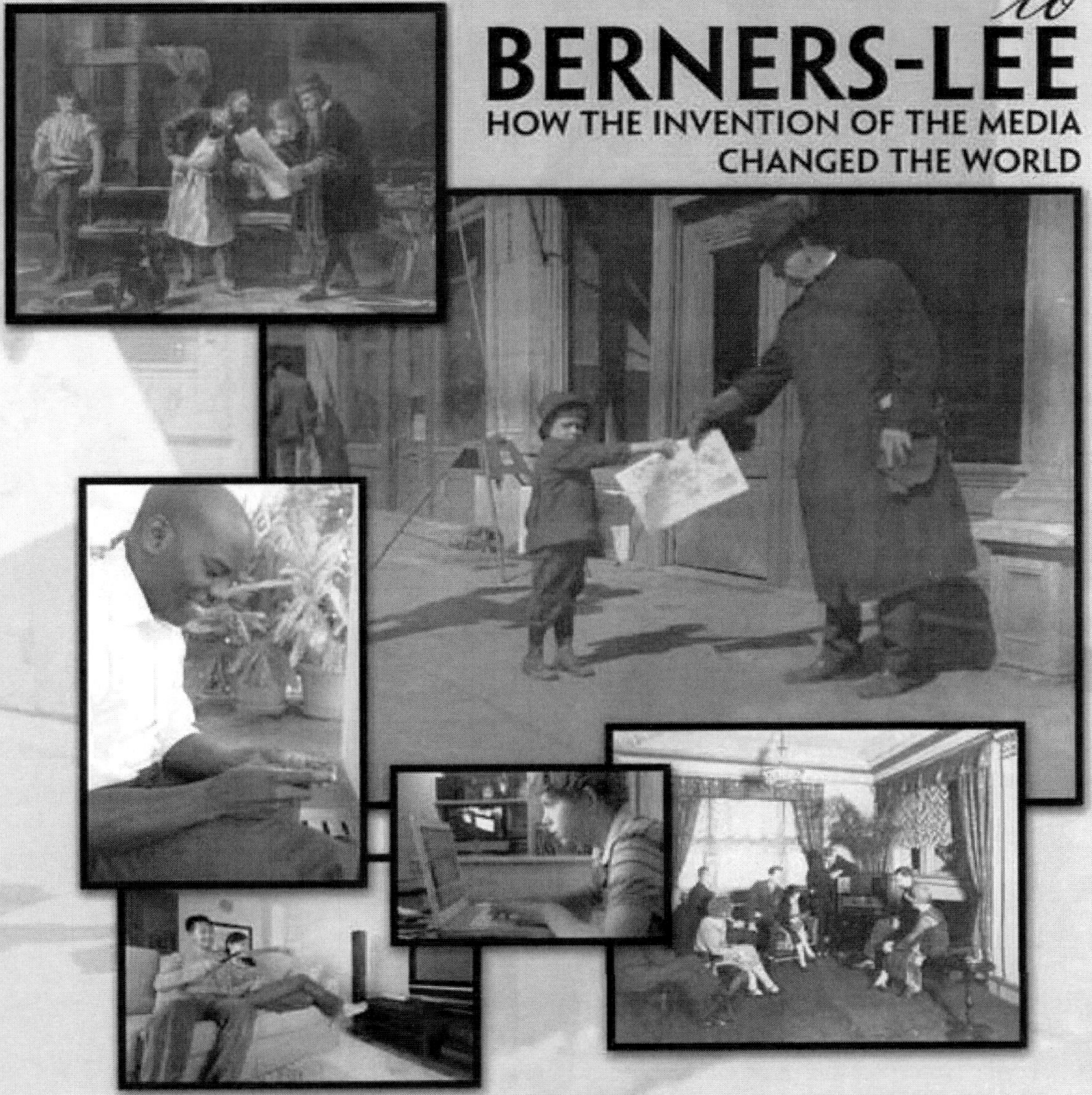

RICHARD F. TAFLINGER

Kendall Hunt
publishing company

Cover images courtesy of the Library of Congress

Kendall Hunt
publishing company

www.kendallhunt.com
Send all inquiries to:
4050 Westmark Drive
Dubuque, IA 52004-1840

Printed in the United States of America
10 9 8 7 6 5 4 3 2 1

CONTENTS

INTRODUCTION

*I*f there's anything people are good at, it's talking. Day and night, by mouth, by phone, by computer, by book and newspaper and magazine and web site, by text and Tweet, people are continually trying to get what's on their minds into other people's minds. Other creatures on Earth send out and receive messages, but humans seem to be particularly obsessed, and over the millennia they have been quite inventive in coming up with new ways to do it. These new ways we call the media: printing, radio, movies and television, the new media created by the invention of the electronic computer, the transistor and the integrated circuit chip.

And every time people were inventive, their societies—the rules of behavior and thought, the way they viewed the world and the people in it, their very sense of reality—changed.

The purpose of this book is to trace the history and development of the various media and the effects on the societies blessed, or in some people's minds cursed, with their introduction and use. It's often a crooked path, with many detours and backtracks, since no invention springs full-grown, as from the forehead of Zeus (whose story, along with those of his compatriots, influenced hundreds of years of social belief). There's the occasional surprise, the occasional breach of conventional wisdom, the occasional retelling, reformatting or recasting of the stories people have heard, and believed and lived by, for centuries.

You might ask: "Why so much about history and science? We have all these media—do we really need to know where and how and why they came about?" Well, communication has been central to being human for hundreds of thousands of years. The arrival of each new medium has changed what it means to be a human in a human society. By tracing that path we learn where we've been to get to where we are, and we make it possible to make some predictions about where we may be going and how we want to get there.

"Then why all the science?" Many people seem to believe that things just happen, that someone has a flash of genius and creates something new out of nothing, especially those things that those people have and have used for years or even centuries—after all, they've always been there. The fact is, they haven't always been there—it just seems that way. That flash of genius that created—let us say, the computer—required a long string of flashes of genius that created other things, like glass and water power and pipe organs and textile looms and paper and the theories of electricity, et cetera, et cetera, et cetera, which had nothing to do with computers. At some point, someone looked at all the bits and pieces of ideas, facts and artifacts by people who came before and thought of a way to put them together in a new way to create something new—the computer. Understanding the process of creation will help us understand the impact of science and technology on our lives and societies.

At the end, there should be a better understanding of where and how we were to get to where and how we are now. And with that understanding should come a better ability to cope with our ever-changing and ever accelerating world.

And what more could we ask?

A BASIC LOOK AT COMMUNICATION THEORY

*E*veryone knows how to communicate. Or at least, they think they do on a subconscious level: speak, write, type, and they've communicated. But do they really know what's happening? Perhaps not. So let's take a look at basic communication theory and clarify it.

First, we need a definition of communication: Communication is the transmission of a message from a source to a receiver. Seems simple. But is it?

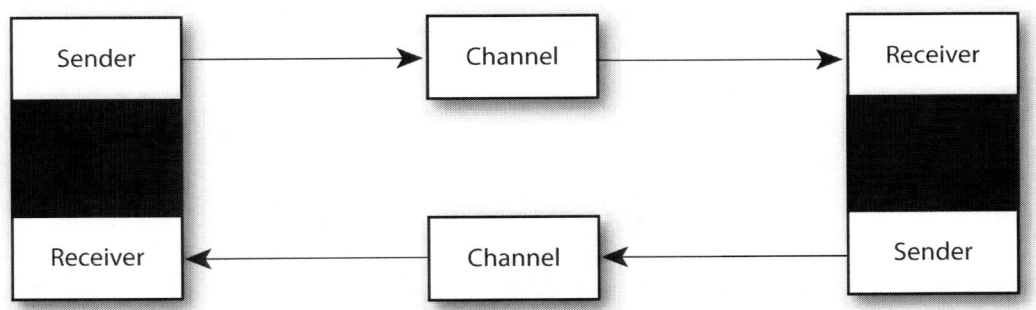

Let's take a look at the standard model of communication. First of all, there needs to be an originator of the message. This is the sender, who, of course, sends the message to a receiver. The receiver may respond, becoming a sender and sending a message to the first sender, who now is a receiver. Each of these messages is transmitted through some kind of channel.

Now it can get interesting. Both sender and receiver have a "black box," which is the way they interpret (also known as decode) the messages they receive and compose (also known as encode) the messages they send. It's in this black box that all the weird things happen, like misunderstandings or selective perception or rationalizations or any of the

Ants

other myriad ways in which we can misunderstand each other. What happens in that black box will be a big part of this book.

But let's start by looking at the channels of communication, the methods by which messages travel from the sender to the receiver and back again.

To start with, all creatures communicate in one way or another, through a variety of channels. For example, ants communicate with chemicals: They lay chemical trails that other ants can follow or emit chemical signals that other ants can pick up, and in this way they **share information and instructions**. That's communication.

Other creatures communicate by smell. For example, the cockroach: A female cockroach emits a smell that will draw males from all over the house. Male butterflies can be drawn by a female's pheromones from miles around.

Then there's visual communication. Bees dance to show direction and distance to food. The direction she faces when waggling her abdomen is the direction to the food, and the speed of the waggle gives the distance. Other creatures using visual communication include fireflies, which use their flashing lights to attract mates and prey. In fact, there is one female firefly that imitates the flashing of a female of another species. When the

Cockroach

Bees

males flock toward it, the firefly catches and eats them—talk about a femme fatale. And the skin of a squid is filled with pigment cells called chromatophores. By changing the size of those

Firefly

Squid

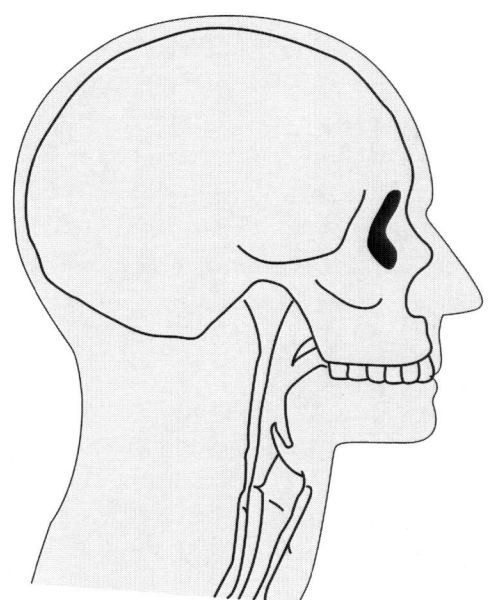

Human skull

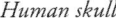
© Kendall Hunt Publishing Company

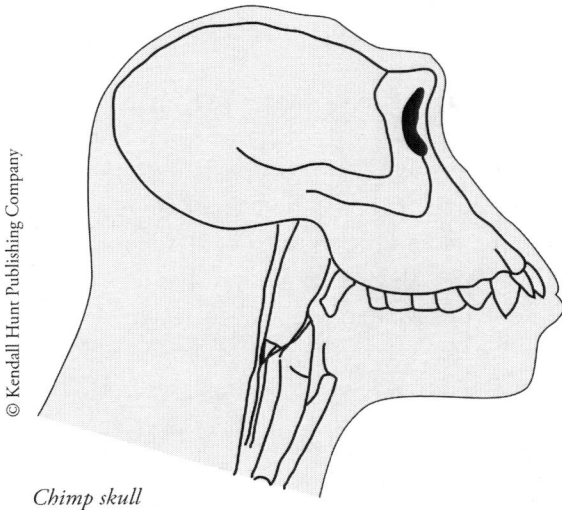

Chimp skull

cells, a squid can almost instantly change its color and the patterns of color on its skin. It does this to attract mates, to camouflage itself from predators, and to get food.

Then, of course, there's communication by sound, which is very popular throughout the animal kingdom. All kinds of creatures use sound, such as dolphins, whales, birds, monkeys, apes—and people. There're chirps and cheeps and whistles and growls and screams and . . . well, you get the idea. And, of course, there's talking.

So what is talking? Talking is the intricate manipulation of oral sounds to convey meaning. Many animals can manipulate sound, and they definitely convey meaning by doing it. So, are they talking?

Well, it can be a matter of vocabulary. Let's do a comparison. Birds—a few words, maybe 35; monkeys—perhaps 50 words; chimpanzees—perhaps 300 words; humans—in English alone, 750,000 words. Why this humongous difference?

A major difference is the way people are built. If we look at human and chimp skulls and necks, we can see big differences. First is the base of the skull. Note the arch in the human skull on top but not in the chimpanzee skull on the bottom. This creates a resonance chamber that permits a greater variety of sounds in terms of timbre. In fact, this arch is one of the first things anthropologists look for to see if an unknown skull belongs to a human or an ape.

Next, look at the placement of the larynx in the throat. It's high in the throat of a chimp, but low in the throat of a human. This lengthens the pipe, sort of like the difference between a flute and a piccolo. Again, it makes a greater variety of sounds in terms of pitch, how high or low on the musical scale a sound can be.

Finally, the human tongue is attached much lower and farther back in the mouth, allowing a greater range of movement. A human thus can enunciate with greater subtlety, making distinctions between *d* and *t,* and *s* and *sh,* and *guh* and *kuh,* and long and short vowels and schwas. People can create many more varieties of sounds than other creatures, and that feature allows them to say many more words.

■ WHY COMMUNICATE?

But why communicate at all? Well, the purpose of communication is to make connections between other members of your species. The greater the need is for connection, the greater the need is for a vocabulary to provide shades of meaning to improve that connection.

So, what are the needs?

First Need: Survival

The first and most basic need is self-protection, the instinct for survival. Every creature on earth wants to survive long enough to reproduce. There are a couple of ways to do that. First, there are numbers. In numbers, there is safety, which is why most prey animals, like cattle, sheep and gnus, band together in the hundreds and thousands. Although the individual is at risk, the greater the numbers that individual hangs out with, the lower its odds of being the one at risk. And with hundreds or thousands of paranoid partners all looking out for danger, it's likely to be spotted quickly, and the first to sense that danger will run from it, communicating to the other members of the group to take off in the same general direction to get away from the danger. With that many individuals rushing off in confusion, it's harder for a predator to zero in on a victim.

If you don't have numbers, then be the biggest badass in the neighborhood. Having claws and sharp pointy teeth, like lions, or a huge horn attached to a bad temper, like a rhino, or just plain size, like an elephant, will pretty well convince possible attackers that it would be a bad idea to annoy you.

The problem is that hominids, including humans, have neither option: They don't gather in huge numbers (chimpanzees and bonobos have troupes of twenty-five to thirty), nor do they have much in the way of natural weapons. Gorillas, of course, are badasses, and chimps have big canine teeth. But our human ancestors, when they were evolving into humans, had neither numbers (gathering in groups of perhaps only ten to twenty-five) nor claws (look at your fingernails and imagine using them to rip open a zebra), nor sharp pointy teeth, nor speed (can you outrun a rabbit—or a leopard?).

So, our hominid ancestors died out and we're all figments of our mutual imaginations.

Well, that obviously didn't happen, so what did? What our ancestors, and now us, could do is cooperate. That is, they could work together toward a common goal. This is unusual among hominids: chimpanzees don't cooperate except when the males go hunting or to war, and gorillas, orangutans and gibbons essentially want to be left alone. They certainly don't cooperate when it comes to food. Why share your fruit when all another chimp has to do is reach out a hand and pluck one of his own?

What about other animals? Lions, hyenas, wolves, wild dogs, all cooperate, but only when they're caring for young, or hunting, just like chimps. And hunting skills are best learned through example and practice: the adults demonstrate techniques;, the young copy and practice them. But hominids didn't hunt; they were hunted.

What our ancestors did was learn to cooperate in other areas other than hunting. They probably evolved in marginal conditions. The following is the reasoning behind that statement:

Our primate ancestors probably behaved similarly to today's primates. Genes guide how a body develops; bodies develop to cope with the conditions in their environmental niches; and we are 99.6% genetically like chimpanzees. (Sagan, 1992) It is reasonable to assume that humans, at one time, lived lives similar to chimpanzees'. As Carl Sagan and Ann Druyan say in Shadows of Forgotten Ancestors, "If we want to understand ourselves by examining other beings, chimps are a good place to start."

Now, chimpanzees live a comparatively relaxed life. They sleep, play, form social bonds, forage for plant foods augmented by the occasional meat acquired through hunting. It is the latter—the difference in how chimps and protohumans (meaning the hominids that will eventually evolve into human beings) gathered food—that caused a great break between them (Leakey 1978).

Chimps (and other apes) eat plant foods when and where they find them. They don't gather them or share them—each ape feeds rherself.[1]

However, when meat is available after a hunt, it becomes the center of attention. The other chimps gather around, "asking" for a share (actually, they hold out a hand in hopes they'll be given a piece of meat). Whichever chimp brings it in shares it however he wishes. It is probable that protohumans did the same thing with meat.

How protohumans handled plant foods is how they differed from other apes. Instead of an individual foraging for rherself and eating what rhe finds on the spot, protohumans began gathering the food and bringing it back to a central area. Here they shared it among the other members of the band.

Why would protohumans change the way they handled food from what is obviously a perfectly acceptable method for chimpanzees? The answer probably lies in the environment in which the protohumans found themselves. Chimpanzees inhabit tropical-zone forests where plant food is near at hand. It's so near they need merely stretch out and grab it. The search for food is more for favorites than for needs. Chimps live in an environment where resources are relatively abundant.

Protohumans changed their way of dealing with food. Since they did so, it must have been an adaptation to their environment to improve their ability to survive. The most logical reason for a change in the pattern of "eat what comes to hand" would be a lack of food that came to hand. That is, the protohuman must have evolved in a marginal environment, one in which food was scarce or difficult to gather.

It's in marginal conditions that every member of the troupe has to help every other member to find food and care for the young or they'll all die. This requires not only cooperation and coordination, but planning, thinking of the future. The best way to do each of these things efficiently is to communicate through sound rather than through example and practice. For instance, how do you tell the members of your troop that there's no more food in the area? You can't do that through example, like dragging them from place to place and pointing at the lack of food. Do you just let everyone find out for themselves, and starve in the process, while you go in search of food on your own and get eaten by lions because you now have no support? A mutual support group is a complex thing, and the more complex the cooperation became, the more complex the sounds needed to be.

Second Need: Reproduction

A second need for connecting with others is for reproduction, better known as sex. For most animals sex is straightforward, unambiguous and uncomplicated: She goes into heat, he responds. He may know she's in heat because of a scent she exudes (remember pheromones?), or her rear end turns bright red (remember visual communication?), or he dances around or builds a bower or jumps up and down or beats up every other male in sight (again, all visual cues), and she goes, "Ohhh, he's the one for me!"

It just doesn't work that way for people. Women don't go into heat, exuding a scent doesn't automatically mean they're ready and willing to have sex, despite what the Axe spray and Chanel perfume ads imply. There are no unambiguous, straightforward visual cues that say to one and all, "here I am, come and get me."

In all animals, the female chooses her mate based on criteria that the male must meet to demonstrate his superiority to other males and thus make him the best choice. The superior male will donate superior genes to any offspring. Her criteria can include strength or health as demonstrated through combat, or skill through building the best nest or catching the most food, or surviving despite handicaps, like the peacock's tail.

However, humans are weirdoes in the animal kingdom. A woman's criteria can include those used by other animals, but remember that humans are the most social creatures on earth. For humans, a man's superiority to other men is shown less through the physical than it's shown through the social. So a man has to demonstrate his superiority in those areas that the society in which the woman and man live deems important. For humans, those areas are less likely to include strength or fighting ability, but will include such things as money, power, social position, the proper political or social attitudes, self-confidence, education and who will donate, if not superior genes, then a superior chance for her and her offspring to thrive not just physically but socially—anything she thinks are signs of a superior man.

That last point should not be taken lightly. Human children have the longest childhood of any animal on Earth, measured in years, not in days or months. In most animals, the male's only job is to get the female pregnant; then he should disappear—his participation in the rearing of young is minimal to none. But for humans, the man's participation is vital to the success of offspring, providing resources that the mother and children need to succeed. So for a woman, a man's suitability as a mate isn't based only on his genes, but what else he brings to a long-term relationship.

So what people have is dating and courtship and romance. It's through these that women determine which men will satisfy their criteria for sexual compatibility. And a major element of all three is conversation. It's through talking to a man that a woman determines what kind of man he is and what he will bring to a relationship.

Third Need: Bind the Group Together

The third need for communication is to bind the group together. Remember the ants and how they share chemicals? Each colony of ants has its own specific chemical signatures, and this is how one colony of ants separates itself from another. Each species of firefly has its own sequence of lights, each species of frog its own croak, each species of bird its own songs and plumage. Each of these binds the individuals of a group together as belonging to the group and keeps out intruders. Just like the old saw, "birds of a feather flock together."

People don't use chemicals or lights or feathers. Instead, people use talking. People tend to divide themselves into groups, and use their language as a way to show they're part of the group and that people who don't use that language aren't part of the group. For example, young people, those in their teens and twenties, tend to come up with a new slang that will exclude people who aren't part of their age or social group.

Today much of that kind of slang comes from texting, like LOL and OMG and BFF. People in their teens and twenties are far more likely to do a lot of texting for social rather than business reasons than people in their thirties and older, so sprinkling their conversation with text acronyms shows they're young and "hip" and "with it," and not old fogies.

Of course, the moment old fogies start using the current slang, it's time to change the slang.

Everybody puts themselves in a group, and separates themselves from other groups. That's easy when it comes to language—the Germans speak German, the Italians speak Italian, the Japanese speak Japanese, the French speak French.

But it's not just the language; it can be the dialect of the language. You can have the British cockney, or the upper class English, who speak with different and distinct accents. Even in egalitarian America, we use language distinctions to separate people. For example, if you speak with a Southern accent, you are clearly not from the Northeast or the West, and thus you probably have different sociopolitical ideas and beliefs than people from either of those two places.

Just listen to lawyers, or doctors, or mechanics, or computer nerds, or professors nonchalantly tossing out terms, phrases and entire sentences that they fully expect, and indeed often hope, no one else will understand.[2]

The point is that people use language as an identity tool to establish themselves as part of a group, and to separate themselves from others. We **can** use appearance, such as clothes and make-up and hairstyle, but the main tool we use is how we talk.

So what does all this have to do with the theory of communication? Well, it all comes down to that black box in the model of communication. It's in that black box that we encode any messages we transmit, decode messages we receive, and encode any response. In that black box are our instinctive responses to danger, or sex, or group identity, and we filter the contents of any message through that black box.

So what's in that black box? It sure isn't the ability to follow chemical trails like ants. After all, what kind of trail could people put down—vomit? And would you want to follow it? Unless it's a really close friend.

How about pheromones? Well, humans can detect pheromones (women are much better at it than men), but they really don't have a specific meaning. And with our addiction to bathing we don't put out many pheromones anyway.

Visual cues are possible. We recognize smiles and frowns and scowls, and a variety of gestures, but they don't provide a lot of specific information, like a bee dance. Can you tell someone which direction and how far away the nearest McDonalds™ is by waggling your butt?

That leaves sound, and at that humans really excel. We've brought speech to a high level, and the ability to formulate and decipher speech is in that black box.

However, remember that talking is just noises coming out of the front of your face. Those noises have to be processed into meaning. If you don't recognize the noises as words, they're meaningless. For example, I say, "*ave, Caesar imperator, morituri tu salutant.*" But it's still just a noise to most if not all of you unless you speak Latin. The Torah says that Jehovah punished humankind for daring to be like gods by building a tower to heaven, saying, "Let us go down, and there confound their language, that they may not understand one another's speech." (Genesis 11:7 KJV) In other words, if you don't know what the noises mean, you can't communicate, and all of the advantages of oral communication disappear.

So the black box contains our ability to translate noises into meaning—but only if we speak the language. And then we have to go the other direction—translate our own thoughts into noises we can make, and hope the receiver of those noises can decipher them.

But now we run into a problem. Let us assume both the sender and receiver speak the same language, but—*do* they speak the same language?

No, that's not a contradiction. You see, the problem with words is that almost all of them have two meanings: the denotative and the connotative. The denotative meaning is the dictionary definition, the one that almost anyone can understand who speaks the language.

Let's take an example, like the word "chair." It has a denotative meaning: a piece of furniture designed for one person to sit upon. Anybody can point at such a piece of furniture and the audience will respond with "chair" (or whatever word means "a piece of furniture designed for one person to sit upon" in their language). It's this denotative meaning that students learn in foreign language classes so they'll know the word "chaise" means "chair" in French.

However, the connotative meaning is the personal definition of the word to the person who says it or hears it. That is, it's the definition each person conjures up in rhis mind in response to hearing or reading the word. That definition can be denotative in effect, but strictly individual. For example, someone hearing the word "chair" will rarely think, "Aha, a piece of furniture designed for one person to sit upon." Instead, rhe'll picture in rhis mind what rhe considers a chair to be. It could be a Queen Anne wing chair, a dining room chair, a desk chair or whatever image appears in rhis mind that represents a "chair." This is not a specific image common to everyone, but a general concept dependent on the individual.

So, the connotative meaning of a word can be denotative in effect. However, of far more importance is that the connotative meaning of a word can have a strong emotional content. In other words, a person can respond emotionally as well as intellectually to a word.

Let's take the example of the word "snake." The denotative definition, a cold-blooded legless reptile, has little emotional content. The connotative definition can have a strong emotional impact, depending on a person's perception of what a snake is. It could be a cool, dry pest eliminator, or a cold, slimy, yucky monster. Another example is "spider." Did you think "an eight-legged dual-segmented arachnid"? Unlikely. Or did you have an emotional reaction, like "a silent pest killer" or "a creepy, crawly, hairy beastie, yuck, keep it away from me, Kill it!" Whichever response you had, that's your connotative definition of the word.

Why is this difference between the denotative and connotative definitions of words of such importance? It is because the greatest impact of words comes from using the connotative meanings to affect people's emotional responses. One reason for this is that you cannot argue away emotions because they do not respond to logic. Thus, if you can make your audience agree with your point of view on an emotional level, your opponent's logical arguments won't sway them about why they shouldn't feel that way.

An example that just about everybody can relate to: You're in love; he-she-it is the most wonderful, perfect person in the world, flawless, faultless ("love is blind" is not only a cliché, it is a truism). Then he-she-it dumps you; tears, wailing, depression, etc., ensue. Your friends gather around and tell you that he-she-it is a jerk, a poltroon, not worth the tears, that he-she-it does not deserve the trauma through which you are putting yourself. You nod, agree, then you burst into tears anew, exclaiming, "but I can't help it, this is how I feel." All the logical arguments in the world about why you shouldn't feel bad about being dumped have no effect on your emotions. That's how you feel.

Aren't denotative and connotative meanings the same? In many cases, yes. In many other cases, absolutely not. There are concrete words, words that you can say and then point to an object and say, "That's what I mean when I use the word." This is handy for words that have concrete referents, like chairs and desks and cars and trucks and dogs and cats and sunsets.

But what if a word doesn't have a concrete referent? These kinds of words are abstractions, and they are really, really fuzzy in their meaning. Abstractions are almost entirely defined by their connotations. That is, fuzzy words mean whatever they mean to the speaker—and to the listener—and so they mean different things to different people. So when they use words such as truth and justice and beauty, what they intend to say may not be what the listener thinks they're saying.

Let's take an example. What is "beauty"? Well, beauty truly is in the eyes of the beholder, is dependent on culture and changes from time to time and from person to person. For example, the ultimate in feminine beauty to cavemen was a woman about as wide as she was tall. This was also true in the late Renaissance, as seen in the paintings of Reuben and Titian. The closer a woman came to being spherical, the more beautiful she was. This is true today among the Annang people of Nigeria.

For men in the eighteenth century, a woman should have wide hips, so women wore panniers that would make them up to eight feet wide. In the nineteenth century, she should have a big butt and so she wore a bustle. For the 1920s, she should have virtually no shape whatsoever.

So what's the definition of beauty? It's whatever you think it is, so when you hear that word, or any other fuzzy word, used, you may not hear what the speaker intended.

The problem with this in our little black box is that we often think we're talking about the same thing when we're not. We rarely define what we mean when we use a fuzzy word—we just assume it means the same thing to others as it means to us, which is not necessarily, and often is not, true.

Then there's another problem with "do we speak the same language." Remember when I discussed vocabulary above? Our vocabulary, the words for which we understand the definitions, is also in the black box. Well, if two people trying to communicate don't share a vocabulary in their shared language, they won't understand one another. If I say, "Michael's jejune blatherskite caused me to snirtle, yet censure his immaturity," would you know what I'm trying to tell you? Yes, every word in that sentence is in English, but they don't appear in most people's vocabulary, at least those that don't do *The New York Times* Sunday crossword puzzle—in ink. It's possible to adequately communicate with a basic vocabulary of 700 to 800 words. You can't have much in the way of a deep philosophical discussion, but you can get by for all practical purposes. Newspapers use a basic vocabulary of 2,500 words. So does the Bible. The average American uses about 3,000 words for everyday conversation. Shakespeare used 12,500, which is one reason many Americans don't understand his plays—they don't share the same vocabulary.

When you move out of the social arena and into the work arena, vocabulary gets even more strained. Just take the word "work." We all know (you know—"everybody knows"?) that work is what you do that isn't done for fun. We go to work, work on a project, do housework, etc. We all know that—unless our work is to be a physicist. In physics, work is the energy that is transferred to a body when it is moved along a path by a force, a very specific definition that the average person doesn't know. So if a physicist and an artist talk about work, they're not talking about the same thing.

How about the word "flat"? Do you work in a garage on a flat [tire]? Are you a stagehand working on a flat [piece of scenery]? A berry picker filling a flat [of fruit boxes]? An English realtor renting a flat [apartment]? Or do you think: not bumpy. Again, how someone automatically understands a word depends on who rhe is.

Then there are the specialized languages of just about every occupation. Do you know the words soffit, titrate, res loquitur? If you don't work in carpentry, chemistry or law, there's no need for you to know those words, but they're vital to those occupations.

Certainly, the more education people have, the larger their vocabulary is. Each level of education adds words and their meanings that are necessary to understand what's going on at that level. By the time someone finishes rhis doctorate, rhe's almost incomprehensible to average people—or at least that's what rhis students think.[3] But rhe's only using the words that deliver the specific meaning rhe's trying to get across rather than to speak in fuzzy generalities.

Each of these features, denotative and connotative meanings and vocabulary, are in the black box through which we filter all communication. So we filter the contents of any message we receive or send through the black box, selecting words that say what we want, rarely realizing that we aren't necessarily communicating what we think we are, and we're stuck with the old "that's not what I meant" excuse.

The black box contains anything and everything that creates the world we live in—which is not the same thing as the real world. Much of what we think is reality is actually only in our heads. As external realities, the people, the places and the things exist only as a bare framework or skeleton. Starting with the skeleton, a person's mind projects a covering and a shape onto it, along with other attributes the mind itself creates, most of which rhe gets from the society in which rhe lives. Thus, each mind creates its own world of illusion and projects it onto a minimal reality shared with others. The shared reality is those things that people can sense in common: the feel of satin, the smell of a rose, the appearance of a tree, the sound of a violin, the taste of an apple. That which we can't sense, we create in our minds, and that is individual.

However, even a shared reality is only that which people have **agreed** to share. Without the agreement there is no sharing.

People may share reality, but the world built from that reality can and does vary according to each individual's perception. Each person's world conforms to its own set of culturally defined expectations and conforms in such a way that it seems totally real and satisfactory to its creator. The taste of roasted beetle grubs can be delicious or repulsive depending on the taster's culture. The definition of feminine or masculine beauty depends on if your culture is European or Australian Bushman. Arthur C. Clarke said that any sufficiently advanced technology is indistinguishable from magic. So if a culture doesn't include television as a natural part of its world, it must be un- or supernatural. Any report of television to others in that culture is considered unreliable, no matter how much a part of the reality of other cultures television might be.

Preconceptions, prejudices, biases, cultural norms and mores, education, superstition, peer opinion—all play their role in how people create their own realities. I call this process filtering.

No matter what the senses perceive, the mind has to understand the information in terms it can believe. This information filters through the person's experience, education, culture and upbringing. These in turn can affect the person's sense of everything: politics, morality, religion, race, sex, economics, humor—everything. These filters are preconceptions, biases, prejudices and attitudes that influence the way the mind processes information and therefore how the individual constructs rhis world and reality.

For example, several witnesses see a traffic accident no one could survive. Nonetheless, nobody is hurt. All the witnesses see, objectively, the same event. Yet, what they "see" differs according to how they filter the information. A devoutly religious person will see the hand of God sparing victims; a politician may see a necessity for government action to make that intersection safer; an attorney may see a potential lawsuit; and a sexist may blame a driver of the opposite sex. It's a well-known problem to law enforcement and the legal profession: Eye witnesses can't seem to agree on what they saw. It's not the fault of the witnesses. It's simply that what is perceived must be understood, and understanding usually comes through relating new information to old. Whatever the old information is influences how the new is understood.

For another example, take the case of several young black men walking down a street. What are they? A peace gathering? A civil rights march? A street gang? A protest parade? The local black student union? Or are they simply several young black men who, by pure chance, happen to be walking in the same direction at a pace sufficient to bring them close together? Any of the above answers could be correct. They could also all be wrong. Until one asks each man what he is doing, preconception will create the reality of the observer. Of course, even the post-questioning reality can be wrong if one or more of the men lie.

What's important in terms of this book is that many of our filters are created, or at least defined, by what we get through the mass media, from what makes a person attractive to what the rules are of the group we want to belong to—our society. Is an attractive woman skinny or spherical, tall or short, tan or pale, blond or brunette or redhead? Is an attractive man muscular or brainy or rich? What words should I use to fit into a group? Which should I avoid? Should I sound erudite or cool? And should it make a difference? Media messages tell us, and each medium tells messages in different ways because of how it tells the messages. All of those filters are in that black box. And **that** is what this book is about.

■ ENDNOTES

1. No, this word isn't a typo—the spelling is deliberate. A problem with the English language is a lack of neutral singular pronouns, those that have no indication of gender. The usual way to get around this is to use circumlocutions and passive verb forms to avoid pronouns, or use both male and female pronouns at the same time (that is, he/she, her/him, etc.). To avoid both of these often awkward sentence constructions, I will use singular pronouns that are neither male nor female. What I do is add "r" to the beginning of a normal pronoun. For example:

   Rher = him or her (objective).
   Rhis = his or her (possessive).
   Rhe = he or she (nominative).

   In this way, I hope to keep the sentences flowing without falling into the trap of sexist language. Naturally, when a person's gender is important, I'll use normal pronouns.

2. Here is a personal anecdote to illustrate the point. I remember one time when I was hired to play Tevye the dairyman for a professional production of *Fiddler on the Roof.* I was talking to a techie (you know, one of the people who handle the technical aspects of a show), and he was condescendingly telling me what they were doing with some of the lighting. I heard him through, then I said something like, "but the instrument you're pointing at is an ellipsoidal, and it makes such a hard edged light. Wouldn't you get a better effect if you used an 8-inch Fresnel with a slotted gobo and a bastard amber gel, and maybe toss in a frost?" He looked at me like I'd grown another head—and it was smirking at him. After all, I was an actor and playing the

lead in the show, and all techies know that actors, especially lead actors, know nothing about tech—they just complain about it. I just smiled and said, "I designed stage lighting for a living. Don't try to snow a snowman." After that, I was the best friend of all the techies for the run of the show. I had demonstrated that I, quite literally, spoke their language.

3. Here's an example. I teach senior level college classes and have for more than twenty years. When I was given a freshman level class, I didn't adjust my thinking about vocabulary and assumed the words I used without a problem for seniors and graduate students were in everybody's vocabulary. I discovered though when giving exams that freshmen often didn't know words like impetus and demagogue, and so they didn't know what I was asking in the question. Their education up to that time didn't include those words.

2

MEDIA LITERACY

*M*edia literacy is an understanding of what the media are, what they do, how they do it, and **how** what they do can affect their audiences and societies. Always remember that you, the reader, are just as much a part of that audience as anybody else, and you are just as liable to the effects as anybody else. Being media literate allows you to consciously notice what media messages are doing and thereby to make conscious judgments about how, and whether, those messages should affect you and the society in which you live.

First, let's define what we mean by media, especially the mass media. Recall the standard model of communication from Chapter 1. The thing to bear in mind is that it's the model of interpersonal communication, not mass communication. In other words, the standard model shows what happens when one person communicates with one or at most a few others.

This model changes considerably when we start examining mass communication. It looks a lot more like the one pictured on page 14. There is one sender, but many receivers: hundreds, thousands, millions. The same message goes out to each of those receivers. However, what happens in each receiver's black box—how the person interprets that message, what rhe thinks it means and what its effects are—is individual.

Now look at the return message. Note that it doesn't go directly to the original sender. In mass communication, the original sender can only infer what any or all of those receivers send back in reaction to the message.

Let's take an example. If I'm giving a lecture to a large class, say to five hundred students, that is mass communication—I'm the original sender, and the students are the receivers. Now, I know what I'm trying to get across to them. But I have no idea how they are interpreting what I'm saying. Do they understand the concepts? Are they confused? Are they bored to tears? I can only infer how they are receiving my message. For example, if they fall asleep, I may infer that they're bored. Then again, they may have just

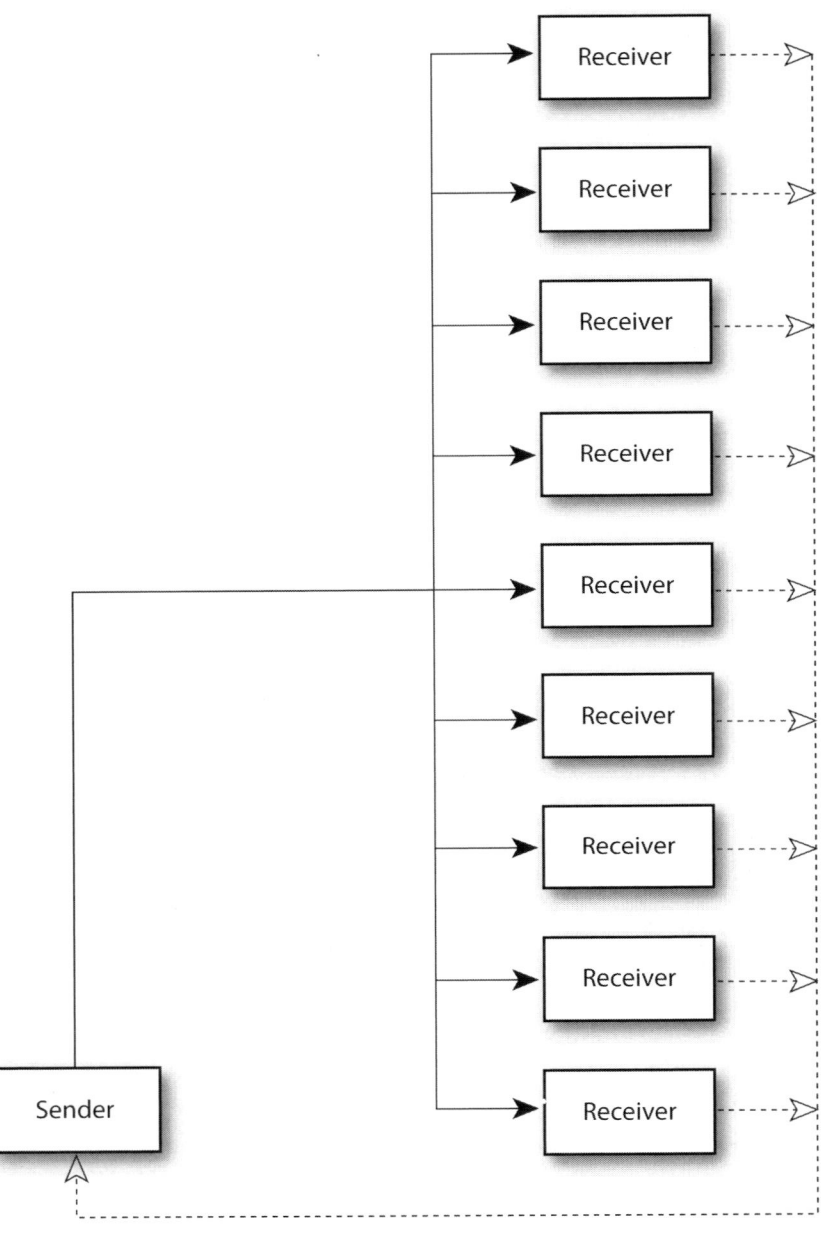

**MASS MEDIA MODEL
OF COMMUNICATION**
Communication without personal
interaction between sender and receivers

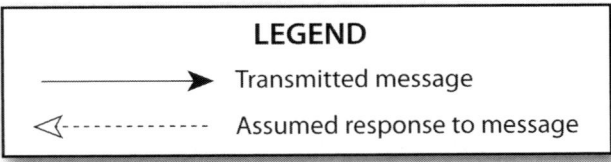

LEGEND

Transmitted message

Assumed response to message

eaten lunch, or they were up all last night partying, or they just wish they didn't have to be here. There's no way I can tell which, if any, of those inferences are right. That's why I give exams—they're the only fairly clear feedback I can get. And even those may not be an accurate reading. The answers may not tell me how well my message is getting across, but may depend on how well the students study, or if they read the book—or if they were up partying all night before the exam. It may even be that what I believed was a set of clear, well-communicated questions wasn't all that clear and well-communicated to the students, due to such factors as vocabulary or syntax that I believe everyone knows, but that it turns out some don't. So in the end I can only hope they're getting the message I'm sending the way I want them to get it, but there's no way I can actually know.

Of course, if the class is smaller, it's still mass communication, but the feedback becomes much more direct. A class with fifty people or fewer has the opportunity for comments and questions from the students that could tell me a great deal about how at least those students who participate are receiving my message. In even smaller classes, say fifteen to twenty, there's a lot of one-on-one discussion, much more like the standard model of communication.

Now that's mass communication. What about the mass media? Well, the model is the same, but the channels change (see Model page 16). See all these lines from the sender to the receiver in the diagram? Those are the channels through which a message travels from sender to receiver. For a lecture, the channel is speech—I'm talking, the students are listening. For this book, the channel is the printed word. Mass media are the mechanical channels that have been invented over the last few thousand years—writing, print, radio, sound recording, movies, television and modern electronic media. We'll be looking at those in depth. But the feedback is even more indirect and inferred than it is in a classroom. For example, the average TV executive needs to wait at least a day, and sometimes a week or a month, before rhe[1] can get any idea of how the show is getting across, and then rhe only sees the ratings, the percentage of possible TV sets that are tuned to rhis channel at any particular time, and the share, the percentage of possible TV sets that are turned on and tuned to rhis channel at any particular time. Note that those only measure how many sets are tuned into the show, not whether people liked the show or not, or what they got out of it, or even it they actually watched it or just left the set on while they did something else. So executives can only infer what they need to do to improve a show based on a string of assumptions: that a statistical sample representing less than half a percent of the population is valid; that if a set is on and tuned to a channel people are watching the set; and if they're watching, it's because they like what they see.

There are other channels of feedback, but they're usually not an accurate reflection of how the majority audience has interpreted the message. Such feedback may be from critics, but critics know a lot more about the medium and how it works, and pay much more conscious and educated attention to the message, and thus don't respond the way the average audience member would. Another type of response is letters and emails from readers, listeners and viewers, but those are not an accurate reflection of the average audience member either. Letters and emails only come from a tiny minority of audience members, and only from those that really, really hate or really, really love the message. The average person just won't go to the bother of sending in comments or complaints—they'll either continue watching the show or stop watching, or continue or stop reading the magazine or newspaper, etc., and never tell the sender of the message why.

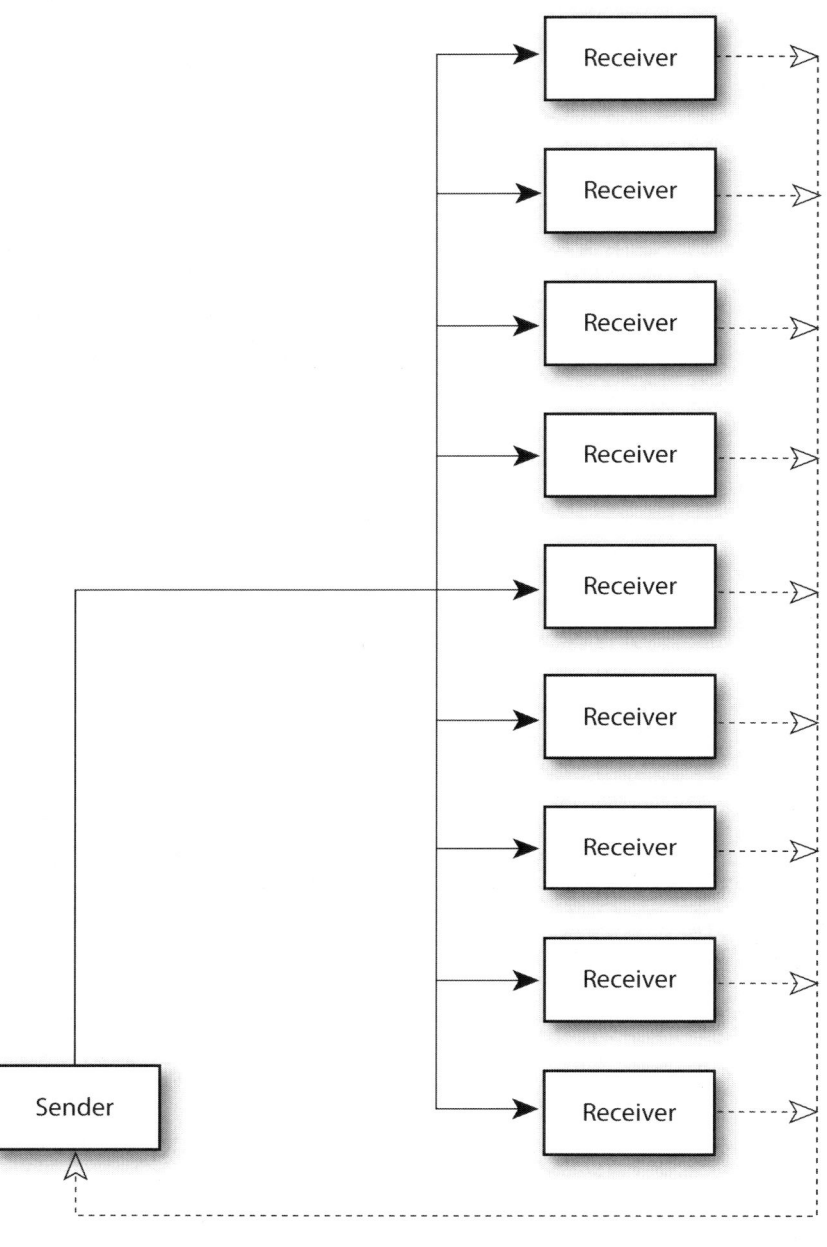

**MASS MEDIA MODEL
OF COMMUNICATION**
Communication without personal
interaction between sender and receivers

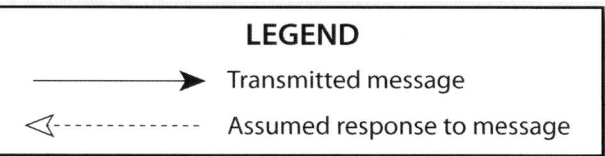

LEGEND

Transmitted message

Assumed response to message

This lack of feedback means that mass media can't quickly respond to their audiences' reactions and make corrections to improve the message. So mass media are conservative in their approach to communication. They go with what worked in the past and keep doing it. For example, when the movie *Animal House* came out and became a hit with movie audiences, TV networks quickly had three shows on the air using an approach like that of *Animal House.* When *The Cosby Show* became a hit, the next season there were three Cosby clones on the air. In each case, there was the assumption: "if we do something resembling what the audience likes, they'll like it as well." This assumption has rarely panned out.

So mass communication and mass media have some differences. However, both have major effects on their audiences. It's necessary to understand how the model of communication works to understand how mass communication works through the mass media, and also to understand those effects. In other words, it's necessary to be media literate. So let's look at media literacy.

We'll start with the basic elements of media literacy.

First, media literacy is a **critical thinking skill** (Baran 2010). By thinking critically about media messages, audience members can make judgments about those messages. So, what does that mean?

Well, the average person interacts with the media without consciously engaging with them. In other words, rhe doesn't **think** about what messages the media are sending rher, but simply absorbs the messages. People may just sit in front of the television, often using it as a background noise, or just leaf through magazines and newspapers, seeing and reading bits and pieces, or use the radio as a background to doing something else, or surf the web at random, going to sites that strike their fancy, or watch YouTube videos as they arise one after they other, or spend time on Facebook, or they text and tweet ad nauseum, spending minutes or hours sending out random thoughts to whoever wants to read them.

Think of a fifteen-year-old girl from Iowa who won the national texting championship. My first reaction is, "who puts on a national texting championship? Do the competitors take steroids to build up their thumbs?" Anyway, back to the winner. She sends an average of 14,000 messages a month. This would mean that, even taking only 30 seconds per message, she would spend four hours a day just texting. What could she possibly have to say to send an average of 500 messages a day? And what did she say about her achievement? "Let your kid text during dinner! Let your kid text during school! It pays off!" I suppose it depends on how you define "pays off."

Notice the wording in this element of media literacy: "critical," "thinking" and "skill." **Critical** doesn't mean, "I don't like it." It's entirely possible you may not like "it," whatever **it** is. But why don't you like it? Can you explain your reaction to it? Can you put into words why you don't like it? To understand and explain means you must examine a media message for its content, its intent and its effect on the audience—including you.

But to examine a message, you must **think**—consciously—making an effort to understand the message below the surface. This requires that you not just react emotionally to a message—"I don't like it," or "I love it," or "how dare they do that?"—but put into words what you see and hear and how what you see and hear may affect an audience. Remember at all times that we think in words, not in feelings. Feelings aren't amenable to logic or reason, can't be changed through discussion, are visceral rather than intellectual. However, feelings are easier than thinking. Feelings are just automatic, instinctive reactions—no thinking involved. Thinking requires a conscious effort, an effort that many people are, or at least seem to be, unwilling to put forth when interacting with the media, either because it's too much work or because they see little value in it.

So this conscious thinking is a **skill**, one that must be cultivated and practiced until it becomes automatic, no different than learning to play a sport or a musical instrument—or to text at 70 words a minute.

Second, media literacy requires an understanding that **media messages are deliberated designed and constructed to affect their audiences**. Every word and image is a deliberate decision on someone's part. There are no accidents—someone sits down and consciously thinks (there are those words again) about every word, every image, every camera angle, every element of the message with the deliberate intent of affecting the audience in a certain way.[2]

Add to that the fact that each medium has its own way of delivering those messages. How those messages are constructed and delivered affects how the audience perceives what they're saying. For example, the process of print media is the use of words in sentences and paragraphs, using the syntax and grammar of writing to deliver their messages, often combined with still photographs. Television also uses words, but it uses the syntax and grammar of **speech** rather than of writing.

You may ask yourself, "is there a difference between written and spoken syntax and grammar?" and the answer is yes. I've done a lot of scholarly writing, and I've written it to be read. This often means using long sentences, lots of subordinate clauses, long words. It's common when writing to put 30 or 40 or even 50 words in a sentence. Why? Because when someone reads, rhe sees the words and thinks about them and can handle long, convoluted sentences.

However, speech is different. The average person, in English, speaks at a rate of approximately 140 words per minute. This means a listener can only hear about 17 words in a row and remember how the sentence started—it's an artifact of short term memory, which lasts just long enough, about 7 to 8 seconds, for you to look up a phone number, dial the first five numbers, then hang up and have to look it up again.[3]

Writing to be said rather than read requires shortening and simplifying the text. A reader can always go back and reread a sentence if rhe doesn't think rhe understood it the first time. However, a listener can't go back and rehear one. So when I've delivered papers at conferences, I've completely rewritten them, turning them into something to be said, not read.

So, print media is written to be read. Print is a linear form of communication that follows a thought from beginning to end in order to communicate in sentences with a logical structure and to place the words in the proper order to convey meaning. For example, in English there's a big difference between a housedog and a dog house (and an even bigger difference between a house cat and a cat house). Note that the order of the words determines the meaning. In addition, print requires descriptors to clarify how the reader should interpret the intent. For example, you read a character's line in a book: "It's a beautiful day." What does it mean? Without descriptors, there's only one way to interpret the line, it's obvious, overt meaning that the person is pleased with the weather. However, let's try it with the descriptors:

"It's a beautiful day," he said sarcastically, staring at the leaden sky pouring rain.

Suddenly the meaning is entirely different. In print, there's no way to tell the intent without the descriptors.

Broadcast writes to be said, and TV combines the words with moving images. This means that TV is a gestalt, communicating an entire idea in a single burst of image combined with either supporting or negating words not necessarily delivered in sentences. It's a mass of information given in a single shot with no way to follow a thought. The thing is, images often have a greater impact on the audience than the words. An example was an ABC News report on President Ronald Reagan. The words were critical of Reagan. The report pointed out things that were going wrong, or legislation that wasn't going anywhere, or foreign policy problems. However, the video accompanying the voice-over words showed a smiling and animated Reagan meeting and greeting people happy to see him on the street and in bars and restaurants. The **intent** of the story was to be critical, but the **effect** was positive. In fact, Reagan's press secretary thanked ABC News for their positive report on Reagan—the moving images attracted and held the attention of the audience far more than the voice-over narrative, turning that narrative into just a background noise to the pictures, which was not ABC's intent at all.

The print examples above demonstrate the point. A simple picture of a house dog, a dog house, a house cat or a cat house is not only instantly recognizable without any further discussion, but it will conjure up in the audience's minds a variety of related images and concepts that don't appear with mere printed words. The scene of a man standing under the clouds getting soaked and saying sarcastically, "It's a beautiful day," requires no other words—although to make that point I obviously had to use a lot of words to make up for the fact that you're reading this, not watching it.

The next element of media literacy is the need to be aware **that the media, the messages they carry and how they deliver those messages, have an effect on the individual and, by extension, on society** (Baran 2010). Most people think the media are just "there" and that they really have no impact other than using up time or entertaining or providing some information. Well, that's true, but it's not the whole story. Yes, the media do use up time and entertain and provide information, but the effect can go far beyond that. Think of advertising—it doesn't just provide information about products or services, it tries to create a desire for those products or services.

News doesn't only provide information, it tells us what's important and worth thinking about—at least, in the minds of those who give us the news. But what they **don't** consider important or worth thinking about, the audience doesn't either. Indeed, they don't even **know** there are other things to think about. For example, at one point Paris Hilton, the celebrity famous for being famous, was sent to jail. When she was released a short time later, CNN News spent the next 90 minutes, without a commercial break, showing her limo driving home, following it with a helicopter the whole way. Apparently, the most important thing in the world during those 90 minutes was Paris Hilton driving home. Forget wars and finance and politics and crime—Paris Hilton driving home was the only thing CNN apparently believed people should be thinking about.

Third, media literacy requires a person to **develop strategies for analyzing and discussing media messages** (Baran 2010). For the majority of people, the interpretation of a media message is in the hands of the creator, not the consumer. Few people consciously notice and think about the effect on themselves of such things as lighting or camera angles, or the choice and placement of pictures in a magazine or newspaper, or the music and sound effects in movies or on TV. Thus, if the audience doesn't develop a strategy to analyze messages, the creators of the messages have all the power in determining how to affect the audience.

Media literacy is taking that power into your own hands, not being a passive receiver of someone else's meaning. It means figuring out the meaning for yourself, and whether and how it will affect you. For example, there is an ad for a cosmetic product called Erace line filler. It's an unretouched picture, which means it wasn't airbrushed or Photoshopped to remove the wrinkles, of a woman's face. Clearly, the product works because there are no wrinkles on the side with the make-up, but there are plenty on the other side. However, the average person doesn't notice the lighting—after all, light is how we see things in the first place and so we don't really notice it. The thing is, we can see wrinkles because of the shadows they make, and in this picture all the light is coming from the woman's left side, the side with the make-up, so the wrinkles are washed out. All the shadows are on her right side, so the wrinkles show. If you don't consciously notice the lighting, you could be misled into thinking the ad is saying one thing—that the make-up will cause your wrinkles to disappear—when it may not be saying that at all. Unless, of course, you carry your own lights around with you everywhere you go.

Fourth, media literacy means cultivating the ability to **enjoy, understand and appreciate media content** (Baran 2010). This one might be perceived as an elitist approach, that everything in the mass media is aimed at the lowest common denominator in the audience, in other words, the stupid and low class, and therefore is beneath consideration. Well, that's not true. True appreciation and enjoyment of media messages come from seeing below the surface and discovering the many ways in which a message can be perceived and meaning derived.

For example, my all time favorite author is Terry Pratchett, a British writer who was England's most popular author before J. K. Rowling hit the big time with her Harry Potter books. I've got a copy of every book he's ever written, and I've read them all at least ten times—that's how much I enjoy them. They're funny—laugh-out-loud funny, and how often do you laugh out loud while reading a book?

What makes Pratchett's books my favorites is not the fantasy or the laughs, although those are a big part of it—it's the depth that's in them. They're not just fantasy and laughs but filled with the finest social satire since Jonathan Swift and his *Gulliver's Travels.* Pratchett takes on everything: politics, social unrest, rock and roll music, theatre, religion, the press, fairytales, everything. He takes what people accept as right and natural and "the way it is," and he stands it all on its head. This allows the readers to examine their most fundamental beliefs and begin to analyze them, understand them and even question them. You could read Pratchett's books just for the fun—and they are a lot of fun—but the real enjoyment comes from the appreciation of what they say about us and the societies we live in.

Think of the *Daily Show with John Stewart* or *The Colbert Report.* They could be enjoyable if you don't know what's happening in the world, although I doubt it, but the shows are designed and created for a more sophisticated, media literate audience, people who interact with and understand on a deep level a wide variety of media messages, including the news and popular culture. If you don't know who people like Ahmadinejad or Berlusconi or Netanyahu are, or Dick Cheney or Barbara Bachman or Mark Sanford, and what they've done and what they've said, you wouldn't get half the jokes on *The Daily Show* or *The Colbert Report.*

Family Guy, an animated situation comedy on Fox, is filled with popular culture references, including television shows, movies, books and the celebrity culture. *The Simpsons* and *South Park* also take on social and political issues. All three are aimed at the media literate. You might enjoy them on a surface level, but the real enjoyment comes from spotting and understanding the deep references.

The news is firmly rooted in the beliefs and worldview of the society for which that news is produced. In addition, each news organization targets an audience that holds certain beliefs about how society does, or should work, and angles what it presents as news to fit that audience's views. To be media literate is to recognize this fact and to filter what is presented as news through that recognition. Realize also that word and image choices can slant what look like facts into an expression of opinion that has the intent of altering or hardening a particular point of view in the audience.

You can look for the deeper meanings, and explorations and discussions of society and its beliefs, in almost all media messages, and if you can't find anything else, they're probably not worth your time. You may enjoy the action and explosions and just plain noise in many action movies, such as *Transformers II,* but is there anything else there, or is it all just "sound and fury, signifying nothing"? You might be amazed if you looked deeper.

Fifth, to be media literate requires the **ability to create media messages**, not just absorb them (Baran 2010). Here I'm not talking about becoming a writer or a director or a film editor or another professional in the world of producing media messages. If you want those skills, you go to schools that teach those subjects. No, in this case I'm talking about the production of communication forms that all of you will be doing for the rest of your lives.

Can you write effectively? By this, I mean get what's in your mind into someone else's mind efficiently and accurately, with proper organization and spelling and grammar and syntax and punctuation? Or do you just throw words in a row until you think you've said it? Can you create a presentation for class or work? Can you make a YouTube video or a web page? Just about everybody thinks they can write a TV show (I certainly get enough emails from people asking how to get their shows on TV—the answer is: you don't), but when people get into my screenwriting class, they realize just how hard it is and how much you have to know to do it properly.

Necessary production skills have changed over the years. Of course, everyone starts with pencil and paper, but they needed to learn what to do with them, like read and write the alphabet and use punctuation. By the 1940s, learning to type, on a manual typewriter, became necessary. Math was done with a slide rule, because electronic calculators weren't invented until the 1970s, and they were the size and weight of a brick and only did arithmetic. Want to make many copies of a document? Learn to use a mimeograph duplicator—that doesn't even exist anymore. Then computers came along, and media literacy required learning spreadsheets and word processing. Today there's the need to create web pages and video edit and upload and download to the Internet and know many other skills. All of these production skills are necessary in today's world if you want to succeed. All the new media require all the new skills. Without them, welcome to the wonderful world of fast food—where you *still* have to know how to use a computer—or at least recognize a hamburger so you can hit the right key.

Sixth, a person who is media literate can **make informed decisions about the performance of the media** (Baran 2010). In order to do that rhe needs to understand the pressures on media people as they try to do their jobs, the ethical and moral obligations under which they operate. For example, it's legal to show violence on TV, but is it ethical? Do the media have a moral obligation to do nothing that may offend someone, like using sex appeal in ads or having gay characters in TV shows? But who determines what is offensive, and to whom? What one person finds offensive may not bother someone else at all, and vice versa. So, whose morals rule?

Add in the fact that all media must be able to financially support themselves, and there may be conflicts the media have to deal with between reporting the facts and losing their sponsors. For example, Glenn Beck pushes his audience's buttons with loaded language and appeals to emotion. He also freely admits that what he's doing is entertainment—that he gives his audience what it wants to make money for Fox News—and for himself. Without understanding all this, how can you have anything but a knee-jerk reaction, an illogical, emotional gut reaction? Or how can you create reasonable arguments about what to do about what the media produce? Answer? You can't.

As an analogy to help understand how media literacy works and its importance, let us say you play a sport, like soccer. You know the rules, you know the player positions, you know various offensive and defense play and strategies. When you watch a game, you make informed judgments about how well or poorly a player is doing or a play is progressing because you know those things, and you often imagine how you would do something else than what the players are doing. In other words, you enjoy watching the game. Now take someone else, myself, for example. I don't know the rules, I don't know the player positions, I couldn't tell a good play from a trip over a divot. I don't enjoy watching soccer—to me it's just a bunch of guys in short pants running around at random and kicking a ball.

The analogy holds true for media literacy. Let's continue the analogy.

Understanding soccer is a **critical thinking skill**. You must be able to consciously notice the performance of each individual player and what is happening in the game at each individual moment in order to evaluate what is good or bad, or how those performances contribute or detract from the ultimate end, which is scoring or defending a goal. Without that skill, the game is meaningless activity.

To appreciate a game of soccer requires knowing that the movements and placements of every player are **deliberate, designed and constructed to affect the outcome of the game**. Otherwise, it just looks like random running and kicking.

Game literacy requires **developing strategies for analyzing and discussing game play** in order to improve your understanding of rules and plays and outcomes.

Game literacy allows fans to **enjoy, understand and appreciate** game play.

The **ability to create game strategies and plays** allows for greater enjoyment of not only watching but playing the game.

Game literacy allows a fan or a player to **make informed decisions about the game**.

Notice how, just by changing the word "media" to "game," all of the elements of literacy apply, and so media literacy isn't so alien a concept after all. In addition, media literacy can have a greater impact on your life than understanding soccer. You may like the game, but the media affect and indeed shape your entire view of the world and everyone and everything in it. That seems important.

Now comes the hard part. The above are things a media literate person must know. However, to become media literate, there are things a person must **do**, and most of them require making a conscious effort and changing how rhe thinks—about the media, about society and about rherself.

First, a person must **be willing and able to pay conscious attention to media messages** (Baran 2010). By paying conscious attention, rhe will be able to not only to understand the content, but to filter out much of the noise that is the bane of all communication. It's easy to veg out in front of the tube, just letting it wash over you while you do other things, like eat or talk or read. But just because you're not paying attention doesn't mean there's no effect on you. Anything that distracts you from the message being presented to you is noise, not just sounds that interfere with concentration. Noise could be thinking about what to make for dinner, or if you forgot something, or if you'll get a chance to talk to that cute person in class, or the phone ringing, or a knock at the door, or any of a myriad of other distractions both internal and external. Any kind of noise makes it more difficult to consciously understand that message. It takes effort to actually pay attention, but without that effort you're a passive receiver of whatever the message may do to you.

Second, **understand and respect the power of media messages** (Baran 2010). Much of mass media is banal, rather silly, and even stupid, so it's easy to dismiss media content as beneath serious consideration or too simple to have any effect or influence on its audiences. However, even the silly can have an effect if you're hit with it often enough. I remember when the top show on TV was *Friends*. Apparently everyone was watching it. And everyone was singing the theme song, "I'll be there for you . . ." Do you imagine for a moment that anyone deliberately set out to memorize those lyrics? Or did they just hear them so often they got stuck in their heads? The songs you listen to most often on your MP3 player have the same effect; you can sing along because you're heard them so often. That is a passive effect, and it can be detrimental since people tend not to guard themselves against things they don't pay any attention to.

There's also a thing called the third-person effect. This is the attitude that "**other** people are affected by media messages, but I'm not." This is, of course, delusional. Remember that those people you think are affected are the same people who think you are affected. And all of you are right. Media messages are deliberately **designed** to affect their audiences, and nobody is totally immune. The only thing you can do is to be consciously aware of the power of messages and that they **can** influence you. Only then can you counter them.

Third is the **ability to distinguish emotional from reasoned reactions when responding to messages, and to act accordingly** (Baran 2010). Many if not most media messages are designed to cause an emotional reaction. But always remember that emotion does not react to nor can it be countered by reason and logic. In other words, you can't talk yourself out of an emotion. Just try to talk yourself out of love, or to develop an effective, logical argument that will remove the pain of a breakup or the loss of a loved one. It can't be done.

The only thing you can do is to realize that you are reacting emotionally and try to figure out why. What is it about those pictures or sounds or words that make you feel pity or fear or all warm and runny inside? The message is punching your buttons—How? Remember that we think in words, not in feelings. So once you can put your reactions **into** words, you can think about those reactions.

Fourth is **developing a heightened expectation of media content** (Baran 2010). There's a concept in TV watching called the L-O-P—Least Objectionable Program. Most people don't expect much from watching TV. There may be a few favorite shows watched on a regular basis, but what about the rest of time the set is on? Most people consider it just a background to their lives. So they're more likely to just flip through the channels until they find something passable—the least objectionable program—than to check the listings to find a specific show to watch.

If you expect more from your media, you consciously seek out those messages that give you the greatest satisfaction instead of just going with "what's on." I watch a lot of

TV—after all, it's my job. But I seek out shows that satisfy me in some way: good writing, good acting, good direction, great entertainment or messages that can impact and inform my world. My favorites include shows like **House** and **Bones** and **Eureka** and **So You Think You Can Dance**; **Mythbusters** and **Dirty Jobs** and **Modern Marvels**; just about anything on the Science Channel and the History Channel and the Discovery Channel. Out of the 187 channels I have available, I watch perhaps 25 on a regular basis. Most of the rest don't meet my expectations. But just in case, I do check the listings to make sure I don't miss something I think will meet them, and often I find something. I rarely just channel surf. Now that's a waste of time.

Fifth is to **know genre conventions and learn to recognize when they're being mixed** (Baran 2010). Genre refers to the different categories into which media messages can be divided, such as TV sitcom or TV evening news or horror movie or entertainment magazine or mystery novel. Each genre of media message distinguishes itself from other genres through such elements as appearance (use of color and light and sets, etc.—the spectacle element of neo-Aristotelianism); sounds (music, sound effects, etc.—the music element of neo-Aristotelianism); language (the diction element of neo-Aristotelianism); and others that are distinct to that genre. When an audience encounters them, they immediately know what to expect. Think of **these** elements: a dark, foggy night; a dirt road winding through a dense forest, Spanish moss hanging from the tree limbs and dripping water; ominous arrhythmic music consisting of bass strings and the occasional high pitched violin screech; a car approaches, seen only by its headlights dimly illuminating the path; cut to view through the windshield at a young, worried-looking couple. I'm sure you recognize these elements, conventional ones used in many horror movies, and you'd be right (it's from **Friday the Thirteenth, Part Six: Jason Lives**). However, what if the scene started in a bright, sun-lit wheat field with upbeat happy music instead of dark ominous woods with equally dark ominous music? It would be confusing since it would be mixing the conventions of a horror film with those of a comedy. So which is it? If the conventions are mixed, how do you decide? You need to understand the conventions, but you also must consciously examine the content to make a decision.

For example, watch the first scene from Steven Spielberg's classic **Jaws**. It starts out with the conventions of a beach party movie, but suddenly the conventions change to that of a horror film, thereby increasing the fear factor by surprising the audience with the unexpected.

Sixth is to **think critically not only about media messages, but about the credibility of those who produce and distribute those messages** (Baran 2010). We live in a democracy, a form of government dependent upon the informed participation of the citizens. However, as discussed before, people get most of their information through the media rather than through personal experience. Thus, it is vital that people be able to trust the media to tell the truth and not distort information through distortion, selective editing, omissions or falsehood. This is why news media are often referred to as the fourth branch of government, the watchdog over the other three. But does that mean we should believe everything they report? Simply because Fox News is "Fair and Balanced," or MSNBC is "The Place for Politics," should we accept everything they say as reliable, or even credible? News media, just like all media, are owned and operated by people, and all people have their own biases and prejudices and, given a forum, can fall prey to using that forum to promote their own agenda. In addition, news media need an audience to pay the bills. So all media slant their messages in some way to appeal to an audience, constructing their messages to reflect what their audiences already think or believe. The degree that messages are slanted depends a great deal on the agenda of those who control the media, as well as the biases of the audience they wish to appeal to—the greater the underlying bias, the greater the slant to appeal to that bias. Remember that just because something is said doesn't necessarily make it true.

Finally, **gain an understanding of media content as a text that provides insight into our culture and our lives** (Baran 2010).

This, in terms of this book, is the biggie. The media have always had major influences on culture and society throughout history. The mere fact of the invention of a medium of communication has irrevocably altered every society that has received the benefits, or to some the detriments, that that new medium has introduced. It is this aspect of media and society that this book will concentrate on—the invention of the various media, and the effect those media had on their, and our, society.

Of course, the first thing we need to understand is what a society is, and how it becomes a society and maintains itself. That will be the topic of the next chapter.

■ ENDNOTES

1. No, this word isn't a typo—the spelling is deliberate. A problem with the English language is a lack of neutral singular pronouns, those that have no indication of gender. The usual way to get around this is to use circumlocutions and passive verb forms to avoid pronouns, or use both male and female pronouns at the same time (that is, he/she, her/him, etc.). To avoid both of these often awkward sentence constructions, I will use singular pronouns that are neither male nor female. What I do is add "r" to the beginning of a normal pronoun. For example:

   Rher = him or her (objective).
   Rhis = his or her (possessive).
   Rhe = he or she (nominative).

   In this way, I hope to keep the sentences flowing without falling into the trap of sexist language. Naturally, when a person's gender is important, I'll use normal pronouns.

2. The exceptions are live events on TV, radio or streaming on the Internet. Here the provider of the message has no control over the specific contents of the message, which can lead to controversies such as Janet Jackson's "wardrobe malfunction" at the Super Bowl, or the occasional "f-bomb" at an awards ceremony. However, today live media are not actually live. The standard is to record a live event and send the recording out on a seven-second delay, providing the time to block, bleep or blur anything that the audience might object to. This again is a case of deliberate decision making.

3. Note the sentence you just finished. It contains 59 words. If I had spoken those words you probably wouldn't remember how it started, about the 17 words in a row. However, that's not a problem when reading the sentence. Well, actually it is. Many people today tend to hear the words silently in their heads when reading, as if they were reading them aloud. This means their reading speed is no faster than their speaking speed, and the problem with short-term memory remains. Try an experiment: Keep track of how many times you have to go back and reread a sentence to understand it (a common problem for students reading textbooks). If the number is higher than one, you're reading too slowly and might as well move your lips. Your mind is perfectly capable of extracting the meaning of the text if you look at the words without saying them, letting your eyes scan along the lines. With a little practice it will become automatic. Once you start reading at 300, or 400 or 1,000 words per minute, reading becomes a joy, not a chore. Try it.

STORYTELLING

"Suppose you'd watched the slow accretion of snow over thousands of years as it was compressed and pushed over the deep rock until the glacier calved its icebergs into the sea, and you watched an iceberg drift out through the chilly waters, and you got to know its cargo of happy polar bears and seals as they looked forward to a brave new life in the other hemisphere where they say the ice floes are lined with crunchy penguins, and then wham—tragedy loomed in the shape of thousands of tons of unaccountably floating iron and an exciting soundtrack…

"You'd want to know the *whole* story."

(Terry Pratchett, *The Thief of Time*)

oes the above confuse you? Did you think, "That's not the way it goes"? It's not the story you expected, is it? The *Titanic* from the perspective of the iceberg, not the ship? Why did you think, "That's not the way it goes"? The answer is, you know how the story goes; after all, you've read about the sinking of the *Titanic* or seen at least one of the movies made about it, and it's always from the point of view of the ship and passengers, not the iceberg and any animals that may have been on it. However, if you think about it, the story could be told either way—the facts, the *reality* of the event, would be the same, but the *story* would be different. An understanding of the role that stories play in the creation and maintenance of societies, and (of especial interest to us) how the media communicate those stories, is important in understanding the creation and maintenance of societies, and in terms of this book, media literacy.

There are many different techniques used to analyze the media. However, they are not part of this book. Nonetheless, there is one that we'll find important to this book, and that is a technique called neo-Aristotelianism.

Neo-Aristotelianism is based on Aristotle's work *Ars Poetica,* or the *Art of Poetry.* What he did was analyze Greek plays to find what they had in common in telling their stories. He found that all stories contained six elements: action, character, thought, diction, music and spectacle.

■ ACTION

Action refers to what happens in a story. There are six parts of action that must occur in a certain order for there to be a story. First is **exposition**, the information you need in order to understand what happens later, like time and place and who the major characters are. It establishes the status quo in the universe of the story where there's nothing wrong and the world is in equilibrium, in balance.

There are many ways the exposition can be delivered to the audience. Shakespeare sometimes used a character, as in these opening lines of *Romeo and Juliet*:

> PROLOGUE: Two houses, both alike in dignity,
> In fair Verona, where we lay our scene,
> From ancient grudge break to new mutiny,
> Where civil blood makes civil hands unclean.
> From forth the fatal loins of these two foes
> A pair of star-cross'd lovers take their life;
> Whose misadventur'd piteous overthrows
> Do with their death bury their parents' strife.
> The fearful passage of their death-mark'd love,
> And the continuance of their parent's rage
> Which but their children's end naught could remove,
> Is now the two hours' traffic of our stage;
> The which, if you with patient ears attend,
> What here shall miss our toil shall strive to mend.

The opening crawl of text up the screen for the *Star Wars* movies is another example of revealing the exposition. For most television shows, the opening credits provide the basic exposition of locale, dates and main characters and their relationships. For example, the credits for the program *CSI* show each member of the regular cast of characters working on forensic science experiments, analyzing crime scene evidence to solve crimes. There are also brief shots of Las Vegas to establish location, and crime scene tape to establish that this is a police show.

With the exposition establishing the universe in which the story will be told, it's time to go to the next part of action: the problem.

The problem is something that arises that upsets the equilibrium, throws the universe of the story out of balance. It could be a crime (crime dramas such as *CSI*), a couple of people that meet (romantic dramas and comedies such as *You've Got Mail*), a need to find something (the Indiana Jones movies), the arrival of something dangerous (e.g., *Independence Day* and *Armageddon*). Whatever the problem is, it needs to be solved, and the rest of the story is about solving the problem and restoring the balance.

Of course, there's nothing straightforward about solving the problem. The protagonist, the main character, says and does things to explore the problem to find a solution. At a point, a crisis, rhe thinks rhe knows enough about the problem to know how to solve it and rhe applies that solution. Naturally, it's the wrong solution—rhe doesn't know enough (the crime evidence is incomplete), or the application of the solution reveals a new facet of the problem (the couple discovers that there's something about the other person that divides them), or the antagonist, the one who caused the problem in the first place, does something to interfere with a solution. This results in a complication, an obstacle to solving the problem (need to find more evidence, need to change the other person, need to fight the villain). So rhe has to continue exploring, but now the solution must not only take care of the original problem, but the complications as well. Rhe keeps applying the wrong answer until finally, in the climax, rhe applies the correct solution and the problem is solved. We're now back at an equilibrium, where there are no more problems and everything's wonderful.

There may or may not be a denouement, which is a final short scene that simply shows there are no problems as life goes on.

■ CHARACTERS

Characters are the agents that carry out the action. Now, there are two words that you need to know and remember in order to understand how stories work, and they are part of character. The first of those words is: **Want**. Every character must want something, and every character must want something different. For example, the villain wants to take over the world, and the hero wants to prevent that.

This, naturally enough, results in the next word: **Conflict**. Because everyone wants something different, it results in conflict between the characters. This is important to remember: Without conflict there is no story. The problem sets the conflict in motion; the conflict between the characters drives the story as they work to either solve the problem (the protagonist) or prevent the solution (the antagonist), and the climax resolves the problem, thus ending the conflict. So when the conflict's over, the story is too.

■ THOUGHT

Then there's thought. Thought is why the story is being told. A story affects the way people see the world and their place in it. The way a story is put together can follow the rules of society, define the rules of society, or even create the rules of society if the storyteller has enough power.

Remember want, conflict, and thought. They'll be important later.

The last three elements of neo-Aristotelianism are how you tell the story. **Diction** refers to the dialogue, the words used and how they're said. **Music** refers to what we hear, all the sounds including music and sound effects. **Spectacle** refers to what we see, including things like scenery and lighting and costumes and make-up and relationships between things and camera angles and any other visual elements of the story. Each of these elements can have an effect on how an audience perceives the action, characters and thought.

■ SO WHAT?

So, why is all this important? Well, it's because humans understand themselves, society, the world, and even the universe through stories, not through facts. People should possibly be classified, not as Homo sapiens, the wise man, but as pan narrans, the storytelling chimp (Pratchett 2002). Understanding stories can help us understand ourselves and how stories affect us.

Let's see how that works. Look at this. Obviously, it's the Moon. But when you see it hanging in the sky—what on Earth would make you think it's hanging? When you look up into the night sky do you think about selenology (that's the Moon equivalent of geology) or gravity or ballistics or orbital dynamics or the other aspects that keep the Moon from either spinning off into space or slamming into the Earth? Of course not. Instead of considering the scientific aspects of the Moon, we make up stories about it, and those, in our thoughts and beliefs, is what the Moon is.

Used under license of Shutterstock, Inc.

We've been doing that since—well, since a protohuman looked up in the sky, saw the Moon and said, "Ook ook ook!" What? You thought it would speak English? Only in stories. However, a rough translation is, "What the hell is that thing?"

So. It's there. It needs an explanation, one that people can easily understand despite the fact that the explanation has nothing to do with objective, scientific reality. People begin to tell a story about it. It's a hole in the darkness that we see daylight through. It's where our ancestors live. Oh, wait, that's the stars, which are the campfires our ancestors sit around. It's the goddess Heru, protecting the pharaoh. It's the goddess Selene riding her horse through the sky. Or maybe the goddess Luna. Oh, wait. When it's full it causes people to turn into werewolves.

Move forward a few centuries and to the invention of various scientific instruments such as the telescope and the moon is now a world. But like the world that people know—the Earth—the Moon must have similar characteristics, such as people and animals and forests that we want to see. And we can get there, with the proper number of swans hooked to our chariot or eagles hooked to our chair. Or we can get there by firing ourselves out of a big cannon, like Jules Verne wrote in his story, ***From the Earth to the Moon***. Finally, in the 1960s we got enough swans (well, actually liquid oxygen and hydrogen) and a chariot, a Saturn 5 rocket, and headed for the Moon.

So why did we go? Because we had told ourselves stories for centuries about going there. So we went, and everyone was ecstatic—the first man on the moon!

And then people lost interest. Why? Because the **problem** of "can we get to the Moon" had been solved. The **climax** of the story had been achieved; there's no more conflict, and the story was over. All that was left were scientific exploration and research, which were never a part of the story, and thus not of interest to average people, only the scientists. Without the support of the average people, who were paying for the exploration with their taxes, the trips to the Moon were over.

Time for a new story.

How about Mars? Scientifically, that would be a good next step after the Moon. So why isn't there any excitement about going to Mars the way there was about the Moon?

Because we haven't been telling ourselves stories about Mars and possibly going there for millennia. We can recognize the Moon as a possible place to go. But Mars hasn't been seen as a place; it's been a spot of light or a god. And you don't go to spots of light or gods; there's no place to stand. So we have no stories about going there. Thus, it doesn't fulfill a desire to finish a story, only a desire for scientific knowledge—and what kind of story is that?

We live our lives with stories. A student gets up at 7:30 so rhe can get to rhis nine o'clock class. Why? Because rhe has to get up at 7:30 **because** rhe has to get to class at nine. It's a bizarre form of cause and effect—the future affects the past—the effect creates the cause. Rhe has told rherself a story in which the climax is getting to class, so the problem must be getting up in time. And so rhe does—to get the story started.

Does this story have a basis in reality? Only very loosely. After all, getting up on time doesn't guarantee getting to class on time. Rhe could miss the bus—or get hit by it. And yet people live their lives as though the story **is** reality.

We tell the future through our stories. Humans have a great sense of past, present and future. We remember the past, compare it to the present, and then, on the basis of the comparison, write a story about the future: I remember when things were like they are now, and this is what happened, so if I do the same thing now I'll have the same future. Unless, of course, what happened was something I didn't want, so I do something other than what I did before, assuming that will change the future. But, note that in both cases you've created a story, with a beginning, a middle and an end, a problem and a climax. Even though people have no control over what will **actually** happen—they might get hit by a bus—their sense of reality, of how the world works, is controlled by the story.

In fact, our entire sense of reality is based on stories, not facts. Let's look at history.

George Washington was an honest man; he could not tell his father a lie—he chopped down the cherry tree with his little hatchet. Well, George couldn't lie, but this story is a lie—it never happened. Nor did George have wooden teeth—they were ivory, but they didn't fit well and hurt, which is why he never smiles.

James Watt invented the steam engine—except he didn't. It was invented by Thomas Newcomen—except it wasn't. It was invented by Thomas Savery—except it wasn't. It was invented by Thomas Somerset. Except it wasn't. It was invented by Hero of Alexandria. Aha! We've found the person who invented the first steam engine.

So why are we told that Watt invented the steam engine? Because it makes a better story, just like most of the stories about the brilliant inventor solving a problem on his own. That virtually nothing has been invented by a single person is irrelevant. Being the last in a long chain of "heroes" working on solving a problem isn't a good story. You need the hero working to solve the problem from the beginning, like Batman going after the Joker. Batman appearing in the story for the first time only at the end and finishing what three or four other people started just isn't satisfying. The story says Thomas Edison invented motion pictures, but reality has at least eleven other people actually inventing bits and pieces that Edison simply put together. The story says Marconi invented radio, but there were at least twelve people who created the parts Marconi put together.

The point is, every society knows what it is by the stories its people tell themselves, and those start early in life. For example, take magic (Pratchett, Stewart, Cohen 2002). There are three kinds of magic. First, there is a sense of awe, like at the Grand Canyon or at a beautiful sunset, the "magic" of nature. Second, there is a spell, where when you say the right words what you want happens, turning a verbal instruction into material action. And third, there is the magic we use everyday—technology, like changing the channel with a remote control. You don't think that's magic? Do you know how it happens? Could you explain it to an engineer? How about your phone? Do you actually know how it does what it does? Or is it just magic? You push a button, and what you want to have happen—happens.

Most of us think of the second kind, spells, as magic, and not the first or third, awe or technology, although they're just as magical. And, of course, we know magic in the Harry Potter sense isn't real. Or do we?

Remember when you were a little kid and hearing fairy tales? All cultures use such stories to teach their children, and they don't teach facts, they teach magic. For example, all cultures use animal characters, like bears and wolves and lions, and these animals act—and talk—like people. You don't think so? How about Goldilocks and the Three Bears? Little Red Riding Hood or the Three Little Pigs? *The Chronicles of Narnia*? Talking animals? Mickey Mouse, Donald Duck, Bugs Bunny, Daffy Duck, Elmo, Big Bird—Spongebob Squarepants—a talking sponge. That's not reality, that's magic.

And what these animals say happens. It becomes magic spells, and kids learn that saying what they want makes what they want come true, not only in the stories but in real life. Parents grant their children's wishes, from food appearing on the table when they're hungry to toys and other gifts on birthdays and Christmas. You just have to add the "magic words," like "please" and "thank you."

To a child, magic does work in the world. Writing to Santa Claus makes presents magically appear on Christmas morning. The Easter Bunny, a magical creature, leaves eggs and candy to find. "Trick or treat" is a perfect magic spell to induce adults to give out candy on Halloween. It's not surprising that we grow up still thinking that magic spells work—that all we have to do is ask or say the magic words, and what we want happens. That happens in my classes. After every exam, people come to my office, thinking that if they just say the right words, their grades will magically go up, despite the fact that it doesn't happen. But as people get older, their belief in magic alters, at least to some degree, by the fact that the world refuses to bow to their desires. The grades they get are the grades they earn, no matter how many times they say "please."

Still, we live as if we're in stories and that saying the right words will solve our problems. Where this becomes important, especially for this book, is finding out which words, which actions, which thoughts, are the right ones to solve our problems. The right solution is one that arises, not out of being human, but out of the rules of the society as they are defined, spread and ingrained in the people of that society. Stories tell people the rules of magic, and those magic rules are what make a society a society.

But what kind of society? Again, the stories we tell ourselves can determine the kind of society we have, and the kinds of minds we have that will fit in that society. As Pratchett, Stewart and Cohen explain in their book, ***The Science of Discworld II***, there are three basic kinds of society. The first is the **tribal society**. It's generally small in numbers, collective in thought and parochial in its view of the world, and tells stories that solve the problem with a climax that says, "do this because we've always done it that way and it works," and "don't do this because it's taboo, evil, and we'll kill you if you do." *Little Red Riding Hood* and *Hansel and Gretel* are such stories, at least in the original versions. There, the wolf eats Little Red Riding Hood (there is no woodsman who saves the day) because she strayed from the path that authority said everyone must follow, and the witch cooks and eats Hansel and Gretel because they didn't obey their parents. They die because they didn't follow the rules of their society.

The second kind of society and mind that fits it is the **barbarian society**. That kind of society is personal rather than collective in thought, and tells its members to strive for personal honor and wealth, at the expense of others if necessary, especially those not in the individual's social group. Stories such as *Aladdin and the Forty Thieves, Mad Max, the Bourne Identity,* the Indiana Jones movies, or almost any video game, create this kind of society, one where the hero prevails, usually after a lot of pain and fighting, but he or she still wins in the end.

In the stories, the hero must pass some kind of test, given by a supernatural being like a witch or wizard or god, to win out. Think of *Beauty and the Beast.* The hero turns away a witch because he's a jerk, gets turned into a beast, and to win out he must get someone to love him despite his being a beast. When he changes his attitude, he turns back into a prince and wins the beautiful girl.

We learn how to **be** in society through this kind of story—don't be a jerk. The hero also often gains control over the supernatural to help in his quest to create the proper future outcome. Aladdin has his lamp, Arthur his sword Excalibur, the kids in *The Chronicles of Narnia* have their sword, bow and medicine. How many of you have a lucky charm of some kind, like a coin or a religious medal, or wear your lucky hat or shirt or underwear? You learned to use them from stories.

Think about the TV show ***Friends***. Every problem the characters had was caused by the character refusing to give in, to lose rhis honor or rhis sense of personal self by accepting another character's wishes. Ross makes a list to decide between Rachel and Julie and decides on Rachel. Rachel's happy about that—until she finds the list. Her self-esteem won't allow her to accept that he would make such a list and she dumps him—again.

When such stories are applied in the real world, they can cause a lot of grief because they are personal rather than collective. This sort of behavior can be seen in the recent housing bubble and banking scandals, where people in the financial industry saw no problem inventing bogus financial instruments to amass wealth for themselves, even though what they were doing was harmful to the overall economy of nation after nation. Those who lost out weren't part of their society and thus weren't worth considering. Members of such a society always see themselves as the heroes, not the villains, gaining what the stories of their society tell them is most important: personal honor and gain.

The third kind of society is **civilized**, in which learning from the mistakes you or others make to achieve your goals is the solution to the problem. Stories like *Three Billy Goats Gruff,* where each goat learns from the others how to bypass the troll, or *The Three Little Pigs,* where the third pig learns from the examples of the first two how to avoid the predations of the wolf, are models—the third pig learns from the mistakes of the first two to build his house of brick. Dr. House determines the correct diagnosis through the mistakes he and his team make; so does the CSI team.

So we think in stories and build our societies on them. And what tells us most of our stories? That's right—the media. And that's what this book is about.

SOCIETY

*E*veryone knows what society is: It's what we live in. It's the people around us—who we talk to, interact with, love and hate. It's the world surrounding us that everybody knows. But just what is it that "everybody knows"? "Everybody knows" means they don't have to think about it—it just is. That's why, at this point, we should understand just what it is that "everybody knows," and especially how they know it.

A society is a group of people with an agreed upon set of rules and mores and customs and traditions of speech, of behavior and thought, a set of rules so ingrained that they are simply known and understood without the need for any thought or examination or question. Things are because—that's just the way things are.

Combine all of these rules and customs and traditions, and the result is a shared **perception** of reality among the people living in a society that may be, but often is not, a reflection of **actual** reality, an ingrained belief that "this" is the way the world and everything in it simply is.

This shared perception of reality is often commonly known as: "commonly known as," "common sense," "they say," and the popular "everybody knows."

Let's examine these one at a time:

First, common sense says, "[whatever] is self-evident—what else could it be?" Well, common sense isn't. The color white is the absence of all color, which is true—if you're using crayons. Use a prism and white is the presence of all colors. The sun rises in the east—except it doesn't. It neither rises nor sets, the earth rotates under it.

How about "They say . . ." Who are "they", and how do they know? And how do you know what "they" say? Other than "they say" that's what they say.

Everybody knows . . . How do you know what everybody knows? And I don't, so everybody doesn't know.

People in a society don't question common sense or "they say" or "everybody knows." That's because those things are what make the society that society and not some other. Because people share the reality that "everybody knows" implies, they can recognize they belong in the society where "everybody knows," on a subconscious level, the same things.

■ WHY BOTHER WITH SOCIETIES?

But then we have to wonder: why bother with societies in the first place? Well, they exist because they serve a vital function for people. Let's explore what that function is.

Humans are weak. Horses are faster, chimps are stronger, eagles can see better, dolphins can hear better, dogs have a better sense of smell, cockroaches have a better sense of touch. Humans don't have natural weapons, like long pointy teeth and claws to fight off predators. Based just on survivability, humans should have died out long ago.

So what allowed humans not only to survive but also to take over the world? Sociability, the ability to band together in mutual support pacts. Humans are the most social creatures on Earth.

But humans are also individuals, and like to be considered as individuals, and to act and speak and think like individuals. This seems contrary to sociability. So why are people sociable?

Let's look at it by building a society, starting with:

The individual:

An individual can do whatever rhe wants: drive at a hundred miles an hour; shoplift; sleep in and skip class; be flatulent in elevators. People do what they want because they get something out of it: fun, an adrenaline rush, money, sex, power. Whatever. Everybody wants something because it feels good or avoids feeling bad. And there's nothing to tell an individual not to do whatever rhe wants, because there are no consequences. Well, you can kill yourself, but—that's the chance you take.

Let's see what happens if we add another individual to the mix.

Two people:

If two people are together (let's say they're roommates) and do whatever they want, they'll soon argue, hate each other, kill each other. One takes the other's clothes or money, that other is going to be pissed. One stays up all night singing show tunes while the other wants to sleep—and hates show tunes; one drinks and the other is a teetotaler; one smokes and the other wants to live . . . Eventually, if they're not going to kill each other they have to come up with some rules of interaction: Don't take each other's stuff, don't lie to each other, and, of course, don't pound the crap out of each other just because you're pissed. Sound familiar? Thou shalt not steal, though shalt not bear false witness, thou shalt not kill. Rules—they allow people to get along.

More than two people:

The more people that hang out together, the more rules are necessary. The rules are designed to lessen the friction between the people who hang out together; otherwise, they would all get on each other's nerves and conflict would ensue. Of course, the more rules there are, the more they curtail the freedom of the individual to do whatever rhe wants for the good of the group. As *Star Trek's* Spock says, "The good of the many outweighs the good of the few—or the one."

So, the first purpose of the rules is to reduce friction between the people in a society.

A second purpose is to separate one society from another. One thing that all societies strive for is a sense of identity, that "my" society is different from "your" society, usually expressed as us versus them. My society, of course, is better than your society: I have better rules, better rule makers, better rule enforcers, my rules make sense while yours don't, there's something wrong with you.

Remember that human societies arose as mutual protection pacts—numbers were too low to act as herding animals and gain relative safety as part of a large group, and natural weapons like fangs, claws and speed were missing. The one thing that humans had was cooperation—mutual support.

Let's see how this worked. For about 100,000 years (300,000 if we include Neanderthals, a million if we go back to Ergaster), people got together in small groups, say 15 to 25, as many as could be supported by the resources like food and water and shelter that they could find in their environment. Why they did this could use some explanation, so let's go back to before people were people.

Our ancestors probably evolved in marginal conditions, changing the way they gathered food from the way other great apes do, i.e., eat whatever was near to hand. The search for food was more of a desire for favorites than a need for calories. This led to a basic change in the relationships between the members and the social life of the band.

Cooperation

For the first time (as far as we know), apes began working together to gather food. This was probably an adjustment to the band living in those marginal conditions. Where resources are abundant, there is no need for cooperation. An individual can get what rhe needs on rhis own. In marginal conditions, a cooperative group can do a better job than individuals in exploiting what resources there are.

Cooperation allowed the group to better exploit its environment. When each animal is foraging only for itself, it must personally find all its needs. In an environment where this isn't possible, some animals will find enough and others will fail (read: die). However, cooperating in such marginal conditions allows each animal to gather what it can, rather than everything it needs. If it falls short of what it personally needs, it gets the rest from the surplus others have found.

Cooperation led to two things. The first was the camp. Most apes are constantly on the move, following the food supply, foraging as they go. Wherever evening overtakes them, they stop for the night. With abundant resources, there is no need to scavenge everything in an area to survive. The band merely needs to follow the line of least resistance, or of the most resources.

However, sharing food requires a central place to which the animals can return to do the sharing. Such a place, a camp, serves two purposes. First, it is a convenient place where all the members of the band know the others will eventually be, particularly the males who may be gone for hours or even days on their hunts. This also makes it easier to share the food found.

Second, it allows the band to better exploit its range. The members of the band can radiate out from the camp in different directions every day, eventually covering the entire area. When, after a few days, the band has exhausted the area, they can move on and find a new camp.

So humans cooperated for mutual support. They were gatherers and hunters, wandering the landscape, camping in one place until they had used up the available food supply and then moving on to greener pastures. They had few possessions, only what they could carry around with them.

Occasionally, they would meet another band and camp together, swapping stories and mates, and then separate again. If one group found a particularly good place, with lots of food, water, shelter and other resources, they would try to hang onto it rather than move on to someplace maybe not as good. If anyone else entered that environment, they would be competing with the original band for the available resources. So, strangers would have to either join the group or be driven off. If the resources were at their limit, the group couldn't accept new members, and they would drive off any strangers. Thus was born xenophobia, the fear of strangers.

This was society as it was for most of human history.

Let's take some hypothetical place where human society completely, and irrevocably, changed. We'll call it—the Nile. As a drought occurred about 12,000 years ago at the end of the last ice age, people wandered down from the highlands and from the woodlands that were changing into the Sahara Desert to the river where there was water and where plants grew. There things continued as normal for a while as bands of people wandered up and down the river in search of food. During this time someone probably noticed that plants like wheat or barley grew where grains had been dropped on the ground during a previous visit to the area, and made the leap of imagination that dropping the seeds would lead to having a guaranteed food supply later. This was refined over the centuries to include putting the seeds in the ground rather than just scattering them on the surface where the birds could get at them.

Then, somewhere around 8,000 years ago, something new was added that completely changed all human social life and interaction—the plow (Burke 1995). Before the plow people probably planted seeds by poking a hole in the ground and dropping in seeds, a very inefficient way to grow food. With the plow, the ground was broken; people could just throw seeds over it and grow more grain and cereals. Add to that the need for something to pull the plow and you have the domestication of animals such as cattle. And if you can domesticate cattle, you can domesticate goats and sheep. Prior to the plow, the only domesticated animal was the dog. The food supply, both plant foods and meat, grew enormously. This meant more people could be fed and the population boomed. Instead of people wandering the countryside gathering and hunting in small bands, they began to gather in larger groups.

Realizing that plants need water to grow, someone had a brainstorm: Make little rivers by digging ruts running between the plowed rows and fill those ruts with water to water the plants. This is called irrigation. So improvements in agriculture such as irrigation led to having even more food that could support an even larger population. To improve the irrigation, they built canals of stone to feed water to the fields (Burke 1995). To make irrigation and canals work, there needs to be an understanding of elevation and slope—the invention of hydraulics. There also needs to be an organization of people into work gangs to do all the work of canal and irrigation channel building that only one or two people couldn't do.

There arose a need to administer these fields, especially since the Nile had a tendency to wash away all field markers every year. A political structure was invented to oversee the proper allocation of land and the organization of people. To do this, the officials, called adj mer (literally "diggers of canals"), had the power to decide who owned what (Burke 1995). However, how did they know who owned what? They had to invent surveying, which requires an understanding of counting, in other words arithmetic. Before this counting probably consisted of one, two, three, many, since a conscious understanding of specific large numbers was probably unnecessary.[1] They also needed standard measurements of length and widths and angles, known to us as geometry and trigonometry—mathematics had been invented.

Agriculture also meant people now stayed in one place to grow their food instead of wandering around in search of it. This meant they needed a way to store food between harvests since they couldn't go someplace else to find more food. So they invented pottery (Burke 1995), a way to store food much more safely than just leaving it in a pile somewhere. They then invented a place to store all the pots of grain—the granary. To supervise the granaries—to ensure a sufficient supply of pottery, to know what and how much of each grain was stored and distributed—officials were needed.

Now they needed someone to administer all the other officials. With small bands there was a chief, but with hundreds or thousands of people they needed someone with much more power, say, someone chosen by the gods—voila, the pharaoh.

And for the pharaoh to show his power, he began to build things, which is possible since they now had the math and the stone working and the organization of people and the surplus of food and you got—the pyramids. Society went from small groups of hunter/gatherers wandering the landscape to stone pyramids in less than 2,000 years.

Over the next several millennia, the new social structure developed to handle agriculture, which arose not just in the Nile valley in Egypt, but in the Tigris and Euphrates River valley in Mesopotamia, the Indus River valley in India, and the Yellow River valley in China. This led to the formation of villages, then towns, then cities and nations.

Okay. So there's a surplus of food and fewer people required to produce it. For the first time, not everyone had to find food, and it was possible for a group of people to support specialists, people who were especially good at a particular task such as pottery or carpentry or tool making or storytelling. These people could now devote all their time to that job rather than doing it part-time when not otherwise busy hunting and gathering.

Trade began as one group traded its surplus of food or superior pottery or woodwork or tools for another group's goods.

Of course, with all these people there had to be more rules, and people to make the rules and to make sure the rules were followed. So, with rules come rulers: chiefs, overseers, pharaohs.

As societies matured and added more rules, strangers were even less likely to know and follow those rules—they were different, they were "other," they might even be dangerous. So societies often added rules that logically don't make sense, but do allow the members of the group to identify who are their own and who are strangers. For example, Leviticus 19:19 in the Torah instructs the Hebrews not to wear two different fabrics, like wool and linen, together. Leviticus 19:27 says don't cut your hair or trim your beard. Leviticus 19:28 says no tattoos (probably because the Egyptians did have tattoos). Note that in each case it makes it easy to tell who's part of your society and who isn't—the rules require differences that are visible to one and all.

Other rules may seem odd, depending on one's culture. For example, when entering a Catholic Church, men have to uncover their heads, and women must cover them; when entering a Jewish synagogue, men must cover their heads and women must uncover them.

If you think about it, there's no reasonable or logical or biological reason for those rules; following them won't increase your food supply or clean the water or prevent disease, like the rules against eating pork or rare meat or fruit until five years after planting the trees. That leaves only having such rules to separate your people from other people.

Even within a supposedly homogeneous culture there are subcultures that differentiate themselves from others in that society by insisting on following certain rules. For example, in ancient Rome only the nobility could wear purple, and prostitutes had to dye their hair red. In medieval Europe, there were rules to separate the social classes, such as who could wear what, how long the toes on shoes could be (the longer the toes, the higher the class you belonged to) and what kinds of buttons they could put on their clothing. Only royalty could wear expensive materials like ermine and fur, or silk, velvet and brocade. Chinese nobles grew extremely long fingernails to show that they didn't have to do any manual labor, or indeed any work at all. The 1960s in America was the era of the shorthaired redneck and the longhaired hippie pinko freak. Today we have jocks and nerds, Goths and Vampires, college students who are either Greeks or dormies or independents. There are hardhats and blue collar and white-collar workers, bosses and employees, each with their own style and attitude and slang to separate themselves from others who aren't "them."

So, if there are rules, and if people are going to follow those rules, especially if the rules aren't logical or about survival, then there must be consequences for breaking the rules.

Without consequences there's no reason not to break the rules. Just as each society determines what the rules are, so it also determines what the punishments are: fines, ostracism, exile, shunning, imprisonment, death. Such punishments serve three purposes: They tell the wrongdoer he did wrong, they drive home that a repetition of doing wrong will bring more punishment, and, perhaps most importantly, they teach everyone else in the society that violating the rules will result in punishment. Each punishment is deemed to be the appropriate response.

However, there is a problem—who does the punishing? It could be your peers (think back to high school—everyone belonged to one group or another, called cliques by those who didn't belong to that group); or the justice system—police, judges, jailers; or even yourself (attacks of conscience).

But what if nobody knows you broke the rules? You don't say anything, no one saw you—you lie. A survey showed that 54 percent of people would pretend their cell phone dropped a call to end a conversation; 63 percent of people say they would take a sick day when they're healthy (*Parade Magazine* poll, February 2009). In many societies, the answer is to have a punisher who is all knowing and all seeing, and all-powerful—a god.

For the ancient Egyptians, there was Thoth and Anubis, who weighed the heart of the dead against a feather, and if they balanced the soul was ushered into the presence of Osiris (read: an afterlife); but if the heart was heavier than the feather, the heart, and thus the soul, was fed to the monster Am-mit, destroying the chance for an afterlife. Thus, an Egyptian's life better follow the rules of society or rhe'll have no afterlife. That's a pretty good incentive.

And just listen to Leviticus 26 on the results of not following God's commandments: "If you will not carry out these commandments, and if you despise my statutes, I will bring upon you sudden terror, wasting diseases and fever that will destroy your sight and drain away your life. I will set my face against you so that you will be defeated by your enemies. I will send wild animals against you, and they will rob you of your children, destroy your cattle and make you so few in numbers your roads will be deserted.

"I will send a plague among you.

"You will eat the flesh of your sons and the flesh of your daughters.

"I will turn your cities into ruin.

"I will draw out my sword and pursue you.

"Anyone left will be so afraid that the sound of a shaken leaf will put them to flight.

"You will die."

Well, *there* are a few consequences. And when you're dealing with a power that knows everything you do, say or even think, that's a good incentive to follow the rules.

Who Creates the Rules?

Individuals create their own rules. Two, or three or a few more people can simply sit and talk about how they're going to interact with each other and what the rules are for their little group.

It's when a society grows large, say fifty or more people, that such an informal approach doesn't work. People are so different in what they want and how they think they should get it that there needs to be an authority of some sort to decide what should and should not be allowed to reduce the conflicts between people.

Who that authority is depends on the rules of the society. When the ultimate authority is a god, it's the priests. In Iran it's the mullahs, the Islamic religious leaders. In medieval Europe it was the Catholic Church. In ancient Egypt it was the Pharaoh.

When the authority lies in the society itself, it's whoever has control over the society. In ancient China the Emperor, in ancient Greece the people—well, everyone except children . . . and women . . . and slaves . . . and men who didn't own land . . . and only in Athens. But except for 80 percent of the population, the people made the rules. In the United States, that authority is the government elected by the people.

As you can see, the authority had to fit the rules of the society. Iran operates under Shariah, the Islamic holy law, which supersedes and thus can overrule the elected government, including deciding who gets to run for office in the first place. This is much like the medieval church, which could overrule kings and princes by threatening them with excommunication, a ticket straight to hell. Henry II of England had to accept the church's decisions on running his country. Henry VIII turned England Protestant, once there was that non-Catholic option for him, because the Pope wouldn't grant him a divorce, which the Church ruled was against the rules of society as the Church saw them.

Egyptian pharaohs were living gods—and male. So when Queen Hatshepsut took over the kingdom and became Pharaoh, she wore men's clothing and glued on a fake beard to become a man. The rules of the society refused to accept, or even see, a female Pharaoh—a queen, yes; a Pharaoh, no.

Even the elected government of the United States has had to follow the unspoken rules of the society of the time. Originally only land-owning men could vote, but when non-land owning, but powerful men grew in power, men like merchants and bankers and craftsmen, that rule changed. It took the Fifteenth Amendment to allow blacks to vote, the Seventeenth before senators were selected by a popular vote of the people instead of state legislatures, and the Nineteenth before women could vote. When the Constitution was written, the rules of society said that blacks were only three-fifths of a person (Article 1, section 3), the "rabble" (i.e., the common people) weren't trusted to select the equivalent of the American House of Lords, the Senate, and women were chattel, possessions of the men in their lives, and not independent people in their own right. An interesting case is the Eighteenth Amendment in 1919, known as Prohibition, which prohibited the manufacture, sale or consumption of alcoholic beverages. Some people in American society saw alcohol as evil and detrimental to society and got it banned. However, many more people saw no problem with alcohol and disobeyed the law by the millions—they simply didn't agree with a social rule that others wanted to impose on them. It was a rule that was so universally ignored, and that created so many social problems, like the rise of organized crime to supply the booze, that in 1933, the Twenty-first Amendment was ratified to repeal the Eighteenth.

As you can see, societies change over time as the old rules no longer work or are unacceptable to a majority of the people in that society—or are no longer enforceable because the people simply won't follow them.

When different societies have different rules, those societies often come into conflict with each other. After all, my rules make sense and are good (after all, they're my rules), and your rules are nonsense and are evil (because they're not the same as mine).

The rules of fascism and Nazism led to conflict with the rules of democracy (read: us) and communism, and thus we had World War II. Then the rules of communism were in conflict with the rules of democracy (read: us), and thus we had the Vietnam War and the Cold War with the Soviet Union. Each side thought it was right and the other side wrong, not on the basis of reason or logic or biology, but on the basis of ideology—how each side thought the world should, and therefore ***must***, work. For example, a belief in the dignity of the individual ran right up against a belief in the state and the position of the individual as a faceless cog in the social machinery of the state.

We're subject to that today. Think of Al Qaida and the West; Sunnis vs. Shiites; Catholics vs. Protestants in Northern Ireland; Palestinians vs. Israelis; the Taliban vs.— well, anyone who doesn't think we're living in the eleventh century. "If you don't agree with my rules, you have to die."

These beliefs are so ingrained that they don't even have to be thought about—they simply are. Think of what I said above— "the dignity of the individual versus the individual as a faceless cog in the social machine." You undoubtedly thought, "how could anyone think the latter way?" Well, look at the society you're a part of and there's your answer—you don't have to think about it, it just is.

But what happens when the conflicting rules aren't external, like democracy versus Nazism or communism, but are internal? When people living in the same place, and ostensibly the same society, have differing ideas of what the rules should be? Once again, there's conflict.

So, what do you do? Go to war? Well, yes. Sparta vs. Athens; Rome vs. everybody; The War of the Roses; The English Civil War; The American Revolution; The French Revolution; The Civil War. All these wars started because one group of people believed that their rules were better than the rules of other groups of people living in that same society.

Of course, I find it interesting that these attempts to prevent changes in society through violence always fail. The Inquisition and the Thirty Years War didn't stop the Protestant Revolution. The British didn't stop the American Revolution. The nobility of France didn't stop the French Revolution. Attacks on women didn't stop women's suffrage. Attacks on blacks and civil rights workers didn't stop civil rights. When the time comes for change, change comes. Turning back the clock, or even stopping it, especially through violent means, just doesn't seem to work.

But we see shadows of this today in American society, with the conflicts over such issues as smoking and gun control and abortion and immigration and taxation, and the calls for the deaths of blacks or Jews or Hispanics, or of doctors who perform abortions, or "I just don't like you." Think of Timothy McVeigh and John Allen Muhammed. McVeigh blew up the Federal Building in Oklahoma City, and Muhammed shot down people at random in Maryland and Virginia. Look at how the rules of our society, based on the stories we tell ourselves, what we *believe* is true whether or not it actually *is,* made it harder for law enforcement to catch these two murderers. "Everybody knows" that terrorist attacks, such as blowing up a federal building, are carried out by Middle Eastern foreigners, since "everybody knows" terrorists are Arabic. Eyewitness accounts that it was a white man who parked the van with the explosives and ran away were ignored—he was white, not Middle Eastern. It came as a shock to quite a few people that a terrorist could be a home-grown white guy. And everyone ignored the idea that the Washington Sniper could be a black man, or that Aileen Wuornos, a woman, murdered so many people, because "everyone knows" that only white men are serial killers. It doesn't fit our worldview that black men or women can be serial killers.

Just think of James von Brunn's attack on the Holocaust Museum because he blamed Jews and blacks and gays and liberals for changing the rules of society from what he thought they should be. Think of Scott Roeder's murder of Dr. Tiller for following the changed rules about abortion. Think of Jim David Adkisson's murder of two people and wounding of six others in a church because he didn't like that they followed the new social rules, and thought he could turn back the clock by killing "liberals," people who believed society should be different from what he believed it should be.

However, there is another way besides violence, and that way is to talk, to write, to communicate. And the ways we communicate have been major catalysts in how societies change and redefine themselves, and how people learn the rules of that new society.

■ ENDNOTE

1. When people are in small bands, you don't have to count noses; you can see quickly whether everyone that should be there is there. You don't have to count a herd when hunting, just have a good sense of whether there are enough. Perhaps shamans would have a way of counting to keep track of days between events like the solstices, but for the average person numbers were unnecessary.

5

HISTORY AND DEVELOPMENT OF WRITING AND PRINTING

*I*n the fifteenth century a man made a bad business deal, something like buying a house to flip just as the housing bubble burst. This wouldn't have been a problem if he hadn't borrowed the money, and now his creditors wanted their money back. He had to come up with an idea, and do it fast. He did—and changed the world.

People have tried to get information out of their own minds and into other people's for quite a while. We're not sure whether Homo ergaster talked, but the evidence for their social groupings indicate that they had some form of communication, perhaps limited to gestures and a few sounds, much the way chimpanzees do today.

Certainly by the time Neanderthals showed up, talking was a method of communicating. Fossilized hyoid bones show that Neanderthals had much the same vocal equipment we do, although they probably had high voices due to the position of their larynxes.

And without a doubt Cro-Magnons talked.

Of course, conversation is face to face, interpersonal communication, the kind that fits the standard model of communication. But there was probably also a desire to communicate at a distance. In other words, people went looking for channels of communication other than just talking.

The most common form of communication at a distance was the kind of noises you could make, and those are still in use. For example, the Swiss yodel was a way to communicate across the valleys from one mountainside to another. Yodeling carries farther and is more penetrating than shouting, as you've all probably experienced listening to some country music. Of course, words weren't yodeled; musical tones and intervals between those tones carried the information in the messages. The vocabulary was somewhat limited, but adequate to the purpose.

Another kind of noise is whistling. In the Canary Islands, the islanders' whistling can be heard for miles, their equivalent of a phone call, although you might not want to be too close if you want to keep your eardrums.

But as humans became more handy, like Homo habilis (which means "handy man"), various media were invented. One of the first was probably the signal fire, which is still in use today. They were certainly in use fairly early in civilization—Homer talks about their use in 1200 BCE in the Iliad. But there are problems with signal fires. First is that they're only really useful at night when they can be seen. Second is that the amount of information is limited. A fire only carries one piece of information—whatever message was prearranged between the sender and receiver—like "the enemy is coming." It's hard to have a deep philosophical discussion when there's only one word—now. Or maybe three—here I am.

Now, someone undoubtedly noticed that fires make smoke, and got the bright idea that smoke could be seen by day. Thus the signal fire became a twenty-four hour warning. Then, with the use of a blanket over a smoky fire, you could send smoke signals, puffs of smoke of varying lengths and intervals that could send more complex messages, much like a telegraph, although words wouldn't have been spelled out as with Morse code. For example, the sender and receiver may have decided beforehand that three short puffs would mean "they're coming through the eastern pass in two hours," and a long puff and three short puffs may mean "they're coming through the western pass in three hours." Another time, the same sequences would carry different meanings, depending on the circumstances and prior arrangement. Indians of the American southwest used smoke signals late into the nineteenth century.

Then there's just making noise. Gongs, drums and horns could carry a message a long distance. Of course, gongs were the sound equivalent of a signal fire. However, drums and horns can carry far more information by varying the beat or the length and pitch of the sound. They were the form of long distance communication for millennia, especially by the military. In the Book of Joshua, Chapter 6, the shofar, or ram's horn trumpet, is given credit for bringing down the walls of Jericho. The Romans gave commands to the troops with a bucina, a large deep-pitched brass horn, in much the same way the bugle was used for centuries, right up through the twentieth; the Romans also used large drums like tympani. And various African and South American tribes used log drums, large hollowed out logs beaten with sticks in various rhythms.

Visual means were also tried. One that worked well for long-distance communication was the semaphore, invented in 1791 by Claude Chappe. Set in a tower, the semaphore could rapidly send messages as far as the next tower (which was as far away as possible while still being clearly visible through a telescope) by positioning the arms in different configurations. Napoleon thought they were a great idea, and he set up chains of towers across France—to make sure the country knew the results of the French lottery as quickly as possible. But the military also saw a use for them, especially along the coast of the English Channel, to keep an eye on the British Royal Navy and to let the French navy and merchantmen know when the British were around. It drove the Royal Navy nuts—they weren't able to catch the French out of port. It didn't stop the British from putting up their own semaphore towers though.

But no matter how hard people tried, they really didn't have mass distance communication. And they sure didn't have a way to save anything that was said—you can't trap smoke and read it later. So something had to be done. And it was. People learned to write.

So, what is writing? It's essentially turning speech, which is composed of sound symbols that are gone the instant they're said, other than in the memory of the listener, into permanent symbols that can be turned back into speech later.

People have been creating permanent symbols for thousands of years. At first, those symbols were pictures of a concrete thing—in other words, a concrete noun with perhaps a hint of a verb.

For example, in the photo on the left we have a few horses and an auroch bull running. Of course, we don't know what they're running to, or from, or why the artist drew them. So in terms of interpreting the symbols, they're pretty clear—horses and a bull, realistically rendered—not a lot of guesswork involved. However, they pretty much don't tell us anything but that there were horses and bulls that could run. The symbols are clear; the message isn't. Is it a teaching tool (this is what a horse looks like)? A spiritual artifact (drawing an animal will lure it to the hunters)? An animal census by an early zoologist? No one can say for sure since no one reads Cro magnon.

Below we see an early example of abstract symbolizing rather than realistic drawing to transmit a message nonverbally. This stone slab from around 19,000 years ago, found in France, is believed to be a kind of marriage contract: two women are transferring to the Bison clan. Note how it symbolizes rather than realistically depicts its message: the two women are represented by *the* physical difference between men and women, the Bison clan by an etching of a bison head, and the transfer represented by a series of dots. The symbols, and their meanings, are fairly straightforward and understandable thousands of years later. However, the symbols are still of concrete things, like women and a bison. But words are not only of concrete things; there are also abstractions.

Egyptian hieroglyphs

Speech is full of abstractions, words that refer to things that nobody can actually point at and say, "That's what I'm talking about," which help the interpreter to understand the message being communicated. However, abstractions can also be symbolized, often by combining them with other symbols.

One of the first examples of this is Egyptian hieroglyphs, as seen in the photo above. Hieroglyphs use pictographs, just like the Lascaux cave paintings, but they are used to stand for something besides what they picture. For example, a kneeling man means "man." Put a pitcher on his head pouring out water and it means "purify." A falcon means "soul."

However, as shown on the left, over time the Egyptians starting using pictographs to represent the syllables in words rather than entire words, and then they used them to represent letters in words. The problem was, the Egyptians used all three methods at the same time, mixing symbols for things, ideas, words and letters at will, thus requiring the reader to determine what a symbol meant from context. A simpler way had to be found.

And it was. The hieroglyphic pictographs were simplified and abstracted. As you can see from the chart on the next page, the pictographs have gradually evolved, like the pictograph of a bird. They changed bit by bit until they became cuneiform. It took far less time to write a word this way, using a wedge shaped stylus and pressing it into clay, than drawing a pictograph with a paint and brush. However, it still took as much time to learn what all the cuneiform mark-

A B C D
E F G H
I J K L
M N O P
Q R S T
U
V
W X Y Z

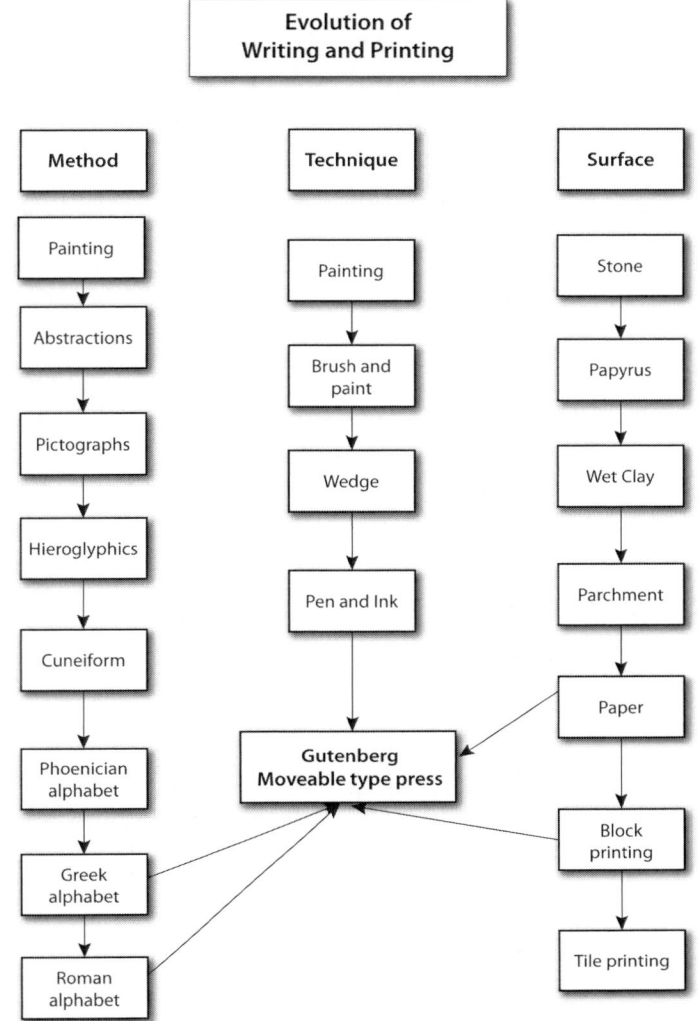

Cuneiform

Phoenician alphabet

ings meant and how to read and write them. Also, it required clay instead of papyrus or parchment to write on, something that wasn't always available or viable, especially at sea.

Something even simpler than hieroglyphs or cuneiform was necessary, especially by traders and merchants who needed to keep records in any language they encountered and to keep them instead of having them melt in the damp. The greatest traders of the ancient world were the Phoenicians, who traveled all over the Mediterranean Sea and even into the Atlantic, the Red Sea and the Indian Ocean. They developed the first real alphabet, having one simple sign for each consonant sound in a word. Note that none of these symbols are pictographs or even abstractions of pictographs. They're just random symbols. Not only could any language be transcribed with this alphabet, it was easy to learn and use.

There was only one problem with the Phoenician alphabet—you may notice it doesn't have any vowels. Look at this word.

ST

What is it? Sat? Set? Sit? Sot? Sut? Stay? Sty? Stow? Stew? Sate? Seat? Site? Maybe you're good at license plates or IM Speak and can figure it out. But are you sure?

A, α	Alpha	E, ε	Epsilon	I, ι	Iota	N, ν	Nu	P, ρ	Rho	Φ, φ	Phi
B, β	Beta	Z, ζ	Zeta	K, κ	Kappa	Ξ, ξ	Xi	Σ, σ	Sigma	X, χ	Chi
Γ, γ	Gamma	H, η	Eta	Λ, λ	Lambda	O, o	Omicron	T, τ	Tau	Ψ, ψ	Psi
Δ, δ	Delta	Θ, θ	Theta	M, μ	Mu	Π, π	Pi	Y, υ	Upsilon	Ω, ω	Omega

It was the Greeks who added to the Phoenicians' alphabet by adding vowels. Now there was no guesswork involved. If it could be said, it could be written, especially after the Romans added the F, H, Q and V.

With this final development, writing became far simpler and more accurate. You might not be able to transcribe every sound in speech, like the swallowed "n" sound in French or the guttural "k" sound in Hebrew or Erse, but you could at least approximate every sound, for example Caen, l'chaim, and loch (as in Loch Ness), at least to the point you could figure out what words were intended.

So now that there was an alphabet, writing became quite simple, and people could handwrite anything they wanted, which is exactly what they did.

Handwritten texts were the norm for the next thousand years. Sometimes the writing got a little fancy, as when the pages were illuminated by adding adornments such as decorated initials, miniature illustrations and margins filled with filigrees and chatzkes, but the writing was still readable and transmitted what was in one person's mind to other minds over the course of years and even centuries. The only thing that would prevent that transmission was the deterioration of the parchment or ink, or the loss or destruction of the text.

This last shouldn't be taken lightly. When everything was handwritten, there were few copies of any particular text since each copy took a lot of time and effort to create. There

Handwritten text

might only be one or two copies in existence, so if they were lost or destroyed the text was gone forever.

A way of making copies quickly, at least more quickly than handwriting, had to be found. That came in 888 CE, when the *Diamond Sutra*, a Buddhist scripture, was printed using block printing. This is carving all the words and illustrations that would be on an entire page into a block of wood, inking the block and smoothing a piece of paper over it.

Block printing

However, this kind of printing required a different block for each page of the text. Imagine the number of blocks you'd have to carve to create this book—more than two hundred—and the time it would take to produce each page, especially with all the tiny letters that make up the words.

In 1041, Bi Sheng in China invented an alternative to carving an entire page to block print. He made clay tiles, each of which had one word raised above the surface on it. Now you could simply ink each word tile and press it onto the paper, much faster than hand drawing every word with a brush, or carving the entire page onto a block of wood. However, this still required that you have a different tile for each word—over 40,000 in Chinese (although you only need about 7,000 for all practical purposes). Still, imagine the equivalent of a keyboard with 7,000 keys! Hunt and peck taken to a ridiculous level.

Of course, with a written language that's pictographic rather than alphabetical, there's not a lot of choice—you need a different symbol for each word. That's the advantage of a written language that's alphabetic. An alphabet has a minimal number of symbols that one can combine in any number of ways to create words. This was the advantage the Phoenicians were looking for and that they created to avoid all the disadvantages of the pictographic hieroglyphs and cuneiform. You'd only need twenty-four tiles to print in Greek. However, you'd either quickly get finger cramps handling those tiny blocks for each letter, or you'd end up writing really, really big, with only a few words per page. This would be an expensive proposition when your only writing surface was parchment, made from the skins of sheep and goats. That's impractical, so handwriting continued.

Let's take a little side trip that might help us along our journey toward printing—the Black Death. What does the Black Death have to do with printing? Give me a moment and you'll see.[1]

The Black Death hit Europe in 1347 and proceeded to wipe out between a third and half of the population. It was a pretty miserable four years.

When it ended in 1351, people were, shall we say—relieved. Try thinking of it in terms of finally getting to the weekend—it's party time! Ramp that up a few thousand times and it gives you an idea of how the survivors reacted to the end of the Black Death.

One of the first things the survivors had was lots of money, the result of inheriting the property of their relatives that had died. Even if most people had little in the way of property before the plague, if you are the only survivor out of a family of twenty, your inheritance is substantial, certainly far more than you had before. With a sudden increase in wealth comes a desire to spend that money in celebration of still being alive. So suddenly people came up with ways to celebrate, like parties and fairs, and of course if you're going to a party you want to dress up in the fanciest clothes you can afford. The upper class went for silks and gold wire, the middle class went for wool, and the peasants, the largest class of people, could afford linen, made from the flax plant. But one thing everyone could afford now was—underwear (Burke 1995).

So, what do underwear, and other linen products like bed sheets and shirts and over-skirts and aprons, have to do with printing? Well, what was necessary for printing was paper. Remember, the only thing available to write on up to this time was parchment, made from the skins of goats and sheep, which made it scarce and very expensive. The thing about linen sheets and clothes and underwear was they wore out. So they were thrown away. That might seem like a waste, but it wasn't. All those huge heaps of worn out linen could still be used—because they could be recycled and turned into paper.

This is how. First, all those rags were turned into even smaller rags by cutting them up with a knife. Then they were quite literally beaten to a pulp in a mixture of water and glue in a water-powered hammer mill for about forty-eight hours. Once thoroughly pulped into a thin gruel, the slurry was sloshed onto fine wire screens and allowed to drain for a moment. Then the thickened slurry was placed between layers of wool cloth. When the stack was high enough, the apprentices were called in and proceeded to squeeze all the water out in a paper press, a new use for the ancient wine and olive presses. When the water's out you take apart the stack and—voila—paper (Burke 1995).

So now there's plenty of nice, cheap paper, and everybody's using it for things like contracts and recordkeeping and writing to each other. However, because of the Black Death, there weren't enough scribes—the people who knew how to read and write and did so for a price—left alive to do all that paperwork, handwriting the hundreds and thousands of forms and copies necessary for the new, bustling post-plague world. So once again, something had to be done.

Something was. The greatest change in the history of the written word since the invention of the alphabet, invented by a goldsmith with a cash flow problem.

Johannes Gutenberg was a German goldsmith who set up a scheme to sell religious souvenirs to pilgrims at a religious fair in the town of Aachen. Investors gave him the money, he bought an inventory, and he set out to make his fortune. Unfortunately, he got the year for the fair wrong and missed it. Now he was stuck with all these souvenirs and investors knocking on his door wanting their money. Gutenberg needed a plan, a cheap plan, and he needed it fast (Burke 1995).

It's at this point that Gutenberg completely changed the world. As a goldsmith he certainly knew how to handle metals and tools for working metal. He also knew about the metal punches craftsmen used to stamp symbols like makers' marks into metal. Using this knowledge, he worked out a procedure. First, he filed a letter in reverse into the end

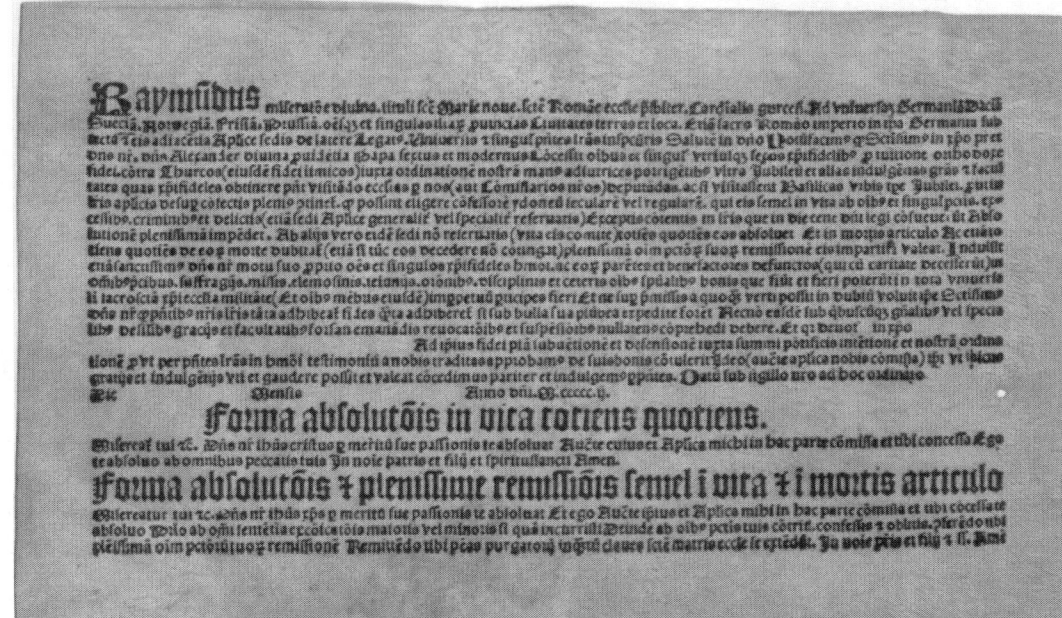

Early printed page

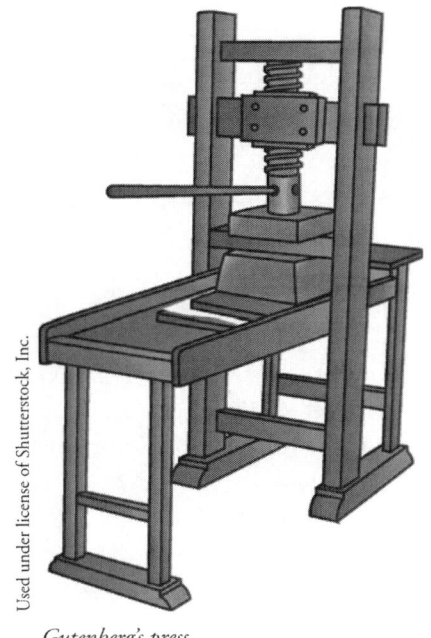

Gutenberg's press

of an iron punch. Then he used the punch to impress that letter into a bar of soft copper. Placing the bar into a mold, he poured in a molten lead-tin alloy. After letting it cool for a moment, he broke the mold and removed a piece of moveable type (Burke 1995). Make a large number of those letters, and other symbols like numbers and punctuation, and put them in a font, a case full of pigeonholes to hold the type. Then you can select individual letters and line them up in a holder the width of the page you wish to print. Enough lines and you have a block of text that you put in a press, lock down, ink up, and press paper down on it, thereby creating in moments a full printed page of text.

With this system, you can print entire pages by the tens, and the hundreds, and the thousands, hundreds of times faster than it could be done by handwriting. And when you're done with printing all the copies of a page you need, you can simply take the block of text apart into its individual pieces of type and rearrange those pieces to quickly put together a new page—and continue the process. The written word was now incredibly cheap. A printer could produce a hundred copies of a page of text for the same price as a scribe would charge for one.

Word of Gutenberg's press with moveable type spread rapidly, and new printers sprang up everywhere, moving from town to town on carts and printing whatever was brought to them. Other printers opened shops and became the world's first capitalists, a new way of thinking about how to do business.

Before the advent of printing, the usual business model consisted of a young teenager going to work as an apprentice for a master in a field, such as a goldsmith, a carpenter, a grocer, a stone mason, or any other field of endeavor. As an apprentice, he would work without pay with the master craftsman, learning the trade in exchange for his labor. After several years, the apprentice would take an examination of competence and graduate to journeyman. As a journeyman, he could hire himself out to anyone who would hire him, including his original master, and earn the money he would need to open his own shop. Eventually, he could become a master himself and take on apprentices of his own.

The print shop was one of the first truly capitalist ventures (Burke 1995). Before this there really wasn't much in the way of entrepreneurship. There were craftsmen who would make things to order, like the blacksmith or the boot maker or the tailor, but these were pretty basic, simple businesses. A print shop, on the other hand, was expensive and complicated. First of all, the physical plant was costly: you needed the press, of course, and the thousands of pieces of type made up. A master printer would naturally have apprentices learning how to be printers. But the printing business required more, especially the money necessary to start up. The printer or his partner was often a successful merchant who was responsible for finding investors who, in exchange for supplying the money, would receive a share of the profits with no other connection nor even knowledge about the business.

The printer had to hire academically qualified assistants who could read, write, and edit material. These assistants may know nothing about printing, but they did know how to prepare the texts to be printed, a role in the business no twelve-year-old apprentice could fill. Even a printing journeyman or the master himself may not have had the necessary knowledge. This was really the beginning of employing specialized workers in a craft for what they knew rather than for what they did as craftsmen.

Then there were the tasks of organizing supplies and labor, setting up production schedules, coping with strikes. And after all this he had to analyze the market to find out what printed texts people would buy. And then he needed to have an inventory of those books already printed up and ready for purchase when a customer came in. That meant tying up lots of money in the materials and labor to print those books in hopes that they would sell. The printer was also in intense competition with others who were doing the same, and he was obliged to risk capital on expensive equipment. And it shouldn't be surprising that printers pioneered the skills of advertising, putting out book lists and circulars promoting their shops (Burke 1995). And that's capitalism.

One such printer was William Caxton, who opened his printing operation in England in 1476 and was the first to print books in English. Of course, there was a problem, one we have to live with today. Before printing, spelling was idiosyncratic. That is, people spelled words any way they wanted. There exist five authenticated Shakespeare signatures, and they're each spelled differently. So when Caxton started printing in English, how did he spell the words? Well, he was from Kent in the very southeast corner of England, where the dialect of English could be considered rather thick. So naturally, when Caxton printed his books, he spelled the words the way he pronounced them—after all, there was no other way. For example, we pronounce "knight" as though it was spelled "nyt." He pronounced it "kah-NEEGH-t." We pronounce "knife" as "nyf"; he pronounced it "kuh-NEEF-uh." Naturally, he spelled words the way he pronounced them. Other printers did the same thing, following the Elizabethan pronunciations of words (which was not the same as we pronounce them today), and we're stuck with those spellings now.

When printers churn out thousands of books with those kinds of spellings, especially books like dictionaries, those spellings become the norm. So we can blame Caxton and printers like him for the spellings of English words and years of grade school misery.

In addition, the old block print didn't go away, but it was used in a different way in the Gutenberg press. It was now possible to reproduce in vast numbers things like drawings. Simply carve the drawing into a block of wood and put the block in with the block of text for the page and you have illustrated text without having to individually hand draw that picture in each copy of the book. This ability would do its part to change the world.

Now anything that could be written could be printed cheaply and in vast quantities to be read by anyone who could read, even those things that had never been read by the general public before. For example, the stage plays of the Elizabethan period weren't printed for the public to purchase and read. Plays weren't considered literature, not the way we consider them today—they were the television of their day, and they wouldn't be published any more than we would publish the scripts for "Gilligan's Island"; literature was poetry. What playwrights would do is write one copy of the play, then copy out what are called "sides." A side is where each actor gets only his own lines of dialogue and the cues for those lines, not the entire play. The publisher of the *First Folio of Shakespeare,* which was published after Shakespeare's death, didn't go from the script—there wasn't one. Instead, he gathered together as many of the actors from the plays as he could, and they recited their lines to be set in type. Of course, this meant that if an actor couldn't be found, or was found but couldn't remember all of rhis lines, those lines aren't in the book and are lost forever. *Macbeth* is the shortest Shakespearean play because not all the actors could be found and so their parts are missing. We could be missing entire works of Shakespeare and other Elizabethan playwrights for this reason. (Wasson 1978)

With paper and printing so cheap, not only books were printed. New forms of information other than books became available, like the news of the day in newspapers, or informative articles in magazines, or general information in essays on politics or nature or society or whatever an author, and a printer, thought readers might be interested in.

The only step left was to increase the speed of printing, which came with the industrial revolution, and the use of mechanical rather than muscle power to run the presses. The invention of the power rotary press in 1863 allowed printers to turn out pages as fast as they could feed in sheets of paper, allowing the printing of a hundred double-sided pages in the time it took Ben Franklin to print one. The roll-fed rotary press in 1866 raised that rate a hundred times to 10,000 or more double-sided pages a minute. This kind of press is in use today.

In 1884 Mergenthaler developed the linotype machine to replace typesetting by hand. Then in 1951 setting metal type was entirely eliminated by photolithography which creates printing plates through photo-etching. Finally, the setup of the press matches the speed of the printing itself.

Books were, of course, the first major use of printing. But as I mentioned earlier, other forms soon appeared. Let's take a look at each of these new forms, one at a time, starting with newspapers. People getting the news is nothing—well, new. Even the Romans had what I suppose could be considered a newspaper, the ***Acta Diurna***, or actions of the day. However, it was a tablet posted on a wall after each meeting of the Senate relating what the senators had done that day. So, the circulation was a bit low, a grand total of one, and there's no way to know what the readership was. Nonetheless, it was news, and it shows that people have always wanted to know what was going on.

During the Dark Ages after the fall of the Roman Empire, the news was delivered by troubadours, traveling musicians who would sing songs and stories and legends and whatever information they had picked up during their travels. After all, writing and literacy was down around the zero range, so news in writing was also zero.

But that, of course, wasn't a permanent condition, especially after Gutenberg. The roots of what we would consider newspapers began in seventeenth century Europe. One-page news sheets called **Corontos** were printed in Holland, and in 1620 English-language versions were imported to England by British booksellers who were eager to satisfy customers' demands for news about what was happening on the European Continent.

English printers started publishing their own news sheets with regular, daily accounts of local news starting in 1641. These were called diurnals.

The thing to bear in mind about these news sheets is that they made no pretense of objectivity. They were clearly and unabashedly partisan, reflecting the political and social views of their publishers. Today we wouldn't call what they published news but editorials, slanting their reporting of events in favor of the publishers' or sponsors' viewpoints (and the sponsor was often the government) and against those of their rivals. English newspapers had to be licensed by the government, a law instituted by Henry VIII in 1530 to control the contents of books. Publishing without a license could result in fines, mutilations and imprisonments, so toeing the government line in news coverage to get and keep the license made sense.

This continued into the American colonies, where at first the only source of news was news sheets imported from England. However, printers soon started setting up shop. The first printing press arrived in America in 1638, operating as the Cambridge Press, but their output consisted of only religious and government documents. It wasn't until 1690 that America got its first newspaper, *Public Occurrences Both Foreign and Domestick,* published by Benjamin Harris. If you think newspapers have it bad today, *Public Occurrences* lasted only one edition. It was shut down because it was critical of local and European dignitaries, and Harris neglected to get the required license from the government.

In 1704, the first newspaper that lasted more than one issue started up in America. The *Boston News-Letter* continued until the Revolution. It was dull, and it was expensive, but it did establish the newspaper business in America. Of course, it did have an advantage—the government subsidized it. But with government support came government control, so whatever the government wanted the people to know, that's what they got. And what the government **didn't** want the people to know, the people didn't hear about.

At least, they didn't until the *Boston News-Letter* got some competition. In 1721 James Franklin started the *New-England Courant,* which he operated without a government license. The *Courant* was popular and controversial, but part of that came from the fact that Franklin used it to criticize the royal governor of Massachusetts. Franklin was thrown in jail for printing "scandalous libels" (read: facts the governor didn't want people to know). To get around the government's ban on the paper, Franklin installed his brother as publisher. That brother was Benjamin Franklin. When he moved to Philadelphia and opened his own print shop, and then started his own paper in 1729, the *Pennsylvania Gazette,* Ben was launched on his career as printer, publisher, writer—inventor, statesman, ambassador, rebel leader, etc., etc., etc. Without Ben, the *Courant* soon closed, but its existence established the idea that a newspaper with popular support could challenge authority.

The *Pennsylvania Gazette* had an advantage: It was supported by Ben Franklin's very successful printing business, a fair amount of which was government contracts. Ben also sold advertising space. This led to the *Gazette* having a large degree of financial independence, which led to editorial independence.

A third newspaper was John Zenger's *New York Weekly Journal,* which started in 1733 in competition, both financially and editorially, with William Bradford's government-supported *Gazette.* Zenger was soon arrested for seditious libel for his criticisms of New York's royal governor William Cosby. What's important about Zenger is his trial. He was guilty under the law that said printed words could be libelous, even if they were true, if they were inflammatory or negative toward the government or its officials. However, he was acquitted with his defense argument that truth is a defense against libel.

The effects of these three newspapers, the *Courant,* the *Gazette* and the *Journal,* are still in force today. First, a newspaper with popular support could challenge authority; second, financial independence can lead to editorial independence; and, finally, government should not control the press because it can stifle the truth. These effects, which gave the press an independence from government control and the right to have no limits on freedom of expression, is enshrined in the U.S. Constitution as the First Amendment.

Of course, in any case, newspapers were an expensive and rather elite proposition, even with advertising to pay part of the costs of publication. Average people just couldn't afford them. But in the nineteenth century, with rising literacy rates and population densities in the cities, the time was ripe for a newspaper for everyone. On September 3, 1833, Benjamin Day started publishing *The Sun,* the first of the penny papers. These were newspapers intended for just about everybody. They sold for a penny and thus just about everybody could afford them. *The Sun* contained less of the elite political and business information of the previous newspapers, and more of what we today would consider news: police and court reports, crime stories, and entertainment and human interest news. Another penny paper was James Bennett's rather sensationalistic *New York Morning Herald.* Bennett started the correspondent system, sending reporters to other cities and other countries to gather news. Horace Greeley's *New York Tribune* avoided sensationalism and aimed at issues, demonstrating that newspapers could be a medium of social action.

In 1883, Joseph Pulitzer bought the *New York World* and brought a crusading, "something-needs-to-be-done" style to social problems. His coverage was usually light in tone and sensationalistic, relied heavily on illustrations, and used publicity stunts like an around-the-world balloon flight to raise circulation. (This approach was satirized in the 1965 movie *The Great Race,* in which a New York newspaper sponsors an around-the-world car race). Such an approach to the newspaper business worked well.

In fact, it worked so well he soon had competition from a California newspaper publisher, William Randolph Hearst, who opened the *Morning Journal* in competition with Pulitzer. The war for circulation between these two was so intense that it came close to destroying the credibility of newspapers and journalism as a whole with sensationalized sex, crime and disaster news, giant headlines and lots of illustrations. There are many historians who believe Hearst engineered the sinking of the *Maine* in order to create a war, The Spanish-American War, so his papers could cover it and increase circulation. When he ordered one of his photographers to Cuba to take pictures of the war, and the photographer said there was no war, Hearst is said to have replied, "You furnish the pictures, I'll furnish the war."

As you can see, objectivity was not a primary goal of newspapers, and it hadn't been since they were invented. But in 1923 the American Society of Newspaper Editors issued their "Canons of Journalism and Statement of Principles" in hopes of getting back some credibility lost after the Hearst/Pulitzer wars. The first sentence is "The right of a newspaper to attract and hold readers is restricted by nothing but considerations of public welfare." This was the beginning of the ideal of journalism today: Be objective, avoid sensationalism, serve the public interest.

Let's now turn to the next printing invention: magazines. Magazines began in the seventeenth century, and they were aimed at the literary elite. Instead of covering the events of the day like newspapers, they contained articles of general interest, fiction, poetry and essays, and they were quite popular with those who could afford them.

Hoping to cash in on that popularity, two American publishers started magazines. Andrew Bradford published his *American Magazine,* and Ben Franklin his *General Magazine.* They mostly reprinted material from British magazines. These magazines had several things working against them. They were expensive, they were aimed at an intellectual elite that was only a minor part of the American population; and since there was no postal system their distribution was limited to those people who could come to the print shop to buy them. So neither magazine lasted long. Nonetheless, they set the stage for other magazines, with forty-five appearing between 1741 and 1795. These magazines didn't have much more success.

However, in 1821 a magazine appeared that did succeed—for 148 years. It was *The Saturday Evening Post.* What really helped the *Post,* and the magazines that followed, were several changes in American life. First was a growing literacy rate. A goal of the United

States in the nineteenth century was universal literacy, and major attempts were made to ensure that everybody got at least a basic education in reading, writing and arithmetic.

Second was the cost. Cheaper printing methods lowered the price enough that they were accessible to more people than just the elite. Later, the invention of the roll-fed powered rotary printing press lowered the price of printing magazines astronomically.

Third was the rise in various social movements, like abolition and labor reform, which generated a great deal of interest. They also included in-depth looks at a type of news that had been pretty much ignored—crime. It was a modern idea to examine the reasons for and the effects of crime, really only presented in magazines such as *True Crime Stories* in the nineteenth century. Only later, under publishers such as Hearst and Pulitzer, did newspapers begin to cover crime in such detail. Each of these movements made for compelling reading and attracted a lot of attention.

Fourth was the use of specialty writers, which means writers who were well trained and educated on certain topics, like women's issues or politics or health or science or religion. Thus, they were able to write articles in their specialties with great depth and understanding. This was quite different from newspapers that used general reporters, who often had no deep understanding of the topics on which they reported.

Mass circulation magazines really began to prosper after the Civil War. In 1865, there were 700 magazines; by 1870 there were 1,200; and by 1885 there were 3,300. A major reason for this was the increase in women's magazines, like *Lady's Home Journal* and *Good Housekeeping*. The rise in factory-made consumer goods after the Industrial Revolution, goods in which women had great interest, had manufacturers anxious to advertise their wares. Magazines were a perfect medium for such advertising, and advertising support lowered the magazines' price for readers even further.

Two other things really helped. First was the Postal Act of 1879, which permitted mailing magazines at a cheap postal rate. The second was railroads expanding all over the country, going to every town, and able to carry magazines wherever there were people wanting to buy them.

The result was that the magazine became the first truly national mass medium. Books were personal, newspapers were local, but the same magazines were read everywhere by everyone.

Of course, this couldn't last. After World War II, magazines faced their greatest rival—television. There was no way a magazine could match the reach of TV, nor its timeliness.

But magazines could do one thing that no other medium could—specialize. General interest magazines like *The Saturday Evening Post* and *Life* lost their audiences, but magazines that aimed at niche audiences could provide whatever those audiences wanted, with articles—and ads—about their interests. Today there are magazines for knitters and skateboarders and guitar players and cat fanciers and astronomy buffs and computer nerds and do-it-yourselfers and financiers and news junkies and whatever anyone is interested in. About 6,700 magazines cater to these special interest readers, and if a new interest develops, you can be sure a new magazine will soon follow.

Books, newspapers, and magazines are the print media that have ruled for centuries, but they've always been dependent on the physical plant, the presses, to churn out their products, and that means money—lots of money. But today things have changed.

The advent of the personal computer, computer printer and photocopy machine in the last thirty years has meant that everyone can be a publisher, printing as many copies of their own work as they can afford. And, with the Internet, anything written can be placed in front of hundreds and thousands of people for almost nothing.

In the beginning, we could only express our ideas to those near to us through speech. But over the last few thousand years we've been able to freeze that speech in writing and then print, allowing us to speak over the miles and over the years. There's a common saying: "If we see farther than our ancestors, it's only because we stand on their shoulders." If we hadn't been able to capture the thoughts, ideas and dreams of our ancestors through writing, we'd still be in small groups scratching out a precarious living. For the first couple of million years our ancestors wandered the landscape and made tools out of rocks. With the invention of writing, we advanced in the next 6,000 years from that to nation states and world exploration and water power and metallurgy. And with the invention of printing, we went from that to the moon in 500 years. Only 8,000 years from caves to space. The invention of printing has allowed us to spread knowledge, not just to an elite few but to anyone anywhere in the world willing to read. And what you read, you can build on. Just look at the way we lived in the long-ago past and see how writing and printing have completely changed the world and the people who live in it.

■ ENDNOTE

1. Much of the following discussion is based on James Burke's excellent examination of history, ***Connections*** (1995).

6

PRINT AND SOCIETY

Print media have been such a central part of our society for so long that we often forget print wasn't always around. For millennia people went without it, and as far as we can tell it didn't do them a lot of harm. But, then again, its lack may have held them back in many ways. So let's examine the effects of print on society. We'll start by looking at what people did before printing.

■ BEFORE PRINTING

Here is a painting from the caves at Lascaux containing a bull, a bird, and a man. However, what do they mean? How do you "read" them? Hunting magic? Animal spirits or gods?

hypenose-kikh.de

Teaching tools? Memorials to the dead? The man on the left doesn't look all that healthy.

Maybe it was the TV of their day (let's watch the horses tonight)?

What story are they trying to tell? The creator of the painting knows, but without that person there to explain it, could anyone else?

Eventually something more concrete and less open to individual interpretation was necessary, and people invented hieroglyphics to write things down. Over time, the Egyptians realized that painting in black and white was quicker and easier than painting in color. Then, because whenever you can write things down more things are found that **need** to be written down, they

started simplifying hieroglyphics and finally created what was almost a shorthand. Then, in order to create longer lasting documents and not need brushes and ink, they invented cuneiform.

However, all these forms of writing were specialized skills that required years of training. Egyptian and Babylonian records indicate that youngsters spent twelve years in scribe school to learn their craft. It must be admitted it makes sense that it would take a long time to learn to be a scribe. They had to memorize thousands of word symbols and how to draw them, so only people who **had** to know, knew how write. This included the scribes and architects and supervisors and artisans and artists working on things like temples and pharaohs' tombs. It did not include average people. They got pictures painted on walls.

A major effect of this is that it led to a very conservative society. This included the ability to communicate. Egypt had symbols that stood for things (a drawing of the thing itself), for words, for syllables, and for letters, and they used all four at the same time—they never let go of anything. It would appear that, to the Egyptians, letting go would alter a society that was incredibly stable and established. They wouldn't change to something else, even something easier and more efficient, because they saw no need.

However, it also slowed any kind of improvement, not just in society, but in **any** area, including government, science and trade.

Science was basically "if it was good enough for great-great-great-grandpa it's good enough for me," and "the gods do it." After all, that's what all the priests and wall drawings said.

Trade was stifled by a lack of quick and easy recordkeeping that all traders could use. Traders didn't have the time to learn hieroglyphics or cuneiform, and trade was basically simple and local. They essentially bartered the actual items that were present at the time, such as bushels of wheat for bolts of cloth. Bartering is an inefficient form of trade, since the person who has what you want has to want what you have to trade. If rhe doesn't, you have to find someone else who does have what the first person wants that wants what you have. For example, you want cloth and have wheat, but the person with cloth wants onions. You find someone with onions, but he doesn't want wheat, he wants a goat; so you find someone with a goat who wants wheat, make the swap, take the goat to the person with onions and make the swap. Then you take the onions to the person with cloth and swap the onions for the cloth. So much for that day.

When it came to altering their writing, the sheer power and inertia of the bureaucracy, especially that of the scribes and their privileges, prevented any change.

It could be that such extreme conservatism well suited the Egyptians when one considers their situation. They lived in an area where everything was unchanging and predictable. The desert was the desert and didn't change. They were so close to the equator, the seasonal changes were close to nonexistent. The Nile flooded every year at approximately the same time and to approximately the same height, bringing the same nutrients to the soil. It was a society in which today, and this year and this century, was very much like yesterday and last year and last century. Over the centuries they had faced problems and solved them quite satisfactorily. For instance, they solved needing more food with irrigation and pottery. With an "if it ain't broke, don't fix it" attitude, it's little wonder they didn't make changes, since any such changes would only be incremental and may cause new and unexpected problems. This is why Egyptians only really changed when it was forced upon them. For example, they only began using chariots in war when the chariot-using Hyksos conquered them. When the Egyptians finally drove the Hyksos out of Egypt about a hundred years later, the war chariot became the Egyptians' most important weapon.

Everything came to an abrupt change with the Phoenicians, the greatest traders in the ancient world. They traveled everywhere and traded with everyone. They needed a method of writing for recordkeeping that was easy to learn and use, easily understood from one end of the Mediterranean Sea to the other, and could transcribe any language. With the Phoenicians' invention of the alphabet, where each letter represented a spoken sound, a consonant, they could accomplish all these goals.

Things improved even more when the Greeks added vowels to the consonants of the Phoenician alphabet. Now there was no need to guess from context what word was intended.

This altered society all over the Mediterranean because it was now possible to communicate through writing, not just through face to face conversation. Such a simple method of writing could be learned by anyone in a relatively short time. It was measured in days or weeks, not the years necessary for pictographic forms of writing such as hieroglyphs and cuneiform. Literacy rates rose and communication of all types became possible, not just bureaucratic records or religious tracts, but personal communication over great distances and time. This led to expanded trade as the Phoenicians and then other cultures—such as the Cretans, the Greeks and even the Egyptians, once they saw the advantages—bought and sold goods throughout the Mediterranean world. Trade meant greater contact between different cultures, leading to a mixing of those cultures and their ideas, innovations, stories, traditions, religion—all the things that make a society a society. The entire Mediterranean world became more homogenous.

■ THE ALEXANDRIAN LIBRARY

The Alexandrian Library in Alexandria, Egypt, was of real importance. Founded in 288 BCE, it contained a copy of virtually every book in the world, estimated at about 100,000, and the library had a deliberate intent to *have* a copy of every book. There was even a law that whenever a ship arrived in Alexandria, it was searched for books and scrolls, and if any were discovered that weren't already in the inventory, they were confiscated to be copied for the Library. For six hundred years the library was a center of learning and research in such fields as science, literature and philosophy. During this time scholars built upon the knowledge already collected and added to it. Knowledge of all kinds grew as people explored and thought and shared their discoveries.

And then in 391 CE the library and its contents were burned to the ground. No one is sure how it happened, although theories abound. Maybe Julius Caesar did it when he torched Cleopatra's brother's fleet, although Caesar died three hundred years before the library burned. Maybe the early Christians did it, fearing that the library contained pagan ideas contrary to their beliefs. Maybe Muslims did it because they believed that the Koran contained everything anyone needed to know, and thus it was the only book that was necessary and therefore should exist—except for the small detail that there were no Muslims in 391, and there wouldn't be for the next two hundred years. Maybe, just maybe, it was an accident. Whatever the cause, burning the library was the beginning of the beginning of the Dark Ages in Europe and the Mediterranean world.

There were, of course, other libraries, like the Ulpian Library in Rome, but they were pale shadows of the Alexandrian. Much of the knowledge of Sumeria, Babylonia, Egypt, Greece and Rome was lost, as there were few copies of any book in existence. For example, we only have thirty-one of the great Greek tragedies, such as *Oedipus Rex* and *Medea,* out of the hundreds that were written. The Alexandrian library probably had a copy of all of them, but all those plays were lost with its destruction.

■ THE FALL OF ROME

With the fall of the Roman Empire, traditionally set in 476 CE, literacy plummeted. Society collapsed in on itself. Travel pretty much ended as the Pax Romana (the peace of Rome) ended, which for centuries had patrolled the roads and maintained law and order throughout the empire. Safety meant staying home. Most people never traveled more than seven miles from home, as far as they could walk in any direction and still be able to get back home before dark. The world for these people became the village and its immediate environs, under the control of the local lord. Just about everything else became nothing more than stories and legends and superstition. People were more concerned with surviving than bothering to learn to read and write (assuming they could find someone to teach them), and they saw little use in reading, anyway. As far they were concerned, they already knew what they needed to know.

The fact that few people were able to read or write meant that knowledge was in people's heads (Burke 1985). History was what people remembered, and thus most of the knowledge of what had occurred in the world in the past disappeared as the people who could remember it died. Stories were told to explain what no one could remember, such as who and how Roman architectural works were built, which the stories now said were built by giants who had lived before living memory. However, most people were more worried about immediate survival, and the past beyond what was needed to maintain the local social group was irrelevant. Knowing about Roman or Greek society or law or architecture or engineering wouldn't help grow crops or stave off the wolves (sometimes literally) at the door. Law was whatever people said it was, and it was the local lord who had the say. Facts were what people believed they were, whether or not they had any basis in reality.

There was no need for books or reading—everything anyone needed to know was local: when to plow and reap, how to build a house or barn, who owned what. You just asked someone in the neighborhood who remembered.

No reading and writing meant that knowledge was oral, that people said aloud what they knew. This led to the firm belief that truth was carried in the spoken, not the written, word. That's still part of our belief, and language, today. Taxes and other forms of finance are audited, which means they are heard—audit comes from the word audio. That means you're supposed to **tell** an auditor (which means listener) about your taxes, not show rher your papers and receipts for rher to read. Courts hold "hearings" where they hear testimony, and eye witnesses telling what they saw still carries more weight than forensics—despite what you see on CSI. (Please note though that in court the experts must tell the jury about their findings by explaining them out loud; the findings can't stand on their own.) There are still rules, for instance, that the jury isn't allowed to write things down, and the judge must explain to the jury the rule of law that applies in the case. He must speak his instructions—the jury isn't allowed to read them.

In a period without writing, which meant a lack of written records, old people were vital to society. They could go into a court holding a hearing and testify with information about the past from their own memories that went back years and decades to help judges make decisions. And they used things such as knives or rings, not something written down, as reminders to trigger those memories, sort of like the old "tie a string around your finger" approach. Everything was dependent on old people's memories to arrive at an answer. There simply weren't any trustworthy documents to rely on.

This also meant that, without writing, memories were prodigious. When you don't have writing you **have** to commit everything to memory, and anything that might help a person remember was vital. Fortunately, people had a method—poetry. Poetry is easier to remember than prose because of the rhythm and rhyme. An example is "The Iliad," the epic poem about the Trojan War. It was not uncommon for people to be able to recite the thousands of words of that poem from memory. Homer didn't write the poem; he wrote it down after it had been carried in people's memory for hundreds of years.

We still have poems as aids to memory, like "Thirty days hath September, April, June, and November," or "Early to bed, early to rise, makes a man healthy, wealthy and wise."

Even nursery rhymes tell us about events in history: "Ring around a rosie, a pocket full of posies, ashes, ashes, we all fall down" is about the Black Death, where the first signs of the disease was a ring around a red spot, people carried flowers thinking the scent would hold off the disease, they burned the bodies, the ashes covered everything, and everyone fell down dead.

"London Bridge is falling down, falling down, falling down. London Bridge is falling down, my fair lady" is a reference to the bridge's decrepit state when, after standing for four hundred years, it caught fire in 1633. "Mary, Mary, quite contrary" is about England's Queen Mary the First, known as "Bloody Mary," and her torture of Protestants (the "silver bells and cockle shells" refer to torture instruments).

"Little Jack Horner sat in a corner, eating his Christmas pie. He stuck in his thumb and pulled out a plum and said, 'What a good boy am I.'" Jack Horner was a real person, the secretary to the Catholic Bishop of Glastonbury. When King Henry VIII decided to strip abbeys of their lands and wealth after he converted England to Protestantism, the bishop sent the king a bribe—a Christmas pie containing the deeds to twelve church properties in hopes the king would let the abbey keep the rest. Only eleven deeds arrived— Horner "stuck in his thumb and pulled out a plum"—he opened the pie and stole the deed to the richest of the twelve properties. "Oh, what a good boy" was he! Horner's descendents still own that property.

So poetry was the language of memory and society. It was the great aid to memory in a society without writing and the way to spread what little actual knowledge there was.

For example, what news of the outside world people got came from itinerant musicians, the troubadours, who traveled from place to place and entertained the nobility and peasantry alike with songs and poetry, telling the stories and sagas and legends of their society—and the news, like who was king now. When bands of troubadours met, they would sit and eat and share new songs and stories and whatever news they had learned in their travels.

Now, even in an era when everyone by necessity had great memories, these people were ridiculous, able to remember a thousand words or more on one hearing. That would be the equivalent of having someone read you two pages of this book and you remembering them and being able to repeat them, word for word, days, weeks and months from now.

That memories were the repositories of knowledge does not mean there were no books, but such books as existed were pretty much one of a kind, hand copied by monks in monasteries. Note that I say "copied." New books, ones containing new, previously unwritten material, were rare, and they were mostly monastic histories and chronicles, like the Venerable Bede's *Historia ecclesiastica gentis Anglorum* (**Ecclesiastical History of the English People**). Naturally, he wrote what he knew, and, being a monk, what he knew all about was the Church.

So books were copied, but not to spread knowledge—after all, there was no one to read them but other monks, and for them books were not for knowledge. For the monks, the copying was a form of prayer, and their tools were symbolic of worship. A twelfth century sermon said:

> "You write with the pen of memory on the parchment of pure conscience, scraped by the knife of divine fear, smoothed by the pumice of heavenly desires, and whitened by the chalk of holy thoughts. The ruler is the will of God. The split nib is the joint love of God and our neighbour. Coloured inks are heavenly grace. The exemplar is the life of Christ."[1]

So **what** was copied, the content of the book, was far less important than the **act** of copying, and content was pretty much irrelevant to that act.

Of course, when a copier isn't concerned with content, errors would also creep in. A monk may make a mistake in copying, especially if the exemplar being copied was old and faded, or poorly inscribed, or if it was full of abbreviations, which was common when everything was handwritten. And if the book was copied again, the error would also be copied. There was little attempt to ensure accuracy because, again, the **copying** was important, not the **contents** of the book. Add to that the desire to illuminate the pages with decorative elements, which was also done as an act of devotion, and the words making up the text became less important than the appearance of the page.

Once a book was done, it was bound and then just randomly put on a shelf or in a cabinet and forgotten, gathering dust until some monk decided to copy it again.

Because the purpose of copying was just to copy, there was no attempt to organize information, or even to keep track of what was in any book. They would write a title of sorts on the page ends, and that was it. For example, the page ends might read "Sermones Sebastiane." However, what was really in the book? The sermons created by St. Sebastian? The sermons created by some other person named Sebastian? Maybe it was sermons copied by a Sebastian. Or maybe sermons copied by somebody from a church of St. Sebastian.

They could just be sermons preached by or belonging to someone named Sebastian or sermons by various people of whom the first or most important was somebody named Sebastian. It may be only the first thing in the book, or even only the first line or first **word**, like the title of the book Genesis in the Bible (genesis means "birth" or "in the beginning," in Latin), and the book actually contains a miscellaneous assortment of unconnected content. Because the title of a book really provided little information about what was in the book, it was hard, if not impossible, to find anything in the books. You had to open and look through every one to see what was in them (Burke 1985).

Because there was no realistic way to find what had been written before, there was no written history on which everyone could agree, only widely differing views of what had happened in the world beyond the walls of the monastery. To the monks, the only thing worthy of inclusion would be how what happened in the world affected the local monastery, like the Venerable Bede's book. There was no geography, or natural history, or science because there could be no sure way of verifying the information on which such subjects depend—it couldn't be found if it existed at all. Thus society was a realm of memory, hearsay and fantasy.

However, that didn't worry anybody, since in a society in which the only thing that was certain in people's lives was the Church, the only true reality lay in the mind of God, who knew everything that needed to be, or indeed could be known, and whose reasons were inscrutable.

This is not to say that there was no writing at all. Some writing was necessary since not everything could be committed to memory. Nobles (virtually none of whom were literate—they considered it beneath them) would occasionally hire a monk or a lay brother from a monastery to do what writing they needed, such as estate records and contracts.

However, society was completely turned on its head after the Black Death of 1347, which killed a third to a half of the population and slaughtered the elderly—and their memories. The problem was the matter of inheritance. Depending on people's memories, especially dead people's memories, to determine who owned what was impossible. Oral traditions were completely inadequate and writing took on an importance again.

Add to that the fact that the Black Death spelled the doom of the feudal system. The Black Death took a major toll on the peasants who worked the land. The reduced number available to work meant that, instead of peasants being essentially the property of the nobles, trading their labor for food and housing, the peasants' labor became a valuable commodity in and of itself—and the peasants knew it. Abandoning their feudal duties of trading their labor for a share of the food they raised, they would hire themselves out for money to whoever would pay them the most, and if their former lord didn't like it, there wasn't much he could do about it except offer an even higher wage.

Suddenly, the common people, not just the upper class, had money—that they wanted to spend. And days off—that they wanted to spend spending money. Trade and commerce boomed, villages became towns, towns became cities, and, for the first time in centuries, people, through their own efforts, could change their position in life, from serf to merchant.

As trade resumed, with money constantly moving from place to place to facilitate it, banking became vital, and if there's one thing banks need, it's accurate records of complex transactions. There was a move away from the feudal system of "I'll take care of mine, and the hell with you" toward large monarchies, as well as the incumbent need for tax records and to keep the burgeoning bureaucracies happy.

With the introduction of cheap paper in the fourteenth century to replace the expensive parchment, the need for literacy bloomed. Schools were founded to train scribes and clerks. The Church usually ran them, as, after all, it had the only people trained in reading and writing. Scriptoria, or writing shops, opened everywhere to supply the demand for documentation from merchants and governments and lawyers and notaries and anybody else that needed something written down.

The biggest problem was there was far more need for forms and records and books than the scribes could handle, as so many of them had died off in the plague, and their fees became astronomical. Something had to be done.

And something was—Gutenberg and his moveable type printing press.

■ AFTER PRINTING (1450+)

Johannes Gutenberg introduced moveable type printing in 1450. Within fifty years, there were 20 million books in print, more than all the books that had ever existed in the world before then (Burke 1985). Printing rapidly expanded communication because so many copies of—well, anything—could be created in a very short a time and very cheaply, certainly more cheaply than a roomful of scribes could do it.

Let's take a look at just one result of how printing changed society. One of the first and biggest users of the printing press was the Catholic Church, which printed sermons and prayer books and breviaries and other documents, and especially what are called indulgences, essentially a get out of hell free card. For a nominal fee (i.e., what the market would bear), anyone could buy an indulgence that the Church said was forgiveness for all past sins.

Prior to printing, an indulgence had to be handwritten, which was a time and labor intensive job. However, with a printing press you could churn them out very quickly and cheaply by the hundreds and thousands, with blanks to be filled in with the name of the sin and the name of the sinner. The money just rolled into Church coffers.

However, there was a German monk who didn't like the idea of indulgences. Indeed, he wasn't too happy about quite a few things the Church and its hierarchy were doing. So Martin Luther made a list of his complaints, and in 1517 he nailed his 95 Theses, or criticisms, to the door of the Wittenberg church. He also sent a copy of his theses to a few friends, fully expecting a civil discussion of his objections. His expectations were a bit too optimistic. Those friends immediately printed copies of his theses and started spreading them around. Within two weeks they were all over Germany. Within a month they were all over Europe (Burke 1985).

Thus was born the Protestant Reformation, the greatest threat ever to the most powerful force in Europe for the last one thousand years: the Catholic Church. Naturally, the Church fought back, and in 1518 the first real propaganda war began, Printing presses churned out essays and broadsides for both sides, including tasteful little cartoons of German Protestants breaking wind in the face of the Pope.

The printing press really accelerated the conflict. By 1520, there were 300,000 copies of Luther's books in print, including his Bible, the first written in a local language, German, instead of the Latin that had been the norm since the Church had settled itself in Rome. Luther even said that printing was "God's highest and extremest act of Grace, whereby the business of the Gospel may be driven forward."[2]

Imagine what that would mean. For the first time, average people could read for themselves the most important single guide to their lives: the Bible. They were no longer dependent on their priests to interpret the rules of their lives for them—they could read and determine them for themselves. They could examine them, discuss them, dispute them—they could decide for themselves what the Bible told them to believe and how to lead their lives. This resulted in a major reduction in the power of the Church to direct the course and beliefs of society, the stories by which that society defined and sustained itself.

To fight this reduction in power, the Church instituted new practices that previously had been not only rare, but virtually unknown. For the Church, printing became the enemy. So, it would excommunicate people for writing, or even reading, banned books. That meant it would declare someone as no longer in the Church, which would essentially condemn that person to hell. It started the Inquisition, a division of the Church with the mandate to find, expose and gain confessions of apostasy (denying the dogma of the Church, in this case by reading or writing anything contrary to that dogma), often through torture; and it burned books that put in doubt the primacy of the Church. And, if they didn't burn the writings, they burned the writers.

A society that had been stable, and indeed stagnant, for hundreds of years, was sent into a turmoil of religious divisiveness. The warfare between Protestants and Catholics resulted in the deaths of millions, a wholesale abandonment of faith in anything and a growth of uncertainty in everything.

Let's take just one example from the Thirty Years War, which raged all over Germany from 1618 to 1648. Ostensibly, it was a battle between Catholic princes to restore the Church in areas that had turned to Protestantism, and Protestant princes to remain Protestant and replace Catholicism with Protestantism in Catholic areas. Actually, it was really more of a land grab as little German princelings tried to seize a few more square miles, or even acres, of land to rule, using religion as an excuse. There were some rulers fighting on either side that were devoutly religious in their motivations, like Frederick II of Bavaria, but most were just greedy little jerks. However, the result of these battles raging back and forth across the landscape was a complete disruption of society.

For example, there was the concept of "cuius regio, eius religio," which meant that the ruler of an area determined the religion of that area and could compel the people living there to follow that religion. But with all the battles between these rulers (and there were 225 of these princelings in Germany), the areas kept changing hands and thus the religion the inhabitants were required to follow. Imagine how secure their faith would be if every other year they had to believe a different one. This would be particularly difficult when the armies fighting to keep the people Catholic or Protestant didn't care what religion those people were. For instance, when the Catholic general Tilly attacked Magdeburg in 1631, his Catholic army burned and looted the city and massacred the inhabitants, slaughtering 25,000 of the 30,000 people who lived there—most of whom were Catholic.

These religious conflicts still exist today—think Northern Ireland and the conflict between Catholics and Protestants, or Iraq and the conflict between the Sunni and Shi'a sects of Islam, or Israel and the conflict between Jews and Muslims. These conflicts arose through different interpretations of how a religion should be followed. However, without the printing press, the millions of books, pamphlets and broadsides that fueled the dispute wouldn't have been possible. They spread each side's arguments and propaganda far and wide and to millions of adherents.

Religion wasn't the only aspect of society that was altered irrevocably by the introduction of printing. The new power to disseminate opinion on any subject was seized eagerly by anybody with a desire to influence others. The printers themselves had shown the way with their advertising. Now the broadsheet radically changed the ability to communicate, not just to the few, but to the many. Broadsheets were pinned up everywhere, stimulating a demand for education and literacy by those who couldn't read them. Mass public opinion was being molded for the first time, fuelled by anonymous appeals to emotion and the belief that if it was printed it must be true.

Centralized monarchies that took over after the collapse of the feudal system used the printing press to enhance their control over the people and to keep them informed of new laws and edicts and tax collections. Since each of the increasingly large numbers of directives in circulation originated from clearly identifiable printing houses, it was easy for the Church and state to impose controls on what could and could not be printed and thus read (Burke 1985).

The corollary, of course, was that dissidence now **also** had a louder voice, whether expressed as nationalistic fervor—itself fostered by the local language being established in

print—or as religious fervor. The persecution and religious wars that ravaged Europe in the sixteenth century were given fresh and ongoing impetus by the press, as each side used propaganda to whip up the frenzy of its supporters. Indeed, even the word "propaganda" originated in the Catholic Church. In the seventeenth century, it set up its Congregatio de Propaganda Fide, the "congregation for propagating the faith," in an attempt to counter the Protestant Reformation.

In politics, printing provided new weapons for state control. As people became more literate, they could be expected to read and sign articles of loyalty. The simple oath, which during the period before printing was accepted as binding, was no longer sufficient, and in any case it was always possible to deny making it. People couldn't deny their signatures at the foot of a clearly printed text. This represented the first appearance of the modern contract, in this case between the state and the individual, and later extended to business and trade. With it came the centralization of the power of the state as it laid out the rules of such contracts and the penalties for violating them.

In addition, through the press the monarch had direct access to the people as his edicts were published and circulated. He didn't have to worry about whether the nobility under him were delivering them or ignoring them to maintain their own power. The political structure of society changed from the local to the national, and with it came politics and politicians. Political songs emerged, as did political slogans and catch-phrases, as politicians attempted to influence public opinion on how government should be run and what it should do.

Other major changes in society, and indeed in the entire world order, came about because of printing. The American Revolution is an excellent example. American propaganda attacking British rule fed the discontent in the British colonies. Paul Revere's engraving of the Boston Massacre inflamed the American colonists against the British. Look at how the line of British redcoats is just mowing down the people. However, it's a completely inaccurate representation of the event. In fact, John Adams, one of the leaders of the American Revolution, acted as defense attorney for the soldiers involved in this so-called "massacre" at their court-martial and got them acquitted. What actually happened is that the officer tried to keep his small troop of soldiers calm, unlike the one in the engraving who's directing his soldiers to fire, but in the face of the taunts and rock throwing of the crowd, one young soldier in fear for his life fired his musket. This led to the other soldiers doing the same, thinking the order to fire had been given. However, in the face of thousands of copies of this engraving, the facts were buried beneath the flood of anti-British sentiment.

The story of the Boston Massacre was just that, a story, and remember how societies tell themselves stories to tell themselves who they are. Let's analyze this story and see how it created a *belief* about what reality is rather than an objective understanding about reality. The exposition in this story was about the British ruling the colonies; the problem was the British slaughtering innocent Americans to maintain that rule; the solution to the problem, the climax, would be independence. The problem as presented is false, but the story says that it is true and provides no implication to the contrary. Thus, in the minds of those who receive the story, the only information they get about the event, the problem is true and thus the climax must be the correct one.

Tom Paine's essay *Common Sense* further encouraged revolution by retelling the story and ingraining it further in the American sense of reality.

The Declaration of Independence is itself a story that laid out for one and all why a revolution was necessary. As Thomas Jefferson wrote in 1825, the purpose of the declaration was "To place before mankind the common sense of the subject, in terms so plain and firm as to command their assent" (Whitman 1940). But the Declaration is also a story, complete with exposition: "We hold these truths to be self-evident, that all men are created equal;" introduces the problem: "The history of the present king of Great Britain is a history of repeated injuries and usurpations, all having in direct object the establishment of an absolute tyranny over these states;" then it continues through a list of crises and complications listing the tyrannical acts of the king; and it ends with a climax: ". . . These united colonies are, and of right ought to be free and independent states; that they are absolved from all allegiance to the British crown, and that all political connection between them and the state of Great Britain is, and ought to be, totally dissolved."

Look at the effect of these documents and the stories they tell. They created a new view of reality and the world, one in which, for the first time in history, common people could take control of their own lives and create their own society instead of being ruled by nobility and royalty. It was an appealing and persuasive worldview, and it led to many people supporting the revolution. It was the first step toward the political world we live in today, as the American story spread across the world. And again, it was printing that accelerated and fed this upheaval in the world.

■ GROWTH OF KNOWLEDGE

Of course, printing created another kind of revolution, one that wasn't all about war or religion or politics. That was a revolution in knowledge.

First, a little background. After the fall of Rome, the Arabs saved and improved on much of the knowledge of the Greeks and Romans that Europe lost during the Dark Ages. When the Arabs conquered most of Spain in 711, they brought that knowledge with them. For example, the library in Cordoba had 400,000 books, and there were 69 other libraries in town (Burke 1985). When the Moors were driven out of Spain in 1492, the conquerors discovered the books, and as the books were translated and printed and circulated across the continent, European thinkers quickly adopted the knowledge they contained. Suddenly everything Greek and Roman was the **in** thing.

So the advent of printing was one of the most critical events in history, up there with fire and the plow. Printing first and foremost made it easy to transmit information to a large audience without personal contact between those who knew and those who wanted to know, and in this sense it revolutionized the spread of knowledge. Craft technique in particular saw a major growth. "How to do it" books were among the first off the press, written about almost every field of human activity from metallurgy to botany to linguistics to good manners. Printing also made texts consistent by ending the copying errors with which manuscripts were loaded. A corollary was that it placed on the author the responsibility for accuracy, since many more people were now likely to read the material than would ever read a handwritten book or scroll, and who might know at least as much about the subject as did the author.

Let's see how that might work. Remember this page, with the drawing of a plant? Before printing, it would take a day or two to turn out just one copy of this page, as it was individually hand drawn. However, with printing you could turn out hundreds of copies of this page in one day.

Imagine the impact on knowledge. Instead of only a handful of people knowing about this picture, hundreds or thousands of people now could. And once they saw that picture, they could go out in a field and look at an actual plant to see if the picture was correct.

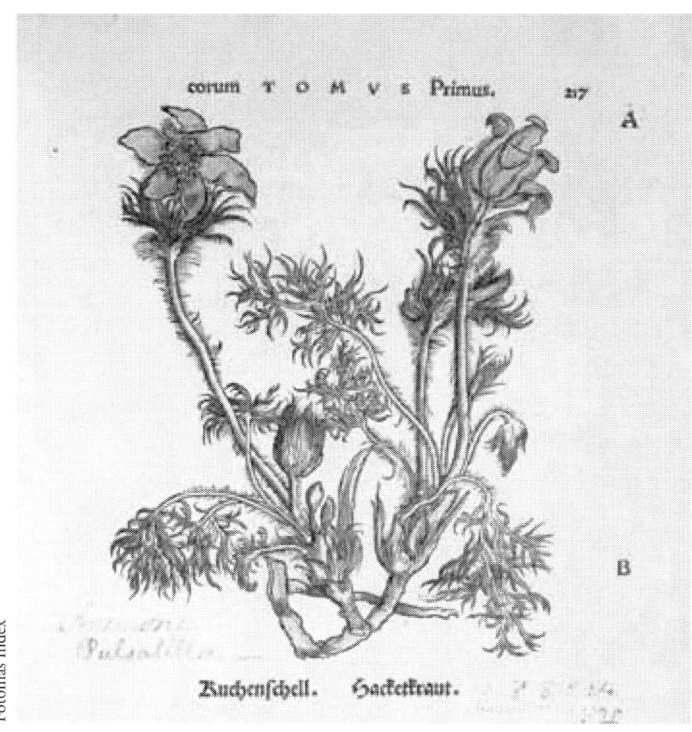

What if the picture wasn't correct? They would probably print their own book with an accurate picture, and possibly toss in a few snide remarks about the person who got it wrong.

More people examining a subject and publishing their results encouraged agreement on the material, and this spurred academic investigation of subjects and the development of academic and practical disciplines, such as botany, biology, architecture, engineering, politics and many others. Individuals who published books on various topics began to be recognized as authors, a variation on "authority," which led to the concept of "mastership" in a subject. In turn this led to knowledge becoming separated into specialized areas, which emphasized the separation of the expert from the rest of the community as someone far more knowledgeable in an area than other people. The earliest books would have been read by men who could doubtless have turned their hand as easily to the violin, the pen or the architect's drawing, and it may be said that with the coming of the book they were the last generation to be able to do so. As the books written by experts began to circulate, carrying ideas to readers who no longer had to have access to a manuscript copyist producing rare and expensive editions, the speed of change coming from the interaction of hundreds and thousands of ideas and approaches to knowledge increased dramatically. This was a far cry from the centuries of the Dark Ages, when all that people needed to know was contained in the Bible, everything else was in the mind of God, and new ideas were discouraged since they might upset the social order.

The coming of the printed book must have seemed as if it would turn the world upside down in the way it spread and, above all, democratized knowledge, and indeed it did. Provided you could pay and read, what was on the shelves in the new bookshops was yours for the taking. Alexis de Tocqueville in his *Democracy in America* discussed major events in history that ". . . promoted equality of condition [a person's position in the social order]. The Crusades and the English wars decimated the nobles and divided their possessions; the municipal corporations introduced democratic liberty into the bosom of feudal monarchy; the invention of firearms equalized the vassal and the noble on the field of battle: *the art of printing opened the same resources to the minds of all classes . . .*" [my italics].[3]

One man really accelerated the process of spreading printed books and the knowledge they contained. That man was a Venetian named Aldus Manutius who had a big idea when the Turks invaded Greece in 1453 and Greek refugees flooded into Venice needing jobs.

At the beginning of the sixteenth century, Aldus sped up the spread of ancient thinking by hiring those Greeks to translate every piece of Greek writing he could get from the Arabs. He then did his second great thing: He started printing. First he printed Greek and Latin dictionaries and grammars so people could read the works in their original languages; then he published the works themselves. But to make it easier and cheaper, he started printing in a new typeface invented by Francesco Griffo, one of his assistants—italics. Aldus could now pack more print onto a page and make the books smaller and cheaper, turning what would have been large heavy tomes into pocket editions, about the size of what are now called paperbacks. These books were easily transportable, and they were— transported, that is. Instead of only one or two books, a person could carry a small library on horseback, spreading their contents even further.

Among all those Greek works that became published were those of the Greek philosopher Aristotle, who was, for more than 1,500 years, **the** authority for all things scientific. The Arabs reintroduced Aristotle to the world, and with the seal of approval from the Church, his ideas became "*the way things are.*" He wrote that dolphins and whales are fish, rotting meat turns into flies and stored grain turned into mice, that it's the weight of an object that determines whether it will float or not, that women have fewer teeth than men, that babies are born healthier if conceived when a north wind is blowing, and that heavy things fall faster than light things.

With the printing of all things Aristotle, naturally there were going to be people who would check on his "facts," like actually counting women's teeth. One such person was Giovanni Bennedetti, who performed the famous gravity experiment of dropping a light ball and a heavy ball from the Tower of Pisa to see which one hit the ground first. Remember that Aristotle said the heavy ball would hit first. Imagine the surprise of Aristotelians when both balls hit the ground at the same time. All of a sudden all things Aristotle were in doubt.

Of course, one of the most famous of those attempting to break the Church's stranglehold on knowledge was Galileo Galilei. Aristotle said that the universe consisted of perfect crystal spheres upon which were mounted the stars and planets, all circling around the Earth, the center of everything. The Church agreed with this interpretation of the universe, as it supported their contention that the Earth and people were the pinnacles of God's creation and thus would of course be the center of everything. When Galileo, with the latest scientific device, the telescope, found moons circling Jupiter, it contradicted Aristotle's, and therefore the Church's, teachings. When Galileo published his findings in his *Siderius Nuncius,* with its illustrations of his discoveries, the Church banned the book and put Galileo under house arrest.

However, the book had been published. Before printing there might have been only one or two handwritten copies that could be easily suppressed. But with printing there were thousands of copies, the word was out, and there was no way to stop it.

So what was the problem with Galileo? It wasn't his facts—even the Church acknowledged that his view of the universe made the math easier to figure out holy days. It sure beat the Ptolemaic earth-centered system. No, what the Church was bothered about was that Galileo was telling a **new story** about the universe, one that contradicted the Church's story. For a thousand years the Earth was at the center of everything, just where God had put it in the beginning, and by Church dogma it had to stay there. The Church and the society it built was a tribal one, built on tribal stories—the old "that's they way we've always done it, and if it was good enough for great-great-great-grandpa, it's good enough for us." So the Earth had to stay in the center of the universe: ". . . as it was in the beginning, is now, and *ever shall be* [my italics], world without end, Amen." The Church's fear was that Galileo's new story would supplant the **old** story upon which the Church derived so much of its authority before the Church could prepare people for the change.

Another effect of the discovery of all the Greek and Roman knowledge in the Moorish libraries in Spain is that searches were made of the old monastic libraries for other things to print that the Arabs hadn't preserved. For example, Vitruvius' *De Architectura* from about 40 BCE showed how the Romans built their buildings, leading to a neo-Roman building boom all over Europe. The work of architects like Inigo Jones based on Roman ideas and engineering popped up all over England. Other examples of old knowledge becoming new included Roman weapons, tools, and even fire engines. Once the pictures and instructions were printed, everyone wanted to build and use them.

Also printed were Roman laws and materials about the Roman legal system. Prior to publishing these laws, the law was in the hands of individuals with power, the nobility, backed by the Church. In effect, their **word** was law. The legal system, far from being blind, was individual, and the richer or more powerful or more noble (read: from the right family) you were, the more rights you had, including the right to do whatever you wanted to with no consequences. It was an era of might makes right, trial by fire, trial by combat, trial by torture, trial by being tied up and thrown in the river (drowning was proof of innocence), or no trial at all. The fate of the accused could rest on what the local lord ate for breakfast that morning.

In addition to there being no criminal or civil laws beyond the local lord's whim, laws dealing with contracts, banking and trade were virtually nonexistent. During the Middle Ages a merchant tended to treat each transaction as a separate thing, having little or no connection with any other transaction. Trade law was a patchwork of local law, verbal law, Church law, local customs, things that would only make sense where they were created (Burke 1985). Trade increased by leaps and bounds after the Black Death because of all the loose money lying around after the survivors inherited, but nobody knew what rules applied where.

Roman Emperor Justinian's *Corpus Juris Civilis (Body of Civil Laws)* would have helped. However, this book had been lost since the year 603, and with it the legal system it laid out. Only two copies existed (remember the problem with hand copying everything) and nobody knew where they were. When a copy was finally discovered in the monastery of St. Stephen, it changed everything. With the publication of Roman laws, people began to realize there was another way of handling law, one that gave everyone some rights and obligations, and that the same laws could, and should, apply to everyone and everywhere.

Trade also began to make sense. The same trade laws began to be applied everywhere as the printed texts of Justinian's civil laws spread across Europe. Add to that the publication and spread of the Arabic accounting system, especially Arabic numbers and the concept of the zero to replace Roman numerals, and trade got much easier. It spread far and wide, and with ease came greater wealth and a sharing of ideas and cultures.

Knowledge blossomed. Indeed, it exploded. Anything anybody knew about—well, anything—hit the books. For a while, in the 1500s, it was possible to know everything—just buy a copy of every book and read it. This was the era of the "Renaissance Man." It didn't last long. The number of books on the number of topics grew exponentially until it was impossible to read a copy of everything. People started looking for the information they needed instead of learning everything there was to know. Specialty publications helped, such as Ben Franklin's *Poor Richard's Almanac* or his *Pennsylvania Gazette* newspaper, or the *American Magazine* containing enlightening articles.

However, there was one problem with this burgeoning of knowledge—there was now so much that an old problem reappeared: How do you find what you're looking for? Remember that was the problem with the old monastery scriptorium. A new tool was invented to making finding things much easier—the index. Now you could just look in the back of the book at an alphabetical listing of topics covered to see if it contained what you wanted instead of reading the whole book to find it.

Then the next step took place—the creation of the cross index. Think of it as the print version of Google. Look up one topic and the cross index lists a set of related topics. Not only did it make finding things easier, it led to a completely different way of **thinking**, one that did not view things as separate entities with no relation to any other, but that viewed all things as related in one way or another, like the game "Six Degrees of Kevin Bacon." For example, astronomy is not a separate science. It's related to optics through telescopes, and to physics through gravity and radiation, and to electromagnetism through light. By combining several apparently unrelated ideas and finding relationships between them, an altogether new idea can arise. To be academic about it, you combine specialization with generalization and get synthesis, the discovery of something new.

Let's see how this would work. Take astronomy, the study of the sky. You study the sky by looking at the light, which is physics and the electromagnetic spectrum, through the optics of a telescope. Now add in something new. Two Bell Lab scientists, Arno Penzias and Robert Wilson, were trying to figure out how to clean up the static in radio waves. However, there was some noise they just couldn't get rid of, no matter what they did with their antenna, including pointing it everywhere in the sky and cleaning out all the pigeon crap. Finally they concluded that the noise wasn't in their equipment, but actually there. It turned out to be the background radiation of the universe (and remember that radiation is physics) and the remnants of the Big Bang creation of the universe—and we end up with an entirely new story about the universe. Now we combine astronomy, the physics of radiation and the electromagnetic spectrum, and telescopes, and come up with a brand new idea— radio telescopy, astronomy by radiation **other** than light. This is an example of how crossing fields of information, like in a cross index, can lead to something new and unexpected.

Printing had yet another effect on society, a far-reaching one. Remember William Caxton, the first printer to use English? Well, there were printers like him working in every language. Spelling and grammar were whatever people wanted—they wrote the way they spoke. Before printing, virtually all communication between people was spoken, and because most people stayed in a limited geographic area, there was no problem as they all spoke the same language because they learned it from each other. In another place only hundreds or even tens of miles away, the people may speak with a different accent, a different dialect, or even a different language, even if they all purported to speak the same language. However, since these separated groups rarely interacted, there was no problem as long as those that did interact shared enough words in common for their purposes, such as trade, perhaps speaking a pidgin. People thought of themselves as belonging to their community, not to a nation, and they saw no need for a common language. The educated and the nobility commonly spoke more than one language so they could communicate with one another, and one language they all spoke in common was Latin, a relic of the Roman Empire.

But with printing, especially such books as dictionaries, which set the spelling and usage of words, and grammar books, which established how you string words together to create sentences—and add any books written in the local tongue—languages such as English and German and French and Italian and Spanish and—well, you get the idea— became set and regional, and Latin disappeared as the universal language. As a local language became the norm, it tended to bind together those who spoke it and exclude those who didn't. This shift in language led to a sense of nationalism: "We all speak English (or German or French or Italian) and therefore are alike. You don't speak English (or German or French) and therefore are different. We are 'us'; you are 'Them'. We are the English nation, and you are—well, whatever you are—but you're not English."

The upshot of writing, and then printing, was a complete overthrow of the previous social structure. For the Egyptians, first the plow changed their society from a nomadic one to a stable one. But it was still one where everyone worked together doing the same things for a common cause, the good of the clan or tribe. But to take advantage of the new agriculture, a new relationship between the people was required, especially the keeping of records to know who owned what and who did what and who **owed** what to whom— which of course required writing. It was just too much and too complicated to commit to memory. So those who could read and write became the ones in charge, resulting in a social structure of workers who took orders and managers who gave them. Thus was born a society of classes, of peasants and professionals and nobles, and of royalty to keep everything going. The world of everyone equal to everyone else was gone forever.

Printing changed the entire backward-looking view of society. When knowledge is carried in people's memories, and its concomitant reliance on face-to-face communication and what worked in the past, innovation is stifled and there's an oppressive respect for the achievements of the past. When knowledge is carried in hundreds and thousands of books that can go anywhere and require no personal contact with the authors, society is turned into one that looks forward to progress and improvement. This new world view led the increasing pace in discovery of the world, from science to politics, including getting on ships and looking for what was over the horizon.

The Protestant ethic, spread by the presses, extolled the virtues of hard work and thrift and encouraged material success. Printing underlined this attitude. If one could now pick up knowledge from a book, the age of unquestioned authority was over. A fifteenth century history (printed of course) expressed the new opinion: "Why should old men be preferred to their juniors when it is possible, by diligent study, for young men to acquire the same knowledge?"[4] The cult of youth, with its belief that what the world needed was young ideas and approaches built on the new knowledge and not on the hide-bound traditions and dogmas of the old, had begun, and it has been with us ever since.

Specialization also arose. The presses made it possible for specialists to talk to other specialists and to pool their resources. They also began to write for each other in the language of their disciplines, vocabularies composed of new words and precise meanings that average people not in those disciplines didn't understand—the so-called gobbledygook of modern science. As knowledge in all fields grew and diversified, fewer and fewer people could clearly comprehend how their world worked, and they began to feel left out and behind.

Printing gave us our modern way of ordering thought as the syntax of writing replaced the syntax of speaking and the cross index made new connections. It gave us the mania for the truth "in black and white." It moved us away from respect for authority and age towards an investigative approach to nature based on empirical observation.

Of course, by removing us from the old collective memory of the community, printing isolated each of us in a way previously unknown. No longer was society the shared association of personal relationships but the shared association of impersonal knowledge. Yet it also left us capable of vicariously sharing a bigger world than just the local community.

So that's what books did to society. But there are other media that use printing, so let's see what effect newspapers and magazines had.

Newspapers

Humans have always been a nosy bunch, always wanting to know what's going on, spying on their neighbors and spreading rumors, the juicier the better. In a way, those things are news, information we don't already have that we want.

For millennia, we got that information by talking to each other. This, of course, meant that the information was only local, but that was satisfactory because the only information that anyone **needed** was local, like "the ice on the river is breaking—let's go take a bath again," or "there are new neighbors—let's go get some mates," or "the mammoths have entered the valley—let's go kill a bunch and stuff our faces." This was news worth hearing.

When the drought hit 12,000 years ago, the news that a river valley "over there" had food was also good news. And spreading the information about the invention of the plow—and irrigation—and a new pharaoh—was also well worth hearing.

But all of this kind of news was word of mouth. Other than wall carvings and paintings, there wasn't much in the way of "printed" news. This was the case for thousands of years.

Newspapers, or more properly news-sheets, only appeared with the invention of the moveable type printing press. These sheets contained information that was unsuitable for books, information that wasn't extensive enough to deserve a book, like new discoveries in botany or architecture or weapons making, or that only had a limited "shelf life," by which I mean information that became irrelevant after a little time had passed.

This kind of information was intended more for the wealthy than for the common people. The Dutch Corontos newssheet of around 1600, and the soon to follow English-language diurnals, contained news that was of importance to merchants and bankers, like shipping news and commodity prices and political news about all the wars in Europe. This is what business people needed to make business decisions.

The common people made do with rumors or with visitors telling stories about what they'd seen or experienced. This was fine as far as the "powers-that-be" were concerned, like the merchants and the nobility and the governments. After all, there was no sense in upsetting people with news about things they could do nothing about—other than perhaps getting upset and to begin doubting whether the merchants and the nobility and the government knew what they were doing, and perhaps overthrowing them.

Even when newspapers containing more than information intended for business people began to be published, they weren't for the common people. Newspapers like *Publick Occurrences* and *The Pennsylvania Gazette* were intended for the literate and well to do. Such newspapers were expensive and carried what their publishers, like Ben Franklin, thought the upper middle class would want to know. Franklin aimed his *Poor Richard's Almanack* at the regular people—that was the kind of information **they** needed to know, like tide tables, calendars, weather predictions, and farming and household hints.

And, of course, newspapers made no pretense of objectivity, of providing what people needed to make informed decisions. Newspapers promoting one political candidate or another were often scathing. For example, during the 1796 and 1800 presidential campaigns between John Adams and Thomas Jefferson, newspapers supporting Adams called Jefferson an atheist, demagogue, coward, mountebank, trickster and Franco-maniac. One paper said about Jefferson that he was "a mean-spirited, low-lived fellow, the son of a half-breed Indian squaw, sired by a Virginia mulatto father."[5] Of course, Jefferson's supporters returned the favor, spreading rumors that Adams planned to marry one of his sons to a daughter of King George III, start an American dynasty and reunite with Britain. Well, maybe the newspapers simply followed the lead of the people they supported. Adams said about Jefferson that "if he is elected, murder, robbery, rape, adultery and incest will be openly taught and practiced."[6]

I get the impression that these two men weren't terribly fond of each other.

When John Quincy Adams ran against Andrew Jackson in 1824, one newspaper promoting Jackson called Adams a pimp (Remini 1966, 100), and another promoting Adams wrote that Jackson's wife was a slut, and that "General Jackson's mother was a common prostitute, brought to this country by the British soldiers who afterward married a mulatto man, with whom she had several children, of which number General Jackson is one!" (Remini 1981, 330) Well, all this is "fair and balanced" reporting, isn't it? Of course, sometimes it can backfire. When Jackson was called a jackass, he adopted it as his party symbol—he was a democrat.

It wasn't until 1833 that someone realized that there were a lot more "regular" people than well to do, and those regular people might want to know things too, and that quantity has a quality all its own, especially when you try to sell something. That was when Benjamin Day began publishing *The Sun,* the first newspaper that just about anyone could afford. It sold for one cent per issue, and it was the beginning of the penny press. Day also realized that the middle class were less interested in financial, commercial, or political news because few of those people were involved in those areas beyond, "Am I getting paid?" and "Am I going to continue to be paid?" So Day filled his paper with things that did impinge on middle-class life, like crime and what was being done about it, and employment and prices, and what kinds of entertainment were available, and human interest stories to appeal to both men and women. This last was a change in attitude toward women, that they could read and may want to know things. Of course, the attitude was rather patronizing, one that felt women wouldn't be interested in important things such as crime and politics—they wouldn't be able to understand them anyway. But recipes and house and childcare and other "women's things" would be fine—especially since advertising for household goods was just starting up and the woman's section of the paper would be a perfect place to put it, resulting in income for the paper.

Day also started the trend of not being so blatantly and fanatically partisan as newspapers prior to *The Sun* often were. If he wanted to appeal to the largest audience possible to sell the most papers possible—which of course would make the most money possible—he couldn't afford to offend his customers by promoting a particular socio-political point of view with which they might not agree. It didn't mean there was no partisanship—it was just soft-pedaled and had less "foaming at the mouth" diatribes.

The success of *The Sun* led other people to see that the money was in mass instead of in elite circulation. Soon newspapers aimed at mass audiences sprang up everywhere, from cities of thousands to small towns of only a few hundred.

Of course, partisanship couldn't be completely avoided, as the majority of a local newspaper's readership may have held certain opinions and want their newspaper to reflect those views. Southern papers were rabidly against Northern attitudes and ideas, and Northern papers were rabidly against Southern attitudes and ideas, especially during the Civil War. Northern papers, not all but most, were abolitionist, anti-slavery. Southern papers denounced Northern intentions to destroy the South's culture, civilization, and "peculiar institution" (as they called slavery). This was only natural, since the papers reflected the attitudes of their readers.

Again, it's a matter of the stories being told. Papers tell the news that supports the prevailing social "story." The story Southerners had been telling themselves for two hundred years was that the South was the home of the American aristocracy, it was the only civilized part of America, and slavery was only right and natural because the superior but kind plantation owners took care of those pure, benighted, uncivilized savages that were incapable of taking care of themselves. They not only feared losing their culture, many actually feared for their slaves, that they would be thrown out into the cruel world without someone to take care of them. This was the way they saw the world; it was their reality because of the story they told about their society.

When George Pulitzer bought the *New York World* in 1883, he deliberately set out to change America's stories about itself. He saw many of the social problems that the old stories either created or perpetuated, such as labor problems, laissez faire (perhaps best described as "anything goes, and screw you") business practices, the growing gap between the rich and poor, and other things he thought of as bad for the country. His news articles were often about crime and social unrest, frequently gave emphasis to problems by sensationalizing them, and provided a climax by showing what, in his opinion, needed to be done to solve them. By adding a lot of illustrations, he could increase the readers' emotional reactions much more than unexciting blocks of text could, because pictures aim right at the emotions and text at the mind.

This change of the story didn't go unnoticed, especially by William Randolph Hearst, who knew how to sell papers: get people worked up about the story by playing off their prejudices and biases, aiming at their emotions rather than their intellect. If he could make it sound patriotic, all the better. The greatest example of this is his promotion of the Spanish-American War in 1898, when he touted the sinking of the US battleship *Maine* in Havana harbor as an attack by the Spanish. Hearst was telling a new story to the American people, providing a problem: "America is under attack by foreigners"; and then providing a climax: "We have to fight back to show how powerful America is." It was an extension of the American story of "Manifest Destiny" to the entire world. This story was the one that sent Americans into the West and said that America is the greatest country on earth and should be in charge, a sort of rebirth of Rome. Manifest Destiny is a story defining America for Americans that has continued for more than a century.

However, the battle between Pulitzer and Hearst and others to tell stories to create an American social reality as they believed it should be reached such a fevered pitch that it almost destroyed what credibility newspapers had built up since Day's *Sun* had turned away from partisanship. In the 1920s, the American Society of Newspaper Editors believed it needed to combat the Pulitzer/Hearst approach in order to regain the place of newspapers as a source of information rather than of passion, and they started a new story about newspapers and their place in society—objectivity in the news. This is the story that society believes in today, that news providers simply tell people the facts and let them, their consumers, make their own decisions based on those facts rather than on what a publisher tells them those decisions should be.

Of course, this story is often contrary to other stories, those that create the worldviews of conservatives (whose stories say that change is wrong), moderates (whose stories say some change is okay, some change isn't), and liberals (whose stories say everything needs to change). If newspapers are going to be objective, they can't promote any of those ideologies, which of course makes them targets for all of those ideologies. An ideology says that its worldview is the only right one, and anyone who doesn't follow it is wrong. In the minds of those people who follow a particular ideology, if a newspaper doesn't specifically say that their ideology (whichever one they happen to follow) is right and other people who follow a different ideology are wrong, the newspaper is by default promoting that other ideology. It's the old "you're either with me or against me"—a statement that denies the possibility of objectivity. So newspapers can't win.

Magazines

What about magazines? Well, magazines started up because there were things that people wanted to read that weren't as ephemeral as news, but they weren't extensive enough or in depth enough to need an entire book.

Like newspapers, they were originally intended for an elite readership and contained what that audience would want: poetry, essays, articles of general interest for the "Renaissance Man" who wasn't concerned with knowing everything but wanted to know something about a subject. Remember him? The person who could know and do everything because rhe could read books on everything?—at least for a few years before the number of books and topics outstripped what anyone could absorb. That kind of man—and woman—still wanted to know things but just couldn't cope with the sheer amount of reading if books were rhis only option.

Magazines filled that void by providing short articles that gave overviews of subjects instead of the in depth coverage of a book. So it was still possible to, if not know, then know **about**, a subject. This is still the purpose of many magazines. For example, you may not be a computer engineer, but you can read articles in computer magazines to learn how to do many things. For the seventeenth century person, it would be architecture, animal husbandry, agriculture, weapons and their uses, and the like.

You might think the average person would want the same thing—and you'd be right. However, magazines were expensive and only available from booksellers. Expense and lack of access were their major drawbacks for the next two hundred years.

However, a change in the social story, kicked off by the American Revolution, came at the end of the eighteenth century. That change was that average people were the equals of rather than inferior to the social and financial elite and should have the same advantages, if not financially then socially. Universal literacy was a major goal of the United States so everyone could participate in the new country, and with that **ability** to read came a desire to **have** something to read.

In addition, the price of magazines dropped as printing methods improved, and the new postal system meant that magazines could be mailed, giving everyone access to them—they didn't have to go to a bookseller to buy a magazine.

Now that magazines were available to anyone, they really took off by doing what Pulitzer would later do with newspapers: They started focusing on social issues like abolition and labor reform to retell the American story. Unlike newspapers, however, which angled the news reporting to focus on the social causes and effects of events, magazines went straight to the issues. They examined them on their own merits, separate from any particular events that may have arisen because of them. They promoted attitudes and beliefs about the issues with articles written by experts, once again changing the social story as people fit them into their understanding of what society was and could be.

Magazines also focused on women. Women were a prime audience for magazines because they provided information that all women wanted, like childcare, cooking, cleaning, home remedies, the proper role of a subservient wife and how to keep your husband happy. Yes, that's the story that most magazines perpetuated in the nineteenth and early twentieth centuries, reflecting the beliefs about society prevalent at the time. There were exceptions, but not many, and it was a hundred years before the story of women's place and role in American society changed.

The greatest change in magazines came in the 1950s as they started niche marketing. General interest magazines just couldn't compete with television, so magazines specialized, aiming their content at a specific audience. Not only did that give the magazines sales, but it also had an effect on society—it segmented it.

No longer did magazines act as a single binding force that everyone at least knew about, magazines such as *Life*. *Life* magazine could be found in just about any home, and it created a single vision of the world for the whole country. Everyone knew the same pictures, which were icons of a shared life. Through the pages of *Life,* America shared visions of society, visions of war, visions of idols, visions of highs and lows and ultimate triumphs.

Magazines no longer contributed to a shared idea of society and the world. Instead, people went off into their own little worlds that only included others like them, others who shared the same ideas, information, attitudes—and stories about reality.

And that's magazines.

With the invention of printing, a world that was local became regional and then national. A world that was completely rural became urban. A world of lore, legend and superstition became objective, inquiring and scientific. A world that was static and unchanging became dynamic and ever-changing. This is the story and the world people live in today. And it was printing—the first mass medium—that created it.

■ ENDNOTES

1. As quoted in Burke, J. 1985, p. 104
2. As quoted in Postman, N. 1985, *Amusing Ourselves to Death.* New York: Penguin Books, p. 32
3. de Tocqueville, A. 1956. *Democracy in America,* trans. Richard D. Heffner. New York: The New American Library, p. 28.
4. As quoted in Burke, J. 1995, p. 123.
5. Hazard, Thomas Robinson. *The Jonny-cake Papers of "Shepherd Tom,": Together with reminiscences of Narragansett schools of former days.* (Boston: Printed for the subscribers, 1915), 232–233.
6. millercenter.org/president/jefferson/essays/biography/3, retrieved 17 Jan 2011.

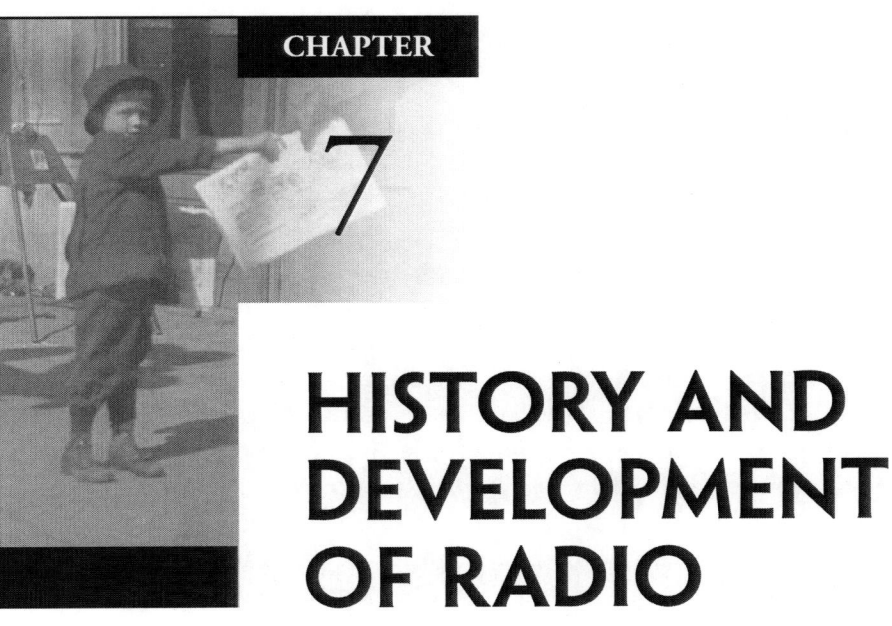

7

HISTORY AND DEVELOPMENT OF RADIO

*F*or thousands of years people dug metals like copper and tin and, of course, gold out of the ground. However, metal wasn't the only thing in the ground, and this fact led to a whole string of ideas that would do their part to change the world.

Before we get into that, let's start with a basic definition of what radio is. Radio is sending sound through the air by piggybacking it onto electrical noise. To see how that happens, let's start back at the beginning with electricity.

People have known about electricity for thousands of years. Of course, they had no idea what it was other than lightning, which was the gods being angry. Someone may have found a use for it about 250 BCE by inventing what's known as the Baghdad battery, a pottery jar holding an iron bar in a copper sleeve surrounded with some kind of liquid acid like wine or lemon juice. Such a construction would produce a mild electrical current, enough to plate base metal medallions with gold or silver, or maybe to give a mild shock to believers in temples to show the power of the gods.

But a couple of thousand years later people started to actually think about electricity as more than irritated gods.

Actual research into electricity began in 1641 when Evangelista Torricelli invented the barometer to measure air pressure. People digging mines discovered that there was water in the ground, and that it had a tendency to flood the shafts. Naturally, they tried to pump the water out since drowning wasn't high on their list of "things to do." However, they also discovered that water pumps couldn't lift water more than 32 feet and wanted to know why. Torricelli determined that it was the weight of the air pressing on the water that pushed it up a pipe, and that the air could only apply enough pressure to lift water—you guessed it—32 feet. He experimented to test the idea, using mercury instead of water because mercury was fourteen times denser than water and he could work with much smaller equipment that way.

The experiment, carried out by Torricelli's assistant Vincenzo Viviani, worked. He upended a six-foot tube full of mercury into a dish of mercury, and the column of mercury dropped until there were about 30 inches left in the tube. The weight of the air pressing down on the pool in the dish held up that 30 inches of mercury in the tube.

About this time you may be asking yourself what all this has to do with electricity. Well, what's important to continuing this discussion is not the column of mercury, but what was left in the tube after the mercury dropped, or rather what wasn't left—anything. The top of the tube now contained a vacuum, a sealed space containing nothing.

It's now that we turn to electricity. The barometer was the new scientific toy for many people. One such person was French astronomer M. Jean Picard of the Paris Observatory, who was walking home one night in 1675 and swinging his mercury barometer. He was somewhat mystified when he saw that the barometer started glowing when he swung it. He didn't know what caused the glow, but he thought it was cool and spread the word.

Other people ran experiments to find out what caused the glow, and in 1705 Englishman Francis Hauksbee determined that it was caused by the mercury rubbing against the glass, and that other substances, like amber rubbed with wool or a cat skin, would also glow. He also noticed that there was a crackling sound, like lightning, when he put his hand near the glow, and that it would attract things like fluff and metal filings. He was producing static electricity at will.

In the eighteenth century people, began to play around with electricity, mostly as a toy. Ben Franklin flew his kite in a thunderstorm to see if lightning actually was electricity—it was. Other people seemed to be obsessed with rubbing cat skins on glass or amber rods or spinning sulfur balls to generate static electricity and zap everything—and everyone—in sight. In one experiment, a line of monks held hands and when the monk at one end of the line was zapped, the entire line jumped. Maybe these experimenters got turned on by all the pretty sparks—or the yelps of pain. You've got to wonder about some people.

But, eventually, people other than Franklin began to seriously study electricity to find out what it was and not just to play games. It was Luigi Galvani who demonstrated that something could be done with electricity other than just shock people. In 1786, he began experiments to prove his hypothesis that electricity naturally existed in animal muscles in the form of "animal magnetism." In his experiments, he touched rods made of different metals to dead frogs' legs and the legs twitched. *Aha,* he thought. He felt he had proven that there **was** electricity in muscles, and animal magnetism existed.

However, Alessandro Volta thought Galvani had gotten it backwards, that touching the different metals to the frogs' legs created the electrical impulse instead of the legs containing the electricity and releasing the impulse. He tested this idea in 1796 by creating his pile, a stack of alternating zinc and copper disks in a mild acid solution, a rediscovery of the Baghdad battery, and it created an electrical current. He proved that electricity could be created chemically. He also provided the world with the first workable battery (if you don't count the Baghdad battery), and that invention enormously improved the ability to research electricity. No more rubbing cat skins on glass rods.

One idea that people had was that, since electricity could attract things like iron filings, electricity was linked with magnetism. Among the researchers was Hans Christian Oersted. He didn't accept the idea that electricity and magnetism were linked. In a lecture demonstration in 1820, he decided to demonstrate there was no link by putting a compass needle near an electrical circuit. He was somewhat chagrined when, upon turning on the circuit, the compass needle swung. He had demonstrated the opposite of his hypothesis and proved that electricity and magnetism were indeed linked.

William Sturgeon solidified that link when he created the first electromagnet. In 1825, he wrapped a wire around a soft iron bar and, when he sent electricity into the wire, the bar attracted metal—the 9-ounce bar lifted 7 pounds of weight.

In 1826, Michael Faraday reversed Sturgeon's process by running a magnet back and forth through a wire coil, thereby producing an electric current. Between them, Sturgeon and Faraday clinched the connection between electricity and magnetism.

So what do you do with this knowledge? Well, Samuel F. B. Morse had an idea. In 1836, he first sent electrical pulses down a wire by opening and closing a circuit. In 1844, he sent out the message "What hath God wrought" over his system and completely changed the way the world communicated at a distance. No longer was it by shouting or written letters or running horses. For the first time, information could travel miles in an instant: Just press the key, making it touch an electrical contact and closing a circuit, and an electrical impulse the length of time the key touches the contact is sent down a wire where that impulse causes an electromagnet to pull on a piece of metal that clicks onto the magnet for that same length of the impulse. The pattern and length of the clicks represent letters and numbers—you just have to translate the pattern and length into the letters, write them down, and you've got a message. Ta Da. The telegraph.

A	•-	Q	--•-	1	•----
B	-•••	R	•-•	2	••---
C	-•-•	S	•••	3	•••--
D	-••	T	-	4	••••-
E	•	U	••-	5	•••••
F	••-•	V	•••-	6	-••••
G	--•	W	•--	7	--•••
H	••••	X	-••-	8	---••
I	••	Y	-•--	9	----•
J	•---	Z	--••	0	-----
K	-•-	Error	••••••••	.	•-•-•-
L	•-••	Wait	•-•••	,	--••--
M	--	End Msg	•-•-•	:	---•••
N	-•	End Work	•••-•-	)	-•--•-
O	---	Inv Xmit	-•-	(	-•--•
P	•--•	/	-••-•	?	••--••

However, it required skill to send those clicks and learn what is essentially a foreign language—morse code—to create and understand such messages. For the average person, it wasn't an easy way to communicate—fast, yes, easy, no.

Two men realized there was another way—to send not electrical impulses to create dots and dashes, but actual sound down that wire. But to get to that point we need to take a little detour.

In 1840, Johannes Mueller was researching physical senses—sight, hearing, smell, touch, taste—to see if they all could detect the same things, or if each detected a different thing. He examined sensations, such as, could you feel colors or hear shapes or smell sounds? He found that each sense detected different things. This may seem obvious, but until Mueller did his research nobody had ever actually ***proven*** that such was the case. Remember "common sense"?

In 1857, Mueller's pupil, Herman Hemholtz, continued the research, this time concentrating just on sound, and he discovered that sound produced vibration by singing into his piano and causing a string to vibrate in response. He also investigated whether different rates of vibration had different frequencies. That is, did different rates of vibration create waves with crests and valleys closer together or farther apart? They did. That being the case, sound traveled through the air at different frequencies. Then he pulled the big trick—he used an electromagnet to attract the arms of a tuning fork, causing it to vibrate and produce sound.

Okay, time for yet another detour. While Hemholtz was singing into his piano, Leon Scott de Martinville was also playing around with sound in France. His approach, however, was visual. What he did was place a bristle on the end of a stick. That stick was attached to a membrane, which he inserted in the end of a cone. He then put the bristle against a piece of smoked glass—a sheet of glass covered with soot—and spoke into the cone. The membrane vibrated to the sound waves made by his voice, causing the bristle to scratch against the smoked glass and leaving a squiggle etched in the soot. He discovered that different words etched different patterns, and those patterns were always the same for the same word. His cone and membrane system created a way to paint a picture of sounds.

So, let's see where we are. Electrical impulses can be sent down a wire, causing an electromagnet to open and close. Each sense detects a different thing. Sounds are different things that cause vibrations that propagate at different frequencies, no two frequencies alike, a fact that can be seen by using a membrane with a bristle touching smoked glass. Also, you can use an electromagnet to cause metal to vibrate and produce different sounds.

If we put these ideas together, we have de Martinville's cone with a membrane at the small end. Cover that membrane with a very thin sheet of iron and have it vibrate to sounds in an electric field and you have Faraday's electromagnet creating different frequencies of electrical impulses matching the frequencies of the sounds. Send those impulses down Morse's wire to another electromagnet, this time Sturgeon's, which causes the metal membrane in a second cone to vibrate and produce sound, the way Hemholtz showed, that recreates the original sound frequencies. Then, reverse the process. In other words, we have the telephone, and we're back to those two men with a better idea, Alexander Graham Bell and Elisha Gray, who both had the same idea at the same time, but Bell got to the patent office two hours ahead of Gray and thus gets all the credit.

So what does all of this have to do with radio? Well, in a broad sense a radio is simply a telephone without wires. So the history of radio is the history of the telephone, but mostly by attempting to get rid of Morse and his sending impulses of electricity down wires.

Let's start with Heinrich Hertz. Hertz was Herman Hemholtz's student, but he researched electricity instead of sound. Hemholtz had demonstrated that sound traveled through the air in specific frequencies, so Hertz tried to discover if electricity also did. He built a spark gap generator, a device that created an electrical current but had a gap in the wire that the current had to jump, thus creating a spark. He then built a receiver to pick up the spark, if indeed it would.

It did. When the generator fired a spark, the receiver also fired a spark—a much weaker one, true, but still a spark. What was of special interest to Hertz was that the echo

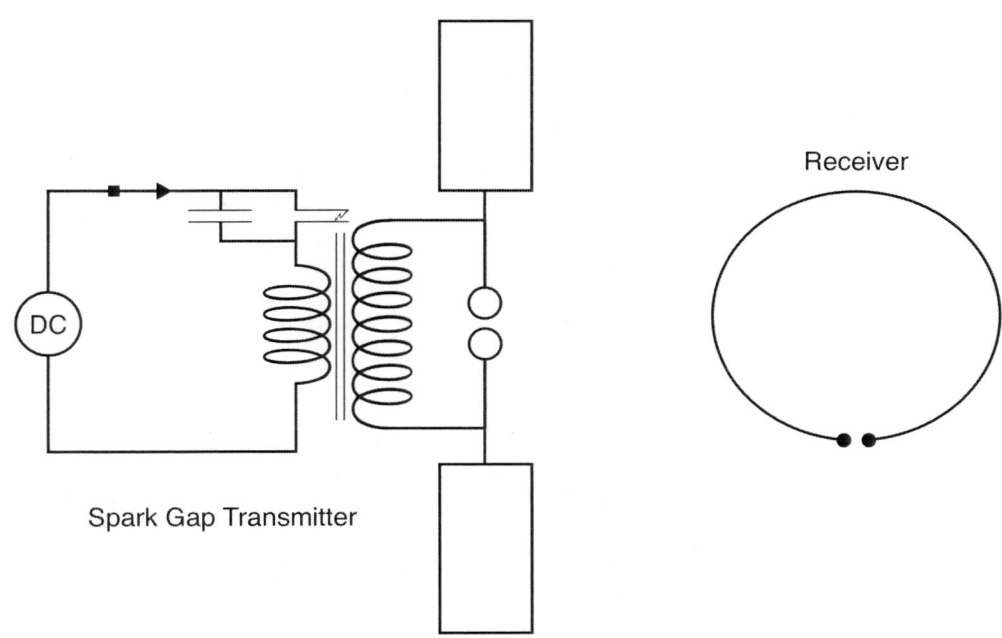

Spark Gap Transmitter

spark in the receiver was stronger at specific and distinct distances away from the generator where the receiver was placed, and much weaker or even nonexistent between those specific distances. This demonstrated that electricity did propagate through the air at specific frequencies, just as sound did.

So now that we've got all the background science out of the way, we can finally get around to radio. Guiglielmo Marconi took all the ideas developed by Hemholtz and Hertz and all the others over the last few decades and put them together. One thing he added to Hertz's spark gap experiment was an aerial, an antenna, to increase the output and allow the electrical waves to be detectable at greater distances. He also boosted the power considerably by adding a step up transformer. With these improvements and Morse's telegraph key, he was able to send long and short bursts of electrical power—morse code—over large distances. Thus, we have the wireless telegraph, also known as radio.

Now it was time for a change in radio that would greatly expand its capabilities. Marconi's radio was essentially a wireless telegraph, only capable of sending dots and dashes by creating electrical impulses propagating through the air that were strong enough to trigger either sparks or electromagnets at a distance. It, just like the telegraph, required knowledge and skill to send and receive messages. Again, this was useless for the average person who had neither that knowledge nor skill. So the next goal was to make possible what the telephone did, send sound.

Nicola Telsa accomplished the first step in the process. A prolific inventor, he created the Tesla coil, the first amplifier. It raised the voltage of an electrical current high enough that the air could conduct the entire current, not just the spikes created by Marconi's radio, thus obviating the need for wires to carry the current. This was the key to wireless sound radio. In 1943, the patent office changed the inventor of radio from Marconi to Tesla because it was Tesla who made wireless telegraphy a viable proposition.

Next up was Reginald Fessenden. He believed that the variation in electrical amplitude could be carried by radio waves just as the telephone's wires carried it. This variation consists of the strength or weakness of electrical impulses through wires used by a telephone, created by the loudness or softness of sound waves created by a voice. In 1900, he sent out the first voice transmission over radio waves. It was short range, only traveling about fifteen miles, and the quality was very poor, barely recognizable as a voice. It could be likened to having a conversation with someone standing at the other end of a football field: shouted vowel sounds like oo and ah will be heard, but not subtle sounds like consonants that make words understandable. However, it was a voice transmission without wires. What Fessenden needed to make it work was far more power to allow those subtle variations in amplitude to be carried clearly.

Ernst Alexanderson provided what Fessenden needed. Alexanderson invented a new generator, the Alexanderson Alternator, which boosted the power up of the electrical signal to 100,000 hertz (one hertz is a unit of one cycle per second of high to low in a wave). With radio waves that strong, Fessenden had enough power to actually broadcast clear sound. In December 1906, Fessenden did the first radio broadcast, sending out poetry, Bible readings, a woman singing opera, and a violin playing Christmas carols. Unlike his previous 1900 attempt, this broadcast could be picked up hundreds of miles away. Sound radio instead of just spikes in electrical noise was born.

Almost. Yes, Fessenden was broadcasting, but the range was still limited and the sound was still not very good. Even more power was needed.

Lee De Forest has often been called the father of radio. This is something of an exaggeration. De Forest was a tinkerer. He was a tinkerer who would take various parts, put them together, and see what happened. In the most famous case, de Forest was tinkering with an English invention called a Fleming valve (valve is what the English call a vacuum tube), and he came up with what he called the audion tube. What de Forest did was add a bent wire to it. This bent wire greatly increased the power of the tube, amplifying the radio signal the way Alexanderson's generator amplified electrical power.

One thing to bear in mind is that de Forest didn't know how his audion tube worked. It wasn't the result of his research in electricity and radio, but the result of putting together random pieces on his workbench. However, another man researched the tube and did figure out how it worked, and once he knew that, he could determine how to improve it.

That man was Edwin Howard Armstrong. He was fascinated with radio from the time he was fourteen, and he constantly tried to improve it. Once he understood how the audion tube worked, he developed what he called "regeneration." Regeneration was the process of feeding the signal coming out of the tube back into the tube up to 20,000 times a second. This vastly increased the power of the tube to output the signal—it was an amplifier, just what radio transmitters needed to increase their range and quality. Fessenden had invented the ability to broadcast sound; Armstrong had invented the ability to broadcast **good** sound.

Of course, a good radio transmitter was of little use without a good receiver, and that was Armstrong's next task. What he did was combine high frequency waves with low frequency waves and feed them back into the system to amplify the signal and increase the sensitivity. The result was the first true home, and later portable, radio. He called his invention the superheterodyne.

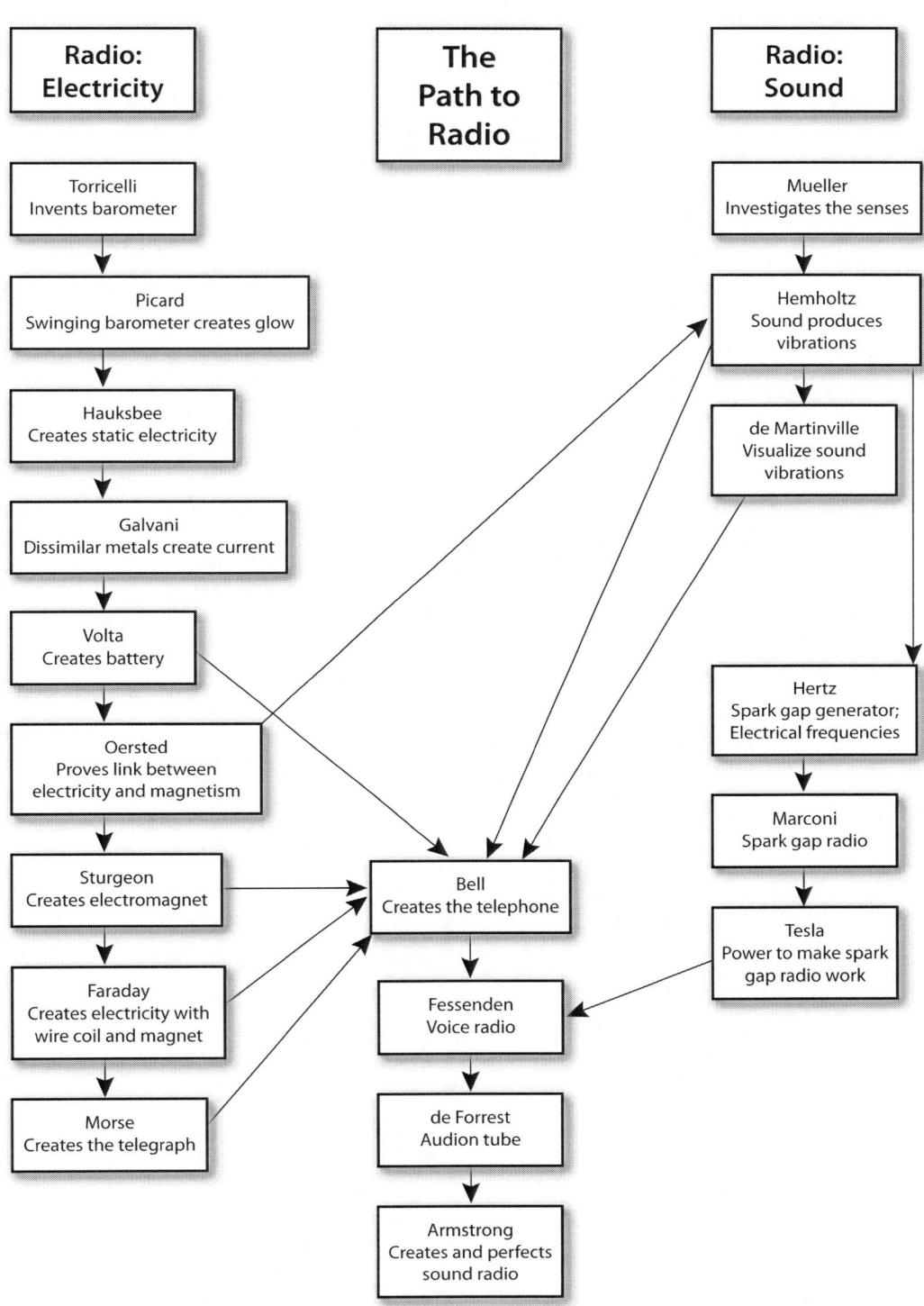

Well, so much for science and invention. Now it's time to get down to business—literally. Radio was a toy for most people as they built their own crystal radio sets and made lists of transmitters they received and how far away they were. Quaker Oats even included instructions on how to turn their round boxes into crystal radios. But entrepreneurs began to see the commercial possibilities of radio, that money could be made off the inventions, and one of the first people to see this was David Sarnoff.

Sarnoff was fascinated by radio from the beginning, but not as an inventor or hobbyist. He just wanted to work in radio. He started with the American Marconi Company, and often bragged that he was the shore operator receiving the messages from the *Titanic* as it was sinking in the North Atlantic.

However, it was when he found out that radio could be used for more than wireless telegraphy that he really got involved. He knew that wireless telegraphy was a point to point medium. That is, its purpose was to send a message to one recipient, in the same way that a letter, book, or telephone call involved one sender communicating with one receiver. However, he also knew that anyone who wanted to listen in to wireless telegraphy messages could also receive the message, not just the person intended; all that person needed was a receiver like a crystal radio or even a spark gap receiver and the ability to read Morse code.[1] He thought it would be a good idea, and a financial windfall, to broadcast to everyone on **purpose** instead of by accident or by eavesdropping. In 1916, he wrote a memo to his employers at American Marconi. That memo is known as the "Radio Music Box Memo." In it, Sarnoff outlined his idea of making sound radio a mass medium rather than a point-to-point medium, putting in every home what he called a "Radio Music Box." His intent was to make a radio receiver like Armstrong's superheterodyne as ubiquitous in homes as the piano or the phonograph. Although the idea was shelved during World War I because the military appropriated all the radios for military purposes, after the war ended in 1919 four American radio manufacturers—American Marconi, General Electric, American Telephone & Telegraph, and Westinghouse—formed a single company to share in all the radio-related patents, especially Armstrong's, and RCA, the Radio Corporation of America, was born. Sarnoff was named as commercial manager, and RCA was soon in business. Very quickly radios, both transmitters and receivers using Armstrong's patents, were manufactured and sold all over the country. To take advantage of this new radio, stations that could broadcast (i.e., send out signals intended for a broad audience rather than the narrowcast point-to-point signals intended for a single recipient) opened.

However, a problem soon arose: What should be broadcast? Stations needed programs, things that people would want to listen to beyond just conversations, which with a point-to-point medium was all there was available. In other words, stations needed to come up with programming that would entertain. Naturally, since they were broadcasting radio anything using sound was perfect, so music and talking were just the thing. Soon every kind of entertainment was on the air. Bands and orchestras played. Actors performed "theatre of the mind," in which radio plays used descriptions and sound effects to help the audience visualize in their own minds scenery, appearances and actions.

Radio performers soon became stars as audiences stayed home and tuned in to listen to their shows. Comedy was very popular, and among the comedy stars were Fibber McGee and Molly, George Burns and Gracie Allen, Fred Allen, and Abbott and Costello.

People also had a desire for drama. Shows such as *Inner Sanctum, Dick Tracy* and *The Lone Ranger* were popular, and people gathered around their radios. During the day housewives were at home, and soap companies, thinking the women were probably cleaning their houses at that time, felt they were a perfect audience for their products. A new form of serialized drama filled daytime hours, the soap opera. The first was 1930's *Painted Dreams*. The plots revolved around morning conversations "Mother" Moynihan had with her daughter and their female boarder before the two young women went to their jobs at a hotel. In 1937, *The Guiding Light* began, running for more than 15,000 episodes (starting on radio and then moving to television in 1952) and ending its run in 2009.

Sometimes dramas didn't work out as planned. Orson Welles' Mercury Theatre thought it would be a good idea to do a production of H. G. Welles' *War of the Worlds*, a story about an attack on the Earth from Mars, on Halloween night. Anyone listening who missed the opening credits didn't know it was a radio play, and many thought it was for real, an actual news report of an alien attack. There were instances of panic all over the country. Really shows the power of radio, doesn't it?

One effect of World War I was an awakened desire for instant, wide-ranging news and information, which may have been why *War of the Worlds* had such an impact. People wanted to know what was going on, and wanted to know **now**. A famous example is the crash of the Zeppelin Hindenburg. Announcer Herb Morrison was doing a live report on its arrival at Lakehurst, New Jersey, when the Hindenburg suddenly burst into flames and crashed to the ground. Morrison tried to report the news but was soon overcome with emotion and had to stop. The immediacy and emotional impact of this live, first-person report affected audiences far more than a sterile news article in a newspaper could ever do.

During World War II, people in the United States heard about the war in Europe through radio, including from one of the most famous voices in the history of radio, Edward R. Murrow. His "This—is London" reports brought the war into American living rooms. They were "theatre of the mind," as Murrow painted word pictures of life in London during the Blitz (the German bombing raids), and his descriptions of his personal ride-alongs on US Air Force bombing raids over Germany during the war. His broadcasts helped make Americans at home feel they were a part of the war, not just observers.

However, after World War II, a new player in the entertainment and news industry appeared that would have a major impact on radio—television, a **new** box in the living room that had pictures as well as sound. It was assumed that radio would be dead, that everyone would be watching TV instead. Indeed, TV took over much of radio's programming, sometimes directly transferring shows from radio to TV, as it did with soap operas and *The Lone Ranger*.

But reports of radio's demise were premature. Radio had one big advantage over TV: Radio was portable. People could take it with them wherever they went. Edwin Armstrong invented the first portable radio in the 1930s, although it was probably like hauling around an anvil. However, advances in electronics, really kick-started by World War II, quickly reduced radios to true portability, about the size and weight of a full lunchbox.

Radio broadcasters also knew they wouldn't get back all the sitcoms and dramas and soap operas that television had taken over, so they came up with new kinds of programming that would appeal to all kinds of audiences and work well on radio but were not well suited to television, especially music in all its varied styles.

Radio also pioneered the long-form talk show, three hours a day of someone with something, anything, to say telling an audience how rhe feels or thinks about whatever is on rhis mind, and allowing audience members to phone in to the show to give their thoughts on the issue. Such shows have insufficient visual appeal to work well on television, but they are well suited to radio. Today, you have advice shows such as *The Car Guys* laughing and joking as they advise callers on how to fix their cars, shock jocks such as Howard Stern saying whatever comes into their minds that might shock people, or extreme socio-political views, such as Rush Limbaugh and Michael Savage and Glenn Beck on the right, and Ed Schultz and Stephanie Miller on the left. These kinds of shows stir the pot, rev up emotions, generally ignore reason, logic and facts, and are extremely popular with their audiences.

Radio was an invention whose time had come. Once scientists really latched onto the idea of doing something with electricity and discovered that it would propagate through the air in specific frequencies the way it did through wires, it was really only a matter of time before someone would put all the pieces together and start sending sound through the air on electric waves.

The invention of radio was full of controversies, contentions and lawsuits, with people making claims they couldn't back up, like Lee de Forest suing Edwin Armstrong several times for stealing his ideas, despite the fact that Armstrong could explain them and de Forest had no idea how what he claimed were his own ideas actually worked. RCA did its best to have a monopoly over radio, but eventually it got competitors.

Nevertheless, more than a hundred years after the first voice went out over the air, radio is still going strong, and indeed it is more popular with audiences than ever.

But what effects did the development of radio as a mass medium have on society? We'll discuss that after we look at the development of sound recording in the next chapter.

■ ENDNOTE

1. This was a problem every military faced. They quickly learned that if they wished to communicate by radio they had to invent codes that the enemy couldn't break, or the enemy would know their plans. They rarely succeeded.

CHAPTER

8

A HISTORY AND DEVELOPMENT OF SOUND RECORDING

*I*n the nineteenth century, a runaway spring on a repeating telegraph triggered an idea that did its part to change the world.

One of the major problems with communication was saving it for later. Writing, and then printing, was the first great step in preserving a person's voice, freezing words so they could be understood miles away and centuries later. Radio could take people's actual voices and extend the reach of those voices to listeners for hundreds and thousands of miles. However, those actual voices couldn't be preserved for later listening. So the next goal was to save spoken words and sounds, not as abstract symbols on a page, but as the actual voices and sounds themselves.

But to understand the history of sound recording, we need to backtrack a bit.

Remember Leon Scott de Martinville. He was the man who developed a way to visualize sound by putting a bristle on a membrane attached to a cone, then setting the bristle against a piece of soot covered glass. When he spoke into the cone, the bristle vibrated and etched a squiggle representing the sound in the soot, thus proving that sound operated at frequencies that could be recorded. In 2009, scientists took one of his squiggles that was done on soot-covered paper in 1860 and were able to produce a 10-second voice recording of a woman singing. So we can say that de Martinville beat Edison to recording sound by seventeen years, although such a technique was completely impractical.

And now we do come to Thomas Edison. There is a story, probably apocryphal, that Edison got the idea about recording and playing back sound from rapidly spinning a disc in a repeating telegraph. Edison himself had invented the repeating telegraph. What this machine would do is receive the Morse code dots and dashes from an incoming message and use those impulses to activate a punch attached to an electromagnet that would poke a dent in a cardboard disk slowly spinning on a turntable. The dents would match the dots and dashes of the message in a spiral pattern across the disk. When the disk was spun again, the punch would now act as a telegraph key, going up and down as it passed over the dents and sending the message out again. As the story goes, Edison was next to a machine when the disk spun at high speed against the punching stylus, and he heard a hum, which sounded, to him, like music. Looking at the disk, he saw the dents and realized they were causing the sound.

This led Edison to try recording sound by creating the equivalent of the dents, only this time by using sound waves instead of a stylus bouncing up and down in response to electrical impulses. He used a version of de Martinville's device. He wrapped tin foil around a cylinder, placed against it a stylus attached to a membrane at the end of a cone, and, with a crank that turned the cylinder and moved it sideways on a threaded rod, he cranked the cylinder around while shouting "Mary had a little lamb" into the cone. The stylus vibrated in response to the sound waves of his voice and created the same kind of dents he saw on the telegraph disk. Moving the stylus to the beginning and cranking the cylinder again played back the recording. It worked.

In 1878, Edison patented his device and began to manufacture it, at first with tinfoil wrapped cylinders, and later with the more durable lead. Each cylinder could record and play back two to three minutes worth of sound.

In 1885, Chichester Bell, a cousin of Alexander Graham Bell, and Charles Tainter invented another type of phonograph, this one using wax-coated cylinders incised with vertical grooves rather than tinfoil.

One problem that both Edison and Bell had with their method of recording was they couldn't make copies—everything had to be an original recording. This would make the machines useful for personal recordings, such as doing dictation or home musicales, but it limited their commercial possibilities.

Then in 1887, Emile Berliner invented a new type of phonograph, using a disk instead of a cylinder. The disk didn't use a wax coating, but instead it was photoengraved with a blank groove. For his machine the stylus would ride in the groove to make the marks to engrave the dents. The next year Berliner introduced an improved gramophone with a seven-inch flat disk with a two-minute capacity. He also developed a way to make duplicate copies of an original recording, pressing hard rubber vulcanite copies from a zinc master disk. In 1896, Berliner discovered that shellac made a better record than hard rubber because it was capable of copying finer detail in the recorded groove, and shellac became the standard material for decades.

The ability to make copies made sound recording commercially viable. A single recording of, for example, a band playing music, could be reproduced in the hundreds and thousands and sold to anyone with a machine that could play it back. Edison and Bell soon realized the possibilities and began making cylinder masters that could make duplicates.

In 1890, the first "juke box" was invented, a coin-operated cylinder phonograph with four listening tubes, sort of like stethoscopes. It appeared in San Francisco's Palais Royal Saloon and set off a boom in popularity for commercial nickel phonographs, and people developed a real taste for recordings.

In 1896, Eldridge Johnson improved the gramophone with an electric motor, replacing the hand-cranked spring driven motor, and created an inexpensive machine that became the most popular phonograph by 1900. He merged his company, Consolidated Talking Machine Company, with Berliner's company to create the Victor Talking Machine Company, with "Little Nipper" the dog as a trademark. The Victrola, introduced in 1906, was very popular—and very expensive. It sold for $200; that would be $4,000 in today's money.

One major problem the Victor machine had was the stylus: It was made of steel, it weighed more than half a pound, and had a tendency to cause heavy wear on the shellac disks and eventually grind away all of the recording marks in the groove. Still, it worked. Then The Columbia Phonograph Company (later renamed Columbia Records), which was founded by Edward Easton, produced a low-cost cylinder based machine. So did Edison, and sales of pre-recorded disks and cylinders, mostly of classical and Tin Pan Alley music, the popular music and songs of the day, began to grow.

From this point on, there was a race to improve the technology in players, cylinders, and disks. Players got better and fancier, the stylus changed from steel to diamond tip and got much lighter, cylinders got easier and cheaper to reproduce as the material they were made of changed from wax to celluloid, and disks got bigger and had longer playing times.

Still, the production of recordings was a problem. To produce a cylinder or disk, it had to be mechanically recorded, just the way Edison did "Mary had a little lamb." The sound had to go into a cone to a membrane with a stylus attached that would etch the dents into the groove of the master, and there could only be one cone. The number of musicians who could get close enough to the cone attached to the recording machine was small or they couldn't be picked up adequately to make a decent recording. This limited the selection of music to what could be played with a very small band or orchestra. Something better was needed.

That something better was electrical recording instead of mechanical, and we're going to bounce around in time a bit to cover this.

■ ELECTRICAL RECORDING

The first step in getting away from mechanical recording was taken by Valdemar Poulsen in 1897 when he invented a way to electrically record. He created an electric current that traveled down a wire at different frequencies with something like a telephone mouthpiece. That current went into an electromagnet that was right next to a thin steel wire. The electromagnet altered the positions of the electrons in the wire, magnetizing and freezing them in that new position. Running the wire past another electromagnet, this time one designed to output rather than to receive electric current, rather like a telephone earpiece, played the recording back. The electrons would remain frozen in place until they were rearranged in another recording—or until someone passed a magnet over the wire.

Poulsen's method may seem counterintuitive. After all, if you take a magnet with north and south poles and chop it up, you get a bunch of little magnets, each with north and south poles, and if you put all those little magnets together you get one big magnet with one north and one south pole. Wouldn't the same be true if you magnetize a steel wire, that it would become just one long magnet? People said Poulsen's idea wouldn't work, but it turned out he was right—the only one who thought so. You **could** magnetize just short bits of a continuous steel wire, leaving unmagnetized sections between each magnetized section, and thus create recordings on wire recorders.

This was the beginning of electrical recording, and wire recorders even started appearing in homes in 1915. Of course, there were problems with wire recorders. First, steel wire is brittle, so it could break. If it did break, there really was no way to splice it back together. That meant you couldn't do "cut and splice" editing. Second, to keep the magnetized areas of the wire far enough apart so they wouldn't blend together into a single magnet, you needed a lot of wire—Poulsen's recorder ran at 100 inches, or 8 feet 4 inches, per second. For a three-minute recording you needed 1,500 feet, or almost a third of a mile of wire. So to keep the spools small enough to be practical, the recorder used very thin wire—which increased the possibility of breakage. Nonetheless, the idea worked, and it worked well despite its drawbacks.

It was another thirty years before this way of electrically recording sound changed. In 1928, Fritz Pfleumer invented a way to apply and adhere magnetic powders, essentially iron rust (or ferric oxide to sound scientific), to long strips of paper or film. Now, instead of magnetizing the medium itself, like a steel wire, you magnetized the coating on the medium. At first, the magnetic particles on the tape are just arranged randomly, with no particular position or orientation. However, as the tape runs under the recording head, which is an electromagnet much the same as Paulsen's, the particles are realigned according to the strength of the signal and remain frozen in these new positions—at least until you re-record on the tape, pass a magnet across it, or the tape rots away. Because it was not the medium that was magnetized but only the coating on the medium, there was no danger of the particles in the coating blending into a single magnet as was possible when using wire as the medium.

A major change was in the recording and playback heads. The smaller you could get the gap between the north and south poles of the recording head, the more information per inch you could get on the tape. This was quite a breakthrough. Instead of needing 100 inches of wire a second, you could record on the paper tape at 32 inches a second. In 1931, Pfleumer and AEG started making magnetic tape recorders for sale. Three years later BASF dispensed with the paper or film as the medium and started using plastic-based tape, the medium still in use today, then they started manufacturing their magnetophone.

■ MICROPHONES

Of course, to record electrically instead of mechanically you needed a way to convert sound into electrical impulses. Alexander Graham Bell did that when he invented the telephone. What Bell used was a carbon granule microphone, the same kind Poulsen used when he invented electrical recording. What a carbon granule microphone, or mike, had was loose granules of carbon held between two electrodes. Speaking into the mike sent sound waves through the air that would cause a membrane, or diaphragm, in the mike to vibrate. In response to varying pressures from the vibration, the diaphragm would press on the carbon granules, the electrical resistance through the carbon granules would change proportionally to the pressure, and the electrical signal was sent down the wire. The quality of sound was not very good—it was common for people to shout into the telephone to be heard at all, so this system wasn't terribly well suited to music. Still, the carbon granule microphone was all that was available for years.

A new kind of microphone, the condenser mike, was invented in 1916, but it didn't really come into use until 1925. The big difference between the condenser and carbon granule mikes was that the condenser mike had a diaphragm that vibrated in a magnetic field rather than putting pressure on bits of carbon. The difference in the quality and fidelity of the sound could be remarkable. The magnetic field could respond to much more, and much more subtle, variation in sound frequencies than could the crude mechanical pressing and releasing pressure on bits of carbon. A condenser mike could detect the difference between 263 hertz (vibrations per second) of the note middle C and 265 (middle C, but a bit sharp); a carbon granule mike was too crude to detect that subtle difference and would send both to the recorder as the same note.

There were, however, a few problems with the condenser mike. First, it required a power supply to create the electrical field between the diaphragm and the back plate that received the changes in the magnetic field. Second, it required an amplifier since the signal was so weak; and third, it was susceptible to moisture. Still, the improvement in sound over the carbon mike made it the definite choice.

Further improvements in microphones came over the years, including replacing the diaphragm with a ribbon that vibrated in a magnetic field, replacing the back plate that detected the variations in the magnetic field with a moving wire coil, and reducing the size and weight. But now with a microphone sending electrical impulses instead of sound waves to move the stylus to etch the recording onto the cylinder or disk, the sound quality improved and it was easier to do recordings. The orchestra, which could now be as big as the room could hold, could sit anywhere in the studio instead of crowded around the recording cone. Microphones could be placed strategically and feed their signals into a mixing board that would combine the signals before sending the output to the stylus.

■ STYLUS

Now we have to get rid of the mechanical etching of the sound pattern on the cylinder or disk.[1] The invention of electrical recording made it possible to dispense with the mechanical etching of the recording medium, like a shellac disk. Mechanical etching used the actual sound waves to move the membrane to move the stylus. That created a poor quality recording.

The first step in the electrical recording of records was to create a new kind of stylus to etch the master. Instead of a membrane that vibrated according to sound waves, the new system moved the stylus electrically by moving the membrane with an electromagnet. As the microphones became more sensitive and capable of a greater frequency range, so did the etching system. By 1931, these changes increased the quality of the recordings, both in terms of reduced noise and greater dynamic range, the highs and lows of pitch.

Improvements in the records themselves soon followed in order to take advantage of the improvements in recording. Going from hard rubber to shellac to acetate to vinyl all allowed a greater fidelity and dynamic range. Finally, life-like recordings for radio and the home were by 1948 a reality.

So, we have recording and a way to play it back. However, there seems to be something missing. That something is a way to hear the recording when it's played back. What is needed is a speaker of some sort.

The first kind of speaker was a simple empty cone. All it did was concentrate the sound, just like a megaphone. It hadn't changed since de Martinville's sound etcher. However, it didn't amplify the sound, just concentrated and focused what went in and out.

To really make recording a working proposition, there needed to be a way to amplify the sound. That came in 1877 when William Siemans created the moving coil transducer and attached a parchment membrane. A moving coil transducer is basically an electric motor. As voltage is applied to the coil, it generates an electromagnetic field. This field is either repulsed or attracted to the fixed field of the magnet, which surrounds the coil, causing the coil to move back and forth, pumping like a piston. Being attached to a membrane increases the movement of the membrane and thus increases the volume of the sound waves being pumped out.

The next step was replacing the membrane with something bigger, like a sheet of tough paper. A shallow cone of heavy paper with corrugations was attached to a speaker rim. The coil is cemented to the back of the speaker cone, which creates sound waves as it's pushed back and forth. Originally, the shape of the cone was convex, with the center of the cone sticking out beyond the rim of the speaker, rather than concave, sunken below the rim.

Another approach to making speakers was Maxfield and Harrison's orthophonic speaker. Here the stylus assembly that rides in the record groove is electromagnetic. The stylus' movement moves a metal membrane in a magnetic field, which moves a membrane at the base of the speaker and pumps the sound through the baffles of the enclosure, ensuring a good range of dynamics. However, volume was still a problem: the speaker was more or less a very sophisticated cone design.

The next change was to add an amplifier to the system, invert the cone of the speaker, and make the electromagnet around the voice coil bigger. Although materials for making the speaker have changed and improved over the years, such as better magnets and cone materials, and the box it goes in has altered configuration in any number of ways, the basic speaker has remained in this form for the last seventy years.

So everything necessary to record sound and play it back is in place. But of course, nothing stands still. Changes and improvements in the technology came about as the decades passed.

The first thing that happened was eliminating the records themselves by going to the alternative—tape. Poulsen's 1897 device was constantly being improved, with better tape, better magnetic coatings on the tape, and better recording and playback heads.

In 1944, 3M (the Minnesota Mining and Manufacturing Company) began experimenting with tape coatings, and they found a better coating than the original coating developed by Fritz Pfleumer in 1928, which was basically rust. They developed gamma ferric oxide (basically a **treated** rust) that provided greater fidelity due to its greater sensitivity.

Then in 1948, Bing Crosby commissioned Ampex to make an improved tape recorder using the 3M tape. The Ampex recorder greatly improved the recording and playback heads. Ampex reduced the gap between the poles of the electromagnet—the smaller the gap the greater the frequency and the less tape you need to record and play back for the same amount of time.

In 1949, Magnecord was making reel-to-reel tape recorders for sale to the general public, and in 1954 RCA was selling the first prerecorded reel-to-reel tapes.

The next step was to make things even smaller, and in 1963 Philips Electronics demonstrated its first compact audiocassette using eighth-inch wide tape that ran at 1 and 7/8ths inches per second. Philips sold them the next year in the US with their carry-corder as a dictation machine, but the company was surprised by the demand for tapes for personal music recording.

Another idea for using tape for music was the 8 track, invented by William Lear in 1962. By 1966, US cars came equipped with 8 track players. That, however, didn't last long because compact cassette players shrank in size to the point that you could easily put them in your car dashboard.

The next change was the personal stereo. In 1979, Sony introduced the Walkman, the first personal, carry-it-with-you, play your own music instead of what somebody else wants to play, form of entertainment. By 1983, more pre-recorded audiocassettes were sold than long-playing records. It was the beginning of the decline of record players and the medium used on them. Today the LP and the stereo phonograph are the province of purists who prefer the sound of vinyl, collectors, and people with large record collections that don't wish to buy their music all over again.

So where do we go from here? To digital, of course. Up to now, everything has been analog—that is, sound was converted to physical changes in either the surface of a medium, like the shellac or later vinyl of a record, or by magnetically rearranging the positions of fine particles of iron on a piece of tape to imitate those grooves.

But there is another way, which we'll talk about in the chapter on modern communication media.

■ ENDNOTE

1. Actually, the cylinder went out in 1913 when Edison conceded defeat and accepted that the disk was the format to use.

9

RADIO AND SOCIETY

he development of radio and sound recording required a large number of people doing a large number of things over a large number of years. But what effects have the invention of radio and sound recording had on society once they were introduced? They went pretty much hand in hand, so I'll combine them in this discussion. Let's start by looking at society before radio.

■ PRE-RADIO

For thousands of years society consisted of the people around you, those you saw and talked to every day. Other people were often pretty much only a rumor—and, of course, nowhere near as good as you. You might bump into another group and discover they were pretty much like you (or completely different from you), but they weren't really a part of your world.

Writing and printing opened up the world to a lot of people—but only those who went to the trouble to learn to read and write and find books to read, and later newspapers and magazines. But in many cases, that was only a minority of the people in the world, the literate and the curious. Even today the book publishing industry is supported by only 5 percent of the people. High circulation for a newspaper or magazine is measured in the low millions—2 to 3 million for a newspaper, 10 to 15 million for a magazine. This is out of a US population of 300 million.

So what did people do for entertainment? Well, mostly they made their own. They might read, or talk to each other, or play parlor games, or even make their own music. A piano was a common piece of household furniture, and larger families would often learn a variety of musical instruments besides the piano, like the violin or flute or guitar, or be able to sing—maybe not well, but they would sing. Certainly, sheet music was a big seller as people tried to expand their repertoires.

Outside of the home, there were a variety of things that could be done for entertainment. There was live theatre, if only a local troupe or the high school. Most towns had at least one and often more vaudeville houses, where a variety of live acts performed, like singers and dancers and comics and trained dogs and dancing mules and whatever anyone could think of to do that they hoped an audience would pay to see. A popular form of entertainment was going to enlightening lectures on a whole gamut of topics, from stories of travel in foreign lands to new discoveries in biology to how to contact the spirit world. Just about every town had a town band that played concerts in the park. Fairs and festivals of all types occurred all during the year. And if all else failed, people could go to the beach or the mountains or the nearest big city. There were also sporting events. People could play a sport, everything from softball to croquet, or be a spectator. Most towns had their own baseball team, and would play their hated rivals from a few miles away, providing a fun-filled afternoon of cheers, jeers—and beers.

The thing about all these forms of entertainment is that just about everything was local, in the home or in the hometown. Communities tended to be insular and parochial, fragmented into small groups with little sense of the larger American society outside of the neighboring area. There was only one medium that could be considered national, affecting most of society, and that was in existence for only a few years before radio entered the social consciousness. That medium, which will be discussed in later chapters, was movies, and their effects on society were quite different from those of radio.

An interesting aspect of pre-radio life is that it was quiet. Most sounds that were heard were natural: dogs barking, birds singing, children at play; the clop of horses' hooves and the rumble of wagon wheels; the occasional laugh, or someone playing the piano. In many ways, it could be considered an idyllic time.

Then came radio.[1] It really was the end of the quiet life. People across the country quickly adopted the radio. And it was on all the time. It was on in homes and restaurants and bars and cars. Businesses, especially those selling radios and records, would set up speakers outside their doors and play the radio to passersby, often resulting in cacophony as multiple businesses would play different stations. The radio became a normal part of life, on and playing all the time. For the first time in human life, sound rather than silence was the norm. There was so much sound, it interfered with human interaction, drowning out conversation or causing people to stop what they were doing to listen to the radio. The world became a noisy place and a more impersonal place, and it has remained so ever since.

◼ THE BEGINNING OF BROADCASTING

Perhaps the greatest change in society was the very basis of communication. Prior to radio, communication was limited and point-to-point. That is, communication was one person communicating with one other person. Books were the authors talking to the readers, newspapers were the reporter talking to the readers, letters were from one person to another, telegrams were from one person to another. When movies finally came along, they may have been seen by tens or hundreds of people at a time, but of course in their case it required an affirmative action on the part of the consumer—that is, the consumer had to consciously decide to see a movie, leave home, pay money, sit in a dark room with a bunch of strangers and concentrate on watching the movie. And even that was local, much like going to live theatre.

However, with radio, for the first time, the entire world was open to everyone with no effort on their part. Let me repeat that: The entire world was open to everyone **with no effort on their part**. This is significantly different from any other form of entertainment. Reading takes an effort, playing music takes an effort, playing a sport takes an effort, even going to a game, live theatre, vaudeville or a movie takes an effort. Radio only required people to turn it on. They could listen to edifying lectures without ever leaving their homes—or their easy chairs. They could listen to opinion leaders. They could participate in national politics by listening to speeches and conventions. A single person's voice, and that person's ideas and beliefs, could reach millions of people, exponentially increasing the impact of that voice. No effort was required on the part of the audience, as it would be with reading or attended a rally—after all, the radio was on anyway.

That could be a good thing, as with Franklin Roosevelt's Great Depression speeches. His Fireside Chats rallied and gave hope to the people.

But it could also allow demagogues the power to influence millions of people. Adolf Hitler motivated his nation to go to war to gain *lebensraum* (living room) by invading neighboring countries and "relocating" the native populations so the German people would have the room for their natural expansion as the "Master Race." The Master Race would also remove impediments to their "natural" place in the world by destroying their enemies, like the Russians, the Poles and the Jews. The result of Hitler's use of radio was a major contributing factor in the deaths of 40,000,000 people.

Such effects of radio didn't go unnoticed. In the 1930s, one of the most popular radio personalities in the United States was Father Charles Coughlin. His radio broadcasts reached millions of people with his populist message. At first, he was a strong supporter of Franklin Roosevelt and his New Deal as a way to fight the Great Depression. But as time went on, he felt that Roosevelt was moving toward socialism, and he became a major opponent of Roosevelt. Coughlin turned more and more toward the fascist[2] ideas of Adolf Hitler, including Hitler's rabid anti-Semitism, and he relied on his radio broadcasts to influence his audience, just as Hitler did, to fight what he viewed as an increasingly liberal government.

The government naturally responded to Coughlin's attacks. It determined that the airwaves were a "limited natural resource," a view that had ample evidence. Radio stations would broadcast on whatever frequency they wanted, with as much power as they could pump out, from 5 watts to 500,000. This resulted in "clutter in the airwaves," as different stations' broadcasts would interfere with each other by overlapping on the same frequency, or one station would drown out others by simply overpowering the others' signals with a stronger one. This was, of course, annoying to audiences, but there was little they could do about it.

In 1927, the government stepped into the growing problem of clutter by requiring all stations to apply for operating permits. The purpose of these permits was not only to give permission to a station to broadcast, but also specify each station's broadcast frequency and power. By doing so, no station's signal would overlap any other station's signal. Such a move, if applied to print media, would have been unconstitutional, violating the First Amendment. Part of the reasoning for giving the government this power to require permits was that radio, as a "limited natural resource," was different from print. Print media could not drown each other out—there could be as many newspapers, books, and magazines as people had resources to print without any one interfering with any other, and any reader could read as many as rhe wanted at any time. Such as clearly not the case with radio broadcasting. Thus, the determination was that radio did not enjoy First Amendment protection since it was now regulated as a publicly owned commons (that is, a resource owned by everyone and thus a single person couldn't control it[3]).

Back to Coughlin. When Coughlin applied for a permit for his broadcast network under the new regulations, it was denied as being against the public interest to allow him to continue his anti-American broadcasts. Thus, it took his voice off the air. Coughlin tried to get around the permit ruling that lost him his national network by buying broadcast time on individual stations around the country, but that reduced size of the audience he could reach and cost him more than he could really afford. In 1939, when Coughlin's diatribes against the U.S. government's attitudes toward Hitler and the war in Europe Hitler had started became more strident, and he increased his anti-Semitism, the National Association of Broadcasters ruled that there should be "rigid limitations on the sale of radio time to spokesmen of controversial public issues." This ruling pretty much forced Coughlin off the air. Although Coughlin continued publishing his newspaper *Social Justice,* which did enjoy First Amendment protection, his influence waned to virtually nothing without the reach and power of radio.

Another interesting case of the power of radio, both figuratively and literally, was that of John R. Brinkley, a diploma mill doctor with a cure for just about everything, but especially for sexual problems. His cure? Transplanting goat glands into his patients.

Something Brinkley noticed immediately about radio was what a wonderful medium it was for advertising. He had had success with newspaper ads, but he saw the advantage of a medium that was always on in people's homes and required no effort on the part of the audience. In 1923, he started his first radio station in Kansas using a 1,000-watt transmitter. Attempts were made to shut him down by the *Kansas City Star* and the American Medical Association, but those attempts failed, and as the old saying goes, "any publicity is good publicity." Brinkley used his radio station to crow about his victories over the *Star* and the AMA, to sell his "medicine" through a chain of kickback pharmacies, and ignored people harmed by his procedures. His business boomed.

In 1930, Brinkley applied to renew his broadcasting license, but his application was denied by the Federal Radio Commission on the basis that his broadcasts were not in the public interest but only for Brinkley's personal gain. Brinkley appealed the ruling on the grounds that the denial amounted to censorship, violating his First Amendment rights, but he lost his appeal. The court decided that the FRC could consider past programming , that Brinkley had used the public commons, the publicly owned air waves, for private gain, and thus it could turn down his application without it being considered censorship.

However, Brinkley didn't give up trying to find a way around the law. Realizing that radio waves didn't respect national borders, he opened a new transmitting station just across the border in Mexico. Since the station wouldn't be on American soil, it wouldn't come under the regulations of the FRC. Brinkley himself, however, didn't move to Mexico to run the station but sent the programming from his station in Kansas over the border to Mexico through telephone lines. The programming itself was exactly the same as he had done before, especially the promotion of his goat gland cures that had led the FRC to deny his license application in the first place.

Brinkley also realized that his audience was in the United States, which was too far away to receive his broadcasts from his Mexican transmitter, so he turned up the power.

He equipped his new station with a high-powered transmitter and huge antennae that pumped out 500,000 watts, and there were rumors that it could be heard in Russia. Other stations that also wished to get out from under FRC regulations that limited their broadcast power soon opened transmitters like Brinkley's.

Then, at the beginning of World War II, Brinkley invited Nazi and fascist sympathizers to broadcast their messages on his station. This led the US government to make a deal with the Mexican government to restrict such over-powered and over-powering stations. The agreement required that any Mexican station receiving its programming from the United States had to be licensed by the FRC. This agreement finally put Brinkley out of business, and he died a year later. Maybe he tried one of his cures.

The above three cases clearly illustrate the power and problems of clutter, demagoguery and the promotion of fraud, brought about by the introduction of radio as a mass medium. Radio could not be considered an open and freewheeling medium the way the print media were regarded. These problems had to be resolved, and the only entity that had the power to do so was the federal government. This gave the government the ability to regulate radio in a way that would be unconstitutional if applied to print.

■ RADIO AS ENTERTAINMENT

Of course, not everything on radio was politics or quack cures. The main programming that dominated the broadcast day was entertainment. David Sarnoff's 1916 memo about the Radio Music Box in every home started coming true, and the music the boxes played was live musicians and recordings. However, there were many other genres of programming besides music.

One element of radio that became immediately apparent was its hunger for material. Multiple stations on the air most of the hours of the day meant a need for something to put out on the air, preferably something other than what competing stations were broadcasting. Dramas, comedies, talk shows, variety shows, game shows—anything anyone could think of that an audience could be enjoy without the need of visual elements.

Naturally, music was a perfect genre for radio. Big band and orchestral music dominated, but radio needed more than they could provide. This led to a major increase in non-mainstream musicians who were unheard of by most people before radio came on the air and attracted the attention of the audience. These included blues singers like Bessie Smith, and Fiddlin' John Carson, whose 1923 "Little Old Log Cabin in the Lane" became the first country hit. In 1925, WSM in Nashville began its *Barn Dance* radio show, which became the *Grand Ole Opry* in 1927. In 1931, Bing Crosby started crooning on the CBS radio network and became one of the biggest stars in the history of radio.

As mentioned above, other genres of programming soon came on the air, including comedies and dramas. This fact led to a fundamental change in how entertainment was done. Prior to radio, books and plays were one-of-a-kind, standalone stories—read or see one and you get the entire story from beginning to end—an exposition setting the universe in which the story takes place, one problem going through a series of crises and complications leading to a climax that solves the problem. There was no need to come back the next day or week or month to see the outcome of a crisis—the story is completely over.

However, radio introduced a new way of telling stories—episodic shows. In episodic shows there is one exposition establishing the universe of the show (time and place that stays the same in every episode, regular characters that appear in every episode and consistently retain their relationships to each other). The only difference from one episode to the next was the problem to solve that was introduced to upset the status quo of the established universe of the show. Such an approach to storytelling had never been done before.

The advantage of doing episodic shows was that the audience quickly grew familiar with the shows' universes and characters, so little time was needed to set up each episode. It also made writing the stories much easier since a whole new universe didn't have to be created every week, just a new disruption of the status quo and the characters saying and doing things to solve that problem. In addition, if an audience liked a particular show, they could be assured of having a new story told in that universe that would be aired every week. This increased audience loyalty, a very good thing for the sponsors of the show, as people tuned in every week to hear the "continuing adventures" of their favorite characters, and turned the actors on the show into stars.

Radio also introduced the first new form of storytelling in history. Remember the structure of a story: an exposition, a problem, the characters going through a series of crises and complications as everything they do and say is directly aimed at solving that problem, a climax that solves the problem, and maybe a denouement. This is the way all stories had been told since Neanderthals reenacted the latest mammoth hunt around the fire 300,000 years ago.

However, radio began airing a genre of episodic show that violated this way of telling stories. That genre of show was the soap opera.

To understand this change, it is necessary to understand the difference between male and female communication styles. Dr. Deborah Tannen did research into this area, and she discovered two major differences:

1. Men use conversation competitively in order to establish their position in a hierarchy. They often approach a conversation as a problem solving exercise to show what they know and their expertise, thus demonstrating superiority.
2. Women use conversation cooperatively in order to form bonds and connections. They often approach a conversation as a way of exploring relationships in order to grow closer to others and arrive at a consensus.

As we look at these differences in men's and women's communication objectives in terms of storytelling, we can see that something immediately stands out: All stories use a male conversation style rather than a female. A story introduces a problem, and every crisis and complication and everything said and done by all the characters is directly related to solving that problem until it's solved, and then the story is over. This is the approach that men use in conversation—when presented with a problem, concentrate on solving it until it's resolved.

The soap opera, or the daytime serial drama, was aimed directly at women, and it introduced a totally new way to tell stories. Instead of using men's conversation style, it used women's. The focus of a story in a soap opera was not to solve a problem, but to explore the effects on the relationships between the characters that the problem, crises, and complications cause. Thus, what happened was irrelevant; what was important was how what happened altered relationships and allowed the characters to talk with each other about that alteration. For example, someone falling in love alters the relationship between not only that person and the person rhe loves, but those two and everyone else they know. All of those relationships may change by taking those two out of contention as a potential loved one, or jealousy may rear its ugly head. Once every permutation of these altered relationships has been explored in conversation between the characters, something else can happen in the story, for instance, perhaps the first two break up, which sets in motion a whole new set of changes in all the relationships.

This change in storytelling from problem-solving to the exploration of interpersonal connections unrelated to solving a problem was the first new way of telling stories in history, and it was an important effect of radio's desire to appeal to audiences.

Then, of course, there was news. Print news was always delayed, arriving before the public a day, and even weeks, after the event reported, which created a lack of immediacy and importance to the moment. There was also the difference between writing and speaking. Writing follows rules of grammar, syntax and punctuation that are required to make an intellectual presentation in order to convert abstract visual symbols into meaning. These rules tend to reduce the emotional content of the words. Speaking, on the other hand, creates an instant emotional reaction as a voice's volume, rate, tone and timbre reflect the speaker's emotions at the time. These tend to evoke those same emotions in the audience. Radio news, using speech rather than writing, and often broadcast as the event being reported is happening, leads the listening audience to have an emotional rather than an intellectual response to the news.

The upshot of radio's rise as a national mass medium is that the country, splintered by region, accent, interest, customs and mores and beliefs, became much more homogenous. Everyone across the country, regardless of region or attitude, was hearing the same things, singing the same songs, discussing the same issues. Differences in the rules of society that were enforced by distance and lack of knowledge started disappearing as the world shrank down to the radio in the corner. The country was bound together by the airwaves.

This, of course, couldn't last. Two things would bring back some of that fragmentation: television, and rock and roll.

■ THE ADVENT OF TELEVISION

In 1947, a new player in communication media started to make an impact—television. At first considered merely radio with pictures, television was indeed radio—*with pictures*. People were fascinated by television, even if all it showed was the orchestra and singer performing the music they could hear on the radio.

A major effect that television had on radio was that television broadcasters co-opted most of radio's programming, especially radio's dramas and comedies and soap operas. TV quickly grabbed radio shows like ***The Lone Ranger***. Of course, this did throw some actors out of work who were perfect on radio but didn't fit the visual wanted. For example, William Conrad played the Lone Ranger on radio, but Clayton Moore who looked more heroic and handsome replaced him.

So radio needed programming to replace those shows that television had taken over, and fill their broadcast schedule. It turned more and more to those things that television didn't do well: music and talking heads.

Talk shows didn't do very well on television because there's nothing very visually interesting about them, and television really depends on pictures. Talk shows are just people sitting and talking, which, even if the topic is important or exciting in an intellectual way, is often very boring to look at since there's little in the way of visual stimulation.

However, talk is perfect for radio. Audiences don't expect to see visual elements on radio, only to listen. So more and more time was turned over to talkers of all types—news, commentators, call in shows. Talk shows have been with us for more than sixty years.

But a major change came in 1947 when the first rock and roll song was recorded: *Good Rocking Tonight* by Roy Brown. In 1949, after observing customers in a bar play the same songs over and over on the jukebox, Todd Storz of Omaha's KOWH Radio created Top 40 radio, a list of the forty most popular recorded songs during a period of time, perhaps every week or month. Then, in 1952, Alan Freed, often called the father of rock and roll, started his ***Moondog's Rock and Roll Party*** in Cleveland after a visit to a music store where he observed teenagers listening to records and dancing. This kind of music was very popular with the youth of the nation, and it led to stations programming rock and roll to attract that audience. With that, rock music became a staple of radio.

Since the 1950s, every kind of music aimed at young people has hit the air, from heavy metal to folk rock to rap. An interesting effect of this has been to **re**-fragment society. Young people loved the music because it reflected what they felt and believed, and older people hated it because it reflected what young people felt and believed. The generation that grew up with Glenn Miller, Bing Crosby and the Andrews Sisters saw nothing but the corruption of society and the decline in the morals of the youth of the nation. **Sex, drugs, and rock and roll** became the jeer of the old and the cheer of the young. By the 1960s, the generation gap widened, fueled by music played on the radio, as rock and roll reflected the rebellion against the old rules of society that youth believed should be shed, the very rules the older generation believed should be maintained.

Over the next three decades, radio continued to grow and thrive, and indeed it is bigger than ever. But instead of bringing society together, it more often than not has divided it. We'll see that later in the book when we look at the media—and society—today.

■ ENDNOTES

1. Here I'm not talking about wireless telegraphy, which was a point-to-point communication medium using morse code, which few people could, or wanted to, personally use. Henceforth, references to radio will mean David Sarnoff's "Radio Music Box," sound radio carrying entertainment into people's homes.
2. There doesn't seem to be a solid definition of fascism, but there is some agreement on certain characteristics: The government holds complete control over the society and is controlled by a power elite, especially in business; anti-democratic; extreme nationalism based on culture, race and history; imperialism; extreme socio-political conservatism; and a fascist society is often led by a charismatic leader.
3. A commons relates to the idea of the village commons, a meadow that belonged to everyone in the village rather than to an individual owner so that everyone could graze their sheep on it. Therefore, individuals couldn't fence in any part of it for their exclusive use.

CHAPTER

10

THE HISTORY AND DEVELOPMENT OF MOTION PICTURES

*I*n the nineteenth century we were running out of elephants. There was also a teacher with a problem and a new idea for an old device. These would play their part to change the world.

People have seen the world in motion from the time they first opened their eyes and focused on what's around them. However, the one thing they could never do was remember that motion in anything but their own memories: There was no medium that could capture motion and play it back at a later time. Print could capture words, recordings could capture sounds, photographs could capture images, but nothing could capture motion. That was about to change, and it all started with an Austrian artillery officer teaching recruits in Vienna.

In 1853, Captain Franz Uchatius wanted to illustrate how a cannonball flew through the air after being fired from a cannon. What he did was make a disc with still pictures of a cannon firing a ball and the ball flying through the air. In each drawing, the ball was a little further along in its arc. He mounted this disk in a magic lantern projector. This was a box with an oil lamp in front of a mirror reflector that would shine a beam of light through a lens that concentrated the light through a picture drawn on a clear or translucent medium like a sheet of glass. This in turn sent an image of that picture through another focusing lens and projected it onto a surface like a white wall or a cloth sheet. When Uchatius spun the disk between the lamp and the lens, the pictures he had drawn passed in sequence through the projector's lens and appeared on a screen. When the disk spun fast enough, it appeared that the cannonball was flying through the air, and persistence of vision caused the audience to see the images as a smooth sequence rather than as a series of individual pictures. What Uchatius had invented to teach his class was a motion picture machine, the first ever.

Uchatius thought little of his invention. To him, it was just a teaching tool. However, another man saw greater potential in the device. That man was one of Europe's greatest magicians, Ludwig Doebler. When he saw Uchatius' invention, he knew immediately what to do with it—steal it. Well, actually he paid the captain a couple of florin for it and took off. Soon all over Europe he was drawing in huge crowds with "his" motion pictures.

Note that Uchatius made drawings to put in his magic lantern. It wasn't until the early nineteenth century that there was a way to make images other than by drawing or painting. To explain this requires another detour into the past.

Aristotle, the fourth century BCE Greek philosopher, wrote about a device that would allow painting with light. What he was describing was the pinhole camera, also known as a camera obscura. It consisted of a closed box with a small hole in one end through which light would stream and cast an image of what the hole was aimed at on the opposite wall.

Around 1021 CE, an Arabic scientist and expert in optics named Ibn Al-Haytham (known to Europeans as Alhazen) explained how it worked. Light rays travel in straight lines and, when some of the light rays reflected from a brightly lit subject pass through a small hole in a thin material like cloth, the rays don't scatter but cross and reform as an image on a flat surface held parallel to the hole. Of course, when the rays cross the image, it comes out upside down. Remember how Arabic knowledge spread throughout Europe? Alhazen's work was included in that knowledge, and people began playing with the camera obscura, including people like Leonard de Vinci.

However, the only thing it was really good for was to create drawings. People would build pinhole cameras up to the size of a room, trace the images cast on the back wall, and create drawings from those tracings.

In 1827, someone succeeded in using the camera obscura for more than drawing. That someone was Joseph Nicéphore Niépce (pronounced "neeps"). He coated a sheet of pewter with bitumen, a product of coal tar created by heating up coal in a kettle and

condensing the steam. He then set the plate into a camera obscura and exposed the plate to light shining through the hole. The bitumen stuck where the light hit, and washing the plate in naphtha removed the excess, resulting in the first photograph. As you can see, it's not exactly the epitome of detail. An additional drawback to Niépce's camera was the fact that the exposure took eight hours.

In 1839, Louis Daguerre improved on Niépce's process. For his technique, he polished a silver or copper plate to a mirror finish and coated it with silver iodide, which was far more sensitive to light than bitumen. He would place the prepared plate in a black box and shine reflected light from the object being photographed through a lens, and the light rays etched the image on the plate. He would then wash the plate in a solvent and produce the picture. Although Daguerre's photographs had far greater resolution than Niépce's, there was still a drawback: The Daguerre process only produces a positive image on the plate, so each picture was one of a kind, and it took up to thirty minutes to do the exposure. No wonder everyone in a daguerreotype looks so uncomfortable; they had to sit or stand still for such a long time.

The problems with Daguerre's technique were solved in 1840 when William Henry Fox Talbot developed several improvements. He used translucent paper instead of a metal plate. Because light could be shone through the paper and create a negative image of the picture, multiple positive copies of a picture could be made using the negative. He also made the silver iodide coating on the paper much more sensitive than Daguerre's, making possible an exposure measured in seconds instead of minutes. Practical photography was finally a reality.

So let's get back to Ludwig Doebler and Uchatius' projector. He brought the projector and his show to America and made as much money as he had in Europe. One person who saw it was Eadweard Muybridge (and yes, that's how it's spelled). Muybridge was a photographer in California. In 1873, the former governor of California, Leland Stanford, made a bet with a friend. Stanford was convinced that a horse at full gallop had all four feet off the ground at the same time. The problem was proving it since the feet moved too fast for everyone to agree on the matter. Stanford turned to Muybridge to see if he could solve the problem.

Four years later Muybridge came up with a plan that he felt would settle the matter. He put a line of still cameras along a stretch of racetrack. The shutters were attached to strings stretched across the track. As the horse galloped down the track it tripped each string, thus taking its picture one after another in rapid sequence. Examining the pictures, he saw in several that clearly all four legs were off the ground, and Stanford won his bet.

Muybridge also found a new career. Intrigued by the appearance of motion from the pictures, he started creating disks with pictures of animals and people doing things like running. Putting the disks in a machine very much like Uchatius' magic lantern, a machine he called the zoopraxiscope, he began putting on motion picture shows.

And now it's time for yet another detour. Enter John Wesley Hyatt.

In the mid nineteenth century there was a problem—we were running out of elephants. The problem was that billiard balls were made of ivory, and you could only get four balls out of a tusk. The billiard industry was desperate, desperate enough to offer a ten thousand dollar reward to anyone who could invent artificial ivory.

Hyatt, a printer, decided to take on the task. What he did was combine alcohol, camphor, and gun cotton. Gun cotton was made by soaking Sea Island cotton in a couple of different acids and letting it dry. Once it was dry it was an excellent explosive, much more powerful and faster than gun powder. Hyatt compressed those materials into balls—billiard balls. He called his material "celluloid." It was wonderful stuff, except celluloid pool balls had an unfortunate tendency to explode when slammed together in a pool game. They were made of gun cotton, after all.

Hannibal Goodwin, a Welsh clergyman, took Hyatt's celluloid and turned it into sheets that would hold photographic emulsion, replacing the old paper backing used by Talbot. George Eastman took those sheets and turned them into strips that he called film. With this final step, it was possible to take a series of still pictures without having to reload the camera for each shot.

Etienne Jules Marey saw possibilities in a strip of pictures. He combined the ideas of Uchatius' rapid projection of a series of pictures, but instead of using a disk, he used a strip of pictures. Marey believed the result would be the same—moving pictures. The only problem was how to pass the pictures in front of the lens in a controlled fashion. His

solution was to punch a series of holes along the side of the strip (he used translucent paper instead of Eastman's celluloid film) and run those holes over a sprocket wheel. By turning the wheel at the proper speed, it pulled the strip in front of the lens, projecting moving pictures onto a screen.

And then everything was brought together by Thomas Edison, the Wizard of Menlo Park, and the most famous and prolific inventor ever. He started with what other people had done. He took Uchatius's idea of passing pictures rapidly in front of a light and through a lens to create the appearance of moving pictures, which Doebler took as a stage show, which attracted the attention of Muybridge, who told Edison about it. Edison then took Hyatt's celluloid, turned into sheets by Goodwin, and then into strips as film by Eastman, and put holes along the strip of film so it could be pulled by a sprocket like Marey did.

Then Edison added his own bits: He used his light bulb as a light source to replace the oil lamp, and of course he marketed the whole thing in 1894 as his kinetoscope.

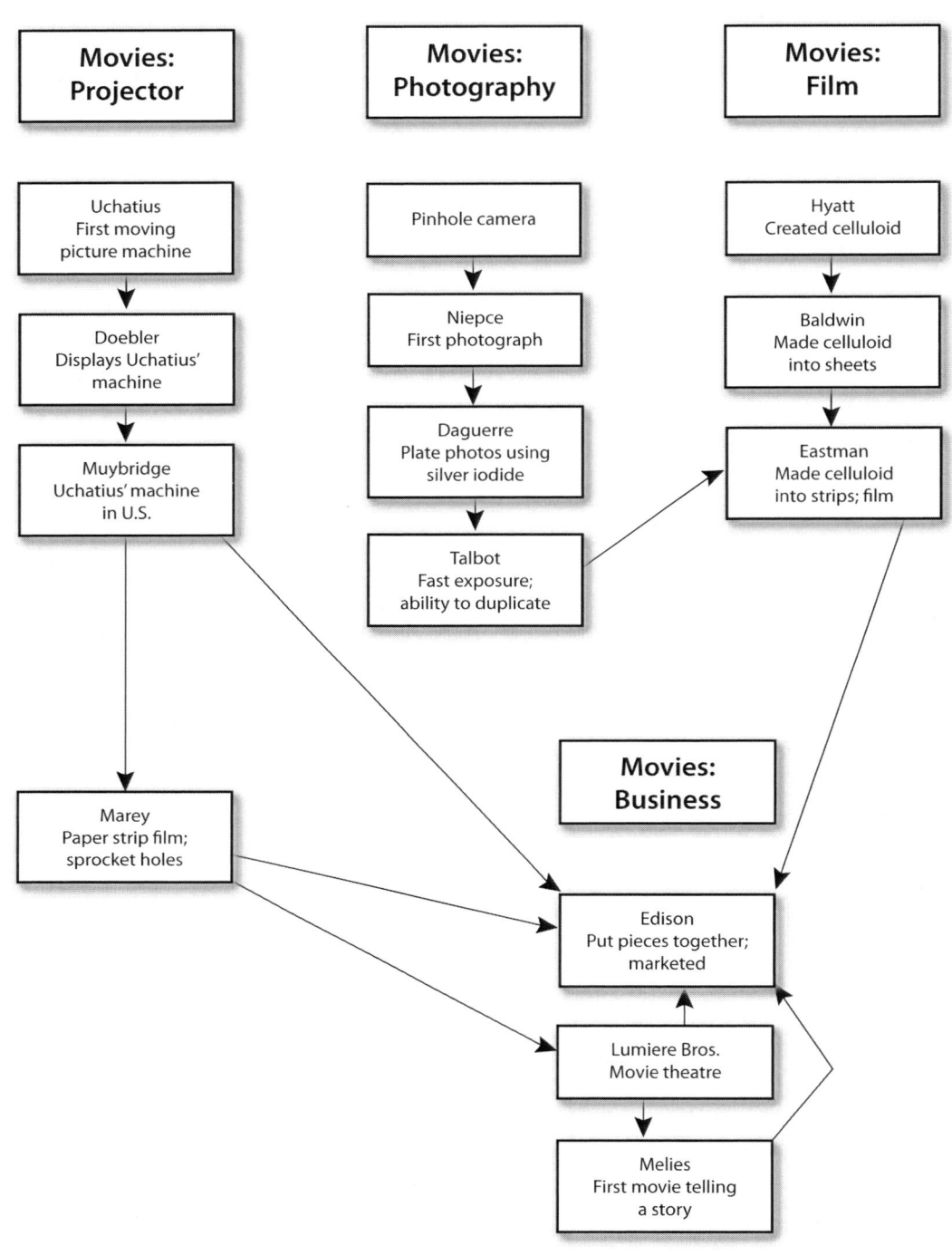

Notice how it works. The film is threaded over sprocket spools in a continuous loop. When the film reaches the top, it runs between the light and a lens. The image shines up into the viewer on top where the customer looks down at the movie. Please note the most important part of the machine, at least as far as Edison was concerned—the coin slot. You needed to drop in a penny to get the thing to run. Entrepreneurs were soon in business, filling rooms called arcades with kinetoscopes for people to watch. Thus the term "penny arcade."

In the beginning, the movies people could watch in the kinetoscope were just short films of regular life: two men boxing; a girl dancing; street scenes; and personal scenes such as a couple kissing. Although the films weren't anything people couldn't see anywhere around them, the novelty of seeing them as movies fascinated people.

Enter the Lumiere brothers, Louis and Auguste. In 1895, they went a step further, adapting the idea of Marey's magic lantern projector to throw an image on a screen rather than Edison's kinetoscope that simply cast the light up through a view piece. Their change from Marey's approach was to use film instead of paper strips. They set up their projector in the basement of a café, aimed it at a white bed sheet hung on a wall, and invited people to gather and watch their moving pictures. They announced their program: *La sortie des usines Lumiere* (workers leaving the Lumiere factory); *Le Repas de bébé* (feeding the baby); *L'Arrouseur arose* (a boy playing a practical joke on a gardener), and finally *L'Arrivée d'un train en gare.* This last one, of a train rushing toward the audience, sent them into a panic, running into the streets screaming, sure that death was imminent.

The movie theatre had been invented.

All these short scenes were fine for a while, but the novelty soon wore off. The realization set in that "the films weren't anything people couldn't see anywhere around them." More than real life was needed to keep audiences interested.

The way to do that was not to just make moving pictures, but to make moving pictures that told a story.

George Méliès believed audiences would flock to stories told in movie form the way they came to plays. A stage artist and magician, in 1902 he made *A Voyage to the Moon,* a movie version of Jules Verne's book. He used imaginative sets, make-up, costumes and even special effects, creating not just moving pictures, but a real experience for the audience. For the first time, they were watching something they had never seen before. Méliès' fortune was made. Well, it would have been, if there were copyright laws. By the time Méliès was ready to start showing the movie in America where he felt it would make the most money, it was too late. One of Thomas Edison's people stole a copy of the movie, and Edison showed it in the US as his own. Méliès didn't get a dime.

Méliès and others followed the Lumieres' example and showed their movies in theatres. These theatres, which were often just storefronts rented for a few days or weeks to show a movie before the exhibitors moved on to a new town, were called nickelodeons—Odeon from the Greek for theatre, and nickel for what people paid to get in. It several years before dedicated movie theatres came into existence.

Edison jumped on the nickelodeon bandwagon by making his own projector, the projecting kinetoscope, and started doing storytelling movies. One of the first was Edwin Porter's ten-minute *The Great Train Robbery,* one of the first movies to use location (i.e., in the real world) shooting rather than being shot entirely in a studio.

Audiences wanted more and longer movies. Filmmakers responded by making two and even three reel movies instead of the one-reelers (that were generally 10 minutes in duration) that were the norm. One of those still remembered—and reviled—today is D. W. Griffith's 1915 epic about the Civil War and its aftermath, *Birth of a Nation.*

There was one thing missing from these movies. There was plenty of action, often a large cast, location shooting and special effects. However, there was no sound. There were only the images, but without the sound there was nowhere near as much impact. Silent movies were usually accompanied by a piano player, and in bigger cities with permanent movie theatres, an organ, but these could not replace the impact of hearing actual sounds like gunshots or, especially, dialogue.

Edison was aware of the lack of sound, and being the inventor of the phonograph felt he could do something about it. He did, but only for his kinetograph. He installed a phonograph in the machine, and the viewer could hear it play during the movie through earpieces like a stethoscope.

In movie theatres, there was also an attempt to add sound by playing a phonograph along with the projected film. However, there was a problem with synchronizing the sound with the pictures. A split second off and the sound of the character's voice was a little ahead or a little behind the actor's mouth movements. This could be very distracting and draw attention to the difference and away from the story. A way had to be found to link the sound and picture.

At this point we go back in time again, to the telephone. Remember that the telephone showed that sound could be converted to electrical impulses and back again by increasing or decreasing the power, or amplitude, of the current.

In addition, an electric light can be made brighter or dimmer according to how much electrical current it gets. Around 1853, Danish researchers discovered that the element selenium would create an electrical current in direct proportion to the amount of light hitting it—the brighter the light, the greater the current created; the dimmer the light, the lower the current created.

Now the necessary elements were in place to make sound using light. Sound going into a microphone, say like the mouthpiece of a telephone, during the filming of a scene is converted to electrical impulses. Those impulses power a light that brightens and dims according to the strength of the impulses. The light is photographed on one edge of the film while photographing the scene. When the scene is played back, a light in the projector shines through that strip on the edge of the film onto selenium, which converts the light back into electrical impulses that are sent into a speaker, like the ear piece of a telephone, but of course it is much bigger and uses a sound amplifier like that developed for radio. Voila, a soundtrack is created that is synchronized with the pictures.

Movies are now complete. Technology would improve, with better lens and cameras and film and sound equipment and special effects, but the basics are all in place. Stories of every kind are being told with pictures and sound, crowds are flocking to theatres, movies become a way of life unknown in history. And society changes again.

11

MOVIES AND SOCIETY

So, what did movies do to society? Well, in keeping with our examinations of previous media, we'll start by looking at society before movies.

There was a lot of entertainment, but it was local and parochial. By that I mean people tended to stay home, or at least in the neighborhood. They would stay home and read or talk or play the piano or play games or recordings (remember that radio wasn't broadcasting yet), but mostly they made their own entertainment. If they did go out, it would be to the local restaurant or live theatre or vaudeville house, and they probably didn't do that very often.

But then came movies. First of all, there was the novelty of thing—moving pictures! What a concept! People were fascinated by it, and they flocked to it, even if at first it only consisted of going to a local penny arcade and peering at scenes of normal life through a viewer on top of a box, or going to a storefront and watching images cast on a bed sheet. It was still something people had never seen before.

However, there was a second aspect of movies that separated them from other media and led to a major effect on society. Movies, as they evolved, required a lot more in the way of money and time to make than theatre or vaudeville. Theater and vaudeville mostly required actors or acts—the outlay in terms of money for the producers, especially in terms of salaries and equipment, usually wasn't that much. But movies required not only actors and sets and costumes, but cameras and lights and film and writers and cameramen and electricians and grips and editors and all the other elements of production, all of which had to be paid for before an audience paid a dime. So, even though every town could have a live theatre, there were very few movie production companies that had the money to make movies, which reduced the number of productions made and exhibited. This resulted in everyone in the country seeing the same movies.

One effect of everyone seeing the same things, and thus receiving the same messages, was that society became more homogenous. Local and regional differences lessened as everyplace and everybody were getting the same stories about society, what the rules of society were and the people living in it should be.

But what were those messages? Well, they reflected the beliefs about society, the rules that the makers of the movies held. After all, those were the stories the makers knew and by which they lived their lives, and believed those were the rules everybody lived by, or should live by. However, those makers tended not to be average, small-town types, but rather big city entrepreneurs. How they believed society worked was the basis of the stories they told in their movies, and thus they instilled those beliefs in the minds of their audiences. This could have a major impact on society at large because everyone was seeing the same movies.

Let's take an example from the early days of movies that can illustrate the point. A major movie that played everywhere in the country was D. W. Griffith's 1915 *Birth of a Nation*, an epic about the American Civil War and its aftermath. What's important about the movie is that it reflects Griffith's beliefs about society, especially what happened in the South after the war. Griffith was a believer in the Confederate cause and in segregation. So *Birth of a Nation* reflects post-war Southern beliefs, such as the view that freed slaves would run amok while supported by the black soldiers from the Union army, and that whites had to protect themselves, their society—and their women—by keeping the blacks in control. Thus, the second half of Griffith's movie extols the creation and exploits of the Ku Klux Klan and shows the white population being oppressed by Northerners, carpetbaggers and free blacks. One powerful black man wants to marry a white woman. In the conclusion of the movie, white men have banded together into the Ku Klux Klan and (literally) ride to the rescue, driving the rioting blacks and their supporting black soldiers running in panic from the streets and saving the woman (again literally) from the clutches of the black man who wants to marry her.

The effect of this movie could be enormous. Before it came out, the Civil War and the KKK were only things people heard or read about (except, of course, those unfortunate enough to have actually encountered them). Now the audience could see the KKK and their actions, and, more importantly, have an emotional reaction to the exciting ride and their rescue of white society. The blacks are portrayed as rampaging animals and the KKK as heroes riding to the rescue. That neither of these things were true was irrelevant. The audience could say "I saw it! It must be true!" This is how a movie maker's vision becomes the beliefs of the audience.

There were complaints about some of the messages that movies were putting before their audiences, but any such complaints about what movie makers did ran right up against the First Amendment—the defense was free speech. However, in 1915 the Supreme Court chimed in on this. In the case of *Mutual Film Corporation v. Industrial Commission of Ohio*, they ruled that the state of Ohio was correct in creating a censorship board to review and approve all movies. The Supreme Court declared that movies were a business, not an art form, and thus did not enjoy the protection of the First Amendment. The decision included the sentence, "They could be used for evil," and as we all know, evil is the violation of what society, or at least those people who can say they represent society, says is right. If those people chosen to sit on a censorship board believed that something in a movie violated the rules of what that society is, or is believed to be, then that something could be considered evil and the movie denied the right to be exhibited.

However, filmmakers could and did get around the restrictions imposed by censorship boards with movies such as ***Intolerance*** by portraying evil (and thus attracting audiences that, no matter what they said, wanted to see evil), but ending with evildoers losing to the good. They showed that evil results in downfall, and thus reinforced society's belief that following the rules leads to reward. Another approach that was taken was to claim historical accuracy, like Cecil B. DeMille's "***Ben Hur***," which showed bare-breasted girls parading down the street strewing flower petals before the emperor. DeMille claimed that that was what the Romans did, and thus it was educational, not evil.

■ THE EARLY PERIOD

From 1900 to 1915, a sense pervaded society that the world was an ordered place, and that everyone had rhis place in that order. Nationalism was rising, with each nation thinking it was superior to every other and needing to show that to the rest of the world. A major element of that was colonialism, as European nations competed with each other to establish a sphere of influence in Africa and Asia. Great Britain had an empire "upon which the sun never sets" with colonies all over the world; the Dutch, Spanish, French and Portuguese in essence ruled large parts of Africa and Asia. But there was a latecomer to the land-grab: Germany. To establish what Kaiser Wilhelm and the German people regarded as their rightful place in the community of nations, they ended up in a war—World War I. This war killed millions of people, especially young men, who marched off for what they had been taught and therefore society believed was the honor and glory of war. They soon learned there was little honor and even less glory, but a lot of blood and pain.

The 1920s

After the war ended in 1919, society underwent a major change, and that change was reflected in the movies. The 1920s was a period of cynicism as people, especially young people—the ones who had gone through the war on the front lines—began to question the way the world was being run. They looked at the traditions and rules of their society and began to think that those rules, created by the same people who started the war and sent them off with dreams of glory instead of the actuality of gore, may be wrong. These young people changed the way they dressed, the way they talked, and the way they acted. Young men started wearing porkpie hats, flared trousers and raccoon skin coats and young women shortened their hair—and their skirts—becoming "flappers." Catch phrases like "oh you kid" and "23 skidoo" and "the cat's pajamas" started springing up, separating the young from the old in their speech; and the youth started dating, and "necking" and drinking and dancing in wild gyrations. All of these changes among the young scandalized and shocked the previous generation that had grown up under Victorian attitudes about modesty and chastity and respectability in dress and behavior, especially when it came to women's behavior and men's behavior toward women. The young took these conventional attitudes about what were and were not the correct ways to be in society and stood them on their heads in a deliberate attempt to throw off what they saw as the chains of outmoded convention.

The movies changed the kinds of social messages they carried right along with the young. One thing the movies did was load up on those things that drew audiences into the theatres—sex and violence. Movies like 1922's ***Manslaughter*** put in orgy scenes, the sort of thing that jaded young people wanted, to break away from the strict Victorian Puritanism of the past.

Other movies reflected the changes in political philosophy in the world. Marxism, based on the socio-political work of Karl Marx, arose in Russia during World War I, as the old tsarist regime collapsed under the weight of aristocratic incompetence and contempt for ordinary people. Marxism caught the imagination of people, not only in Russia but around the world, who saw the rich and powerful and ruthless throwing away the lives of those ordinary people in war just to further their own wealth and ambitions.

Eisenstein's 1925 ***The Battleship Potemkin*** portrayed this revolution (literally) in socio-political thought as the Russian Fleet mutinies against the oppressive upper-class officers and the ordinary sailors take over the fleet. In the most famous scene from the movie, called "the Odessa Steps," the citizens of the Black Sea city of Odessa, who support the sailors in their mutiny, receive the response from the rich and powerful. The citizens gather on the steps to wave and cheer at the sailors. Suddenly, they come under attack from lines of the Tsar's soldiers, who advance down the steps firing on the crowd, deliberately targeting men, women and children and sending them fleeing in panic. Just as the slaughter reaches its highest point, the battleship *Potemkin* opens fire on the headquarters of the Tsar's military, blowing it up and avenging the fallen people. The effects of this movie, and especially scenes like this, on audiences all over the world were quite strong. People who already didn't trust the people in power were left with an emotional sense that although such leaders would destroy ordinary people for their own gain, it was possible to fight back and gain control of their lives and the society in which they lived.

Fritz Lang's ***Metropolis*** (1927) echoed this theme as an allegory of the ruling class crushing the working class for its own gain. Here again, the rich are crushing ordinary people, but if only the rich would find out how the workers were suffering, like the hero in the white clothes, then the world would be a better place. This is illustrated in the film when the son of the richest man in the world descends to the world of the working class, a hell of smoke and steam and endless hard labor, and he sees how the policies and disdain of his own class oppress and even kill people his class knows nothing about. In the end, the working class rises up with the help of the son and turns the world into a workers' paradise, with no classes and everyone equal—the idealistic goal of Karl Marx.

Of course, in the 1920s sound was introduced to the movies. ***The Jazz Singer*** (1927) was the story of a young man who wanted to sing jazz against his father's wishes. The father wished him to be a cantor in their Jewish temple. This again illustrated the 1920s' theme of rebelling against the stifling rules of the past.

The 1930s

The 1930s came in with a stock market crash and an economic depression, leaving many people feeling helpless and hopeless. Misery often leads to a desire to escape from it for a while into a fantasy world where happiness is not only possible, but probably assured. The movies accommodated this desire.

People would often go to the movies once a week, and the theatres would cater to them. The movie house became a community center that provided an interlude to the routine of life. People would make an evening of it, not just going to see a movie, but to be part of a community. There would be door prizes, sing alongs, and community announce-ments. This would be followed by a cartoon, a newsreel providing the news of the day, a short subject film such as a travelogue or stories from history or a documentary, and then the movie, and sometimes two.

The theatres themselves became palaces of entertainment, filled with pomp and vel-vet and gold leaf. Patrons would enter the theatre up a grand staircase that would set the right mood of suspending their normal life for a few hours, and they would enter a world of dreams.

Many of the movies were upbeat and optimistic, filled with music and dance and good things happening to good people. *Mr. Deeds Goes to Town* is the story of a sim-ple man who inherits a fortune and uses the money to help people down on their luck. Naturally, the evil types take him to court to prove he's crazy, but in the end he defeats them and stands up for the common man. *The Wizard of Oz* taught us that "there's no place like home."

Of course, not everything was sweetness and light. From *Frankenstein* in 1931, we learned that tampering with the natural order could lead to disaster. *King Kong* (1933) echoed that, and in 1931, *Dracula* provided thrills and chills.

Romance wasn't neglected. Just consider 1939's *Gone with the Wind*.

However, as a backlash against the openness of the Roaring 20s, which many people blamed for the Depression, there was a call for censorship to rein in what numerous people believed was evil in movies as they violated the social stories these people believed should be the ones told to maintain society as they wished it to be. Of course, it may have been that what many people believed was evil was less the movies than the movie business, such as actors, and Jews (who "everybody knew" ran Hollywood), and other bad influences that have never gotten respect. Nonetheless, they felt they had some grounds for their com-plaints, such as the costumes that appeared in movies in the early '30s. In *Tarzan and his Mate* (1932), neither Tarzan nor Jane wore much more than a scrap of loincloth. In one scene, Tarzan throws Jane in the river to go swimming, and Jane's dress rips off, leaving her to swim naked, as everyone in the audience could see.

In order to combat what many people saw as licentiousness and immorality in the movies, The Hays Code, named after Will Hays, the head of the Motion Pictures Producers and Distributors Association, was first adopted in 1930 from a document created by Father Daniel Lord, a Jesuit priest. However, the code had no enforcement power.

The Hays Office had three general principles:

1. No picture shall be produced that will lower the moral standards of those who see it. Hence the sympathy of the audience should never be thrown to the side of crime, wrongdoing, evil or sin.
2. Correct standards of life, subject only to the requirements of drama and entertainment, shall be presented.
3. Law, natural or human, shall not be ridiculed, nor shall sympathy be created for its violation.

This was followed with specific restrictions that movies had to follow:

1. Nakedness and suggestive dances were prohibited.
2. The ridicule of religion was forbidden, and ministers of religion were not to be repre-sented as comic characters or villains.

3. The depiction of illegal drug use was forbidden, as well as the use of liquor, "when not required by the plot or for proper characterization."

4. Methods of crime (e.g., safe-cracking, arson, smuggling) were not to be explicitly presented.

5. References to alleged sex perversion (such as homosexuality) and venereal disease were forbidden, as were depictions of childbirth.

6. The language section banned various words and phrases that were considered offensive.

7. Murder scenes had to be filmed in a way that would discourage imitations in real life, and brutal killings could not be shown in detail. "Revenge in modern times" was not to be justified.

8. The sanctity of marriage and the home had to be upheld. "Pictures shall not imply that low forms of sex relationship are the accepted or common thing." Adultery and illicit sex, although recognized as sometimes necessary to the plot, could not be explicit or justified and were not supposed to be presented as an attractive option.

9. Portrayals of miscegenation (that is, marrying outside your own race) were forbidden.

10. "Scenes of Passion" were not to be introduced when not essential to the plot. "Excessive and lustful kissing" was to be avoided, along with any other treatment that might "stimulate the lower and baser element." This was an interesting one. Kisses couldn't last longer than 35 seconds, even married couples were expected to have separate beds, if not separate bedrooms, and if a man and a woman were reclining during the kiss, the man had to keep one foot on the floor at all times. This resulted in some of the most interesting pretzel shapes you've ever seen.

11. The flag of the United States was to be treated respectfully, and the people and history of other nations were to be presented "fairly." The flag always got respect, but other nations? That idea got pretty well stretched completely out of recognition in the years before and during World War II.

12. The treatment of "Vulgarity," defined as "low, disgusting, unpleasant, though not necessarily evil, subjects" must be "subject to the dictates of good taste." Capital punishment, "third degree methods, cruelty to children and animals, prostitution and surgical operations" were to be handled with similar sensitivity. Good taste, of course, is subjective, but the rules were followed. For example, a prostitute usually had to die by the end of the movie, usually after performing a redeeming act, like saving the life of the hero. That happened in "***Destry Rides Again***," a Western starring Jimmy Stewart as Destry and Marlena Dietrich as the prostitute. In the climax, she leaps in front of a bullet meant for Destry, saving his life and dying in his place, thereby atoning for her sinful life.

So changes appeared in movies. Recall Jane's costume in 1932. Now, after the Hays Office got involved, her costume changed from near nudity to a modified Mother Hubbard, a modest, distinct difference.

Another aspect that came into play that shows how society felt wasn't as overt as how characters dressed. For example, ***Reefer Madness*** (1938) was produced to combat the evils of drug use. In it, a young man descends into madness and murder as he becomes addicted to marijuana and turns into a paranoid maniac. Interesting how evil "the weed" is, isn't it? Too bad this depiction is completely inaccurate. If anything, marijuana reduces the odds of getting angry, and reduces even more the odds of turning manic and getting violent. That's why modern anti-pot ads show stoners essentially vegetables on their couches and vowing to do something—tomorrow.

So why is **Reefer Madness** so incorrect in its portrayal of the effects of marijuana? Why does it say that pot is worse than opium or heroin? Why was it made a Class 1 narcotic? Especially when for centuries the marijuana plant was so useful and grown by everyone, including George Washington and Thomas Jefferson? Hemp was often grown as a cheap substitute for linen rags to be made into paper.

There's a clue. A major force to ban marijuana was the forestry companies, which sold the wood to paper companies. They didn't want hemp available since it would cut into their profits. Drug companies were also against marijuana since their profits would drop if everyone could grow their own sedatives and pain relievers instead of buy pills.

But probably the most insidious reason was the perception of who used marijuana. It was the drug of choice of jazz musicians—and they were black. To many people, that evil Negro music jazz was corrupting the youth of America: It made them think—and act— black. That was the evil, not the effects of marijuana. It was just plain racism.

The 1940s

As World War II gripped the world, the 1940s started as a period of propaganda in the movies. Under propaganda minister Joseph Goebbels, the German National Socialists Party, the Nazis, became masters of using movies to promote their ideology. Leni Riefenstahl's monumental (in every sense of the term) **Triumph of the Will** extolled Nazism as the ultimate expression of civilization, with vast crowds and massed soldiers under flying banners and flags saluting Adolf Hitler, their Fuehrer or leader, as epic music stirred the souls of the audience. In **Der Ewige Jude** (*The Eternal Jew*) Goebbels justified the deportation and murder of Jews everywhere in the world by comparing them to diseased rats. As scenes of hordes of scurrying rats juxtaposed with shots of Jewish men and women, the narrator tells the audience what they should believe about what they're seeing: "Wherever rats appear they bring ruin, by destroying mankind's goods and foodstuffs. . . . They are cunning, cowardly, and cruel, and are found mostly in large packs. Among the animals, they represent the rudiment of an insidious and underground destruction—just like the Jews among human beings." That last little distinction is quite interesting. It fits right in with Goebbels' concept of "the big lie"—tell a lie often enough, and loudly enough, and no matter how big the lie, people will believe it.

Of course, the Nazis weren't the only ones churning out pro-war propaganda. After the Japanese attack at Pearl Harbor, Hollywood immediately went to work, with actors, directors, cameramen, and entire studios joining the fight. Warner Brothers, MGM and Disney Studios made cartoons to show before movies with Bugs Bunny, Daffy Duck, Donald Duck, and even Tweety Bird fighting the Germans and Japanese, and hitting Hitler, Mussolini and Tojo on the head with sledge hammers. They tossed in war bond pitches for good measure, with Bugs Bunny singing, "Buy a bond today."

Among the actors doing short subjects for recruiting and propaganda were Jimmy Stewart, Clark Gable, Ronald Reagan, Robert Montgomery, and Robert Taylor. Directors included some of the top in Hollywood, including John Huston, William Wyler, John Sturges, and Frank Capra. Capra himself headed the United States Service Film Units, consisting of movie professionals such as camera and sound men gathered into military companies who made documentaries about the war. These short subjects shown before movies informed the audience about what was happening in the war, but they were done in such a way that they touted the skill and bravery of American soldiers as they faced an implacable, but beatable, foe. Capra also made the multipart propaganda documentary **Why We Fight** that was shown in movie theatres all over the country. It was a patriotic, indeed jingoistic, discourse on what led up to the war, emphasizing the evil motivations of the Axis forces and the need to defeat them.

The cartoons, documentaries and newsreels were followed by jingoistic war movies such as **Wake Island**, **The Fighting Seabees**, **Air Force**, **Go For Broke**, **We Dive at Dawn**, **Destination: Tokyo**, **Thirty Seconds Over Tokyo**, **Bataan**, **Guadalcanal Diary**, and **Gung Ho**. These types of movies, many opening only a few months after the events they portray, all carried the message that there was a big fight, but Americans always pulled through. Many characters died, even the heroes, but they always died heroically, fighting to the last. However the movie played out, they were designed to boost morale on the home front and promote the war effort. For example, in the final scene in **Gung Ho**, starring Randolph Scott, he speaks to his men after a successful attack on a Japanese held island. Toward the end of the scene, he looks directly into the camera and speaks of a great battle between good and bad, right and wrong, but proclaims that in the end right will triumph, which is the ultimate victory of the American way of life. This message was aimed directly at the audience.

Much the same message was sent by movies such as **Casablanca**. In **Casablanca**, the hero, played by Humphrey Bogart, is a civilian who has refused to take sides in the war, believing it's none of his business. However, he finally decides to give up his own life and happiness and the woman he loves to fight the Nazis. The message to the audience is clear: The fight against evil is everyone's business, and everyone should do their part, however small, to defeat it.

Other movies were designed to show the strength and courage of the people the soldiers left behind as they marched to war, the home front. These movies were often tearjerkers with happy or bittersweet endings, like **Three Came Home**, **Mrs. Miniver**, **So Proudly We Hail** and **Since You Went Away**. In the majority of these, the gallant wife or sweetheart stands by, proudly and stoically waiting for her man to come marching home—if he does, and often he doesn't. In the meantime, she willingly puts up with the sacrifices of a country at war because, well, that's what you do. Just like the combat movies, these home front movies were designed to boost morale and promote the war effort. Such movies, propagandistic as they were, changed American society from an isolationist nation that believed "Europe's problems are Europe's problems" and "what should we care what they do over there in Asia" to one of almost wholehearted support for war with the Axis.

Of course, not everything was aimed at propaganda. People needed a break from pain and sacrifice, and the movies provided just that kind of lightweight fare to lift moods and provide distraction. Movies like **The Miracle of Morgan Creek**, **The Maltese Falcon**, **Arsenic and Old Lace** and **Meet John Doe** provided laughs, thrills, and warm sentimentality.

Once the war was over, people wanted to forget the pain and sacrifice and start to feel good again. Movies like **It's a Wonderful Life** (that is in most movie critics' top ten movies of all time) brought a feeling of warmth to everyone, and many a burly he-man teared up at the end. However, other movies looked at one the biggest problems facing society at the end of the war—the returning soldiers and sailors and how to fit them back into society. For example, **The Best Years of Our Lives** looked at how hard it was for returning soldiers and sailors to pick up their lives after going through the war. One of the characters is a sailor who lost both arms in battle, and audiences could see and feel his struggles to fit into normal life again, dealing both with having hooks instead of hands and with people's reactions to his lost arms. The actor who played that sailor, Harold Russell, had actually been a soldier who lost both his arms during the war. He won an Oscar for his performance.

There was also a growing fear in America—the fear of communism taking over the world. At the end of the war, the USSR, an ally during the war, became an enemy, as it declared its intent to defeat democracy and remake the world in its own image. Movies reflected and even intensified that fear by telling stories about what was happening in Europe just after the war, movies such as **Air Lift**. The Soviets closed all land entry to Berlin in an attempt to drive the European forces out by starving the inhabitants. In response, the Americans started the Berlin Airlift, which flew in supplies for the people of Berlin. The movie dramatized the event and showed the inhumanity of the communists, and the humanity of the Americans, reinforcing the belief in the audience of the danger of communism.

Still, people wanted to get back to normal. Movies like **Treasure of the Sierra Madre, Kind Hearts and Coronets, White Heat, Great Expectations** and **Miracle on 34th Street** gave people a sense that, if the movies are back to normal, telling stories in much the same way as they did before the war, so is American life.

Of course, things were not back to normal—or a least they were not back to pre-war. Just like what happened after from World War I, World War II threw society into a turmoil. However, this time the turmoil was beneath the surface, where many people hoped it would stay.

The 1950s

The 1950s were a period when people wanted peace, quiet and stability to counter the tumult and chaos of the '40s; they wanted a period of conformity. Most of society believed in the "Leave It to Beaver", white picket fence, suburban lawn way of life, with everyone content, and no one rocking the boat.

Too bad that's not the way things were. Just like after World War I, people's sense that the world was reasonable, understandable and controllable was completely overthrown, especially for the young and the men who came back from the war.

Veterans had a hard time fitting back in because they didn't feel they did—fit in, that is, with the pre-war attitudes. Many were depressed, others were angry, all thought there had to be more. Many of them took advantage of the GI Bill, went to college, got a job—and a white picket fence and suburban lawn.

But quite a few didn't. They started rebelling against the society they felt had ruined their lives by starting a war and sending them to fight it. This rebellion was reflected in the movies. For example, **The Wild One** was the story of a veteran who became the leader of a motorcycle gang that rides into a small town and terrorizes it until he's brought down. It ends with a restoration of the status quo when this gang leader gets taken down and beaten by the "normal" townsfolk, a desirable outcome for the average audience member as order is restored. But the fact that the main character, the hero of the story, is a rebel against that very status quo shows that everything is not quite as idyllic as believed. So what is he rebelling against? As he says in one scene, "Wha' d'ya got?" This one line sums up the confusion and discontent felt by many as society just didn't seem to fulfill them they way they believed it should.

Another film took this rebellion against conformity into the home. ***Rebel Without a Cause*** had teenagers feeling stifled by what they saw as the demand to conform to rules that they considered outmoded, old-fashioned and designed for their parents, not for themselves. They weren't sure what those rules were, or what to replace them with, but they could see that their parents weren't happy and the kids wanted to avoid that fate. That the rebellion ultimately failed may have mollified the "conformity first" audience, but it was a release for those who wanted more out of life.

This was really driven home by ***The Blackboard Jungle***. Many in society wanted to believe in "Leave it to Beaver's" Wally and Beav and their friends as the models of school kids. Even the budding juvenile delinquents like Eddie Haskell came across as only slightly bad and merely mischievous, sort of like Dennis the Menace. To see that that image wasn't necessarily true in ***The Blackboard Jungle***, that school kids could be vicious, disrespectful of authority, form gangs, be uninterested in education, almost animals in their behavior and thought, came as a shock to many. A very telling scene is the movie shows a gang of teenage boys standing against and peering through the bars of the wrought iron school fence, hooting at an attractive woman walking down the sidewalk. The scene makes it appear that they're in metaphorical cages and implies that's where they belong. This view violated the fantasy that most people had about American life. Some people even thought the movie was a communist plot to make American schools, and by extension American life, look bad. But in the end, it did deliver the message: Don't kill the kids, and don't coddle them—give them a direction and some guidance and they'll make it.

It should be noted that ***The Blackboard Jungle*** had one of the first serious black lead characters in a mainstream movie. Sidney Poitier's character is important to the plot as he is the catalyst to solving the problem: He's a leader of a gang who decides to take a chance on the teacher and follow him. For the 1950s, having a serious black character, one that isn't a maid or butler or waiter or other minor and often comic character, wasn't a cultural shift, it was an earthquake. Of course, life didn't reflect the movie: Poitier was one of the stars of the movie, but he wasn't allowed to stay in the same hotel as the rest of the cast—after all, he was black.

For many people, relying on cultural and social stereotypes to make decisions was the most comfortable way to go—conform, don't rock the boat, don't question. This idea was effectively attacked in ***12 Angry Men*** in 1957. Set entirely in a jury room, twelve men must arrive at a verdict in a murder trial. All but one immediately vote guilty—and that one wants to talk about it, refusing to condemn the defendant, a teenage Hispanic boy, to a sentence of death without at least thinking about it first. As the movie progresses, each man's biases and prejudices are revealed, from racism to disinterest to blindly following the majority because of an unwillingness to rock the boat, which led them to vote guilty, until they finally realize how they let those prejudices influence them. In the end, all vote not guilty, following the actual evidence instead of their unthinking stereotypes and biases. It is hard to miss the message of this movie.

Perhaps one of the most powerful, yet subtle, attacks on the status quo was ***Giant***, the story of a Texas ranch over a generation. It does nothing less than expose America's patriarchal society as a woman rebels against being "the little woman" with no ideas of her own on politics, child rearing, the position of the wife in a marriage and a woman in society. When, after a dinner party, she wishes to join the men in conversation, the men sit in uneasy silence until her husband tells her that "this is man's stuff." Affronted by the implication that she's too stupid to join the conversation because she's "just a woman," she condescendingly says to the other women, "Set up my spinning wheel, girls. I'll join the harem section in a minute." This movie clearly said to the audience, which thought the society of the 1930s was back after World War II, that American society and women's place in it had moved on, and they had better move on with it.

Of course, World War II had overturned just about everything—women's place in society, stifling conformity, and especially a sense of safety. The Cold War with the Soviet Union made it clear to everyone that the world could indeed come to an end, and movies reflected that fear. ***The Day the Earth Stood Still*** reflected people's fear of annihilation if a way couldn't be found to solve the problems between countries. The movie says aliens will destroy the world, but the implication is clear that we could easily handle the job ourselves.

The fear of nuclear weapons became a common theme in movies, often implying that things would change through mutation if the weapons were ever used. A prime example of that is the movie ***Them*** from 1954, in which ants are irradiated by A-bomb tests and grow to giant size. As usual, there's a moral at the end as the mutant ants get killed at the last moment. The scientist who led the fight to destroy them says, "When man entered the atomic age, he opened a new world. What we will find in that new world, no one can predict." This told the audience that no one knows what nuclear weapons will do to the world, again implying that the old certainties that society had depended on are gone.

But there wasn't only fear of nuclear tests—there was fear of the nuclear powers. At the end of World War II, the antagonism between the US and the Soviet Union came to a head as democracy and communism battled for control of the world. This antagonism and distrust resulted in what was called the "Red Scare," and it began to show up in movies in allegorical form. For example, the movie ***The Thing from Another Planet*** was, on the surface, about a potential attack from outer space when a flying saucer is discovered in the frozen wastes of the north and the alien pilot attacks a small band of scientists and military men. However, it is actually about a potential attack from the Reds, again with a moral at the end as a reporter who happens to be at the outpost files a news story about the fight and the victory over the alien. The most important part of that story appears to be his warning to "Keep watching the skies." On the surface, this is a warning to watch out for flying saucers, but actually his statement "Keep watching the skies" is a reference to watching for Soviet bombers and missiles, not UFOs.

Another major change in movies and society took place in 1952. In the 1915 Supreme Court case ***Mutual Film vs. Ohio***, the court ruled that movies were a business, not an art form, and they could be used for evil by corrupting their audiences; therefore, they didn't enjoy First Amendment protection. This ruling laid the groundwork for localities to set up censorship boards all over the country that could prevent the showing of any movie the local board deemed immoral by whatever standards they wished to apply and to deny it a license for exhibition.

However, in 1952 a New York board of censors denied a license to the movie ***The Miracle***, calling it sacrilegious. The movie's exhibitor, Joseph Burstyn, sued the board, and the Supreme Court overturned its 1915 decision. In ***Joseph Burstyn, Inc. v. Wilson***, the Court ruled that movies, even if they are a business, were also an art form and a form of expression, and therefore as a form of expression they enjoy First Amendment protection. The result of this ruling was to deny a legal basis for all those censorship boards and for the rules of the Hays Office. At bottom, they were based on a belief that society, as they believed it should be, needed protection from those who might think otherwise, and those others should not be allowed to have their views heard. This was clearly a violation of the First Amendment.

Further attempts to censor movies arose, such as in the case of *Jacobellis v. Ohio* in 1964. Ohio tried to ban the film *The Lovers* for obscenity, but the court ruled that it wasn't obscene. The court couldn't define how they determined that though, other than that the movie wasn't "hard core pornography," and only that would be obscene. As Justice Potter Stewart so famously said about pornography, "I can't define it, but I know it when I see it." Such a rule is clearly too vague to be of any judicial use because it is based on personal opinion, yet it is still the only guide to whether something is obscene or not.

With such Supreme Court rulings on their side, movies were now allowed to be more open, to cover more controversial topics and portray most, if not all, of the things the Hays Office had banned for the last twenty years, and Tarzan and Jane could take off their clothes again. Indeed, in *Tarzan the Ape Man* in 1981, Bo Derek starred as a topless Jane.

The 1960s

In the 1960s, movies took advantage of the new freedom from censorship and the worry that they might offend someone. For example, in 1962 a movie took on racial bigotry in a big way. *To Kill a Mockingbird*, set in the 1930s, showed the effects of bigotry as a black man, Tom, was accused of assaulting a white woman. Although the trial clearly showed he not only didn't do it but that he couldn't have done it, and that the woman was covering up the fact that she kissed a black man and was beaten by her bigot father for doing so, Tom was convicted because of the bigotry of the jury and most of the town. Tom's lawyer, Atticus Finch played by Gregory Peck, was not only threatened, his children were almost killed because he stood up for that black man, defying the social rules in force in his community. *To Kill a Mockingbird* was a powerful condemnation of prejudice and of the people who hold such views. This was quite a statement in the early '60s, when such views still held sway in many parts of America, and especially in the Deep South.

In the Heat of the Night (1967) continued this look at racial bigotry, as a black Philadelphia cop, Vergil Tibbs, gets arrested for murder in a small southern town. A rich white man was considering opening a factory in the town, something the town wanted, but then he was murdered. While waiting for a train in the middle of the night, a deputy arrests Tibbs on suspicion of being black, with the assumption that he was probably the murderer. When the local police chief interrogates Tibbs, he finds out that Tibbs is a homicide detective from Philadelphia, Pennsylvania. Knowing that Tibbs won't be able to catch a train home for a while, the chief solicits his help in solving the murder. Tibbs suspects a rich white bigot, and when he tells the chief he's going to nail the man, the chief brings Tibbs up short by accusing Tibbs of being just as prejudiced as everybody else. Removing his own blinders, Tibbs opens up his investigation and ends up solving the murder, despite the overt racism of everyone he meets. Although Tibbs pushes the police chief's buttons, by the end of the movie, not only has Tibbs solved the crime, he's earned the respect of the chief and his cops through his sheer competence and unwillingness to bow to racism. Like *To Kill a Mockingbird*, the movie In the *Heat of the Night* is a powerful condemnation of bigotry and demonstrates that it has no place in modern society.

Another movie that looked at the mores of the time was *Dr. Strangelove: or How I Learned to Stop Worrying and Love the Bomb*, which appeared in 1964 just after the

Cuban Missile Crisis that brought the world to the edge of nuclear war. This satire was hilarious and frightening at the same time, as it showed how easy it would be to allow politics, fear, and warmongering to lead to the destruction of the world. When a communications glitch causes the United States to launch a nuclear attack on the Soviet Union and one of the bombers gets through to drop its bomb, the end of the world is imminently possible. The military fears a weapons gap—that the other side may have more weapons—and want to finish the job. The final scene is particularly ironic as the President's council turns its attention to surviving the war in deep mine shafts and realizes they must avoid a mine shaft gap to preserve the American way of life. As the scene cuts to a series of mushroom clouds, a song plays:

> "We'll meet again, don't know where, don't know when . . .
> Keep smiling through, . . .
> 'Til the blue skies drive the dark clouds far away."

This satirical counterpoint drives home the point that governments must get serious about nuclear disarmament or the world is doomed, and it won't be pretty.

Other social mores were also held up to scrutiny. For example, in 1967 ***The Graduate*** examined suburban life and how adrift in life young people were. They lacked interest in the strictures of the '50s, but they didn't know what they wanted in their place—although sex looked like a good plan. And speaking of sex, which people didn't in the 1950s, ***Bob and Carol and Ted and Alice*** looked at sex as a game, violating all the social mores that had ruled for decades.

A major element of American society in the 1960s was the Vietnam War, which at the end of the '60s was on the minds of everybody, especially the young who were the ones who were going to have to go fight it. This was the beginning of the "Generation Gap," which was the complete misunderstanding between parents who had grown up during the Great Depression and World War II, and who carried the social rules of that society into the age of conformity of the 1950s, and their children, who felt stifled and even crushed by the social traditions and mores their parents insisted upon. That those children should have to go fight a war they didn't believe in, for *reasons* they didn't believe in, drove a wedge between the generations that has lasted for decades.

Movies reflected this break in the worldviews of the different generations. In the 1950s, ***Rebel Without a Cause*** showed young people as adrift and unsure. In the 1960s, young people were still adrift, but they were sure that whatever their parents wanted was not what they wanted. In 1969, ***Easy Rider*** showed this rebellion against the Establishment, the name the younger generation called the people and institutions that perpetuated the social story they were rebelling against, and the potential effects of that rebellion. In the final scene, Wyatt and Billy, the long-haired counterculture heroes of the movie, are riding their motorcycles down a rural highway when they are passed by a pickup truck holding two short-haired men. The characters represent the divide in culture during the 1960s: the long-haired hippie rebelling against the old social story and the short-haired redneck determined to maintain the old story. The rednecks decide to scare the hippies. As the driver turns the truck around, the passenger takes a shotgun out of the rack in the back window. As the truck passes Billy, the passenger fires at him and blows Billy off the road. Wyatt, noticing that Billy is gone, goes back to him, and the rednecks kill Wyatt as well. This scene clearly illustrates the conflict between one worldview and the other, between the rednecks and the longhaired hippy pinko freaks. Society in the 1960s was fragmenting into groups with opposing views of what that society should be.

The 1970s

The 1970s brought an examination of the myths that hold a society together, and it explored which myths should be held dear and which should go. One myth was the trustworthiness of the government to always work in the public good. The Watergate scandal that brought down President Nixon shook that confidence. The Democratic National Committee had offices in the Watergate building. Burglars broke in searching for anything that could be used to discredit the Democrats and help re-elect the Republican President Nixon. Nobody investigating this crime knew why the DNC offices would be burglarized. The film, *All the President's Men* (1976), based on the book of the same name, traced the investigation by *Washington Post* reporters Bob Woodward and Carl Bernstein. Woodward and Bernstein discovered that the burglars were in the employ of people close to the White House, and as they continued to investigate, they found that the crime could be traced to the highest levels in the Nixon presidency, including Nixon himself. In the end, several people went to jail and Nixon himself resigned from the presidency. This political scandal, going to the very top of the American government, left people with a sense that politicians did whatever they had to in order to hold onto power, and that they were more concerned with that power than with the people they purported to represent. The previous trust that people had in the government and their belief that politicians only worked in the public interest have never returned.

Other myths that were explored included crime with *The Godfather* and teenage angst and a desire for stability with *American Graffiti*. *Jaws* in 1971 showed that there are powerful forces out there that are out to get you, and you must battle with them. *Jaws* was the first of the summer blockbuster movies. Before *Jaws*, studios tended not to release big movies in the summer because they believed it would be the slow season because audiences had far more to do than go to movies. *Jaws* demonstrated that there were big audiences for big, exciting movies, the so-called blockbusters, and it set a trend to have blockbusters come out every summer.

Of course, there are the battles between good and evil that must be fought, and these appeared in one of the biggest blockbusters of all time, 1977's *Star Wars*. This movie almost didn't make it to the screen as the studio had no confidence in it and wanted to cancel production. As is often the case, the bean counters got it wrong. *Star Wars* still ranks as the fourth highest grossing movie of all time, and its five sequels and prequels are in the top forty-five (*Movie Times*).

All of the above movies of the 1970s helped to bind back together a society shattered by the racial and social turmoil of the 1960s, for they provided common myths that all people could embrace.

The 1980s

One problem for the movie studios, or at least for the studio accountants, arose in the 1980s—messages were bad for sales. As movie studios merged and were bought by non-movie industry companies more concerned with profits than with art, the movies slacked off on trying to examine society and moved toward putting bodies in seats, especially the bodies of teenagers with time on their hands, disposable income, and a desire to get out of the house and go on dates. There were movies about teenagers, like *16 Candles* and *The Breakfast Club* and *The Boyfriend School* and *Pretty in Pink* and *Valley Girl*. There were scary movies with teenagers in peril like *Nightmare on Elm Street* and *Terror Train* and *Prom Night*. There were action movies, like *Die Hard* and *Alien* and *Raiders of the Lost Ark* and *The Adventures of Buckaroo Banzai*. They pretty much reflected the social beliefs of their audiences, but not of the society at large.

There were still a few movies aimed at adults. For example, the Vietnam War for the first time became a possible subject. Unlike during World War II, virtually no movies other than 1968's jingoistic *The Green Berets* promoted the war—most, like *The Deer Hunter* in 1978, were anti-war. In the 1980s, movies examining the war came out, mostly showing that it was a bad idea and really messed up the people fighting it. These included *Platoon*, *Full Metal Jacket*, *Casualties of War* and *Good Morning, Vietnam*.

Splashy technical effects really took off, too, now that the production of *Star Wars*, especially *The Empire Strikes Back* in the 1980's, showed how to do it, with its computer controlled cameras and extremely detailed models. Computers began to be a major element in moviemaking, and *Young Sherlock Holmes* took computer generated images to a whole new level in 1985, creating such scenes as a knight made of a stained glass window leaping from the window frame and stalking a priest. It was the first movie to have purely CGI (computer graphic) elements, and *Star Trek: The Motion Picture* alone turned out three sequels. Still, most of these movies were simple treats for the eyes rather than deep explorations of society.

The 1990s

The 1990s were a period of establishing new myths or reinforcing some of the old ones while knocking down others. Certainly *Schindler's List* and *Saving Private Ryan* reinforced our old myths about World War II, the enemies we fought and the heroism of the people who fought them. They harkened back to the 1940s without the extreme jingoism. *Apollo 13* did the same for the space program.

Other movies established new myths. *Dances with Wolves* broke with the image of Native Americans as rampaging savages attacking white settlers and preventing the spread of civilization that had, in the main, been the ruling paradigm in movies. *Wolves*, on the other hand, portrayed Indians as victims of, rather than as impediments to, white western expansion, and the heroes of decades past, the US cavalry, as the rampaging savages. *JFK* touted a conspiracy to assassinate President Kennedy, instead of it being the act of one man. It often made up characters and conversations. It did this so persuasively that the myth has pretty much replaced the actual evidence for many people.

One thing that really became important to the movie industry in the 1990s was the blockbuster, which was no longer relegated to the summer slow season. Again, money rather than art was the driving force, and the more tickets that could be sold the more money that could be made. Some the biggest of these blockbusters were *Braveheart*, *Armageddon* and *Jurassic Park*, but they pale in comparison to *Titanic* in 1997, which is still listed as the second biggest grossing movie in history, just behind 2009's *Avatar*.

Another change to the movies was the re-emergence of animation as a major form of film, which started in 1937 with Disney's *Snow White and the Seven Dwarfs*. A driving force was the savings that could be realized using computers to do the backgrounds and much of the animation, rather than having every frame hand drawn. Disney Studios restarted their dominance in animation with such movies as *The Little Mermaid*, *Aladdin*, *The Lion King*, and the Oscar-nominated *Beauty and the Beast*. These movies retold the stories, the fairy tales, of our youth, the ones that tell us so much about who we are and who we should be. Of course, a lot of these retellings bore only a passing resemblance to the original stories: Pocahontas was thirteen years old, not an eighteen-year-old Barbie clone; the Hunchback of Notre Dame was ugly and grotesque, not kind of cute with a great singing voice, and the little mermaid did **not** get her prince—he dumped her for someone else, and she ended up dying on a rock, with legs that didn't work and unable to return to being a mermaid. But the movies reflect the stories told for the society of today, not the society for which the stories were originally intended.

The 2000s

And now we come to today. Today, movies are still delivering a mythology, but it's not one based on our own experience and at least rooted in, if not an actual reflection of, reality as was common in the past. Instead, it's a mythology based on fantasies that were never part of our reality. Incidentally, these movies delivered big at the box office.

The Lord of the Rings trilogy is based on the fantasy books by JRR Tolkien. The *Harry Potter* series is based on the fantasy books of JK Rowling. The *Batman* series and the *Spiderman* series are based on the comic books. The *Transformers* movies are based on toys. Then, of course, there's the *Pirates of the Caribbean*, a trilogy based on the amusement park ride, and the *Matrix* movies, based on, as far as I can tell, someone's paranoid drug haze. Movies like these have no real connection with our lives, and yet they have become a part of our mythology, of who we are, who we should be, and how our society works. They have something else in common—they all come in series. If you make money with one, make two or three—or more.

In the world today, the movie industry has, in the main, gone back to its beginnings and Edison's kinescope, which is less about the art or the message and more about the money. And yet they still enchant, enthrall and provide us with many of the rules by which we live and how we define our lives.

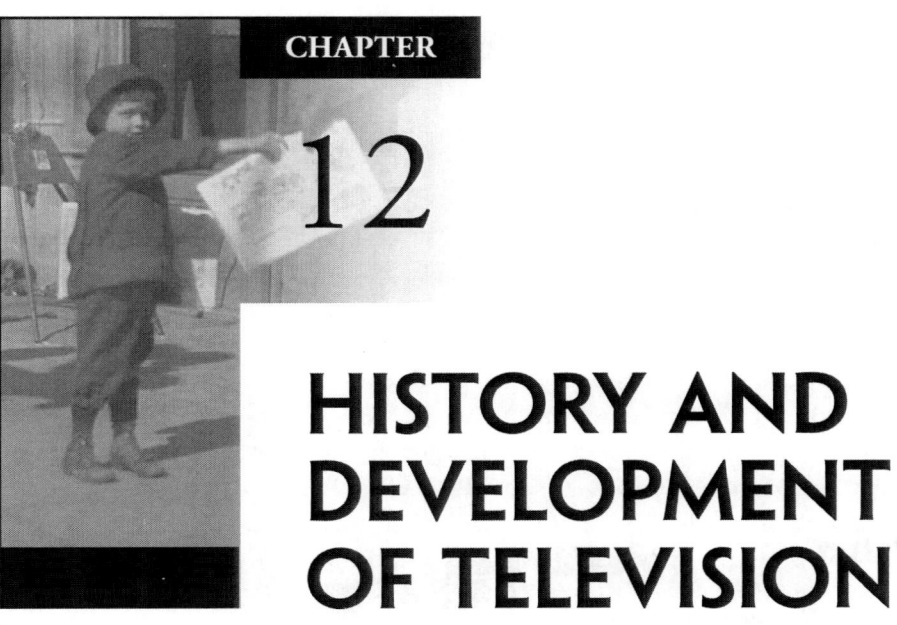

HISTORY AND DEVELOPMENT OF TELEVISION

*A*t the 1939 New York World's Fair the world changed. Television was first introduced to the world at large there, and the media have never been the same since.

So let's start at the beginning, once again with a heavy dose of science.

■ EARLY HISTORY

Television wasn't invented by one man. Or even two, despite what anybody may tell you. It was invented by a long string of people building on the work of the people before them.

We'll start with Julius Plucker. Who's Julius Plucker, you ask? He found a way to make electrons go where he wanted. In 1858, he made a sealed glass tube with an electrical connection at either end. He then evacuated most of the air from the tube. Sending an electrical current into the tube sent electrons flowing from one connection to the other. The flow of electrons caused a fluorescent glow on the walls of the tube, which he could move around with a magnet.

About 1875, Sir William Crooks invented the Crooks tube, a device that has contributed to everything from X-rays to nuclear power. However, for our purposes it was a major factor in the invention of television. Much like the device that Julius Plucker used, it was a vacuum tube with electrical connections, electrodes, at either end. What Crooks did was add a gate, a piece of metal foil with a slit in it, near one end. As the electrons flowed from one electrode toward the other, the gate forced them into a beam rather than simply allowing them to diffuse throughout the tube. When the electricity was turned on, a beam of electrons went from one electrode to the other.

An interesting thing happened when you brought a magnet near the tube—the beam of electrons bent in the direction of the magnet. The upshot is that an electromagnet could control and direct a beam of electrons, a basic necessity for television as we know it.

In 1897, Karl Braun took the next step. He developed the cathode ray tube. He placed an electron gun in the narrow end of an essentially conical vacuum tube, the diode of an electrical circuit that would shoot a beam of electrons toward the anode plate. Past the anode plate, electromagnets would bend the beam wherever he wanted it to go. The wide end of the tube was a curved glass plate, the screen, coated with fluorescent paint. When the electron beam hit the fluorescent paint, the paint would glow right where the beam hit. Using the electromagnets, you could move the beam around and thus create glowing lines on the screen. Braun won a Nobel Prize in 1909 for this invention.

Now we go back in time, as is often the case when tracing scientific developments. We return to 1873, when those Danish researchers mentioned in the invention of sound for movies accidentally discovered that the electrical resistance of selenium varied in proportion to the intensity of the light shining on it. This was quickly recognized as a way of transforming light variations into electrical signals, and immediately a number of schemes were proposed for sending pictures by wire (remember, this was before radio).

The American scientist G. R. Carey proposed the first idea for television in 1875. His idea was a system for using electricity to send a picture from a camera to a receiver some distance away. Carey's system consisted of a number of light sensitive selenium cells in a mosaic that would capture the image in the same way a camera takes a photograph. Wires connected each cell in the mosaic to a battery and an electric lamp. Light reflected from the object being imaged would fall on the cells; the amount of light reflected would vary according to the shape and surface of the object; The cells reacted to the light and would send an electric current in direct proportion to the amount of light hitting them, which amounted to an electronic version of the picture from the camera, down the wire to the electric lamps. At the other end of the wire there was one electric lamp for each selenium cell. Carey envisaged a receiver consisting of the same number of lamps as there were for the selenium cells. The idea was not practical because producing a clear image required millions of tiny selenium cells and electric lamps, and each had to have its own wire.

Practical television required a single selenium cell connected to one lamp. Carey considered this, and, to get away from needing millions of wires, he proposed scanning the cells—that is, transmitting the signal from each cell individually to its associated light, one after another, over a single wire. At the other end, the lamp associated with each cell would light up. If this happened fast enough, persistence of vision would cause the resultant images to be seen as a complete picture.

The next step was to get rid of the mosaic by scanning the image directly instead of "photographing" it. In 1881, Shelford Bidwell demonstrated one way of doing that. He mounted a single selenium cell in a camera obscura. A motor driven cam moved the box rapidly up and down and across the plane of the image. The process worked, but the scanning speed was extremely limited. Maurice leBlanc suggested that the image could be scanned with an oscillating mirror, which would reflect the light onto a fixed selenium cell and would greatly raise the scanning speed.

Then in 1884, Paul Nipkow invented a mechanical "television," the simplest and most workable of the scanning systems proposed. Nipkow's device consisted of a disk pierced with small holes in a pattern going from the edge to the center in a spiral. This disk could be rapidly spun. To "televise" an object, one illuminated it. The spinning disk allowed bits of light corresponding to the bits of the object through the spiral of holes. That light fell on a selenium cell, generating an electric current in direct proportion to the amount of light falling on the cell. That current could then be sent down a wire that caused a light to vary in intensity as it shone through the matching holes in a second disk onto a screen, recreating the light from the illuminated object. Each spin of the disk equaled one frame.

Although the quality of Nipkow's system was pretty bad (only 18 lines per frame compared to today's 525, or High Definition's 1080), it still proved the principle of scanning as a way to capture, transmit and rebuild images.

And then—pretty much nothing happened. It was almost twenty years before anyone did anything with either Nipkow's mechanical disk TV or Braun's cathode ray tube. The first of the experimenters to start working on a different method of sending pictures other than mechanically was the Russian Boris Rosing, who in 1902 starting playing with Braun's cathode ray tubes for image reproduction. In 1907, he managed to build a system in which a mechanically produced picture was viewed on a cathode-ray tube that deflected the beam in synchronization with the sending signal. This was a good accomplishment, but perhaps Rosing's greatest accomplishment was one of his students, Vladimir Zworykin, of whom we'll hear more later. We probably don't hear more about Rosing because Stalin had him arrested and exiled to Siberia.

Other people were working along the same lines as Rosing. In 1908, Archibald Campbell-Swinton was the first to suggest using a cathode ray tube at both ends of the system—not only the receiving end, but the sending end—going one better than Boris Rosing. And, in 1911, A. Sinding-Larsen suggested using radio, now that it was a viable option, instead of wires as a carrier for the picture signals. So now all the concepts for what we think of as "modern television" were ready to go.

And then World War I happened.

It was ten more years before anyone got back to working on television, and one of the first persons to do so was Charles Francis Jenkins. In 1923, he publicly demonstrated his mechanical television in the US. John Baird did the same in England, and he was the first to televise a face and a moving object. Both of these systems used the Nipkow disk and were crude. The resolution was low due to the mechanical limitations of using a disk to scan and transmit an image.

Nevertheless, the possibilities of transmitting moving pictures by radio waves drew the attention of big corporations like AT&T, General Electric, RCA, Dumont and Philco. Prior to corporate interest, the research into developing television was done by lonely inventers working by themselves or in small laboratories. The corporations, on the other hand, undertook major development programs, building laboratories, hiring researchers, and providing the funds necessary to propel the research. However, all of the systems they developed used mechanical scanning, relying upon the Nipkow disk or something similar. The researchers started with 30-line scans, then they increased the number of lines, but the pictures still had poor resolution. Furthermore, the large disks required, some of them 4 feet in diameter, were obviously not practical for home use. The Nipkow disk TV was approximately 50 inches, but the viewing screen was only 4 inches.

Enter Boris Rosing's student, Vladimir Zworykin. He realized that Archibald Campbell-Swinton's suggestion of using a cathode ray tube for both ends of the system, both sending and receiving picture signals, might be a possibility. Zworykin finally developed a cathode ray tube that could pick up images and convert them to electrical signals, and history tells us that in 1923 he patented his iconoscope, the first camera tube.

In the iconoscope the picture to be transmitted was focused on a mosaic of tiny photosensitive cells mounted in the tube. An electron beam controlled by electromagnets scanned the mosaic line for line. The beam rapidly passed over the mosaic, hitting each cell in turn. When the beam hit the cell, it released a small electric charge in direct proportion to the amount of light falling on it, reflected from the object being photographed. Thus, the basic concept of scanning continued. The greatest difference and leap forward was the speed of the beam and the fact that mechanical considerations such as a moving box or a spinning disk no longer limited the number of lines scanned.

Then, in 1929, Zworykin demonstrated his kinescope—a greatly improved cathode ray television picture tube that would receive the signal from the iconoscope, the electron beam hitting the phosphorescent screen. Now, with an iconoscope at the sending end and a kinescope at the receiving end, an all-electronic system was a practical possibility.

In 1927, another man came up with a similar idea. He was Philo Farnsworth, a farm boy from Idaho who is said to have gotten his idea about scanning by looking at the "scanning" lines created by a plow. He also created cathode ray tube cameras and receivers.

At this point, there is controversy. Who actually invented TV, Zworykin or Farnsworth? Both claim credit for developing the same all-electronic television system. Let's look at the record. Remember, I said, "history tells us that Zworykin patented his iconoscope in 1923." That's not entirely true. Zworykin **applied** for a patent in 1923, but it wasn't granted until 1938. Why this fifteen-year gap? Nobody's entirely sure. However, we are sure that Farnsworth challenged the patent in 1934 and won his case. Zworykin's problem was that he had little if any evidence that he had actually invented a device in 1923 that worked, only his word. What is also clear is that Zworykin's working models of iconoscopes and kinescopes only came after he visited Farnsworth's lab in 1930. So, on the basis of the evidence, Farnsworth is the "Father of Television," and Zworykin's role isn't that of the inventor, but of an improver of Farnsworth's system for the Radio Corporation of America.

Did I mention that Zworykin worked for RCA? And, of course, David Sarnoff, whose main goal in life was to make RCA the greatest, and preferably the only, force in radio and television, ran RCA. So if Sarnoff could get the patent rights for all the parts of electronic TV, then RCA would have total control. A problem for Sarnoff was that, if Farnsworth held the patents, RCA would have to pay him royalties for a license to use those patents, something that Sarnoff definitely found less than desirable. After all, he ran a company that was determined to "collect patent royalties, not pay them."[1]

Regardless of the controversy over who actually invented it, television was now a reality. During the 1930s, RCA and other companies continuously worked to improve the quality of television's picture. The measure of their progress is indicated by the increasing number of scanning lines employed in the successive demonstrations made during the period:

1930	60 lines
1931	120
1933	240
1936	343
1939	441
1941	525

In 1939, RCA demonstrated television to the public at the New York World's Fair. This included broadcasting Franklin Roosevelt as he opened the fair, and the public loved it. RCA intended to offer televisions for sale, but immediately obstacles appeared. Other manufacturers complained that RCA was attempting to create a monopoly, and the Federal Communications Commission rescinded its approval for commercial television while an industry committee reviewed the standards for transmission and reception. In the end, this committee recommended the basic RCA system, but it changed the number of resolution lines from 441 to 525. The FCC then approved the start of commercial television. RCA quickly changed its equipment to 525 lines and prepared to make a fortune.

And then World War II happened.

When the war, and the interruption in the commercial development of electronics, ended it was time to get back to work.

In 1946, RCA introduced a new television set for consumers, the "630" with a 10-inch screen and a tremendous improvement in performance. To stimulate production and demand—and by extension the demand for new stations that would need RCA's transmitting equipment to carry the programming for all those new TVs in people's houses—RCA gave other companies the manufacturing drawings. The market exploded. New TV stations came on the air at a rapid pace. Some interference problems cropped up, just as had happened with radio, so the FCC froze new station construction for a time. However, even this couldn't stop the boom. Sets continued to sell, and the number in use skyrocketed. In 1946, there were only 6,000. Only six years later, in 1952, there were almost 22 million in use.

■ TELEVISION STARTS BROADCASTING

So TV started broadcasting. However, what exactly would it broadcast? TV was essentially radio with pictures. In the beginning, the camera basically was pointed at what was little more than a radio show. For example, a singer would just stand in front of the orchestra, no different from what she'd be doing if she were on a radio show.

So TV was radio with pictures. But that was the big difference. Television combined sound with pictures that would grab and hold the attention of the audience in a way that radio could not, and that's what fascinated people. It didn't matter **what** was being shown, only that it was.

But just as the novelty of movies quickly wore off, and filmmakers had to turn to creating stories and adding more action and sound, so the novelty with TV wore off too. Broadcasters needed programming that was more than just pointing a camera at something, so they went with what they knew—radio shows. If it could be done on radio, it could be done on TV—with pictures. So television broadcasters co-opted the programming that radio had developed: dramas, comedies, talk shows, game shows, sports, news, anything and everything.

Just like radio, all TV shows were performed live. The signals were sent out over phone lines to the network affiliates, the independent broadcasting stations that contracted to carry network programs. Since the TV studios and theatres were in New York City, that's where TV shows originated. The shows had to fit in the studio or theatre, mostly because they needed extremely bright lights for the refrigerator-sized cameras to pick up the scenes (sporting events, of course, used sunlight).

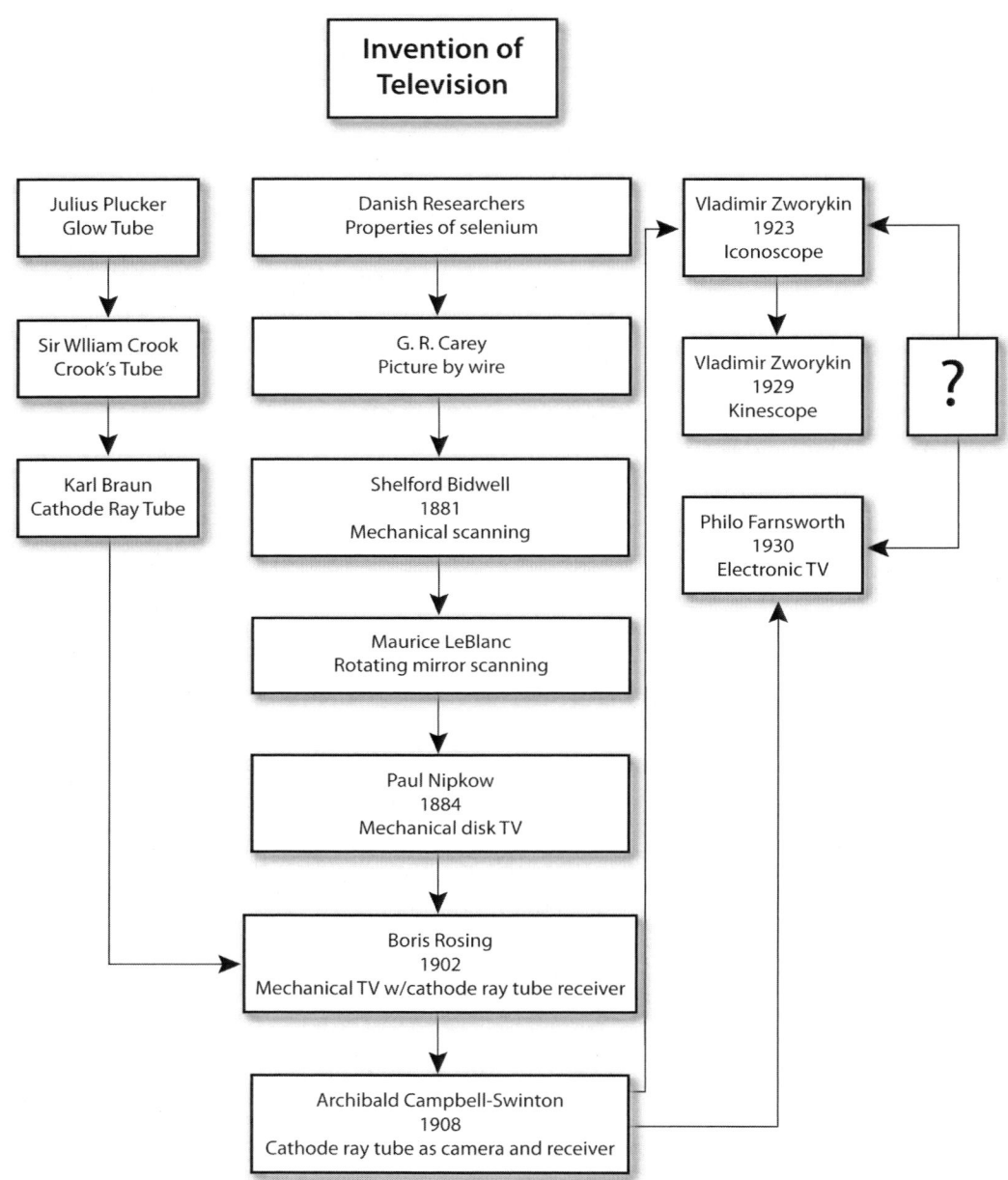

Several genres of programs were popular with audiences. One such genre was the situation comedy, including such shows as *I Remember Mama*, *The Ruggles* and *Mr. Peepers*. The situation comedy, or sitcom, was a half-hour weekly show that used a continuing cast of characters in a continuing "universe" of situations out of which the plots arose (thus, situation comedy).

Another popular genre of show that took advantage of the radio-with-pictures aspect of television were the comedy-variety shows, including such shows as *The Texaco Star Theatre* with Milton Berle and *Your Show of Shows* with Sid Caesar. The comedy-variety show had a varying mix of variety acts, such as singers, dancers and stand-up comedians. It was essentially a vaudeville show in front of a camera, with comedy skits performed by a small company of comic actors. These shows usually had a star that acted as host to the segments, introducing the performers and, of course, performing as well. The host was generally a singer, such as Frank Sinatra, Judy Garland and Perry Como, or a comedian, such as Jimmy Durante, Milton Berle and Sid Caesar. Of course, it was possible the host would have no talent whatsoever, such as the newspaper columnist Ed Sullivan, whose show ran for decades. These shows became so popular that they affected everything else. On Tuesday nights, when Milton "Uncle Milty" Berle was on, movie theatres delayed their starting times until his show was over, and cities noticed a decrease in water pressure during the commercials due to people going to the bathroom.

There were also episodic dramas, such as cop and detective shows, westerns and medical dramas. The schedule also contained anthology series, which, unlike episodic series, presented a weekly stand-alone drama with a cast and story that had no connection to any other week's show. The common label for this early period as the "Golden Age of Television" invariably is referring to these anthology series, as they brought some of drama's finest offerings into people's homes.

But then there was a change, one that would transform television forever.

Two 1940s' Hollywood stars decided they wanted to do a situation comedy and asked CBS if they would air it. CBS was thrilled. TV was anathema to Hollywood, the kiss of death for any actor who still wanted to work in movies. Hollywood hated TV—it took butts out of theatre seats and firmly planted them on sofas. TV was costing the studios money. So to have two movie stars wanting to do a show would give TV the respectability it needed to attract the finest acting talent. CBS immediately agreed and asked how soon those stars could get to New York and get to work. However, bumps in the road immediately appeared.

You see, those two stars were Lucille Ball and Desi Arnaz, and they didn't want to move to New York. They were happy living in Los Angeles. CBS told them they couldn't do a show in Hollywood—the studios were in New York, along with all the equipment necessary to send the show out live over telephone lines to the affiliates. But Ball and Arnaz said they were staying in LA.

CBS still wanted the show, but they couldn't see how it could be done. Arnaz, on the other hand, did, and he told CBS that he and Ball would film their show rather than broadcast it live and send the edited film to New York. CBS could air that. CBS didn't think it could be done. The problem was that it takes a long time to film something. A typical ninety-minute movie took eight to nine weeks to film. For example, let's take a scene: Four people are having a conversation while standing around, say, a Christmas tree. To film this scene, a master shot is set up, covering all four people. Once the master is shot, a new set-up is done, moving the camera and lights to do the close-ups (called a two-shot) on one pair. This may take one to two hours. After that two-shot, another setup is done for another two-shot with a different pair (another one or two hours), then another setup, then another setup. This scene may only take one minute on screen, but it could take a day to shoot. After shooting came post-production, such as editing, to put all the takes into a single scene.

So to film a half hour sitcom would take at least three weeks, and episodic TV series needed a new episode every week, which meant a show would have to be filmed in one week.

This is where Desi Arnaz proved himself a genius. He said they wouldn't shoot the show like a movie. They would do the show like a one-act play in front of a live studio audience. The difference would be that instead of using one camera the way a movie would shoot a scene, they would use three cameras, all three shooting the entire show while it was being performed. Then the three reels of film would be edited together, sent to New York, and go out over the air.

In essence, what he was doing was replacing TV cameras, which commonly used the three-camera technique when shooting a live show, with film cameras to produce a TV show.

CBS still wasn't sure. To prove it could be done, Ball and Arnaz shot their own pilot episode to show it would work. The pilot had very poor production values though. The walls of the set were made of paper, and the doors shook the entire wall when they opened and closed. Ball and Arnaz weren't idiots—they weren't going to spend a lot of their own money on speculation. Still, the pilot worked and demonstrated the three-camera technique was viable. CBS bought both the show and the idea of how to do it, and *I Love Lucy* became TV's first megahit.

There was some fallout from Arnaz's idea. First, everyone wanted to start filming their shows. Of course, to do this, producers needed sound stages and cameras and film processing labs, and the people who had all of these things were the movie studios. Suddenly Hollywood loved television. Studios rented out their facilities and equipment that they weren't using and made a fortune without any cost to themselves. They even got into the TV production business themselves. And of course the studios were in LA, so that's where TV went, and it has been there ever since.

All because Lucille Ball and Desi Arnaz didn't want to leave home. Amazing how things work out, isn't it?

The next step was for television to go from black and white to color. In 1939, CBS had shown a color TV system with a wheel divided into thirds that had a different color filter in each third—red, blue and green. This was rotated at high speed in front of the camera lens. A similar wheel synchronized to the wheel in front of the camera was used in the receiver. This system produced three picture fields—a red, a blue and a green picture—on the screen, in rapid succession. This was called the "field sequential" system. Persistence of vision caused the viewer to see a single full-color picture. The system worked well. However, it, like previous TVs, was mechanical, with the problems of breaking down and going out of synchronization inherent in such a method.

In 1949, the FCC started a series of hearings on proposed color TV standards. The commission viewed demonstrations of the CBS system, as well as of RCA's new all-electronic system, which didn't work quite as well as CBS's.

The problem with the RCA system was that it used three separate pickup tubes in the camera and three kinescopes (one for each color) in the receiver. These required exact—and hard to maintain—alignment. However, this system had a big advantage over the CBS system in that it was compatible with pre-existing TV systems: Black and white TV tuned to the color transmission still produced a good black and white picture. The CBS system would require all stations to install new equipment and consumers to buy new television sets to get color.

The FCC chose the CBS system, and in 1950 it gave the go-ahead for color on this basis. RCA, naturally, sued, but they lost, and in July 1951, CBS went on the air with color transmission. However, the other networks didn't follow their example. The TV industry didn't like the idea of a color wheel in every set, **and** it wanted compatibility with previous sets. Also, by the time it rolled out its system, RCA had developed the tri-color kinescope using three electron guns. Each was devoted to one color, red, blue or green, and each fired an electron beam at the screen, which removed the need for three hard-to-align picture tubes in each set. Within a few months, CBS gave up.

Meanwhile, the industry formed another committee: the National Television Standards Committee, or NTSC. After several months of deliberation, it recommended a set of standards for color TV, and on December 17, 1953, the FCC approved the start of color TV broadcasting based on the NTSC standards.

NBC started broadcasting many of its programs in color. RCA, of course, started selling cameras and transmitting equipment to stations, and color TVs to the public, with other manufacturers soon following.

However, color TV didn't explode with either stations or consumers the way black and white TV had earlier. The problem was money. Producing shows in color was much more expensive than doing them in black and white, and with only a few color sets in people's homes, sponsors that the producers relied on were reluctant to pay the extra cost. And, in a catch-22, people were reluctant to buy expensive color sets when there were only a few color shows on the air. However, there were plenty of black and white shows to watch on the sets they already had. It looked like color TV was doomed.

RCA determined to make color TV a reality though, and it pumped in millions of dollars for promotion. It also subsidized the production of shows in color on NBC and independent stations, but didn't help CBS. By 1962, there were about a million color sets in people's homes, enough for sponsors to feel the extra cost was worth it.

By 1965, there were 5 million color sets in use, and all the networks had gone to full-color. Now color took off. By 1970, there were 37 million color sets.

Since 1953 there have been no further changes in the basic system used in the US. However, there have been huge changes in both sets and telecasting equipment. Cameras have gotten smaller and smaller, TVs bigger and bigger, cable and satellite have changed how audiences get shows and how many shows they can get, and digital has replaced analog. We'll look at all those.

■ ENDNOTE

1. As a side note, I find it interesting that whenever there's a patent argument between two inventors, RCA seems to be involved. Remember how Lee de Forest sued Edwin Armstrong over all those radio patents? De Forest worked for RCA.

13

TELEVISION AND SOCIETY

*I*n 1939, one of the most influential media in history debuted at the New York World's Fair. That medium, like writing and printing, has completely changed the world —yet again. And that medium was television.

Television didn't really start having an effect on society until the late 1950s, when enough sets were in homes. But it once started, the effects were on a par with the introduction of printing.

Starting out as radio with pictures, TV soon created a new form of mass media, one that combined the effects of radio and movies. It was movies in the home—and remember how movies affected society.

The difference is that movies took the myths and stories of what people thought society should be, and they often tested or even stood them on their heads. Television, on the other hand, took the mainstream beliefs of its audiences and didn't stray from them, reinforcing instead of challenging them.

Situation comedies, or sitcoms, show this clearly. One of the reasons for that lies in the rules of comedy, which are probably the best indicators of what the rules are that a society believes. So as I go along tracing how TV has—and does—affect society, I'll keep bringing up sitcoms as examples to show how that happens. But to do that requires knowledge of how comedy works. The following is a discussion of the rules of comedy.

Comedy is that which makes one laugh. This is the basis for any study of comedy. However, just what is it that makes one laugh?

There are six criteria that an attempt at humor must satisfy for it to get a laugh. If any one of these criteria is missing, the attempt at humor will fail. So we'll start at the top.

The six criteria are:

1. It must appeal to the intellect rather than to the emotions;
2. It must be mechanical;

3. It must be inherently human, with the capability of reminding us of humanity;

4. There must be a set of established human or societal norms with which the observer is intimately familiar;

5. The situation and its component parts (the actions performed and/or the dialogue spoken) must violate those norms in some way, and

6. It must be perceived by the observer as harmless.

We'll go through these one at a time.

The first criterion, the *appeal to intellect rather than emotion,* is obvious when ethnic humor is used. Polish (Irish, whitey, gay, fraternity, sorority, etc.) jokes can be hilarious to everyone—everyone, that is, except to the Poles (Irish, whitey, gay, fraternity, sorority, etc.). To the group being ridiculed, jokes at their expense are not funny—they are insulting and rude. People respond to insults and rudeness subjectively, taking umbrage, or, in more simple terms, getting angry, which is an emotion. To those who have no personal interest in the joke, i.e., everybody else, there is no insult and they take an objective, intellectual view of the joke and can respond to the other criteria for comedy if they are met. Thus, one can take the old joke, "How many Poles does it take to screw in a light bulb? Five: one to hold the bulb and four to turn the ladder" and substitute a different group for Poles in each retelling, thus irritating a whole new set of people each time.

Lenny Bruce counted on the intellectual basis of comedy when, in one of his routines, he identified all the races and ethnic groups in his audience with insulting labels: "I see we have three niggers in the audience. And over there I see two wogs, and five spics, and four kikes," etc. As he started the routine, there were gasps of incredulity and even anger—the audience couldn't believe that Bruce would be so insulting and insensitive. But as Bruce continued, and the list grew longer, and it became clear that he was listing everything he could think of, the words lost their connotative, emotional meaning as insulting terms and turned into just noises. In other words, they lost their emotive content and became an intellectual exercise in how words lose their meanings outside of context. At this point, the audience, all of whom had been appalled and angry at exactly the same words, started laughing at them—the audience was reacting intellectually, not emotionally.

Henri Bergson delineates the second two criteria for comedy in his essay "Laughter": that it be *mechanical* and *inherently human.* His theory revolves around a basic axiom, that the laughable element consists of a mechanical inelasticity, just where one would expect adaptability and flexibility. It's humorous when a person acts in a manner that is inappropriate to a stimulus or situation, as in any slapstick comedy routine. It's funny when a chair is pulled out from under someone who is sitting down, because he doesn't adapt to the change in situation and continues to sit in a mechanical fashion. Characters in situation comedies such as Lucy on *I Love Lucy* or the six major characters on *Friends* are funny because they mechanically react to events without thinking about how events have changed the situation.

An extension of Bergson's theory is his idea that comedy is *inherently human.* Something is funny only insofar as it is human or reminds the audience of humanity. The audience may laugh at the antics of animals, such as chimpanzees or horses or bears, but only in direct proportion to the animals' capability of reminding the audience of something human. Thus, animals such as chimps and orangutans are often dressed in human clothing to heighten the reminder, and horses, such as Mr. Ed and Francis the Talking Mule, can talk, a human characteristic, and think better than the men they're around.

One major point that becomes apparent when one examines comedy is that it is based on incongruity—the unexpected with the expected, the unusual with the usual, the misfit in what has been established as a societal norm.

For incongruity to exist, there must be something to be incongruous to. Therefore, for a comedy to work, there must be an established set of cultural, human and societal norms, mores, idioms, idiosyncrasies and terminologies against which incongruities may be found. Such norms may be internal or external. **Internal norms** are those the author has provided in the script. **External norms** are those that exist in the society for which the script was written.

Human norms are those that are simply part of being human, those aspects that every person, regardless of time, place, or culture, have in common. There are few, essentially greed, death and sex.

The most common human norm used in comedy is sex, and, depending on cultural proscriptions, dirty jokes are funny regardless of society or time period. Aristophanes' play *Lysistrata,* written more than two thousand years ago, is still funny. The story is about the men fighting a war that the women want them to stop. When the men refuse, the women go on a sex strike. Finally, the men get so desperate to have sex they end the war. Many of the jokes in Shakespeare's comedies are dirty, and once an audience can get through the language, they are still funny.

Societal norms are those that are particular to a society, the rules and mores that make that society a society (see Chapter Three for a discussion). In this instance, the humor comes from violating the audience's expectations of how people should act, speak and think in their culture.

The major problem is that societal norms change from society to society (of course), and societal norms change over time, unlike human norms. One difficulty is knowing what societal norms exist, and which have become out of date. Many times some people, upon hearing a joke, will respond with "I don't get it." This is because they don't know or understand the societal norms violated in the joke. This is also why you can never explain a joke. To explain, you must first explain the norms, then show how they have been violated. Such an explanation removes any incongruity by illustrating how it works within the norms.

The need for norms also explains why humor can become passé. Stand-up comedians do very few jokes about President Eisenhower's administration because the norms have changed—no one understands topical references to sixty years ago.

Plays and jokes can also go out of date. Neil Simon's early plays depended heavily on social attitudes of the time, particularly those about the relationships between men and women. However, sex roles and attitudes have changed considerably since 1961. ***Come Blow Your Horn***, and the humor in the character of Alan Baker's rather sexist approach to women and sex now evokes an emotional reaction of distaste in many people rather than of laughter. The humor that does work takes as its norms human attitudes and norms that are independent of society and culture.

Nonetheless, a funny play can remain funny even when the norms change. Shakespeare's "breeches parts," such as Viola in ***Twelfth Night*** or Rosalind in ***As You Like It***, evoked great laughter from Elizabethan audiences because their societal norms said that women do not wear men's clothing, and the sight of Viola and Rosalind in male attire was incongruous and therefore funny. Today, women wearing pants is the norm, and therefore seeing Viola in pants is not funny. Nonetheless, there are many things in Shakespeare's plays that are incongruous to today's norms, and thus his comedies continue to be funny four hundred years later. We still laugh, perhaps not at what Elizabethan audiences did, but the plays are still funny because he gained most of his humor from human rather than from societal norms.

Three aspects of incongruity are *literalization, reversal,* and *exaggeration.* In literalization, the joke comes from taking a figure of speech and then performing it literally. When Secret Agent Maxwell Smart (**Get Smart**) asks the robot agent Hymie to give him a hand, Hymie detaches a hand and gives it over, interpreting the instruction literally. On the situation comedy **Cheers**, Coach, and later Woody, the bartenders, take everything said to them at face value. Apparently, they are incapable of recognizing innuendo, hyperbole, or figures of speech.

Reversal is simply reversing the normal, taking what is normal and expected and doing or saying the opposite. When Retief, in Keith Laumer's science fiction novel **Retief and the Warlords**, is subjected to what his captors think are the most horrendous tortures, he is assailed with modern art and smellovision renditions of overheated tires, burnt toast, chow mein, aged Gorgonzola, and the authentic odor of sanctity.

An exaggeration is taking what is normal and blowing it out of proportion. Events occur to which the characters react beyond all proportion: the mountain out of a molehill syndrome. The jealous wife's discovery of a blonde hair on her husband's jacket leads her to build an entire scenario of mad trysts, trips to the Riviera, and a murder plot against her, until he points at the collie sitting at her feet. Such exaggeration is a standard in comedy.

The greatest incongruity is the violation of societal taboos. This violation can provoke the greatest laughter. In American society, the greatest taboos are discussions of sex, death, and biological functions. These are all subjects society has decreed should be discussed seriously, discreetly, and euphemistically, if discussed at all. Much humor is derived from these taboos.

The sixth and final criterion for humor is, as Aristotle states, that ". . . which causes no pain or destruction . . . is distorted but *painless*" (my emphasis). The audience perceives that the comic action causes the participants no actual harm. Their physical, mental, psychological and/or emotional well-being may be stretched, distorted, or crushed, but they recover quickly, and by the end of the performance they are once again in their original state. The Warner Brothers' Roadrunner cartoons are a prime example. Wile E. Coyote is dropped, crushed, pummeled, rolled, wrung, and otherwise punished for his attempts to catch the roadrunner, yet seconds later he is putting together his next Acme widget to carry out his next plan. Wile is never damaged permanently, no matter how high the cliff he falls off or how big the rock that lands on him. The criterion applies to real life, as well. It is funny when someone slips on the ice and falls. People laugh—until they realize that the person broke rhis leg. At that moment, the event is no longer humorous.

In addition, the audience extends the perception of harmlessness beyond the participants in the joke to any and everyone. For an attempt at humor to work, the audience must perceive no harm to the participants, the audience, or to society at large. For example, sexist or racist jokes may be perceived as harmful to the self-esteem or image of the butt of the joke in society, and thus not be funny.

The perception of harmlessness also has the problem of being individual, not universal. What one person may perceive as harmless another may perceive as harmful. Thus, there's no such thing as a joke everyone will laugh at.

The six criteria must all be present for an attempt at humor to succeed: If only one is missing, then the joke will fail. As long as the audience knows the norms and can thus see the incongruity, the participants act in an inflexible manner but are inherently human, no one appears to get hurt in any way, and the audience doesn't take it personally, then an attempt at being funny will succeed.

Now it is time to really start looking at TV, tracing its history and how it influenced, and was influenced by, society.

■ EARLY TV

Early TV shows really were radio with pictures. The problem TV had was the size and weight of the cameras and the amount of light they needed. Cameras had all the mobility of a refrigerator, and they needed thousands of watts of light to pick up the picture.

It was an era of experimentation, as TV tried to figure out what it was and what it could do. Naturally, broadcasters started with what they knew—radio. So they used the formats common on radio: musical shows, interview shows, dramas, soap operas, and comedies.

The most common shows on early TV were musical variety shows like ***Talent Scouts***, ***Arthur Godfrey and his Friends***, ***The Fred Waring Show*** and ***The Frank Sinatra Show***. In these shows, acts would appear on a small stage and simply stand in front of the cameras as though they were on radio. Some shows, like ***The Ed Sullivan Show***, were more expansive, using a theatre instead of a studio, but in its case, it was just a stage show with cameras pointed at it.

Small-scale sports shows, like boxing and wrestling, were also popular, taking up several hours a week of prime time. They were easy to do since all the network had to do was point a camera at the ring. There were none of the close-ups or multiple camera angles used that are common for boxing and wrestling shows today.

Live drama was also popular, with programs such as ***Ford Theatre***, ***Philco Television Playhouse***, ***Studio One***, ***Kraft Television Theater*** and Armstrong ***Circle Theatre***. Note that almost all of these early television shows had the name of the sponsor in the title. That's because these shows had only the one sponsor, which owned the show outright. Imagine the power these sponsors had over the show—after all, without them there wouldn't be any show. These companies did indeed exercise their power. When Reginald Rose, one of early TV's best writers, the writer of ***12 Angry Men***, wanted to explore racism, he showed discrimination against a black man in a New England town. He was compelled to alter his play "Thunder on Sycamore Street," a drama about a black family beset by white racists, because it "was unpalatable to the network since many of their stations are situated in southern states, and it was felt that viewers might be appalled at the sight of a Negro as the beleaguered hero of a television drama."

The sponsor didn't want to offend Southern audiences and forced Rose to change the main character from a black man to an ex-convict. Although the play still deals with mob mentality and attacks on differences from the norm, the racism was gone. In another example, in a production of "Judgment at Nuremburg" about the Nazi war trials and the concentration camps, Hotpoint, the sponsor and maker of kitchen appliances, demanded that all references to the gas chambers be removed, thinking it would reflect badly on their gas stoves. Interference by sponsors could be really petty, such as the insistence of Alcoa (the Aluminum Company of America) that a lynching in "Tragedy in a Temporary Town" on ***The Alcoa Hour*** in 1956 could not be set in a trailer camp because most mobile homes were constructed of aluminum. Writer Reginald Rose had to substitute wooden shacks for aluminum trailers. Phillip Morris, the cigarette maker, insisted that every use of the words "lucky" and "strike" be removed from scripts lest the audience be reminded of Morris' competitor cigarette, Lucky Strikes.

This state of affairs continued until, starting in 1953, Pat Weaver altered the system. Taking his cue from magazines, he started selling time to any company that wished to advertise rather than to single sponsors to pay for a show.

The live drama shows were not really TV shows, but rather plays performed on camera. The entire set for a play would be put up in the studio as though on a stage, with open walls and no ceilings so the lights could be hung and to maneuver the cameras. Several cameras were used, and their use was well rehearsed so they could move to the right position to shoot the scene and set the distance (e.g., medium shot, close-up). The director would select the shot he wanted at any particular moment and that would be sent out over the air. These live dramas are often cited as the crowning glory of the golden age of television.

And it's true that it was the golden age in a sense. Television for the first time brought culture into American homes through some of the finest drama the world had seen, from Sophocles to Shakespeare to Shaw, and many modern plays that would become classics. Plays and performances that average Americans had never seen, and probably would never have been able to see without television, were on the air almost every night.

These dramas are an indication of how television was going in the early years. There were only a few scripted episodic series, like ***The Aldrich Family***, ***The Life of Riley*** and ***Mama***. These half-hour shows required sets and multiple cameras, and they were difficult to do live week after week. The only alternative was to do filmed series, such as ***The Lone Ranger*** with his faithful Indian companion Tonto, but that was expensive and extremely time consuming, taking two to three weeks to film each week's episode, and thus requiring a long lead time.

A major difference between early TV and the TV of today was the number of political and social interview shows in prime time, shows such as ***Meet the Press***, ***Meet Your Congress***, ***Quizzing the News***, and ***America's Town Meeting***. They're totally absent in today's TV prime time network schedule, relegated instead to Sunday morning and cable news networks. Since they consist of only two or more people sitting at a desk, they're very easy to put on TV. But the fact that they've moved from prime time to Sunday morning says a lot about the business of television. The drive was for viewers to get advertisers, and political interviews require concentration and thinking on the part of the audience. That thinking could interfere with the ads as the audience spends the commercial breaks considering what they had been hearing and even talking to each other, so away with talking heads and their conversation.

Programming definitely changed when Desi Arnaz and Lucille Ball made it possible to film a show in a day instead of three weeks. Everything started to be filmed, with the exception of the live dramas. Those still came out of New York studios for several more years.

As I discussed during the chapter on movies, the 1950s were a time when memories of World War II were still fresh in everyone's mind and when people wanted peace, stability and conformity. The ideal situation for most people was a family with 2.5 kids, a dog, and a house in a good neighborhood or the suburbs. In other words, what people wanted was ***Leave It to Beaver***, ***The Donna Reed Show*** and ***Father Knows Best***. In each of these shows, and others like them, the father was the head of the family, the breadwinner and the fount of wisdom, ruling over his family with gentle firmness. The mother was the source of comfort and love, and the children learned from their mistakes with the guidance of Dad and the support of Mom. In other words, these are "dream families" where there **are** problems but everyone loves everyone else and all turns out all right in the end. Mom stayed home, dad went to work, and the kids rarely did anything worse than tell a little white lie. The tragedies were measles, broken household appliances, acne, unfulfilled puppy love and so on.

An excellent example is an episode of ***Leave It to Beaver***. First the problem is set. Beaver, his brother Wally and a few other friends are playing baseball in the street in front of the Cleavers' home. An errant fly ball crashes through a window. While their friends run, Wall and Beav look at the window and worry about their father's reaction when he arrives home from work. He tells them they'll talk about it later as their mother, June, tells them things will be all right. When Beav comments on her making them feel better, she says, "Isn't that what mothers are for?" At dinner, Ward tells the boys they shouldn't play near the house and shouldn't do it again. He then mentions that he had to get the car's brakes fixed that morning because "someone" had driven with the brake on, clearly meaning that June had done it. Notice how June provides loving support to the kids (after all, "Isn't that what mothers are for?") and Ward sets the punishment. I also find it interesting how Ward treats June, his wife, almost like one of the kids for her mistake driving with the brake set.

Of course, it can't stop there. The next day the boys are going to the park to play ball, but Beaver wants to try to hit the ball because he never can. Wally pitches, and Beaver hits the ball into the garage, breaking a side window on the car. The boys broke their promise not to play ball near the house and don't know what to do. Their friend, and the closest thing you'll find to a juvenile delinquent in the Beaver world, Eddie Haskell, advises them to roll down the window, and when it's rolled up again, act as surprised as anyone that it's broken. However, Wally and the Beav are too honest for that, so they try to raise the money to have the window fixed before it's noticed, but they fail.

So what happens? The next day on a drive the window is down, and June says she's cold. Ordered to roll up the window, Beaver says he can't. Asked why, Wally admits they had broken it. Again ordered to roll it up, Beaver does, and the boys are surprised that the window isn't broken. Ward tells them that he thought he had broken the window closing the door, and had it fixed, but he is glad the boys admitted what they had done. So the kids are honest, the parents are loving and forgiving, and all is right with the world, just they way the audience would like to believe the world actually is.

Sociologist Laura Oswald sums up this 1950s ideal perfectly in her article, "Branding the American Family":

> "Regardless of whether programs like *Father Knows Best* or *Leave it to Beaver,* or *The Donna Reed Show* represented the reality of most families, they mirrored an unspoken ideal of white middle-class contentment, based on rather limited roles and expectations of family members and society. Ethnicity, homosexuality, and 'the dysfunctional family' were not yet admitted or discussed openly, and no one was expected to question tradition."

The 1950s were an era not only of conformity, but an era that saw everything in terms of black and white. There was good—us—and there was evil—them. After the battle against real evil in the 1940s, immediately followed by the fear of the Red Menace of communism, it only makes sense.

Television responded to that by doing something that was difficult in radio drama —action. In other words, shows were made containing lots of visually stimulating things happening, starting with *Martin Kane, Private Eye* in 1949. In few other forms could a better idea of good versus evil be shown than in crime dramas, which present a clean structure for quick and easy portrayals of good guys and bad guys. These half hour shows had little time to probe the nuances of character: A hero is a hero, and a villain is a villain. Any prolonged wrestling with conscience would replace time that could be devoted to the more important chase and showdown sequences.

Although these crime dramas were formulaic, many variations could be made on that formula. Nonetheless, however the formula was presented, the central premise remained the same: simple righteousness opposing simple evil. Stirred together with a bit of sex and a bit of violence, or in the case of 1958's *The Untouchables* a lot of violence (in fact, so much that they ran out of ways to kill people), evil is defeated, and the audience basks in the glow that all is the way it should be. That this glow had little resemblance to the real world was irrelevant—what the audience wanted was to believe their worldview is supported.

An exception to this rule was a transplant from radio, a quiet show with no car chases or gunfire: 1952's *Dragnet*. It was created, produced and directed by Jack Webb, who insisted that the actors avoid the normal emotional portrayal of characters and deliver their lines in a deadpan fashion, not memorizing them but reading them off a new device invented for the show, a TelePrompter. The point of *Dragnet* was to enter the story after the commission of the crime, which showed the crime's effects as the detectives worked to solve it.

Webb noticed something else as he watched TV: The small screen wasn't suitable for sweeping, wide scenes, which worked well for movies and their large screens. Such scenes lacked detail and impact. What he noticed worked well on TV were close-ups, a tight focus on a character's face, which allowed the audience to see the slightest nuance of expression. So he directed his show with many close-ups, cutting back and forth between characters as they spoke rather than using wider shots of both characters on the screen, which would lose impact. Thereafter, the close-up shot became a staple of television directing.

Dragnet started off slowly as audiences were unused to this new approach to crime drama, but by its second season it had become a hit, leaping sixteen places in the Neilson ratings, from twentieth to fourth. Soon, it was challenging *I Love Lucy* for primacy on the viewing schedule and in the hearts of viewers.

However, a new kind of action drama almost drove out everything else, one based on that greatest of American myths—the cowboy. *The Lone Ranger* was the first in 1950, and soon Hopalong Cassidy, Gene Autry and Roy Rogers joined him. However, these westerns were aimed more at kids than at adults. Adults didn't really buy into the idea of the hero stopping the action to sing a song.

Networks wanted to appeal to adults—after all, they had more money to buy sponsors' products. So they started producing adult westerns, beginning with shows like *Wyatt Earp*, *Bat Masterson* and *Cheyenne*.

The most popular TV western in history—and, in fact, the second longest running prime-time series with continuing characters in history—was 1955's ***Gunsmoke***, the stories of Marshall Matt Dillon in Dodge City, Kansas. It was the first western to hit number one in the ratings, in 1957.[1] It was on the air for twenty years and surpassed only by ***The Simpsons*** in 2010.

By 1959, there were thirty-two different western series on the air, making the western the most popular kind of show during the 1950s. For hour after hour, TV screens were filled with showdowns, barroom brawls, and heroes in white hats. All over America kids carrying cap guns practiced their fast draws and their intimidating squints.

There were so many westerns that new ones had to keep coming up with gimmicks to differentiate themselves from all the others. You had ***Have Gun, Will Travel***, the stories of Paladin, a gun for hire who smoked expensive cigars, quoted Keats and Shelley, and collected chessmen. Carrying a Colt .44 with a hair trigger, he "dispatched his adversaries not only with distaste but with a unique"—and weird— "combination of epicurean zeal, Spartan valor, and existential boredom" (Shulman, 305).

But pistols weren't enough. There were also ***Wanted—Dead or Alive***, where Josh Randall carried a sawed-off Winchester rifle called the mare's leg, and ***The Rifleman***, where Lucas McCain carried a full-sized Winchester rifle, but twirled it like a six-gun. One of the weirdest gimmicks though was where the hero Sundance in ***Hotel de Paree*** had a hat band made of mirrors that he used to blind his opponents with reflected sunlight.

"But adult westerns weren't all gunplay. In fact, some purists complained that they didn't have **enough** action. There was too much talk. Gene Autry said, 'Television westerns drive me nuts. Too slow.' And messages, of all things, were creeping into westerns—sermons about brotherhood and nonviolence and togetherness" (Shulman, 293).

As more and more westerns came on the air, the old white hats versus the black hats six-shooter solutions to problems were perceived not only as too simplistic, but they made it difficult for the audience to tell which western they were watching. Hats could be any color, and, as for the rest of his costume, he might end up wearing a ruffled shirt, silk vest, and white suit, like Yancy Derringer, and some weeks that six-gun never left the holster. Yancy didn't even have a six-gun; he had a derringer hidden in his hat, which must have made any attempt at a quick-draw problematic.

You even had what I suppose could be called the "anti-western." The hero seldom rode a horse because he didn't like to. He was not only slow on the draw, he was more likely to run from a fight or to try to talk his way out. He had the moral fiber of a wet Kleenex, lacked honor, and was perfectly willing to lie and cheat to get what he wanted. What kind of a hero is **that**? Well, he's a maverick—Bret ***Maverick***, to be precise. He strolled instead of strode onto TV in 1957, and it took a while for viewers to realize that the show was less a western than a satire on westerns. In fact, "many viewers never caught on at all, which was probably the secret of the show's success: it was possible to enjoy it either as a western adventure or a western spoof" (Shulman, 309)

But the western couldn't last. Like having to eat the same thing every day, audiences got tired of having little **but** westerns to watch night after night, and shows got cancelled left and right. Some, of course, **did** last, like ***Gunsmoke*** and ***Bonanza***. New shows also appeared, but in nowhere near the numbers of the 1950s. One was 1965's ***The Wild, Wild West***, a blend of western and James Bond. Although popular, with a 30 rating, it fell prey to an anti-violence push in Congress as the most violent show on television and was cancelled. ***The Big Valley*** was the first show to have two women as the main characters rather than men. One western that boosted civil rights was 1964's ***Daniel Boone***. This show often featured black actors in serious roles, rather than the comic roles of the past, and it emphasized the commonality of all people regardless of race. A subject that appeared in several episodes was Boone helping runaway slaves escape, or even finding and reuniting them with their families.

However, a growing realization in society that the distinctions between good and evil just weren't as clear and clean as portrayed in the typical western made the shows seem too simplistic. Society was beginning to see that there were indeed grey areas between the two extremes.

Perhaps a major influence behind this growing realization was the power of television to expose hypocrisy and the evils of extremism by simply putting those who espoused such views in front of the camera where the audience could see them and let them talk and show themselves for what they are.

The fear of communism caused people to stop thinking and just react, and some people took advantage of this fear to promote their own agendas and, not accidentally, themselves. The driving force of these people in the 1950s was the Republican junior senator from Wisconsin, Joseph McCarthy. As chair of The Senate Permanent Subcommittee on Investigations, he led a witch-hunt looking for communists in the Army, the government and especially in Hollywood, accusing hundreds of people of being secret reds with no evidence and badgering anyone who refused to testify or admit to what **he** called their guilt. These hearings were shown on TV, and the fear spread. However, what people feared was likely not communism, but McCarthy. Even the news organizations were afraid—mostly of being accused if they went after McCarthy.

There was an exception—Edward R. Murrow. Murrow, who established his reputation as the most respected, influential and principled broadcast journalist in history with his CBS News broadcasts during World War II, brought this same sense of integrity to television. Unwilling to bow to the pressures McCarthy brought on anyone who opposed him, Murrow went after McCarthy on his news show ***See It Now***. He played clips from the televised hearings and commented on how McCarthy browbeat and interrupted witnesses. He ended by saying, "This is no time for men who oppose Senator McCarthy's methods to keep silent" (Edwards, 116). CBS gave McCarthy time to reply to Murrow's report. It wasn't an interview with a reporter asking questions and McCarthy giving answers. CBS just set up a camera and let McCarthy say whatever he wanted. What McCarthy wanted to say was not support for his methods or evidence for his attacks; he wanted to make a personal attack on Murrow's integrity. McCarthy showed himself a demagogue, playing off people's fears for his own self-aggrandizement. He lost his following, his power, and his Senate seat. Television, which presented events and people warts and all, brought powerful sounds and images into people's living rooms in a way that no other medium ever had or could have done. And it was a power that TV would never lose.

The 1960s

The 1960s were an era when TV explored all sort of possibilities in keeping with what **society** was doing. Not only were people losing faith in the Great American Dream as represented by the ***Leave It to Beaver*** world, but people who had never had a chance at that dream began to be heard.

In 1960 a new type of show came out—the single parent family show. The show was ***The Andy Griffith Show*** and it started two trends: families headed by single parents (all of whom were widows or widowers as divorce was still a forbidden subject on TV), and the rural comedy.

The Andy Griffith Show played off the stereotype of the innocence of country life —that rural life was cleaner, free of the ills of the urban life with its crime, rudeness and impersonality, and that small town values were the best values. And ***The Andy Griffith Show*** supported this stereotype. Its main character was Andy Taylor, a small town sheriff in Mayberry, North Carolina, who didn't carry a gun and only allowed his deputy Barney Fife to have one bullet, which he had to carry in his pocket, not in his gun. Andy is friendly, easygoing, knows everybody, and teaches his young son Opie life lessons with gentle firmness.

However, Andy won't put up with any guff from big city, big shot types. In fact, the show was a spin-off of ***The Danny Thomas Show***. In an episode of ***The Danny Thomas Show***, Andy caught Thomas speeding. When Thomas not only refused to pay a ten dollar fine but tried to bribe this hick-town sheriff, Andy tossed Thomas in jail—but he didn't lock the cell, and his Aunt Bea treated Thomas to fine home cooking and friendly treatment. Thomas realized that he had been a jerk, paid his fine and went on his way, resolving to mend his ways. This episode was so popular that ***The Andy Griffith Show*** started its run the next year.

The show often explored the changes that were appearing in American society. One of those changes was the rise of women in the public sphere as they shook off the paternalistic attitudes that were so prevalent in America up through the 1950s. In one episode, Ellie, Andy's girlfriend, wanted to run for city council. However, Mayberry's men, including Andy, didn't think a woman belonged there, and said so. The women, in retaliation for this disrespect for women, went on strike, refusing to cook or clean for the men. The men refused to bow to this pressure, declaring they could take care of themselves (although indigestion ran rampant as the men tried to cook for themselves). When, after all the pressure and contempt she experienced in her campaign, Ellie dropped out of the race for council, Opie said, "We won, we beat them females. We kept them in their place. Us men folk don't want women running our town, do we, Pa." Andy is stunned hearing these chauvinistic comments coming out of his young son's mouth, and he realizes the Opie is only repeating what he's heard from the men in town, including himself. It's not the sort of thing he wants Opie to learn and believe. Andy then went to a rally supporting Ellie and made a speech in which he said he was ashamed of himself when he heard Opie parrot his own anti-woman prejudice. He stated that the only reason the men could think of to oppose Ellie was that she's a woman, and that if Ellie wanted to run for office, she had a right to. Sheriff Andy carried a lot of weight, so if he thinks, although grudgingly, that it's all right for a woman to run for office, the rest of the town went along. Ellie continued her run, and the battle of the sexes was over. It was a big deal in the early 1960s for a popular sitcom to present a message in patriarchal America that women had the same rights as men, especially a decade before the beginnings of women's liberation.

This new type of comedy illustrated the clash between the innocence and genuineness of rural life and what many people in American society were starting to see as the ills of urban life—that the ***Leave It to Beaver*** life wasn't what most people were actually experiencing. Two years later, one of the most popular shows in TV history came on the air, and it revolved around this clash—***The Beverly Hillbillies***. This show took the innocent folk from the country and put them in the big city, where they immediately showed up all the backbiting, money-grubbing hypocrisy of big city people.

Two other shows quickly followed that did the same thing: *Petticoat Junction* and *Green Acres*. The latter was sort of a reverse *Hillbillies*. Two big-city types tried to survive in the country, and of course they are pretty much failures at it because the artificiality of the urban life doesn't work when up against "real" life.

However, in 1970, all of these rural comedies were cancelled, despite how well they were doing in the ratings. It came down not to the **number** of people in the audience, but the **kind** of people in the audience. These shows attracted an older demographic, those forty-five years of age and older, and that wasn't the kind of audience the sponsors wanted. That audience was considered too old and too set in their ways to be affected by the commercials. So, out those shows went.

Throughout the '60s and '70s many social change movements took place, such as the civil rights movement, the anti-Vietnam War movement, and the formation of the National Organization for Women. These movements all affected the values of many Americans. Their emphasis on the questioning of social institutions such as government, business and higher education played a part in a new sense of individualism.

Some would argue that these movements and sense of individualism also gave way to a change in the family structure from a hierarchical one controlled by the male head of the household to our current one in which all family members are segmented and decisions flow in all directions. Slowly, more diverse family structures were represented on TV as a reflection of the changing family structure.

In 1964, actual magic started to appear in shows like *Bewitched*. It was the story of a mortal man, Darrin, who falls in love with and marries a witch, Samantha. The series premier illustrates social norms of the period. When Samantha revealed to Darrin that she is a witch, he sought the advice of others, such as a best friend, a doctor and even a bartender, none of whom took him seriously. Finally, he returned home, thinking, "*So my wife's a witch. Every married man has to make some adjustments.*" That adjustment is what's illustrative of the period—it's not Darrin's, but Samantha's, because Darrin insisted that, if they're going to get married, she must stop using magic. In other words, for the sake of the marriage, she must give up a major part of who she is, but as far as we can tell, Darrin doesn't give up a thing.

At the same time, Samantha took a "wifely" interest in Darrin's job as an advertising executive. Whenever Darrin got in a jam, which was often, Samantha got him out of it through her imagination and intuition—and her occasional use of magic. She frequently saved Darrin's job with a twitch of her nose by producing sales concepts on the spot for his clients, or sometimes practicing witchcraft on his clients, like turning them into animals, to prove a point or to buy him time to finish something. As she saved his bacon again and again, she didn't neglect shoring up Darrin's ego and making him feel that it was *his* ideas that saved the day. In this way, *Bewitched* illustrated the social conflicts of the 1960s as society fought over which social story should prevail—the old rules of the family structure with the husband as benevolent dictator and wife as dutiful subordinate, or the new ones that opened up a place for women in the public and private spheres. Society was questioning the old social truths and looking for answers: What is the appropriate woman's role, as equal or subordinate to the man? How should a woman exercise her own agency to the best of her abilities? What do we do with female power? Toward the end of the run of *Bewitched* in the early 1970s, Samantha often took on a role of her own, not just as a helpful appendage to her husband, but by traveling through space and time or meeting historical figures and helping to solve problems, somewhat displacing the centrality of the home and middle class suburban life.

When Darrin said, "So my wife's a witch. Every married man has to make some adjustments," it was actually rather prescient because Samantha, not Darrin, had to make the adjustment. As the 1960s moved into the 1970s, husbands would have to adjust to the increase in women's equality in all spheres of society and the changing social and cultural significance of domestic institutions.

Another example of the changing face of the American family was *I Dream of Jeannie*. Air Force Captain Tony Nelson thought he was the master—certainly Jeannie called him that—but he wasn't. Jeannie herself was in charge, using her magic to get whatever she wanted, which almost invariably wasn't what Nelson wanted, and it caused one problem after another. But in the end, as Nelson was completely trapped in the problem, Jeannie would cross her arms, nod her head and provide the solution. Toward the end of the show's run, women's groups attacked the show as sexist because Jeannie was apparently a "slave" to her "master" Nelson. But those were only the words, not the actuality—Jeannie was the master to Nelson as **her** slave.

There was also an attempt at intelligent comedy with *The Dick van Dyke Show*. Departing from the wackiness of *I Love Lucy* or the warm and runny sentimentality of *Father Knows Best*, *The Dick van Dyke Show* had a loving couple, Rob and Laura Petrie, who had real-life problems that many couples of the period were dealing with. These included whether the wife should work outside the home, or what to do if she opened his mail, or what happened if the wife showed up the husband in a confrontation with a drunk.

In the latter episode, Rob and Laura were in a bar awaiting a table in the restaurant when a drunk harassed Laura. Rob played Galahad and tried to drive off the drunk, and got punched for his efforts. When the drunk turned to Laura, she flattened him with a judo throw and was surrounded by admirers. The next day, Rob got razzed after everyone read a newspaper column recounting the exploits of "the adorable Amazon." One person told him that since the drunk beat him up, and Laura beat up the drunk, that meant Laura could beat up Rob. By the time Rob got home, he had become fed up with the razzing and the praise for Laura. He was proud that she could take care of herself, but his ego had taken a beating. When he saw her wearing slacks, he even said to her, "Why don't you ever dress like a girl?" Insisting that she couldn't beat him up and that he was still man of the house, he pushed her into a fight in which she flattened him with a judo flip.

The next day he asked a friend to teach him some judo moves, turning down the man's offer to "rough her up." That night he insisted he be allowed to show Laura what he'd learned. When she refused to play his game, Rob brought out a giant stuffed monkey—and ended up flattened as he flipped himself to the floor.

This episode illustrates how society was changing in the 1960s. Trying to maintain the old social positions of men and women, of the husband as the man of the house and the gallant defender, and the wife as "the helpless little woman," was disappearing from the social story. The fact that the retelling of the story was a comedy allowed the show to demonstrate how silly such thinking as Rob's can be.

Oh, and you know that reference to "why don't you dress like a girl?" Laura is wearing slacks. So what, you might ask. Well, the mores of the time said women didn't wear pants, and CBS wanted Laura to be just like all the other wives and mothers on TV, modeling themselves after June Cleaver, wearing cocktail dresses and pearls to do housework.

Mary Tyler Moore, who played Laura, rebelled against this. She made CBS write into her contract that Laura could wear pants—in one scene per episode. Sales of Capri pants sky-rocketed as women all over the country saw it was alright to wear pants. Way to go, Mary.

Another great example of the effect *The Dick van Dyke Show* could have is the episode "That's My Boy?" Rob convinced himself that the baby he and Laura just brought back from the hospital wasn't theirs, that their and the Peters' couple's baby were switched. Worked up into a lather, Rob finally called the Peters and asked them over to swap their babies back. When the Peters arrived, they turned out to be black; clearly, the babies weren't swapped. This was one of the biggest laughs TV comedy ever got, so big they had to edit out a chunk of the studio audience's reaction because it went so long. This unspoken acceptance of a black couple as just people, requiring no discussion or explanation, helped push civil rights.

Another show that could be assumed to have shown changes in society was **Julia**. It was broadcast on NBC in 1968 and was the first sitcom to have an African American in a starring role since *Amos 'n' Andy*. Diahann Carroll played Julia, a widowed nurse raising her young son Corey in a multi-racial apartment complex. The show was somewhat successful, lasting three years on NBC.

Despite breaking the color barrier, the show was very controversial and had both black and white critics. Some people thought the depiction of black life was not accurate because so many black people were living in ghettoes and projects while the character Julia Baker was living in a luxury integrated apartment building. Other critics viewed Julia as a sellout because she did not address any of the racial issues of the time.

Julia's producers were very sensitive about the race issue and did not want to depict blacks in a stereotypical way. It was tough for them to do this, because there were few depictions of blacks in television sitcoms that were not racist; the Dick van Dyke episode was one of those rare exceptions. In one of the scripts, the mother of one of Corey's friends was changed from a black woman living in a slum to an upper class black woman preoccupied with money who has no time for her daughter.

Viewers had different reactions depending on their own race. White viewers felt the show was non-threatening, unlike images they had seen in the news about race riots and crime. They also may have watched it to feel good about themselves, sort of a "see how enlightened and non-racist I am—I watch a show with a black lead character."

Many black viewers, however, were unhappy with the show and saw the depiction of Julia as unrealistic because they did not know anyone like her. It seemed, for some, to be a white woman with white problems in blackface.

Overall, *Julia* was an impressive effort to address the issue of putting a positive depiction of blacks on TV, but since there was nothing to compare it to, many people took different meanings from the show. From the different reactions,we can see the different attitudes about race that were present during the Sixties.

The next year Bill Cosby became the first black **man** to be the lead in a comedy series, playing a high school gym teacher.

An interesting thing to note was the disparity between what people saw every night on the news versus during prime-time entertainment in the Sixties. The news was filled with images of war and civil disturbance and protests, while the shows included things like *Camp Runamuck*, *The Flying Nun*, and *Gilligan's Island*. There was even what I consider one of the stupidest shows ever—*My Mother the Car*—in which a man's mother is reincarnated as a 1929 Porter hupmobile and begins to run his life.

It was as if television had a split personality. On one side, the news was showing how society was fighting over just what it wanted and wanted to be, but television entertainment wanted to deny that there were any changes happening. TV networks made their money by selling audience eyes to sponsors, and sponsors didn't want that audience upset—it would interfere with the commercials and sales. So the networks avoided programming that might be controversial, perceived by some as telling the wrong social story, or that would initiate intelligent conversation.

This is the sort of thing Newton Minnow, Chair of the Federal Communication Commission, was talking about when he said to the National Association of Broadcasters: "When television is good, nothing—not the theater, not the magazines or newspapers—nothing is better. But when television is bad, nothing is worse. I invite you to sit down in front of your television set when your station goes on the air and stay there, for a day, without a book, without a magazine, without a newspaper, without a profit and loss sheet or rating book to distract you. Keep your eyes glued to that set until the station signs off. I can assure you that you will observe a vast wasteland." (americanrhetoric.com)

The 1970s

If we thought the 1960s were turbulent, you should have seen the '70s. Not only were war protests growing, but so was the generation gap, as baby boomers, people born after World War II, fought with the Great Depression generation over the direction society should take, what the social rules should be, how the social story should be told. There were those who thought problems were small and easy to solve. There were those who thought the nuclear family should rule, with the father as head of the family, the mother as his stay at home helper to take care of the kids and have dinner on the table, and the kids as polite little urchins, the boys made of snips and snails and puppy dog tails, and the girls made of sugar and spice and everything nice.

However, the wife and kids didn't always agree with this worldview. At the end of World War II, many of those women who had gone to work to free men to fight decided that they liked to work and have financial freedom. This really came to a head in the late 1960s with rebellion against the constraints that the social story put on women in the 1950s.

Television began to reflect this dawning reality. One show that did so was ***The Mary Tyler Moore Show***. It gave every appearance of being just another situation comedy, no better and no worse than any that had gone before. However, it introduced two new concepts to television comedy that had previously not existed. The first was that a woman could reach the age of thirty and not be married and still be happy, and even more importantly, not be celibate. Mary Richards was the first truly liberated woman on television, living her own life on her own terms as she wished. There were network misgivings, of course. For example, the producers wanted her to be a divorcee, but the network, still believing in the past view that divorce was something to be ashamed of and worried that the audience also believed that, didn't like the idea of having a divorced woman as the heroine of a show. In the premiere episode, therefore, Mary moved to Minneapolis because her boyfriend had broken up with her.

The second new concept introduced to TV was the idea that disassociated adults could form a relationship with each other that strongly resembled a nuclear family: Mary, Lou, Murray, Rhoda and Ted were not just coworkers, they were a family.

Mary also contended with many of the issues women were facing in the 1970s. In one episode Mary discovered that a man with the same job as hers was paid more. She asked her boss, Lou, why. His reply was that the man had a family and needed more money. Mary accepted this answer—for a moment. She then asked why another man with a lesser job than hers, received more than her even though he was single. Lou's only response was, he's a man. This was, and to a large extent still is, a problem that women have faced in the workplace—making less money for doing the same job. Bringing this issue up in the early 1970s on a popular sitcom and satirizing the idea that the only reason for paying women less than men is the fact that women aren't men would have caused people to think about that issue.

Then, in 1971, there appeared on the scene two phenomena the like of which had not been seen before. One was *All in the Family*. The other was its creator, Norman Lear. Lear felt that television comedy should be not only funny, but provocative and stimulating. After his first show, *All in the Family*, Lear went on to be a very successful creator/producer of new comedy shows, including *Maude*, a liberal counterpart to the archconservative Archie Bunker; *The Jeffersons*, about an upper-class black family; and *All's Fair*, a show in which an archconservative and a liberal fall in love and, of course, argue from their differing socio-political angles.

The violation of human taboos often provokes the greatest laughter. In American society the greatest taboos are discussions of sex, biological functions such as the elimination of body wastes, and death. These are all subjects that society has decreed should be discussed seriously, discreetly and euphemistically, if discussed at all. When these subjects are **not** treated seriously, they produce embarrassed, titillated, or delighted laughter, or any combination of the three. *All in the Family* often used these taboo subjects as comic fodder, including a frequent use of the sound effect of a toilet flushing followed by Archie coming downstairs. For the first time, TV blatantly showed that people go to the bathroom.

However, *All in the Family* went far beyond bathroom humor. For the first time in any situation comedy, it regularly used such subjects as racism, sexism, and religious bigotry as the basis for plots.

I'd like to illustrate how things were changing in the 1970s. A sampling of plot synopses of sitcoms of the 1950s compared with shows of the 1970s illustrates the freedom that television was beginning to enjoy. For example:

Mr. Peepers (1953). Mr. Peepers decides to buy a new suit, and his mother and aunt decided to help him make the selection; *Hot l Baltimore* (1975). Ainsley, the timid mamma's boy, is romancing one woman while another threatens to name him in a paternity suit;

The Life of Riley (1954). Chester and Gillis decide to swap houses. *Maude* (1975). The Findlays spend a disconcerting evening with a swinging couple that think Maude and Walter would be the perfect couple for a **mate**-swapping game.

Mr. Peepers (1953). Mr. Peepers discovers one of his students can't afford a dissection set. *Welcome Back, Kotter* (1975). Gabe tries to find out which boy in his class is responsible for one of his female students' pregnancy.

Private Secretary (1954). Susie tries to get rid of a cold by testing remedies recommended by members of the office staff. *Good Times* (1976). J. J. panics when his girlfriend tells him that she has a venereal disease and that he is the culprit.

My Little Margie (1956). Margie's boyfriend uses a trick dog to retrieve his golf balls. ***One Day at a Time*** (1976). An entreaty by Julie's boyfriend throws her into a turmoil—he wants to spend the night with her.

It's obvious from the above examples that television moved more and more toward the use of societal taboos as subject matter for plots, and it used ideas rather than pat situations with pat solutions.

Lear's ***All in the Family*** was one of the first situation comedies to regularly violate cultural taboos. ***The Mary Tyler Moore Show*** had as its leading character a woman over thirty who was not married and yet had relationships with men that were more than platonic, an impossibility prior to 1970. Nevertheless, it was ***All in the Family*** that discussed as a regular part of the show racial bigotry, political ideologies (both extreme right and extreme left), sex, death, and societal dysfunctions that had previously been banned from the public airwaves.

What ***All in the Family*** did was present the two extreme positions that could be taken on a social or political issue and then put the arguments for the extremes into words. Archie represented the reactionary, arch-conservative view, and his son-in-law, Mike "meathead" Stivik, represented the ultra-liberal view. Neither of these characters was really likeable, and neither of their extreme views really reflected reality in American society. However, their arguments put many people's feelings about the issues into words. Remember that you don't think in feelings—you think in words. By the show putting feelings into words, the audience could think about the issues and arrive at their own conclusions about them somewhere in between the two extremes represented by Archie and Mike.

A sampling of ***All in the Family*** episodes includes the following: one in which Edith allows a woman whom she is to care for do what she wants to do—die; Edith rejects God after a street gang kills one of her friends, a female impersonator; Archie is upset about the death of a friend's roommate until he finds out that the two women were lesbians; Edith must contend with the problems of sexual assault and its aftermath when she's almost raped; and Archie becomes upset when his niece, who is white, goes out on a date with the boy next door, who is black. Such violations of societal taboos are fertile grounds for comedy, and remember that the first rule of comedy is that it's intellectual. The comedy and the thinking involved really worked for ***All in the Family***, which remained on the air for twelve years.

All in the Family really changed things on the television landscape. No network wanted the show because the bean counters didn't believe the audience would accept a situation comedy that required thought and consideration, and that brought up and discussed social issues. They thought all the audience wanted was mindless entertainment of the ***Gilligan's Island*** ilk. CBS finally decided to use the show as a mid-season replacement just to fill a half hour hole in their schedule, fully expecting to drop the show and put on a new one when the fall season started. It came as quite a shock when the show not only attracted and held an audience, but it became one of the biggest hits in television history, holding the number one spot in the Neilson season ratings for five years in a row, a record never broken.

The show still upset a lot of people, especially those who didn't want the social story to admit that the problems the show dissected week after week actually existed in American society, or to have their beliefs held up to ridicule. But the show clearly demonstrated that large portions of the society believed that it needed to explore its increasingly changing rules, not just passively accept the old and increasingly outmoded ideas.

In 1972, one of the most popular and important situation comedies ever premiered: *M*A*S*H*. Its popularity is obvious from its ratings. It was never below fifteenth, and often it was in the top five during the entire ten years it was on the air. In fact, its final episode still ranks as the most watched TV show in terms of share (the number of sets turned on and tuned to a specific channel) in history. Its importance stems from the fact that it was the first situation comedy that didn't feel that laugh-a-minute scripts was an inflexible rule. It dealt with subjects such as war, death and misery, not only in a humorous fashion, but with a sense of serious examination and compassion. Its primary consideration was not necessarily to get laughs but to be human, which often means being funny. The characters were characters, not caricatures, as is often the case in sitcoms, and they reacted to situations with honest intellect and emotion.

The show really pointed up the disparity between people's differing ideas of the way society should view the world. *M*A*S*H* was clearly anti-war—there was no sense of glory or honor, just a lot of blood and pain and nobody knowing what they were fighting for or what they hoped to gain. This was very much the sentiment of a large part of American society during the Vietnam War, especially among young people. But another part of American society, especially those who had gone through World War II, felt the show was not only not funny, but insulting to the military and those who fought against what they perceived as evil.

I speak from personal experience: I loved *M*A*S*H*. I thought it was funny and touching at the same time. Of course, I was up for the draft at the height of the Vietnam War and just barely avoided going. My father, on the other hand, hated *M*A*S*H*. He was an Air Force squadron commander during World War II. He said there's nothing funny about war. He and I had completely different ideas of what society should believe about Vietnam. And our differences were the same as those that existed throughout American society.

Then came Watergate, the scandal that brought down President Nixon, and society has never been the same since. Woodward and Bernstein, reporters for *The Washington Post,* did the investigative reporting, and they blew the whole thing wide open. However, it was television that really brought the scandal home to the national public and influenced people.

Walter Cronkite, anchor for *CBS Evening News* and often called the most trusted man in America, played a key role in the unraveling of Watergate. Cronkite broadcast two extensive stories on *CBS Evening News* on Watergate in 1972. Ben Bradlee, *The Washington Post* editor at the time of Watergate, said that a lot of "Washington people, people who followed national stories—a lot of them who had not decided that we were right changed their minds because of Walter."

This is part of Bradlee's comments in *Newsweek*: "In October 1972, Cronkite devoted two segments, back to back, to the Watergate story. The first was 14 minutes, the second eight. I think that second night was curtailed by CBS chairman William S. Paley because Paley was scared of it. The fact that Cronkite did Watergate at all (let alone at that length) gave the story a kind of blessing, which is exactly what we needed—and exactly what *The Washington Post* lacked. It was a political year, and everyone was saying, 'Well, it's just politics, and here's the *Post* trying to screw Nixon.' We were the second-biggest newspaper in the country trying to scramble for a good story—whereas Cronkite was the reigning dean of television journalists. When he did the Watergate story, everyone said, 'My God, Cronkite's with them.'" (*Newsweek*) For most of America, Walter Cronkite's reputation for integrity and probity meant that if he said something was accurate, it must be true, and his in-depth reporting on the *Post* investigation of the Watergate break-in implied he supported not only the investigation, but the conclusions derived from it. In addition, Cronkite's national television audience brought what was essentially a local newspaper story to the entire country.

What Watergate did was pretty much destroy people's confidence in government—or at least in politicians. The American social story once again changed. Prior to Watergate, people trusted their politicians to act in the best interests of the country and its citizens. They trusted that when problems arose politicians would work and eventually come together to solve them. Suddenly there was a sense that politicians worked only in their own interests, not in those of the country, and that they would come up with solutions to problems that were aimed less at actually solving those problems than at getting reelected. That distrust of the motivations of politicians is still in play today.

With this sudden lack of a foundation to society—if we can't trust our government, who can we trust?—the old rules seemed to be slipping away, and society really starting searching for new rules. Television went along.

There were attempts to regain the past, a return to a simpler time when social values were more clear-cut, like **The Waltons**, set in the Depression era in rural Virginia. This show about a big family using love and connection with each other to stave off the difficulties of life was a hit, especially with older audiences. However, such an approach was becoming less and less popular as society really started searching for a new direction.

One new direction came out of the sexual revolution of the late '60s and early '70s, as it started showing up on TV, despite the protests of the older generation. For example, in 1977 the first of the T&A ("tits and ass") comedies came on the air. Its title was **Three's Company**. A T&A sitcom is devoted to showing a number of young women with beautiful bodies wearing a minimum of clothing romping about the stage uttering sexual innuendos. **Three's Company** was a prime example of this type of show. Its basic premise was a trio of roommates, two attractive women and one attractive man. However, the apartment they're living in didn't allow co-ed roommates, so they tell the landlord the man is gay. The attempts to maintain this façade in the face of Jack being aggressively heterosexual led to much of the humor. Apparently it was what the public wanted because it rated #3 in 1977, and in the fall of 1978 it became the top-rated show on the air. Other permutations of the T&A formula included **We've Got It Made**, **Blanskie's Beauties**, **Roller Girls**, and **Co-ed Fever**.

This does not mean to say that only sex and T&A were the subjects of situation comedy. There were several shows on the air that had social consciousness as their themes. **Barney Miller** was a police comedy-drama show in the tradition of **M*A*S*H** that illustrated the interaction of people and the police, particularly as it applied to lower- and middle-class Americans, both criminals and victims of crime. Many young people distrusted the police, but **Barney Miller** tried to show that the police have many problems of their own—that they're doing their best, but things can go wrong on all sides.

One Day at a Time was about a young divorced woman coping with the problems and follies of her two teenage daughters. This show reflected a reality that wasn't even acknowledged only twenty years earlier—that people got divorced, that marriage wasn't always for life, and that families were being headed by single mothers, not because their partners had died, but because their **marriage** had. Remember that only four years earlier, before Watergate, Mary Richards on the **Mary Tyler Moore Show** couldn't be divorced but had to have been dumped by her boyfriend—the network felt the audience wouldn't accept divorce. In addition, the two teenage girls faced problems that TV shows of the

1950s and 1960s didn't admit existed in society, problems like popularity, sex and drugs. This more accurately portrayed the realities faced by families.

This isn't to say that the networks overthrew all the old rules. In the fall of 1978, the networks made an attempt to return to the social rules of the early 1950s with such shows as **Apple Pie**, **Who's Watching the Kids**, and **The Waverly Wonders**. However, the viewing public rejected the idea. All three shows were canceled within weeks. Viewers obviously preferred something with some content to it, either intellectually, to give them something to think about, physically, to give them something to watch, or socially, to reflect the newly emerging social story.

The 1980s

Apparently, people weren't finding very much to laugh at in the 1980s. Certainly, sitcoms were having a very hard time. The networks watched the Neilson ratings very closely, and if a show didn't immediately show favorable results it was dropped within days. For example, during the 1979–80 season, eighteen of the thirty new sitcoms introduced were canceled within weeks, **A New Kind of Family** lasted only six. Seven other sitcoms left the air that season as well. Sixteen of the nineteen new sitcoms in 1980–81 were canceled. Twelve of the fifteen new sitcoms were canceled in 1981–82, along with nine from previous seasons. Fourteen out of nineteen new sitcoms were canceled in 1982–83, and seventeen out of nineteen in 1983–84.

Many people in 1984 were saying it was the end of the situation comedy on television, that the audience no longer wanted that form of program, but were looking for something else, such as **Magnum, P.I.**, a detective drama; **Buck Rogers in the 25th Century**, a space drama; **Hill Street Blues**, a cop drama; and **Dallas**, the first prime-time drama with plots that didn't wrap up in one episode but continued over many episodes.

The networks seemed to listen, because for the 1985–86 season there were only nineteen sitcoms on the air, the lowest number since the late 1950s and the battle with the western. There was, however, something on the air, a time bomb from the 1984–85 season: NBC's Thursday night lineup, led off by a quiet domestic comedy, **The Cosby Show**.

What was it about **The Cosby Show** that caused such a turnaround in the fortunes of the situation comedy? **The Cosby Show** was noted for its lack of pretension and gimmickry. It revolved around the day-to-day situations faced by Cliff and Clair Huxtable and their five children. This family was unlike other black families previously seen on television in that it was solidly upper-middle-class. The Huxtables lived in a fashionable Flatbush brownstone, the father was a respected gynecologist, and the mother a successful attorney. Theo, the only son, was something of an underachiever who enjoyed a special relationship with his father. The oldest daughter, Sondra, was a college student at Princeton University. The next daughter in age, Denise, constantly tried her parents' patience with her unconventional preoccupations, from being bohemian to New Age. After the third season, she left the series to attend the fictitious, historically black Hillman College in her own series, **A Different World**. The two younger daughters, Rudy and Vanessa, were uber-cute preteens who acted as foils to Cosby's hilarious childrearing routines. The Huxtable kids steered clear of trouble as they grew up over the series' eight-year run, kept safe from much of the realities of world by loving, protective parents and money. Indeed, *TV Guide* compared the Huxtables' lifestyle to that of other black families in America and described the family as the most "atypical black family in television history."

For many observers, ***The Cosby Show*** was unique in other ways as well. For example, unlike many situation comedies, the program avoided one-liners, slapstick shtick, dumb antics and the other normal ways sitcoms tried to get laughs. Instead, series writers remained true to Cosby's vision of finding humor in realistic family situations, in the little things of human behavior.

In many respects, ***The Cosby Show*** and its "classy" aura were designed to address a long history of negative black portrayals on television. Alvin Poussaint, a prominent black psychiatrist, was hired by the producers as a consultant to help "recode blackness" in the minds of audience members. In contrast to the families in other popular black situation comedies–for example, those in ***Sanford and Son***, ***Good Times***, and ***The Jeffersons***, all from the '70s—the Huxtables were given qualities that its creators thought would challenge common black stereotypes. These qualities included a strong father figure; a strong nuclear family; parents who were professionals; an affluent lifestyle and fiscal responsibility; a strong emphasis on education; a multigenerational family; multiracial friends; and low-key racial pride.

Of course, ***The Cosby Show*** had its critics, just like ***Julia*** had sixteen years earlier. Some observers described the show as a 1980s' version of ***Father Knows Best***, the Huxtables as a white family in blackface. The Huxtables' affluence, they argued, worked to obscure persistent inequalities in America—especially those faced by blacks and other minority groups—and validated the myth of the American Dream. One audience study suggested that the show "strikes a deal" with white viewers, that it absolves them of responsibility for racial inequality in the United States in exchange for inviting the Huxtables into their living room. Meanwhile, the same study found that black viewers tended to embrace the show for its positive portrayals of blackness, but they expressed misgivings about the Huxtables' failure to regularly interact with less well off blacks.

But to illustrate the importance many people placed on this show, we just have to look at an April evening in 1992 when America was being saturated with images of fires, and racial and economic turmoil from Los Angeles in response to the verdict in the Rodney King police brutality trial. Five white police officers had been acquitted of beating Rodney King, a black man, during a traffic stop because King was on PCP. Many black residents of Los Angeles took this as proof of racism in the LA police department and in society in general, and took to the streets. That night, many viewers outside of LA chose to tune in to the final episode of ***The Cosby Show***. However, in Los Angeles, at least, this viewing choice was almost not an option. KNBC-TV's news coverage of the rioting seemed certain to preempt the show, much as the news coverage of other networks' affiliates would preempt **their** regular prime-time programming that evening. But as Los Angeles Mayor Tom Bradley worked to restore order, he successfully lobbied KNBC-TV to broadcast the final episode as originally scheduled, perhaps hoping to show an alternative to the racial unrest running through the streets.

So despite complaints, audiences loved it, putting ***The Cosby Show*** at the top of the ratings almost every week, and putting the sitcom back on as a staple of the television schedule.

A different approach to the family was ***Roseanne***. Roseanne was almost the total opposite of June Cleaver from ***Leave it to Beaver***, and not much like Claire Huxtable from ***Cosby***, especially in handling the kids' problems.

The show was based on the stand-up comedy of the comedian Roseanne Barr-Arnold-Barr. Her character on the show is the opposite of June Cleaver. She is crass, loud, overbearing and overweight. Her husband Dan is an overweight construction worker, and they have three unruly kids. Through depiction of her struggles such as juggling her work and family responsibilities in the pilot, she contradicts the American Dream that is enshrined in the sitcoms of the 1950s. She constantly jokes about getting rid of her own kids because the constant attention they require gets in the way of her happiness. In one episode, she even has a dream sequence where she fantasizes about killing her whole family just so she can enjoy her bath.

Another way in which Roseanne violated the norm for the svelte sitcom wives of the past was by her sheer physical size and her sexuality. Usually overweight women are not depicted as sexual, indeed they are rarely depicted at all, but in many scenes in the series Roseanne is openly affectionate and sexually aggressive with her husband.

As a result of the feminist movement, many started to question traditional gender roles. The critic Janet Lee discussed Roseanne's impact as an inspiration for feminists. She believes that Roseanne "comes across as a woman who knows her own mind and has a strong sense of her power as a working class woman." Roseanne does this by violating cultural norms by being loud, brash, overweight and sexually aggressive, again changing the social story. At the time the show came out, this led to some mixed reactions about it. The feminist Katherine Rowe discussed this using the idea of the "unruly woman." She wrote that, "Through body and speech the unruly woman violates the unspoken feminine sanction against making a spectacle of herself." In other words, by being so "unruly" Roseanne gained power over people who try to control her, who try to make her fit the outmoded 1950s' model of women being quiet and submissive. According to Rowe, this is the reason she offended some critics. Well, some critics may have been offended, but audiences sure weren't—Roseanne was a top five-rated show for six years.

The show **Roseanne** retold the social story, recasting the character of wife and mother—instead of the husband and father—as the dominant force in the family. This started a new trend in television, especially in sitcoms, that of the husband and father as bumbling boob who could only survive with the help of a good woman. This trend was accelerated by the arrival of a new player on the network scene.

■ THE ARRIVAL OF FOX

In 1987, a new variable entered the television equation: a new network, Fox. In order to compete against the Big Three (ABC, CBS, NBC), Fox needed to be different. Seeing that the Big Three were basically conservative in their programming and were not showing programs that were too far out of the mainstream in order to avoid offending anyone in their audiences, Fox decided that being outrageous would be the way to get attention and gather an audience. They started showing programs that went against the norm. If **Cosby**, with its extremely functional family life was the norm for NBC, then it made sense for Fox to do the opposite—put on a family that was as dysfunctional as possible. Thus was born **Married . . . With Children**, the antithesis of **Cosby**. It was filled with sexual innuendo, familial hatred, problems with no solutions, incompetent parents and disrespectful children. Al Bundy was the father and husband in the family, an incompetent, harassed, chauvinistic women's shoe salesman—the perfect job for a man who hates women. His wife was Peggy, a lazy housewife who never cleaned and, when she did cook, she did so very poorly and dribbled cigarette ashes in the food—which, considering her culinary skills, could only have improved the flavor. Daughter Kelly, the sexpot, had an IQ as low as her hemlines were high. And son Bud, although intelligent—indeed the only intelligent person on the show—spent all his time from the age of 11 trying to lose his virginity.

In fact, sex was a major element of the show. Al's bedroom prowess, or lack thereof, was a frequent topic of conversation. The marriage was a disaster, as Al constantly bickered with Peggy about money, the kids' activities, and sex.

Naturally enough, **Married . . . With Children**, the anti-Cosby, generated complaints. Terry Rakolta, a homemaker from Michigan, started a national boycott campaign against Married…With Children's sponsors, clearly believing that the show violated the social story she thought should be the one America should live by, and that was definitely not the one shown in **Married . . . With Children**. Although some sponsors pulled their ads, and a few episodes were pulled as being **too** outrageous, her campaign generated so much publicity that, far from getting the show cancelled, she made the show a hit as millions of people tuned in to find out what she was complaining about, and many of those people liked what they saw.

Much the same thing happened when **The Simpsons** went on the air as a half hour show in 1989. This show continued and even heightened, the trend of the idiot incompetent father. Homer is a fat, lazy, ignorant slob who leaves disaster in his wake. His wife Marge stands by her man and rescues him from one crisis after another while trying to maintain the house and keep the family together. Lisa, the oldest child, is intelligent, talented and frequently embarrassed by being related to Homer. Bart, the second child, is a budding juvenile delinquent with an utter disrespect for authority. And Maggie, the baby, never says a word (well, that's not true—she did say her name once in one episode, voiced by Elizabeth Taylor).

There were lots of complaints about **The Simpsons**, especially about Bart and his disrespectful behavior and how it was such a poor model for kids, but once again, just like with **Married . . . With Children**, people watched to see what all the complaints were about and loved the show. In fact, the show is so popular that it has now surpassed **Gunsmoke** as the longest running prime-time entertainment show with continuing characters in history. And if things continue, it'll probably become the longest-running entertainment show in history, surpassing **The Ed Sullivan Show**.

Despite its family sitcom format, **The Simpsons** draws its animated inspiration more from Bullwinkle J. Moose of the cult cartoon shows **Rocky the Flying Squirrel** and **The Bullwinkle Show** than Fred Flintstone. Like **The Bullwinkle Show**, two of the most striking characteristics of **The Simpsons** are its social criticism and its references to other cultural forms such as TV shows, movies and authors. John O'Connor, television critic for *The New York Times*, has labeled the program "the most radical show on prime time." Indeed, **The Simpsons** often parodies the hypocrisy and contradictions found in social institutions such as the nuclear family (and nuclear power), the mass media, religion and medicine. Homer tells Lisa that it's acceptable to steal things "from people you don't like." Reverend Lovejoy lies to Lisa about the contents of the Bible to win an argument. Krusty the Clown, the kids' show host, endorses dangerous products to make a quick buck. Homer comforts Marge about upcoming surgery with the observation that "America's health care system is second only to Japan's . . . Canada's . . . Sweden's . . . Great Britain's . . . well, all of Europe."

The show, much like **Married . . . With Children**, has been controversial at times. Many elementary schools banned Bart Simpson T-shirts, especially those with the slogan, "Underachiever, and Proud of It." President George H. W. Bush and former Secretary of

Education William Bennett publicly criticized the program for its subversive and anti-authority nature.

In addition to its ironic satires, it is also one of the most culturally literate entertainment shows on prime time. There are references to such cultural icons as ***American Idol***, ***Nightmare on Elm Street***, Susan Sontag, and the movie ***Psycho*** in any given episode. Itchy and Scratchy are Tom and Jerry—with chainsaws. These allusions to other media extend far beyond just talking about them. Because the show is a cartoon, ***The Simpsons*** can go anywhere and any time and do anything. Just think of the annual "Treehouse of Horror" episodes. On occasion, ***The Simpsons*** has reproduced the actual camera movements of the films it models. For example, in one episode Maggie, under the influence of the violent Itchy and Scratchy cartoons, hits Homer in the head with a hammer. As Homer goes down, the scene is straight out of the shower scene from Alfred Hitchcock's movie ***Psycho***, camera shots, music and all. A cartoon able to show what's going on in the characters' heads, such as memories and dreams, has produced some of the program's most hilarious moments, such as Homer's conversations with God. For example, in one episode Homer decided to not go to church but to watch football instead. God sat next to him on the sofa, although we could only see him from the waist down, and wished He could watch football on Sunday, but He had to work.

The unique nature of ***The Simpsons*** reveals much about the nature of the television industry. Specifically, the fact that the show exists at all illustrates the relationship of television's bean counting ratings-are-everything attitude to its degree of innovation in content. It was a program that came along at the right place and the right time, and it appealed to the right demographic groups. Matt Groening, the creator, said that no other network besides FOX would have aired ***The Simpsons***, and in fact that conventional television producers had previously turned down his ideas. However, the degree of competition in network television in the late 1980s helped to open the door. Network television found itself with increased competition from cable television and VCRs. The FOX network, specifically, was in an even shakier economic position than the Big Three. Because FOX was the new, unestablished network that was attempting to build audiences and attract advertisers, the normally restrictive nature of network television's desire to avoid upsetting its audience may have become loosened to allow the program on the air. In addition, the championing of ***The Simpsons*** by James L. Brooks, an established producer with a strong track record, helped the show through the bean counting television filters that might have watered down the program's social criticism. Finally, the fact that the show appeals to young audiences, the one advertisers particularly want to appeal to, also explains the network's willingness to air such an unconventional and risky program. The "tween" demographic, those between twelve and seventeen, is an especially key viewing group for ***The Simpsons***, as well as a primary consumer group targeted by advertisers.

The Simpsons was a watershed program in the establishment of the FOX network. It's been the Fox program most consistently praised by television critics. It was the first Fox program to reach the Top 10 in ratings, despite the network's smaller number of affiliates compared to the Big Three. Fox moved ***The Simpsons*** to Thursday night in 1990 to go head to head against the number one program at the time, ***The Cosby Show***. Eventually, ***The Simpsons*** beat this powerful competitor in key male demographic groups. The schedule change, and the subsequent success, signaled FOX's staying power to the rest of the industry, and for viewers it was a powerful illustration of the innovative nature of FOX programming when compared to what they got from the other networks.

The Advent of Cable

Did you notice something I wrote that drove Fox to offer ***Married . . . With Children*** and ***The Simpsons***? What kept the other networks away from such creative and innovative programming was the rise of cable and VCRs and the competition they offered. The networks felt they had to play it safe, not take any chances.

Although John Walson invented cable TV in 1948, the FCC restricted it to bringing television programs to households that couldn't receive over-the-air broadcast signals. This was to prevent competition for local stations, a regulation that stayed in place until 1972. HBO started in that year, and it was the first TV network to use satellite delivery to cable companies. In 1981, MTV started up. However, it wasn't until the Cable Act of 1984 that cable really became a viable option for a new network.

Fox's problem was that, to broadcast over the air, it needed an affiliate station in the area. Affiliates are television stations that sign an agreement with a network to carry network programming. However, most stations were already affiliated with the big three networks. So Fox's only option was to sign up independent stations, those not already affiliated, but there weren't many of those. However, with cable, a station could be hundreds of miles away—much too far for broadcasting, but not a problem for cable. I remember the first Fox station for Pullman, Washington, where my university is situated—that station was physically in Seattle, Washington.

What cable did was fragment the audience. When there were only three networks, choice was really limited. If someone wanted to watch TV, it often came down to the LOP—the least objectionable program. But with cable, if a viewer doesn't like what's on the big three, rhe can switch to MTV—or WTBS—or A&E—or TLC—or CNN or the Comedy Channel or the Sci-Fi Channel or any of a multitude of others. By 1998 there were 171 networks—4 broadcast and 167 cable, all competing for audience.

With all the possibilities open to the audience, television could no longer play it safe. Each network had to concentrate on a different audience. It began niche marketing, in much the same way that magazines did when television arrived.

What's important is what makes one audience different from another: the social story they live. For example, the WB network concentrated on attracting a black audience, an audience whose concept of American society was quite different from that of the mainstream white audience. Shows like Sister, Sister used the black experience of living in America as the basis not only of plots, but of interactions between the characters. TechTV went for the nerd crowd, all computers all the time, the answer to ESPN. Did I mention ESPN?

So, what happened to the social story as shared by all Americans? There wasn't one. I mean that. There wasn't **one**. For decades most of society followed the same story—except, of course, for those who weren't really let in on it, like blacks, and Asians, and Indians, and gays, and . . . well, you get the idea. But now each group could have something in the dominant media force that reflected their story.

There was some crossover. A major example of that was ***Will and Grace*** on NBC.

Will and Grace was a groundbreaking sitcom from the late 1990s, a period when gay rights moved into the forefront of the national media. The show depicted the relationship between a gay man, Will, and a straight woman, Grace, as well as the friendship between them and Will's gay friend, Jack, and Grace's assistant, Karen. In much of the humor, the butt of many of the jokes was the sexuality of Will and his friend Jack.

There were complaints about the show, that it was "mainstreaming" homosexuality. However, there weren't that many complaints. Most people who saw the show simply saw people. It must be granted that, although Grace had boyfriends, generally speaking Will did not. The fact that Will was gay wasn't shoved in anybody's face. And Jack was so flamboyantly, stereotypically gay that he almost satirized rather than represented the stereotype.

In fact, there were complaints from the gay community about Jack, that he was perpetuating the "flaming gay" man, but he was so over the top that few people could take his performance as a serious reflection of reality.

Now, it's possible that a show like **Will and Grace** can perhaps promote stereotypes and homophobia, but then again any representation on a national show is just as likely to alter that old element of the social story, homophobia, by promoting equality and the recognition of gay people as human beings and homosexuality as an acceptable lifestyle choice.

Then there's that real deviation from the 1950s' story, **Sex and the City**. **Sex and the City** ran on HBO for six seasons. It depicted the lives of four educated women in New York City and their struggles with men. The main feature of this show that deviated from the social story of the past was the frank discussion of many topics concerning sexuality that were, and for some people still are, considered taboo. For many people over fifty years old, women aren't supposed to talk about sex as if they were men.

Mostly, the series focused on friendship between single urban women and the deviance of being single and over thirty. The bond between the women on **Sex and the City** is so strong it's almost like a family.

The show is also reflective of our time in which many women have become highly successful and are able to have fulfilling lives as single women. In his article, "Does Sex and the City Predict the Future of Marriage?" Roderick Duncan refers to the series in how it reflects the growing reality for many college-educated women. He analyzed the statistics of male and female college graduates and noticed that women tend to marry men who have the same college education or greater. However, overall there are more women than men who are graduating from college and consequently less of a dating pool.

The episode, "A Woman's Right to Shoes," touches on this trend and the discrimination in society towards women who are not married. Carrie attends a party at her friend's house who is married with kids and has to take off her expensive Manolo Blahnik shoes. During the party, somebody takes her shoes. Later, she goes back to see if her shoes turned up, and the party host refuses to pay for her expensive shoes, putting her down for her extravagant single lifestyle. Carrie is offended by this attack on her single status, and she later complains that she has spent a large amount of money on gifts to celebrate her friends' marriage, so why shouldn't her friend compensate her for her $400 shoes? Carrie solves this problem by telling her friend that she is getting married and registering for the same shoes at Manolo Blahnik.

Certainly Samantha violated the rules by approaching sex as though she were a stereotypical man: that is, she wanted sex whenever and with whomever she desired just because she enjoyed it, and she wanted no strings attached. In previous decades, she would have been presented as a slut, and under Hays Office rules she would have to repent of her behavior and die. However, in this show she was presented as a supremely self-confident and liberated woman who thought the old rules were just that—old, and not for her. With Charlotte representing the old-fashioned ideal of femininity, the audience is given a choice of extreme stories to consider and to decide where they personally would fall between the two.

In **Will and Grace** and **Sex and the City**, the characters form a sort of family with each other. That is, a family that does not have a mother and father, but one of extremely close friends that support each other in the same way family members usually support one another.

And now it's time to talk about a major effect of all this fragmenting of the audience—money.

When the Big Three, ABC, CBS and NBC, were the only networks and provided all the choices that people had to watch TV, each network got, on average, about a third of the available money pot. But with more than a hundred channels, the amount of money each of those networks could get was greatly reduced. This meant that the networks, in order to remain profitable, had to find ways to reduce their costs.

The main cost, of course, was the programming. A typical show could cost a million or more dollars per episode, especially when actors could ask for thousands or hundreds of thousands of dollars per episode just to be in the show. For example, for the last couple of years of the show **Two and a half Men**, the producers paid Charlie Sheen two million dollars an episode. All six of the actors on **Friends** got a million dollars per episode. Add to that the cost of the other actors and producing the show itself with its writers and directors and producers and crew. This means the networks had to lay out millions of dollars for each episode.

This is one reason shows get cancelled so quickly if they don't generate a large audience immediately. The only way a network can show a profit on TV shows is for them to go into syndication. Syndication is selling the rights to air a show, one that's already had a network run of the first airing and two or three reruns, to individual stations. These stations generally run the shows they license the right to air during non-primetime hours (primetime is Monday through Saturday 8 to 11 P.M., and Sunday 7 to 11 P.M.). That's why it is possible to watch **Friends** or **Two and a Half Men** or **House** between 7 and 8 P.M. every night on one station or another.

The problem with syndicating a show is that it has to have enough episodes to allow "stripping" the show. Stripping means running a different episode every night five nights a week, Monday through Friday. But to avoid running the same episodes too often and losing the audience, there need to be enough original episodes. The rule of thumb is seventy-two episodes, or the show running new episodes for at least three years on a network. That means a show has to have had reasonably good ratings, sufficient for advertisers to continue sponsoring it, for three or more years to be worth syndicating.

The necessity for economy brought about a change in programming, especially scripted dramas and comedies. Scripted shows are the expensive ones, as indicated above. You have to pay the producers, the production crews, the production costs, the writers, and, of course, the actors—that represents a massive investment.

Unscripted shows are a lot cheaper. The biggest costs for scripted shows are the writers and actors. Eliminate them and costs drop amazingly. Game shows like **Jeopardy** and **Wheel of Fortune** are popular for syndication because they're cheap: a single set; simple production at low cost; the crew; the host(s); and simple writing like the questions for which the writers are paid far less than for a script. The rest of the cast for a game show, the contestants, are free, a real savings there. The prizes are a minor cost, a few thousand dollars per episode. Compare that to paying for one actor like Charlie Sheen.

Now the point of all this. In 1973, Public Broadcasting put on a show called ***An American Family***. They simply had a camera crew follow a family, the Louds, through their normal life. They edited down three hundred hours of film to twelve one-hour episodes. What added drama to the show was the break-up of the marriage of the parents, Bill and Pat, during the filming period. It was the first true reality show, showing real life on TV. It was also the last for close to twenty years.

However, with networks needing to save money on their programming, reality TV appeared to be a way to do that. The problem is—what is reality TV? How do you define it? Is it just filming real people doing things and putting that on the air? Wouldn't that make the news reality TV? So does that make ***Survivor*** or ***Big Brother*** or ***The Bachelor*** or ***The Deadliest Catch*** or ***Project Runway*** or ***Dirty Jobs*** news? Well, maybe to some people, but I don't think that's what most people mean by news.

Is it then an unscripted program that shows dramatic or humorous situations, documents actual events, and usually features ordinary people instead of professional actors? Well, that description still fits the news—and game shows.

To try to find an answer, let's take the two big differences between scripted shows and so-called reality shows: scripts and professional actors. Writers and actors are probably the greatest expense for scripted shows. Remember Kelsey Grammer on ***Frasier*** and the cast of ***Friends*** as an example of actors. Then there are writers. In 2002, the top twelve sitcom writers—just the top twelve—made between them 900 million dollars—twelve writers in just one year. The writer Aaron Sorkin, creator and writer of such movies as ***The American President***, ***A Few Good Men***, and ***The Social Network,*** and the TV shows ***Sports Night*** and ***The West Wing***, got an offer from HBO when ***Sports Night*** was cancelled by ABC. HBO wanted to continue the show—but only if Sorkin would write twelve episodes a year. Sorkin turned them down so he could concentrate on ***The West Wing***. HBO offered him 36 million dollars a year, or a hundred thousand dollars a page, and he turned them down. Imagine what he was making to write ***The West Wing***.

So perhaps we can define a reality show as a program with no actors or writers involved. Well, that's not exactly true either. There is the host, and he or she is an actor. Okay, so the rest of the cast are just ordinary people. But are they really? If they are, why do they have to audition? As if they were actors? Look at ***Big Brother*** or MTV's ***The Real World***. Do you think they would get that mix of people by just getting people off the street? There's always the homophobe and the gay guy, the nerd and the jock, the innocent and the slut, the angry black and the bigot. These are hardly ordinary people.

So why do they audition the participants? To get that mix, one that will cause drama, and to get drama you have to have conflict. Remember way back to what I said about storytelling—Every character must want something, must want something different from every other character, and these differences cause conflict.

So-called reality shows do the same thing. The participants are not "ordinary people." They are characters in the drama, and the people are cast to cause the conflict. Think of the ***Survivor*** season with the gay exhibitionist Richard and the ex-marine homophobe Rudy. The producers were undoubtedly looking forward to the conflict. Imagine their chagrin when Richard and Rudy immediately formed an alliance and worked to help each other. Rudy didn't like Richard, but he knew they would improve each other's chances to win. Johnny Fairplay was probably the most hated contestant ever on the show. He even set up a scheme ahead of time so that when contestants' relatives came, his friend should say Johnny's grandmother had died to gain the sympathy of the rest of the survivors and to let

Johnny win the reward. It was a total lie. The producers must have known what kind of person Fairplay was.

The Deadliest Catch, a reality series about crab fishing during the winter on the Bering Sea, demonstrates the principle. The first season was essentially a documentary, cameras placed on crab boats showing the job. However, when the documentary series generated a large audience, the Discovery network made it a series, but they made some decisions. Several crab boats that were in the first season never showed up again. Those boats' captains and crews were simply competent, hardworking and calm. In other words, they generated no conflict other than between themselves and the job, especially the Bering Sea. The boats that appeared after the first season have captains that are extremely competent, but also extremely colorful, like Jonathan and Andy Hillstrand, or volatile, like Sig Hansen and Keith Colburn, or dealing with family and health problems on his boat, like Phil Harris. And of course the crews have their own conflicts, with the captain, with the other crewmembers, and with the Bering Sea.

The first season of ***Big Brother*** illustrates this point about conflict perfectly. That first season the audience voted people out of the house. Naturally, they voted out the people they disliked the most. By halfway through the season, every villainous person was gone, leaving only the nice people, and there went the conflict. Viewership dropped precipitously because the show became boring—just nice people acting nicely. The next season, the people in the house did the voting instead of the audience, and the conflict was everywhere as everyone stabbed everyone else in the back to win.

So while reality shows may not have professional actors, they do have actors: They're just unpaid and expected to act like themselves.

However, what if the actors don't act like themselves? Now we come down to having no scripts. This is not actually true: There's always a script. Before a show can go on the air someone has to decide precisely what the audience is going to see and hear. Consider a documentary on lions. If it were reality, the producers would just turn the camera on and let it run, and all we'd really see are lions sleeping. They only hunt every two or three days, the hunt is over in minutes, then they eat, and then they sleep. Yet the documentary shows very little sleeping and a lot of action; after all, action is what makes it interesting. So a year's worth of film is edited down to the high points—those that have action and conflict and create drama.

The same applies to reality shows. The camera and sound crews shoot hundreds of hours of material, which is then organized and edited into the few hours that appear on the air. That organization is the script. Contestants often say after the show has been on the air that they were made to look bad by editing things said and done out of context. Well, a show needs heroes and villains, and if the people aren't heroes and villains on their own, the editing, laid out in the script, can make them appear that way. The main difference when it comes to the script is that, for scripted shows, the script is written before shooting, and for reality shows the script is written after shooting.

Remember all the way back to when I started this discussion about reality shows that I said it all comes down to money. Well, reality shows are cheap, whether they're documentary style like ***The Deadliest Catch*** and ***Dirty Jobs***, or game style like ***Survivor*** or ***Big Brother*** and ***The Bachelor*** and ***Beauty and the Geek***. The producers don't have to pay for the people playing the characters who, apparently looking for their fifteen minutes of fame, volunteer to go through the pain and suffering, either physical or emotional or both, for the joy of being on TV.[2]

So reality shows are cheap. Even a million dollar prize at the end of thirteen weeks of airtime, as with ***Survivor***, is cheap compared to an actor getting a million a week.

What this means is that reality shows are crowding out scripted shows. In less than ten years, there are twenty-five fewer hours of scripted shows on the big four networks (ABC, NBC, CBS, Fox), all replaced with reality shows. That doesn't include the hundreds of hours a week of reality and documentary programming on cable networks.

The effect on the audience of all this "reality" can be tremendous. Thousands of people have applied for a job on a crab boat. Thousands of people audition for ***Survivor*** or ***American Idol*** or ***So You Think You Can Dance*** or ***America's Next Top Model***. Thousands of people try to get on ***The Real World***. Thousands of people think what they're seeing is real, and they want a part of it, sure they'll get all the fame and fortune. Millions of people just think it's real. But it's no more real than a soap opera or a sitcom. It's just cheaper to do.

So that's television. But that's not the last of the media. We still have what's going on today to deal with. And we'll start looking at that in the next chapter.

■ ENDNOTES

1. By the way, if you're wondering about that record, the longest running prime-time series with continuing characters in history, there are several distinctions. The longest running **non**-prime-time series in history is *Meet the Press,* which has been on the air since 1947. The longest running show **without** continuing characters, in other words without characters that appear in every episode, is *The Ed Sullivan Show,* a variety show that ran for twenty-three years.

2. I'm going to editorialize for just a moment here. On Fox's new "reality" game show ***More To Love***, a version of ***The Bachelor***, sixteen women who have missed out on love in their lives because of their weight compete to have the bachelor choose them. These women have been rejected all their lives—and they are now competing, and being rejected again, on TV. If it was bad enough for them as private pain, as they often say it has been in their lives, how much worse is it as public pain? And what does it say about an audience who gets pleasure out it? Well, so much for my editorial.

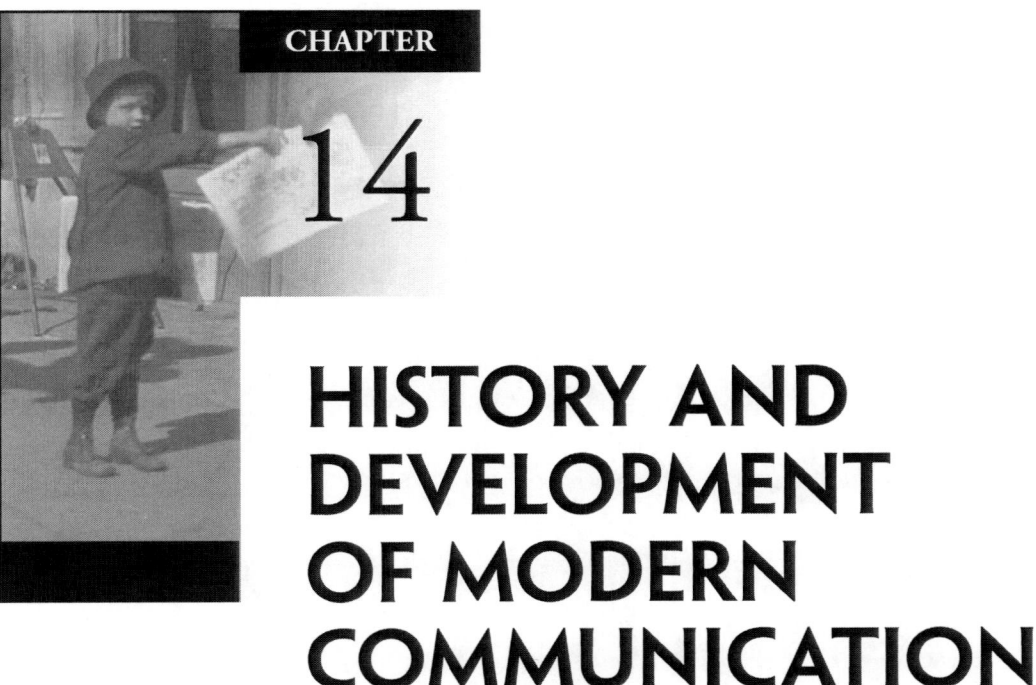

14

HISTORY AND DEVELOPMENT OF MODERN COMMUNICATION

*W*hen I was in college, there was always a need to take notes doing research. While going through books, journals, magazines, newspapers, etc., I would find a piece of information or a quote that would be good to include. The hard part was to remember where each piece of information I needed at any moment was in those notes. However, I found something that helped a great deal, a product called Indecks™.

Indecks™, unlike regular note cards, was a set of 5 × 8 cards with a double row of small numbered holes along each edge. The holes were there for a reason. I could write all kinds of different information on these cards, and different information on each card. But I wasn't worried about how I'd find something I was looking for because of the holes.

I had one card with a list of general categories, and each category had a number. If I wrote something on a card that fit one of those categories, I clipped the hole so it was open to the edge of card. The number of the hole clipped corresponded to the number of the category the information belonged to. I could have hundreds of cards in the stack.

When I went to work on whatever I had done the research for and wanted to find that card again, or any other card in that category, I didn't have to go through the stack and look at each card. I would just stick a thin rod through the appropriate hole and shake the stack. Any card anywhere in the stack that had the hole clipped fell out of the stack and—voila—there's every note I've taken on that category. If I wanted to narrow it down more, I just picked another category and shook out those cards.

You know what the Indecks™ system was? A computer. At least, the only kind of computer you could buy in the late 1970s if you didn't have a few hundred thousand dollars. It operated because of the design of the cards—they were punch cards. All these cards did was answer the question: Does the card contain information I want, yes or no? Yes, the card drops out; no, the card doesn't. And that's really all a computer does, substituting turning an electrical current on and off for the rod stuck through the holes for the answers yes and no.

Common wisdom says that Charles Babbage invented the computer in 1830. What he invented was a device, his integrating engine, which could calculate numbers far faster than doing arithmetic by hand. However, it was analog, not digital. In other words, it used actual numbers instead of yes or no to do its calculations. When we think of computers today, they aren't analog but digital, using a series of yes or no, on or off, questions to do their calculations.

The biggest problem with computing is getting the data in and getting answers out. For that we can start back with water powered pipe organs. Remember the water powered camshaft with pegs inserted into it that raised and then let fall hammers used to beat linen pulp to make paper? The same sort of camshaft was used to run pipe organs. Pegs were inserted into the camshaft that would open and close the organ pipes to play the notes. To change the music played, you changed the placement of the pegs, and to know where to place the pegs, you wrapped the roller with a piece of paper with holes in it where you wanted the pegs and inserted the pegs in the camshaft.

In the eighteenth century, there was a craze for patterned textiles, with images of flowers or animals or other images woven into the cloth. To create those textiles required controlling the colored warp threads in the loom to ensure that only the correctly colored threads desired in the pattern appeared. This was difficult because the desired threads had to be lifted above the shuttle, but only as long as those threads appeared in the pattern. The thread lifters were strings tied to certain threads that, when pulled, lifted those threads above the weft so they would appear in the pattern. During this period, children, who weren't exactly God's gift to concentration, generally controlled the thread lifters. Thus errors in the cloth pattern could easily result.

In 1725, Basile Bouchon realized that the perforated roll of paper that determined where the pegs in an organ's camshaft were inserted could actually be used as a controller for a loom. He built a textile loom that substituted pins for the children. Each pin would control one set of thread lifters by having the control string run through a hole in the pin. When the pin was in the default back position, its string would be pulled down by a comb, lifting the warp threads; when the pin was in the forward position the string wasn't pulled by the comb, and it didn't pull the lifter. A loop of perforated paper pressed against the pins controlled the pins' position. If there was a hole, the pin moved into the forward position and thus didn't pull the thread, but if there was no hole, the pin stayed back, lifting the thread, and the thread appeared in the pattern. No more children, no more errors in the pattern. However, although this system worked, it was limited. The paper control tore or wore out very quickly.

In 1728, Jean-Baptiste Falcon improved on Bouchon's idea by replacing the paper loop with a loop of stiff cards strung together. The cards were much sturdier and lasted a lot longer. However, the system required two people, one to run the loom and the other to advance the cards. It removed the errors, but it also raised labor costs.

Then in 1741, Jacques de Vaucanson automated the system. He went back to the perforated paper roll, but this time he wrapped it around a cylinder filled with rows of holes. When the pin encountered a hole in the paper, it went into the hole in the cylinder. The cylinder was mounted on a rack that, with each movement of the loom, advanced one row of holes by way of a ratchet. This eliminated one worker, but it had the drawback of a limited number of rows of holes in the cylinder.

Finally, around 1800 Joseph Jacquard put all the pieces together. He took Bouchon's loom with its pin system, Falcon's string of cards to control the pins and Vaucanson's ratchet system, and he combined them, creating the loom that has carried his name to this day—the Jacquard loom. As usual, the last one to work on something gets all the credit. His loom could have an unlimited number of cards, and the design could be changed just by substituting, removing or inserting cards in the string.

If the cards with holes at specific locations sound familiar, it should. Just like the Indecks™ cards, the loom cards answered a question yes or no: Should threads be lifted? If there is no hole, yes; if there is a hole, no.

So where am I going with all this? As you know from school, the ability to find information fast is very important. Our current ability to do that started because of a clause in the United States Constitution, Article 1, Section 2, paragraph 3, which requires a census of the population of the United States every ten years to apportion representatives to the federal government among the states.

Doing a census every ten years was a great idea. A census of a country had not really been done since William the Conqueror's Doomsday Book in the eleventh century. However, problems arose in the late nineteenth century when apparently everybody in the world wanted to live in America. Suddenly there were millions more people to count and gather information about. The only way to do that was to interview every person and to write things down, and then to go through all those handwritten records and tabulate everything by hand. The 1880 census took eight years; by the time they finished, it was time to do the next census. This was considered a major problem, especially since there would be even more people for the 1890 census—it might take more than ten years.

Herman Hollerith, who worked for the census bureau, found a solution. He thought: "*There's a better way.*" What he did was invent an electro-mechanical tabulation machine that used—yes, you guessed it—cards with holes in them: punch cards. Hollerith was given the idea of using cards by his boss in the census office, John Shaw Billings, who thought the cards used by looms could carry information.

This is how it worked:

Hollerith constructed a tabulation machine that consisted of four rows of ten dials each, every dial capable of counting up to 10,000. The dials were hooked up electrically to a data recorder.

When a new person was interviewed, the information was written down. Then it was given to a tabulator, someone whose job it was to enter the data on a punch card. The cards were the size of a dollar bill at that time, since paper and holders for that size paper already existed—no sense in reinventing what was already available. The card was covered with columns of numbers and letters, each of which stood for some piece of information. For example, one number or letter could stand for gender—male or female —one for race, one for country of origin, one for state of residence, a column for age, and whatever else the census bureau needed.

The card was then placed in a holder and a hole punched in the card for each piece of information from the interview. After the card was done, it was placed in a recording device, the data recorder, which held a plate covered with holes. The placement of the holes in the plate matched up with the placement of the letters and numbers on the card. Above the card holder was a box containing a spring-loaded pin for each hole, and under each hole in the card holder was an electrical contact. When the box was pressed down on the card, if there was a hole in the card the pin would go through and hit the contact, sending

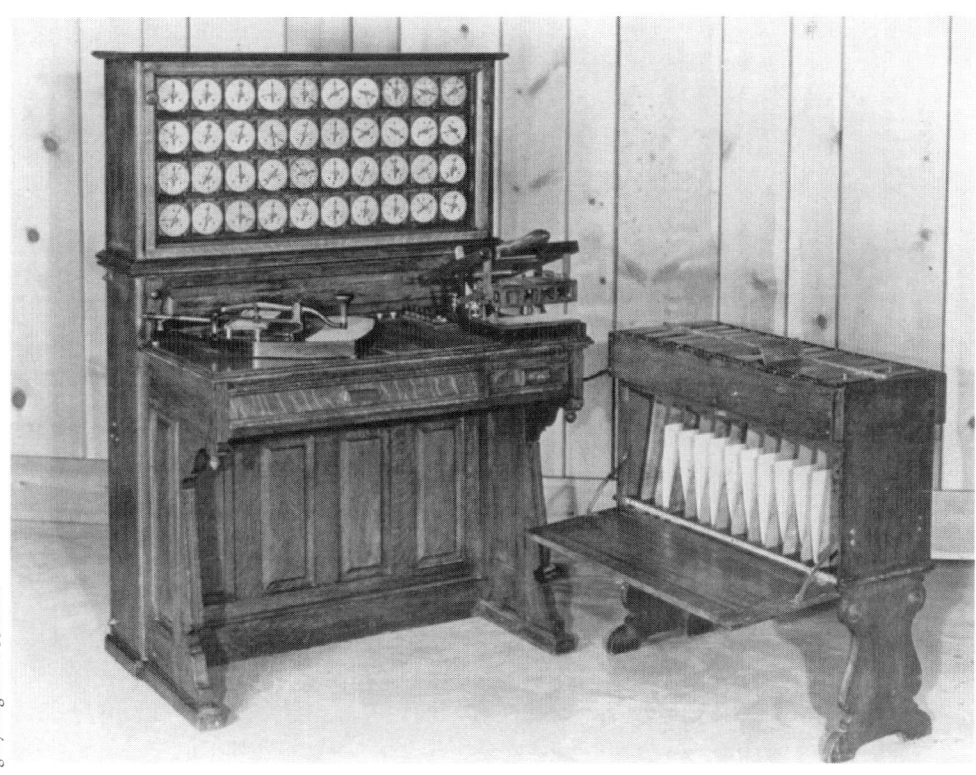

gettyimages.com 3362420

a signal to one of the tabulator's dials, which would click forward one number for each punched hole. Of course, if there was no hole in the card, the pin wouldn't go through, no contact was made, and nothing would happen.

Tabulation of all the data coming in speeded up tremendously. However, so was the retrieval of data. The tabulator could be programmed. That is, each dial could be designated for whatever piece of information someone wanted. Let's say you wanted to find out something about thirty-five-year-old men in Minnesota. You'd set one dial for men, one for thirty-five years old, and one for Minnesota. Then you'd take all the cards and run them through the data recorder. When a card containing a piece of information you were looking for came under the pins, a pin would go through the hole, advance the dial one number, and then pop open the lid of a box containing several cubby holes with lids next to the tabulator. If a lid opened, you dropped the card in the cubby hole. At the end of the day, you took the cards with the information you were looking for out of the box and could run them through again for anything else you wanted.

This system was a great time saver. The 1890 census took only two years. And we entered the computer age, because that's what Hollerith's tabulator was, a computer.

Hollerith applied the same principle as governed his tabulator to many other areas, such as business. He turned his business into a corporation, and it became International Business Machines, better known as IBM.

As is usual, two forces drive most innovations—business and war. Computing was driven mostly by the needs of war. During World War II, the airplane, improved by the needs of war in how high and fast it could fly, became a major factor in battle. A means had to be found to be able to shoot them down, preferably before they attacked. However, to shoot them down, gunners needed to be able to point their guns in such a way that the shells would arrive at the same places and times as the planes: off by a little and the planes would continue on unscathed. This required the ability to compute angle, speed and distance of not only the planes but the shells. Considering the speed at which both traveled, there was no way a person, either in his head or with paper and pencil, could do such a calculation in time to do any good. All a gunner could do was point the gun in the general direction of the plane and hope for the best (or in the pilot's opinion, the worst). However, a calculating machine linked to radar **could** do such a calculation. The radar would give the range and speed of the target, and the machine would combine that with the speed, distance and arc a shell could travel, and it could tell the gunner when and at what point in the sky to fire. A crash program (no pun intended) was started to create just such a machine.

One of the first was the Z3, invented in 1941 by a German, Konrad Zuse. It was an electro-mechanical device using vacuum tubes for calculating. The thing about a vacuum tube is that it's either on or off. By representing every number and letter in an equation, such as the ones used in ballistics to shoot down a plane, as a series of tubes that are either on or off, the equation can be solved at the speed of electricity. Here's an example of how a computer sees numbers in terms of on and off, with 0 (zero) meaning off, and 1 meaning on.

0	0	4	100	8	1000
1	1	5	101	9	1001
2	10	6	110	10	1010
3	11	7	111	11	1011

It's called binary code. So instead of doing math by hand, Zuse's machine could do it with electricity to turn the vacuum tubes on and off.

The British, of course, needed the same thing, and they responded with their computer, the Colossus, in 1944.

As time went on, the usefulness of machines that could do calculations rapidly became very evident. So these calculating machines, called computers, got bigger and bigger in terms of calculating ability; and, because of the number of vacuum tubes necessary, and their size, they were given the ability to be programmed to do tasks other than just angles and trajectories, just like the dials on Hollerith's tabulator. The Eniac, developed during World War II but not completed until 1946, weighed 30 tons, was 8 and a half feet high, three and half feet deep, and 80 feet long. However, by rewiring its inputs and changing the kinds of information the computer was given to work on, it could be programmed for different tasks. This was unlike the Z3 or the Colossus, which had only one function, to figure out how to shoot down a plane.

Efforts were made to make the computers smaller in size and bigger in abilities. Illiac of 1952 at the University of Illinois was much smaller and much more powerful than Eniac, having 8 kilobytes (kb) of Random Access Memory (RAM), the information to work on, and 64Kb of Read Only Memory (ROM), the instructions on how to work on the information. The US Army's Brlesc (yes, that's how they spelled it, and they pronounced it burlesque) had 36 kb of RAM, and it could use tape-based storage of binary data, with each tape holding 315 kb.

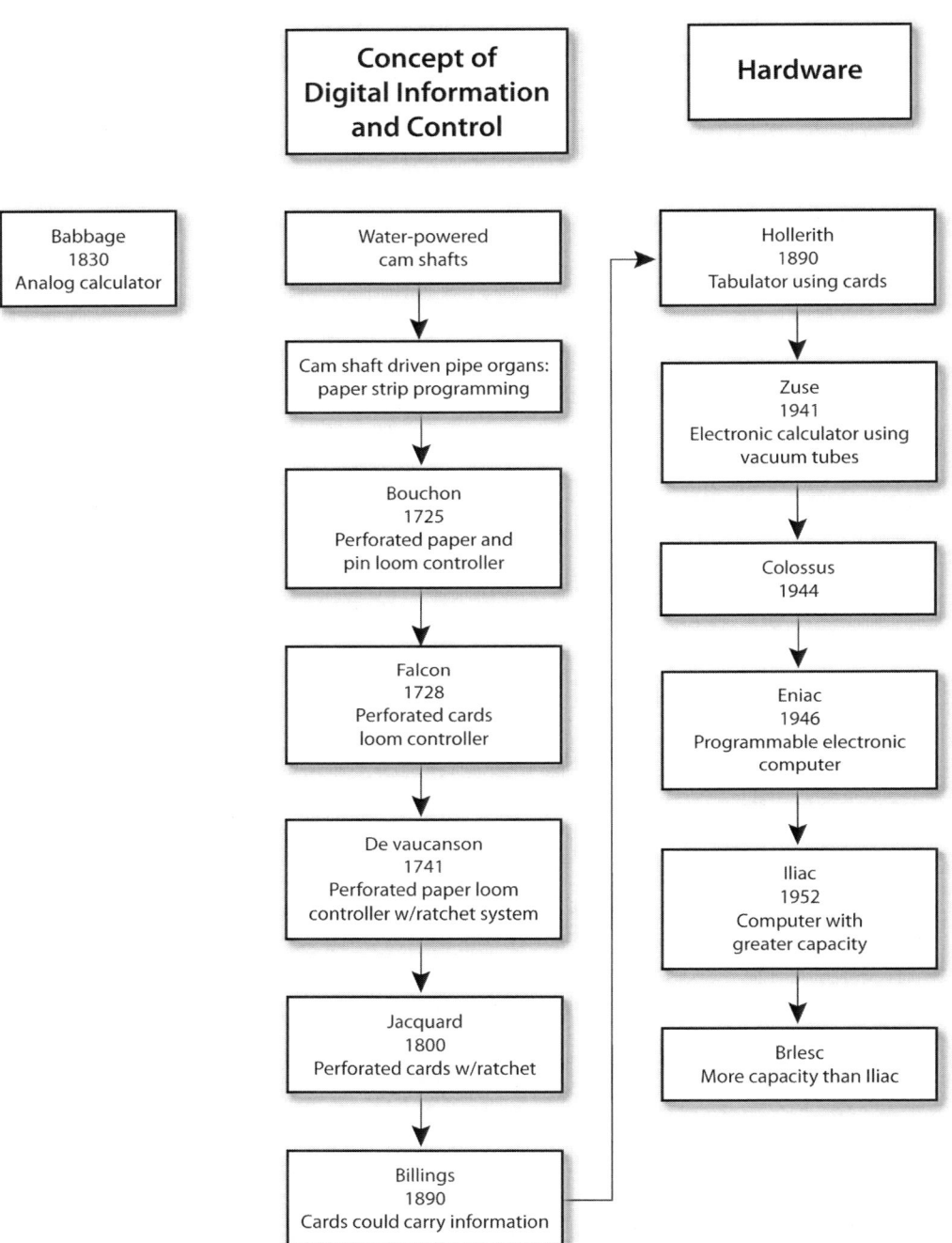

Concept of Digital Information and Control

Hardware

Babbage
1830
Analog calculator

Water-powered
cam shafts

↓

Cam shaft driven pipe organs:
paper strip programming

↓

Bouchon
1725
Perforated paper and
pin loom controller

↓

Falcon
1728
Perforated cards
loom controller

↓

De vaucanson
1741
Perforated paper loom
controller w/ratchet system

↓

Jacquard
1800
Perforated cards w/ratchet

↓

Billings
1890
Cards could carry information

Hollerith
1890
Tabulator using cards

↓

Zuse
1941
Electronic calculator using
vacuum tubes

↓

Colossus
1944

↓

Eniac
1946
Programmable electronic
computer

↓

Iliac
1952
Computer with
greater capacity

↓

Brlesc
More capacity than Iliac

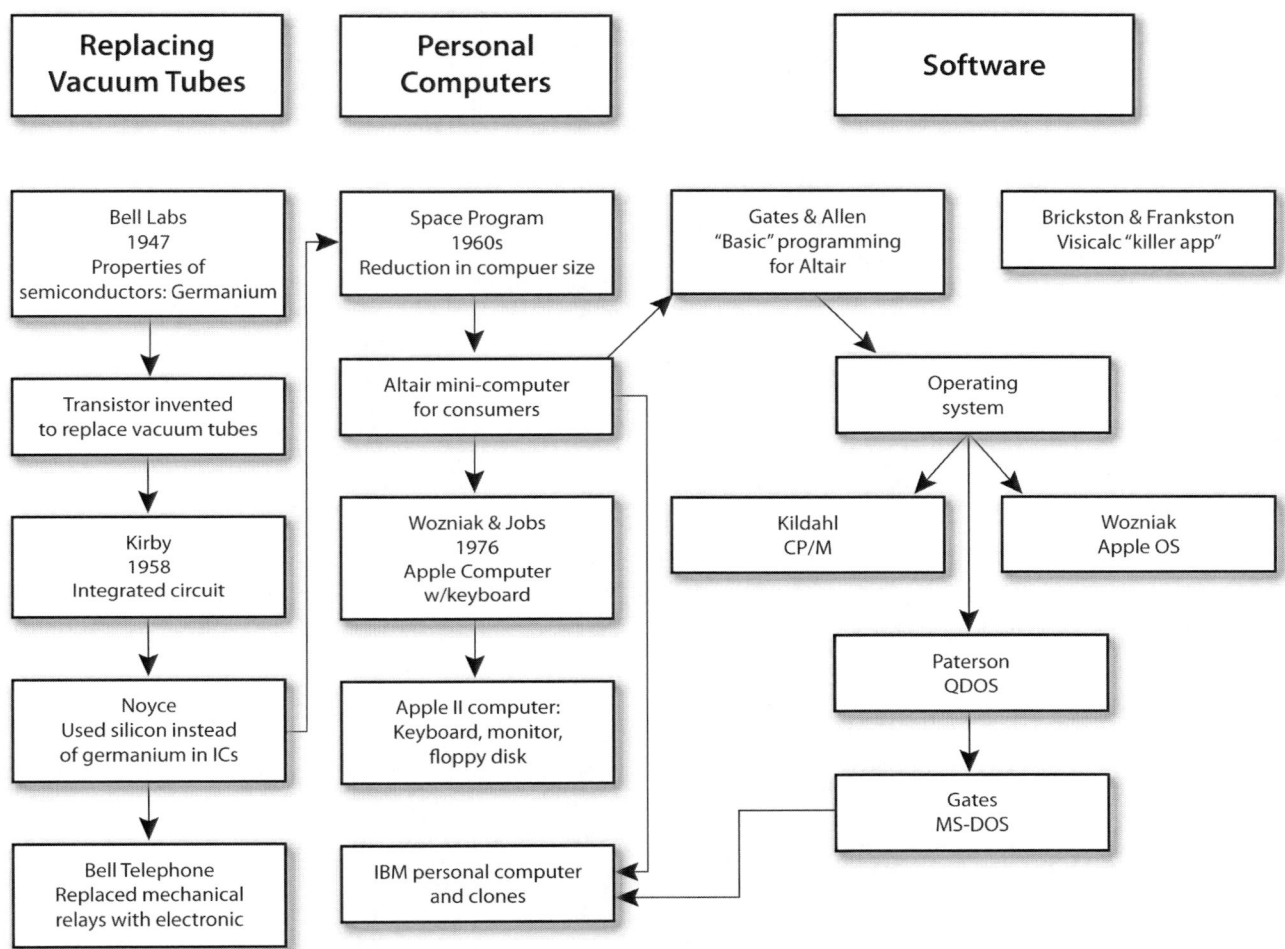

Replacing Vacuum Tubes

Bell Labs
1947
Properties of
semiconductors: Germanium

Transistor invented
to replace vacuum tubes

Kirby
1958
Integrated circuit

Noyce
Used silicon instead
of germanium in ICs

Bell Telephone
Replaced mechanical
relays with electronic

Personal Computers

Space Program
1960s
Reduction in compuer size

Altair mini-computer
for consumers

Wozniak & Jobs
1976
Apple Computer
w/keyboard

Apple II computer:
Keyboard, monitor,
floppy disk

IBM personal computer
and clones

Software

Gates & Allen
"Basic" programming
for Altair

Brickston & Frankston
Visicalc "killer app"

Operating
system

Kildahl
CP/M

Wozniak
Apple OS

Paterson
QDOS

Gates
MS-DOS

Let's compare that to a computer of today. The one a typical student uses, a laptop or a netbook, has at least 28 times the RAM, 510,000 times the storage, runs thousands of times faster and is thousands of times smaller. How is this possible?

Well, computers used vacuum tubes that turned on and off—in other words, yes or no—to do calculations, the same way Hollerith's tabulator either let a rod through to the electrical contact (a yes), or didn't let a rod through (a no), which, of course, is exactly what Bouchon's weaving cards did. But vacuum tubes were not only slow, they would get incredibly hot, and for any kind of calculation a lot of them were necessary. A way had to be found to deal with all these problems. And that way was found.

In 1947, Bell Laboratory scientists discovered the properties of germanium. Germanium is one of a group of elements called semiconductors; the others are boron, silicon, arsenic, antimony, tellurium, polonium and astatine. Semiconductors, when properly alloyed, act like switches and can either block or permit a flow of electrons through them just the way a light switch does. I won't go into how they do that, but the fact they can means what they're attached to can be turned on or off—just like a vacuum tube using binary code. The scientists had invented the transistor, and it allowed them to dispense with vacuum tubes. Transistors are much smaller and much cooler to operate than tubes, and you could pack several of them into the space of one tube. And, just as was the case with tubes, the more transistors, the more powerful the computer could be. The goal became to pack as many transistors as possible into the smallest space possible. This was achieved in 1958 when Jack Kirby invented the integrated circuit, a device that held the internal workings of several transistors and their connections as a single unit rather than as several individual parts connected together. For this, Kirby won the Nobel Prize in Physics in 2000. Robert Noyce improved Kirby's circuit by using silicon rather than germanium as the semiconductor.

The race was on: who could make the smallest integrated circuit with the most transistors. That's still being done today, with IC chips packing millions of transistors and connections into spaces measured, not in meters, but in micro millimeters.

So now that you've got these little chips, what do you do with them?

One of the first places they showed up was in telephone exchanges to replace the mechanical relays with **electronic** relays to connect one phone with another. That only made sense since the transistor was invented by Bell Labs.

But everybody who was using vacuum tubes wanted to replace them with transistors and integrated circuits. Remember the little transistor radios that came on the market in the 1960s? Then manufacturers of television sets got in on the act.

But a place that really needed integrated circuits was the space program. In the 1960s, there was a great space race between the US and the Soviet Union. Both wanted to get there first with the most. To do that, they needed calculating power that could be packed into the smallest space possible at the lightest weight possible. Integrated circuits permitted packing a computer the size of a room into the size of a briefcase—just what the space program needed.

News of these little computers, called mini-computers, spread, especially among the nerds and geeks who wanted their own. They didn't really have anything for them to do, they just wanted one. Although not the first, the most popular was the Altair, which came in kit form and gave the buyer the great joy of putting all the pieces together and soldering them. Flipping the switches on the front plate into various configurations could "program" it to do arithmetic or to play a simple tune. There was no keyboard or monitor, but it really caught the imagination of enthusiasts.

Someone who got in on the mini-computer craze was Bill Gates and his friend Paul Allen. They developed a computer language that could operate the Altair called "Basic." This computer language was the beginning of Microsoft.

A couple of other people who got in on the act were Steve Wozniak and Steve Jobs. In 1976, they came out with the Apple I computer. It replaced the switches that the Altair used with a keyboard and used a version of BASIC that Gates and Allen wrote for it. Then in 1977, Wozniak and Jobs came out with the killer—the Apple II. It had a CRT monitor, color graphics and a floppy disk drive, and it looked like something more than a hobbyist's kit. Of course, it also cost four times what an Altair did—$1,300 (that's about $3,000 today), but it was a usable computer and it looked like one.

About the same time, the Sinclair came out, a tiny computer about the size of a thin paperback book. It was sold as a kit for only $100 and used BASIC. It only had 4 kb of RAM and no monitor, and it used a cassette recorder for storage. But it had a membrane keyboard and an output to a TV set so a user could see what was being typed in to write a program and watch the results as the program ran.

Radio Shack also came out with a personal computer, the TRS-80, using the computer chip developed for the Sinclair. In fact, it was basically a Sinclair with a full-size keyboard and a monitor. However, at half the price of the Apple II, it sold by the thousands. It could even be upgraded to an incredible 16 kilobytes of RAM, a factor that wowed the enthusiasts.

Still, personal computers remained the province of nerds. The average person couldn't think of anything to do with one. The most common comment about getting a computer was, "What am I going to use it for—balance my checkbook?" Then, in 1978, Dan Brickston and Bob Frankston came out with the first "killer app," a computer application that anyone could use, and, more to the point, that anyone would want to use. It was a spreadsheet for the Apple II called Visicalc. For the first time, people could buy a computer to do more than play around with programs and make pictures or play games. People who previously wouldn't even have considered getting a computer now wanted one. With Visicalc they actually **could** balance their checkbooks. And, of course, a whole lot more. Businesses that couldn't afford a main-frame computer could now have one sitting on their desks that handled much of their accounting needs rapidly and easily, and average people found many uses for a spreadsheet.

Of course, now that computers were selling to average people, not just big corporations, who else would want to get in on the action except the biggest business machine company in the world? Of course, it would be IBM, Herman Hollerith's old company. It's now that things took a turn for the weird. Computers need an operating system, a set of codes giving instructions that determine what the computer does to run a program. BASIC, that original programming language that Gates and Allen invented, could act as its own operating system, but it was limited in what it could do, and the user had to do rhis own programming. The most popular operating system for personal computers at the time was Gary Kildall's CP/M (Control Program for Microcomputers) that many companies used, like the Kaypro and the Osborn, two popular personal computers.

A competing operating system was Tim Paterson's Quick and Dirty Operating System, QDOS that could do a lot more with more powerful computers. For example, the maximum amount of RAM or floppy disk storage CP/M could control was 64 K, and it could only run on older, less capable ROM chips. QDOS could handle 128 K and run on the latest ROM chips.

This is when Gates pulled off what is called the "Deal of the Century." He bought Paterson's QDOS for $50,000, tweaked it a bit, called it MS-DOS (the Microsoft Disk Operating System) and promoted it to IBM as just the thing they needed to get into the personal computer business. IBM agreed and offered to buy MS-DOS. This is where Gates really made his deal. He didn't sell MS-DOS to IBM, he **licensed** it to IBM—on a non-exclusive basis. In other words, Gates kept the rights to the system that would run on all IBM personal computers, but he also kept the right to license it to all of IBM's competitors. And that's exactly what he did. Every non-CP/M or Apple computer, not just IBM's, came with MS-DOS installed. The manufacturer paid the license fee and simply added it to the retail price.

Gates also realized that the real money wasn't in the operating system, but in the programs that ran on the operating system. He almost gave away MS-DOS to computer manufacturers, creating a virtual monopoly on the operating system and shutting out other systems. He set to work developing applications, the things the computer could do for the user and the reason the user gets a computer in the first place. These applications that Gates' company Microsoft put out are the applications we all use today.

Wozniak and Jobs, on the other hand, developed their own operating system for their Apple computers. However, unlike IBM and Gates, they kept exclusive not only the hardware of their computers but the operating system as well, not permitting other companies to make clones of their product. This limited their marketing because there were many manufacturers making IBM clones, which caused prices to drop and almost monopolized the market for personal computers. Apple, although it was cutting edge when it came to such things as graphics rather than text interfaces, was the first to use a mouse, as well as to add more RAM and faster speeds, especially with the introduction in 1984 of their MacIntosh computer. Since they had no competition for their particular kind of computer, they also kept their prices high, often double or more the price of an IBM clone.

Software manufacturers outside of Microsoft and Apple, seeing the way the wind was blowing, made sure their programs were compatible with MS-DOS and thus could run on MS-DOS machines. They often only grudgingly produced a version that would run on an Apple machine and its different operating system.

That Gates knew the real money was in applications didn't stop him from constantly upgrading and changing the operating system. Most people—those who aren't using a Mac—are probably using Windows XP or Vista or Windows 7, each several incarnations away from MS-DOS.

Today computers run the world. When was the last time you sent a letter instead of an email? When was the last time you did research by looking in books instead of Googling? When was the last time you shopped for books or videos in a store instead of online? When was the last time you played a board game instead of a video game? When was the last time you were on YouTube? Facebook? iTunes? I used a computer to write this book; twenty years ago I'd have used a typewriter. There are computer chips running everything, from coffeemakers to cars, from electric razors to the national electric power grid, from clocks to corporations.

And computers aren't the only electronic media that we use today that didn't even exist thirty, or twenty, or even five years ago.

■ VIDEO RECORDING

Let's start with something that changed the way people watched TV—the video cassette recorder, or VCR. Video tape had been in use since 1956 when Ampex perfected the video recorder at the behest of Bing Crosby. Ampex's VR1000 was the first practical machine capable of recording video to tape. It used a 2-inch wide reel to reel tape that went at 360 inches, or 30 feet, per second. It was a rather large machine, about the size of three large refrigerators—not the sort of thing you'd want sitting in your living room.

Of course, when the transistor came out, the machine started to shrink, but it was still sizeable—and far too expensive for average people.

However, in 1963 the Neiman Marcus Christmas catalog advertised the first home video tape recorder, the Ampex Signature V. It used 8-inch diameter reels of 2-inch wide tape and a single head helical scan system, and it recorded 64 minutes at 5 inches per second. Of course, it did have some drawbacks. The entire system was nine feet long and weighed 900 pounds. The video portion of the system included the black and white reel-to-reel video recorder with a TV tuner and automatic timer as well as a home television camera. The cabinet also housed a complete audio system, including an AM/FM tuner, a stereo amplifier, a record player, a reel-to-reel audio recorder, and stereo loudspeakers. A color TV was viewable from the front of the console, while all other components were accessed from the top. The $30,000 price tag, the equivalent of $75,000 today, included a personalized plaque and installation by an Ampex service engineer. The video recorder alone weighed 100 pounds. But at least you could record TV in the home.

For the next twelve years, companies all over the world worked at improving video recording, changing the recording and playback heads, the tapes, the tape speed and, of course, the electronics. Networks and TV stations were the primary markets for the systems, but there was a holy grail out there—the home consumers. Professional users are limited in number and, thus, sales—average people aren't.

Then, in 1975, Sony hit the jackpot. They came out with their Betamax video cassette recorder. It used a half inch tape in a cassette about the size of a paperback book that would record an hour's worth of broadcast, and it had a built-in TV tuner that would allow the user to record one program while watching another. It was a bit expensive at $2,295, but that was a lot cheaper than Ampex's Signature V at $75,000.

A year later, JVC introduced a new video recorder in competition with Sony's, called VHS, or video home system, and they put it on the market for $885. It was completely incompatible with Betamax, as it used a larger cassette and a different method for recording and playback that produced a slightly poorer picture and sound, but it was cheaper.

Then JVC, which shared its designs with other companies, and Matshusita developed a way to increase the time a VHS tape could record to two hours. Throughout 1977, tape speed wars saw Sony's Beta II counter with a three hour tape; VHS followed with a four hour length; Beta III then offered five hours; and VHS finally ended the competition with a six hour recording time. Today, a VHS machine can record up to eight hours using the T-160 size tapes.

Sony, having lost the recording time war, turned to aggressive advertising to fight back, claiming in its ads that a Betamax machine "can actually videotape something off one channel while you're watching another channel" and "build a library of your favorite shows." These claims immediately led to lawsuits. MCA/Universal and Disney filed suit against Sony, claiming that it would violate the copyrights they held on their movies and

TV shows if people could not only record TV shows, but keep them for later viewing. The battle went on for years, but Sony finally won eight years later in 1984.

Still, competition from JVC's VHS system really forced Sony to reduce prices. For example, in 1978 a Betamax machine could be purchased for $800.

Sony's Beta format finally lost the war to VHS. Betamax recorded and played back a better picture and better sound than VHS, and it used a smaller, more compact cassette, but its recording time was a bit shorter. However, what killed Beta were rentals. As more and more people bought VCRs, the studios that fought so hard to kill the device now embraced it because they could sell pre-recorded video tapes of their movies. Rental shops popped up everywhere. The shop would buy copies of the tapes and then rent them to consumers. At first Beta was on top in the battle of the formats, with many rental shops only stocking Beta, or only having a small section of the shop stocking VHS copies, but one particular kind of movie producer settled the question. In the back room of many video rental shops, there was a collection of tapes for rent—although few people would admit the room existed, and they certainly would never admit that they would rent anything from it. Nonetheless, it was a big moneymaker for the rental business, and so the pornography industry, which settled on using only the VHS format for its movies, finally drove Beta out of business.

Change Brought By the VCR

So how did the VCR change things? When Sony reduced the size of the video recorder from a room to a tabletop box by developing the Betamax VCR, television programming started to move out of the hands of the networks and into the hands of the viewers. The fact that viewers were able to tape a show and view it whenever they wanted changed network planning. Networks had been doing what is called counter-programming; that is, they would put their most popular shows on at the same time as their competitors' most popular shows in order to steal audience from one another. That's what the Fox Network was doing when it put *The Simpsons* on against NBC's *The Cosby Show*. That's counter-programming, and in that instance Fox won, stealing audience from NBC in that time period.

However, with the VCR, such programming decisions by the networks were irrelevant. The viewer decided not only what to watch, but when to watch it. So if two popular shows were against each other in the same time slot, it didn't matter. The viewer would just watch one of the shows at the scheduled time and tape the other to watch later.

Viewers taking so much control over when they viewed was, of course, a problem for the networks. First, counter-programming no longer worked. Second, people were watching their tapes when, by the networks' lights, they should have been watching the less popular shows. Audiences, however, were watching the tape of the popular show in place of a less popular one, so there went the ratings for those less popular shows. This caused the sponsors to either pay less for advertising time on those shows, or to stop sponsoring them entirely. If that weren't bad enough, there went the ratings—and the money—for the taped shows as well. There was no way to track what was being recorded and when it was being watched.

But the worst thing for the networks and advertisers was that the ability an audience had to tape a show enabled it to avoid commercials entirely. All they had to do was to hit the fast forward button when they appeared and zip through them while watching the tape. The whole point of putting on commercials during TV shows was that, if the audience wanted to watch the show, they had to watch the commercials, too. Well, so much for that idea.

Then there was recording movies off the air—and saving them. That was one of the most common things people did. They would record their favorite movies and watch them again and again. However, that meant the studios that made the movies wouldn't get paid by the networks for all those viewings. It's no wonder that Universal and Disney sued Sony when Sony advertised recording—and saving—movies as a big selling point in its advertising. The studios viewed that as a way for viewers to violate their copyright. They would lose TV rerun income, and, even worse, prerecorded tape income. Rather than rent or buy movies, people would just go to the library of films they had previously recorded off the air. In testimony before Congress in 1984, Jack Valenti, the president of the Motion Picture Association of America, said that the average person owned twenty-eight tapes, but if all they were doing was taping a show so they could watch it later, and only once, they would only need one or two tapes. That means people must be recording programs to keep, and therefore they were violating the producers' copyrights, which was the right to get paid royalties **every** time someone watched something. Valenti had a solution. Every VCR sold should have a royalty payment of several hundred dollars added to the price, and every blank tape sold should have a $25 royalty payment added. That, of course, would pretty well kill the VCR market—which is what the studios wanted in the first place.

In 1984, the Supreme Court (*Sony Corp. of America v. Universal City Studios, Inc.,* 464 U.S. 417)[1] ruled against the studios, deciding that home use of the VCR was "fair use." The VCR became a normal piece of American furniture just like the TV and stereo, and television and the movies haven't been the same since.

First, for TV. Sponsors started wanting deals. According to the ratings, viewership for shows was dropping. It was assumed that people were recording shows for later viewing instead of watching them when they aired, but nobody knew which shows. It was also assumed that people were zipping through the commercials, lessening their impact. A lot of assuming going on there. The networks didn't really listen, insisting the shows, and their commercials, were still being watched. So advertisers started punching up the ads, reducing the words and the talking heads and adding movement and color and spectacle, figuring people would stop zipping past a commercial just to see what was going on. That actually works.

Networks worked to reduce costs while at the same time raising viewership. Any show that didn't immediately get an audience, say within three or four weeks, was cancelled. New shows were often clones of successful shows—like **CSI** generating **CSI: Miami**, then **CSI: New York**, or all the **Law and Order** clones. And of course all the reality shows and game shows and anything else that audiences got hooked on—until they got sick and tired of it. Think about **Lost**. When they shot the pilot, everybody working on the show stayed in hotels because they didn't expect any network would buy the show—it wasn't like anything else on the air. And that's probably what made it a hit. Just like you'd get tired of eating spaghetti for every meal, you'd get tired of seeing one show after another that was just like everything else on the air. So **Lost** was a hit. And how did the networks respond? Of course—with **Lost** clones, like **Heroes**.

And then there's the effect of the VCR on movies. Probably the greatest effect was how it changed what kinds of movies are made. The studios realized that their money comes from putting butts in seats, so the movies went toward doing things that worked best on a big screen. That means spectacles, the blockbuster. Think **Jurassic Park**. Think

Independence Day. Think *Transformers*. Think *Spiderman*. Think *Batman*. Think *Harry Potter*. They are all big expensive movies with lots of action, noise and special effects, and especially with CGI (computer graphics images).

Then there's the broad humor of people like Judd Apatow and Seth Rogan, with *Pineapple Express*, *Step Brothers*, *Superbad*, and *Knocked Up*. And, of course, we can't forget the witty repartee of *Harold and Kumar*, with their search for love, pot, and tiny hamburgers, not necessarily in that order, and Neil Patrick Harris as Neil Patrick Harris, the drug-crazed sex maniac.

And if you're not into that, there's always *Saw*, or *Saw*—or *Saw*—or *Saw*. Just how many horrific ways can you slice someone up? And why would you want to watch it?

Well, clearly someone wants to. And someone wants to watch sophomoric drug and sex and fart jokes, and things blowing up. That audience is the target for many movies—teenage boys.

The main reason for targeting teenagers is that they are the people most likely to go to movies. Why them? They want to get out of the house, to have freedom, to get away from the parental units. And, of course, dating—the bar scene is pretty much out.

So there are fewer and fewer movies that target older adults, people in their thirties and forties and up. Remember all those movies I mentioned a while back? They were targeted at that adult audience. That doesn't mean that teenagers and younger didn't go to them; it's just that they were intended to be deeper, to have a heavier social message, one that adults were more likely to understand and appreciate.

Now, there **are** movies made for adults, movies like *Schindler's List*, *Saving Private Ryan* and *No Country for Old Men*. Such movies aren't really interesting to the big audience, teenagers. But there aren't as many of these kinds of movies as there were before the 1980s.

However, movies of all kinds draw large audiences, despite the VCR. Perhaps the greatest problem with the VCR was the quality of the picture. Although a standard TV has 525 scanning lines, VHS taping only provided 240 lines.[2] So the picture was essentially half as good as the original broadcast TV picture; if you wanted to record more time on the tape, the quality dropped even more. You just couldn't get the quality of the original. This was also true of pre-recorded tapes of movies: they were not the same thing as going to the movies with their sharp, clear pictures. Something had to be done.

But not just yet.

Remember sound recording, and how it went from mechanical to electrical recording and playback? Both methods recorded by etching pits in the grooves of first rubber, then shellac, and then vinyl records with a stylus.

The problem with this way of recording and playback is that the record deteriorates over time. The more it's played, the more the vinyl is scraped by the needle, gouging and smoothing away the pits. This reduces the quality of the sound, adding pops and crackles and hisses as new pits are etched in by the playback needle. Such was the case all the way up into the 1970s and 1980s. As long as the vinyl records were being played back with a needle in a groove, music lovers had to put up with the knowledge that the records they liked most were going to be the first to die on them.

Of course, this changed when Fritz Pfleumer's audiotape became a reality and reel to reel tape recorders came out in the 1950s. In fact, many record collectors would buy two of every record they wanted. One would be carefully wrapped and go into a vault for preservation. The second would be recorded to a tape and then go into the vault.

What these audiophiles knew was that even tape deteriorated. Every time the tape was played, a little bit of the oxide coating would come off as it went through the rollers and passed the electromagnetic recording and playback heads. And, of course, the plastic the tape was made of would age and crack and get brittle over time. So they would listen to the tape until it started producing poor sound, then out would come the second record from the vault and it would be recorded again on a new tape. In this way, a favorite recording could be listened to for years at the same high quality, although it could be an expensive way to go.

This was the case even when the cassette tape came out in 1963, especially since so much information was being recorded on and played back from such a narrow tape. Once again, something had to be done.

So once again it's time to go back in time, back to 1885, and a man trying to light the world—or at least a little bit of it. Gas lamp companies (don't worry, the connection will be made clear in a minute) had a new competitor. The electric light was brighter than the gas lamp, and they needed to increase the brilliance of their own light. The man who did that was Carl Auer Freiherr von Welsbach, an Austrian chemist. What he did was surround the flame in a gas lamp with a loosely woven bag of Sea Island cotton impregnated with various chemicals. When the bag got hot, it glowed with an incandescent light. This bag is still in use in camping lanterns today—it's called the gas mantle.

Welsbach experimented with different substances to impregnate his mantle, trying to get the brightest, longest lasting mantle possible and concentrating on minerals called "rare earths," a group of elements that share certain properties. A mantle impregnated with various chemicals including rare earths worked so well that gas lamps using a mantle were actually much brighter than electric lamps. What's important about this is that, while experimenting with rare earths, Welsbach discovered a new one he called neodymium. And we'll leave it sitting in its jar for a while—say, 75 years.

Time for another little side trip. As a publicity stunt, a glass company called Libbey Glass in Toledo, Ohio, wanted to show what they could do with glass, so they made Georgia Cayvan, the hot Broadway star of the 1880s, a dress made of spun glass fibers. (They made another one for a Spanish princess.) (Burke 1995)

A man named Michael Owens got really interested in what else you could do with glass fibers—like make fiberglass. Michael Owens is the founder of Owens-Corning Glass Company. What he worked on was getting really pure glass—no bubbles, no imperfections, no distortions.

In the 1960s, people got turned on by a new idea, and here's where we get back to Welsbach and his neodymium, and Owens and his pure glass. First, take pure glass and mix in a bit of neodymium. A magnetic field excites the neodymium atoms and they kind of overload and shoot out their excess energy in an incredibly intense beam of light. What you get is the laser, which stands for **L**ight **A**mplification by **S**timulated **E**mission of **R**adiation. Gordon Gould was the first to create the visible light laser, the ruby laser.

In 1962, Robert Hall invented the semiconductor, or diode, laser, the kind we find in all sorts of communication devices, like laser pointers, or CD players or DVD players.

A laser can focus down to a very fine beam, measured in micro millimeters, with absolutely no spread. It's like the difference between using a laser pointer and a flashlight. A laser provides a pinpoint of light, a flashlight a large pool. In addition, the length of a laser beam can be very finely measured, again in micro millimeters. So if pits are burnt or pressed into a surface, the laser can detect if they are there or not, no matter how shallow the pits are. The pits are read by the laser as either being there or not being there, a yes or no answer. A laser can read something that's digital, a "no" as a zero and a "yes" as a one. And we're back at computers running on binary code.

With the arrival of the commercial laser came a whole new methodology in communication. The thing about light is that it doesn't physically touch the medium it's getting information from, such as a phonograph needle touching a vinyl disk or the rollers and heads in a tape player touching the tape. With no physical contact between the player and the medium, there's no wear and tear. Once you've got the recording, it stays the same forever.

Almost immediately the laser-read compact disc, or CD, replaced the record and the tape as the medium of choice for music—as long as you could afford to replace your turntable and tape player with a CD player and buy all your albums again (assuming you could find them) in the new medium. However, prices quickly dropped, and the record and tape have virtually disappeared other than for purists and nostalgia buffs.

It wasn't only sound recording that the invention of the laser impacted. So were television and its companion, the VCR. In the early 1990s, Sony and Philips went head to head against Toshiba to develop a high density compact disc, one that could hold, not just the 700 megabytes of digital information that's the norm on a regular CD, but hold gigabytes of information. These companies came out with two systems that were, of course, incompatible. IBM's president, Lou Gerstner, acting as a matchmaker, led an effort to unite the two camps behind a single standard, anticipating a repeat of the costly format war between VHS and Betamax in the 1980s. So, by combining their technology Philips/Sony and Toshiba came up with a system that could put 4.7 gigabytes of digitized information on a CD, almost seven times more information than on a regular CD. This was large enough to put, not just one, but several albums of music on one disc. It was also enough to record a two hour movie. The digital video disc, or DVD, had been invented, and the first DVD players appeared in retail stores in 1996.

And that rang the death knell for the VCR. Well, it actually did no such thing. Although the DVD could have a much higher quality picture and sound than a video tape, providing all 525 scanning lines as opposed to the VCR's 240 lines, there was a problem— a user couldn't record on a DVD. If rhe wanted to record a show or a movie broadcast on TV, rhe still had to use a VCR. So, although video rental shops quickly switched from prerecorded VHS tapes to prerecorded DVDs, and DVD sales climbed, the VCR was still a part of most people's entertainment systems as a way of creating personal recordings of TV shows.

As far as the studios making TV shows and movies were concerned, the DVD was wonderful. People preferred the high quality pictures and sound, so they stopped building libraries of video tapes and starting building libraries of prerecorded DVDs. The VCR went back to just what Jack Valenti thought it should be for—recording something to watch later rather than to save for multiple viewings.

In 1999, even this use of the VCR started coming to an end when the digital video recorder, or DVR, came out. The first was TiVo, a subscription based service, but it was soon followed by other companies. The DVR converts the analog TV signal into digital information and records it to a computer hard drive instead of to tape. This method keeps the video and audio quality of the original show intact, unlike using the VCR.

Of course, there is a drawback to the DVR. The size of the hard drive limits the number of shows that can be kept. With a VCR you can just stick in a new tape if you want to save something. With a DVR you don't have that option.

Actually, today there is an option. In the 1990s, computer manufacturers started moving away from floppy disks to store data and began making CD burners. These are disk drives that could be installed in a computer and that would "burn" data to a blank CD by altering the properties of a dye placed on one side of the disk. It wasn't long before DVD burners for home computers became available.

A digital video recorder converts the analog TV signal to digital to save it to disk, and then back to analog to play back the recording to the TV. If you could convert the analog TV signal from the DVR back to digital, you could save it on a computer, and once there you could burn a TV show to a blank DVD. There are any number of video cards and dongles that can convert analog signals to digital. This wasn't good for movies since a DVD could only hold one hour of TV data, but it was fine for TV shows. Then manufacturers came out with dual layer DVD disks that could hold 8.5 gigabytes of digital information and burners to go with them, and it became possible to record an entire two-hour movie to your own DVD.

With these capabilities, the VCR as a way of saving video for future use was essentially dead—as long as you had a computer with all the appropriate hardware and software, the knowledge of how to use them, and the time.

The next step was to increase the amount of information that could be stored on a single disc beyond that of dual layer. To do that required making the pits representing zeros and ones even smaller and closer together, a laser with the precision to read and write distances measured in nanometers, and the technology with the precision to place that laser in just the right place so it would hit what it should. That next step was to replace the ruby laser with a blue laser with a shorter wave-length, resulting in what is known as Blue-Ray technology.

So we've got radios, TVs, computers, CD players, DVD players, all based on the work of Hollerith and his census, Fleming and his tubes, Kilby and his transistor, Gates and his programs, Wozniak and his home computer, and all those others who have changed how we receive the media. But it doesn't stop there.

Cell, short for cellular, phones came out in the 1980s. They were the size and weight of a brick—in fact, they were called "the brick" —and they required carrying the twenty-pound battery in a shoulder bag. For the first time, it was possible to have interpersonal communication at a distance at any time and any place. People were no longer tied to a wire plugged into the wall, and they didn't have to search for an unoccupied and functioning public telephone.

The Sony Walkman, another product impossible without the transistor, came out in 1979, for playing tape cassettes. A few years later, Sony came out with a personal CD player. Then, in 2001, Apple introduced the iPod, which dispensed with the need for any medium to carry the analog or digital information. It played mp3s, which are audio files converted to purely digital computer files, and it's gone through several incarnations. The mp3 player is now the personal music machine of choice for the majority of people, and it has added the abilities to carry digital photographs and even digital video that people can take anywhere and watch whenever they want.

In 1993, the must-have gadget for many people was GPS, or the global positioning system. Through picking up satellite signals, the handheld device can pinpoint its location anywhere on Earth within feet, or even inches. People can find out where they are, even if they're not going anywhere.

And then there was the iPhone in 2007, a so-called "smart" phone, which has gone through several incarnations. It now has all the "killer apps" (remember Visicalc?). With a tap on an icon on the touch screen of the phone, a user can not only make a phone call, but send a text message, email, have the phone make fart noises, connect to the Internet, and many other things—the possibilities number in the tens of thousands.

And then there's the biggie just mentioned, the one new form of communication that has changed everything—the Internet.

There are lots of stories about how the Internet came about, from its invention by the Defense Department to its invention by Al Gore.

This is the most common story. President Eisenhower created the Advanced Research Projects Agency, better known as ARPA, in the 1950s to research linking computers into a network to decentralize the computer network in case of a nuclear war. This became possible with three changes in computers: converting phone signals from analog to digital, connecting computers to each other through phone lines, and the idea of packet switching.

Packet switching means dividing a message to be sent into small pieces, a few tens or hundreds of bytes of digital information, called packets. Each of these packets has the same final destination address, called an IP, or Internet protocol, address, attached. Then the packets are sent over the computer network through the phone lines by being added to the data stream wherever there's an opening. Because any individual packet is so small, it doesn't need to wait for a large gap in the data stream. It could be likened to vehicles getting on to a freeway. A compact car is more likely to find a gap in the traffic large enough for it to get into a lane than will a double-trailer semi. What makes packet switching so efficient is that it's irrelevant which path through the system any particular packet that makes up the message takes, just so long as it moves along. When all the packets arrive at the destination address, they are reassembled and the message is received.

Well, that would work if all computers could talk to each other, but they couldn't; only computers made by the same manufacturer could communicate with each other. The problem was that computers were made by different companies and they weren't compatible because they had different basic input/output systems (called BIOS). So what researchers now had to do was to develop protocols, or computer commands in digital code, that would allow computers to communicate with each other regardless of their basic BIOS or their operating system.

Once these difficulties were ironed out, the Internet became a reality. At first, it was used by governments and universities so they could share information, especially research, mainly in the form of email. But there was, of course, interest by people like professors to communicate with people other than their fellow researchers at other universities, and interest by companies to make that happen. Thus was born the Internet Service Provider, or ISP, the first of which was CompuServe in 1979. All you needed was a modem.

A modem is an electronic device that converts the digital message packets produced by a computer into the analog signal that a telephone line can carry. As the packets arrive at their destination, the analog phone signal is converted by the modem at the destination into the digital information the computer can read, the packets are reassembled, and the message is received.

At first the speed at which a modem operated was extremely limited. Many people started with a 300 baud modem. This meant it could send or receive 300 bits per second— that's about 37 characters a second—the number of characters between the dashes in this sentence. That's not many in a second; in fact, at that rate it would take minutes to send the page you're reading.

However, technology improved, and the baud rate of modems steadily climbed: 1200, 2400, 4800. Currently, dial-up modems (those connecting to the Internet through standard phone lines by calling up an ISP) run at 56,000 baud, a definite improvement.

Fewer and fewer people are using dial-up connections to ISPs because the connection is considered far too slow. Today's modems connect through dedicated direct phone lines, TV cables, or wirelessly. Each of these connection types is far faster than dial-up, from 500,000 to five million baud.

There was really no need for such a massive increase in connection speed between a computer and a provider. At least, there wasn't until 1993 when Tim Berners-Lee, who created the World Wide Web in 1989, made it public. The big advance was the creation of HTML, or Hypertext Markup Language, which is a set of codes that tell a computer how to format a page and display it. As you can see below, the codes almost make sense.

<p	Start paragraph	</b>	End bold face	<li	Item in list
/p>	End paragraph	<a href="[URL address]"> [name of link]</a>	Go to link	</ul>	End of list
<b>	Bold face	<ul	Start of list		

The only problem was that you had to learn the codes and make sure you typed them in correctly or the web page just didn't work. In the beginning, it took time to create a page since there were no programs to do the work of putting in the codes.

One real advantage of HTML was hypertext links, or hyperlinks, which are highlighted words or images that a user could just click on and automatically move to another site instead of having to type in, or even know, the universal resource locator, or URL, the Internet address of a Web site. Still, everything on the Internet was text based: words, not images.

Then, in 1993, Marc Andreessen, a student at the University of Illinois, invented the first web browser, Mosaic. It was graphic based, using icons, pull-down menus and colorful links to display documents created using hypertext. Released as Netscape, and making Andreessen a billionaire, the Web became not just a reality but accessible and usable by just about anybody. No special knowledge, such as HTML or protocols or commands, was needed to get on and use the World Wide Web. And, of course, just like VHS beat Beta for videotaping, one of the biggest drivers of the popularity and improvement in the Internet was, and is, pornography. Currently, approximately 12 percent of all websites are devoted to porn.

Since the web browser was invented, the Internet has become central to just about everything in the modern world, from education to business. Today most documents that require distribution are put on a website instead of photocopied and passed out. The first place most people look for something, from a phone number to a fact to a schedule to a price to just about anything, is online. We even have new verbs created by the web, like Googling (the use of the Google search website to find something), and redefinitions of old ones, like surfing and browsing. And email has replaced the letter, the memo, and even using the phone to contact someone.

Each of these devices, whether it's the computers that run our lives, or the computer that eats your homework, the iPod that shuts out the world, or the cell phone that rules your world, has affected not only how we communicate, but how we live. And we'll look at that in the next chapter.

■ ENDNOTES

1. As a side note, the Kaypro and the Osborn were considered portable, like a laptop today, but they weighed a ton. You can put a handle on an anvil, but that doesn't make it portable.

2. S-VHS (Super VHS) machines provided 420 scan lines, a real improvement over standard VHS, but few people bought the machines and it required special S-VHS tapes. So the machines and tapes were generally for use by professionals rather than by average viewers, and since there were few machines, pre-recorded tapes remained in standard rather the S-VHS format.

MODERN COMMUNICATION MEDIA AND SOCIETY

odern communication media really started with the invention of the transistor. It grants everyone the ability not only to receive but to send both interpersonal and mass communication messages, With the invention of the transistor, electronics were no longer dependent on large, hot vacuum tubes, so electronic devices not only shrank in size and cost, they moved out of the hands of the corporations that could afford and house those devices and into the hands of average people. It's true that people did have radios and TV sets, but those were one-sided, passive receivers of mass media messages, not interactive connections, with both senders and receivers able to communicate with each other. The transistor changed everything.

In the 1960s, a popular toy was an electronics projects kit. Kids got these kits for Christmas or their birthdays and immediately started wiring together circuits using transistors. The results were always simple—a radio, a sound-activated light bulb, a light-activated buzzer. But these kinds of kits laid the groundwork for all the geeks and nerds to come who would take electronics to the next step.

With the invention of the integrated circuit, and then the IC chip that put together lots of integrated circuits as a single unit, the road was open for the invention of the communications media that we have today: satellite TV and radio; cell phones that not only connect us to others, but take pictures and videos, let us watch TV and movies and play games, keep track of our appointments, and find our way around; and home theatres with giant high-definition TVs and surround sound audio. And, of course, there's the computer with which people write everything, do spreadsheets, play games, email, Google, tweet, and connect.

So what effect has all this had on society? There are some small ones. For example, how many of you have ever received a handwritten letter from a friend? Or sent one? I'm not talking about holiday or birthday cards, but actual letters in which you write about your life, express hopes and dreams, make a personal connection with the person to whom you write. There was kind of a rush when such a letter appeared in your mailbox, that someone was thinking about you, and thought **enough** of you to take the time to actually put pen to paper, write the address where you actually live on an envelope, buy a stamp, and travel to a mailbox to drop it in.

Think about how it is today. There's no effort in an email or a text. Just sit down (or even walk down the street), type up something and click a button to send it off. Quite often, we just write something off the tops of our heads, not putting much thought or organization behind the communication to put clarity or emotion or real connection into it. And think of all the times that what you wrote was so stupid or insulting or disorganized that you wished there was a recall button so you could get it back.

And there's no thought in a tweet. They're less about making a connection than they are about putting words in a row to show the tweeter is there. I mean, how should you feel about someone telling you they're at the mall? Should you care? Are you supposed to join rher? Should you ask rher to get you something? Or is rhe just so narcissistic and egotistical that rhe thinks everyone is hanging on rhis every thought and action, that rhis input and opinions are that important to the lives of rhis readers?

We've even changed the way we think about communicating. We used to talk, or write on paper. Now we talk—on a phone. We write—on a phone—or a web page or . . . Just to show you how weird our ideas of the way to communicate can get, in September, 2009, two thirteen-year-old girls in Australia got stuck in a storm drain. So did they call someone? No. They updated their FaceBook pages to tell their friends where they were. It apparently didn't occur to them to use their phones to call the police or their parents. What's interesting about this incident is that the girls apparently were certain their friends were on and would see their call for help. For them social media, being on a computer, trumped actual personal contact.

Even proper etiquette, just plain good manners, has changed because of our modern media. Everyday we listen in on other people's private conversations, whether we wish to or not, as they don't even attempt to wait until they're alone or hold their voices down while they talk on their cell phones in public venues. We snoop on other people's private lives online. For example, a woman in Georgia named Stephanie Kahn had just gotten engaged and wanted to spread the news in her own time and her own way. However, her friends had taken pictures at the engagement party and put them on their pages before she knew anything about it or could do it herself. She started getting phone calls from people she hadn't told but who had found out from the web, and who were upset she hadn't told them. (Spokesman 9/26/09)

How about the effect on the family? Before the 1970s, the family would gather for dinner, and then generally do something together, like talk or play games or, since the 1950s, gather in the living room to watch TV. Whatever they did, at least a few hours every day the members of a family would have face-to-face contact with each other.

However, since the 1970s, it's normal for every person in the family to have a TV, and, since the 1990s a computer or a video game console, in their own rooms. They stay there, they eat there, they rarely gather together.

The effect has been to divide the family. Parents have less contact with their children, and vice versa. They've started to lead separate lives, often with very little in common. Before the 1980s and the '90s, there was no such concept as "quality time," in which parents and children **schedule** time to be together rather than gathering as a matter of course. And the whole idea of "play dates," where parents arrange times for their children to get together instead of the kids just going outside and spontaneously meeting their neighborhood or school friends to play, seems more for the parents than for the kids. The very concept of what constitutes a friend has been changed.

And, speaking of TV, the new technologies have made it the center of many people's lives. The artificial satellites and their attendant technologies to build them and put them into orbit made possible by the space race have increased the number of television channels from three to hundreds, and with that increase in channels has come an increase in viewing. Every year the average amount of household viewing goes up, currently to more than eight hours a day. If someone spends eight hours working and eight hours sleeping, that leaves zero hours for anything else.

Clearly, people aren't just sitting and watching TV—they have to be doing other things while the TV is on. This must mean that whatever is on isn't fascinating enough to command and hold a viewer's attention. The old saw, "100 channels and nothing is on," must be true.

So when a show comes on television that **is** a hit, one that does command and hold a viewer's attention, one that everybody is watching, or at least is talking about, it's a special event. But even that doesn't last. ***Lost*** was a major hit its first season, then the audience dropped. ***Heroes*** was a major hit its first season, then the audience dropped. The same happened with ***Grey's Anatomy*** and ***Desperate Housewives***.

The question we have to ask ourselves is—why? Is it because the quality of the shows dropped, or did the audience's interest in the show? Let's look at what shows like those mentioned above have in common. Their storylines—how the plot gets from the problem through a series of crises and complications to the climax that solves the problem—extend over many episodes. This is unlike most shows that have a problem that is solved at the end of the episode (recall the rules of storytelling). Shows that don't wrap up a story at the end of the episode require a commitment on the part of the audience to watch every, or almost every, episode to follow the story.

Let's look at another piece of information. The most popular newspaper in the United States is *USA Today*. Its most distinguishing features are that its articles are short, and it uses a lot of graphic elements like charts and maps to tell its stories, unlike virtually every other newspaper. In fact, *USA Today* deliberately designed its newspaper boxes that sell copies to look like TV sets in order to attract the TV generation.

Another little fact: Research shows that the average length of a sound bite, a statement usually made by someone trying to make a political point in a speech or discussion, has shortened since 1982 from just over 42 seconds to just over 7 seconds in length, or from approximately 100 words to under 20. They've changed from policy statements to bumper stickers with the concomitant loss of depth and meaning.

Add to these facts the 140 character limit on tweets, and we can arrive at a conclusion. Modern communication media and how they're used have caused, and reflect, the fact that people have a much shorter attention span than in the past. People are less likely to concentrate on one thing for any length of time, be it a book, a newspaper, a TV show, or even their own conversations. Have you ever noticed that, if someone you're conversing with speaks at what you perceive as too great a length, you start thinking about what you're going to say next instead of listening?

In addition, people don't concentrate on what they're doing for any length of time. Consider writing an essay for a class. In the past, it was normal to work on it for hours at a stretch, writing a first draft to carry out the idea until it was done. This would be followed by a period of polishing. Today, a student is more likely to write a paragraph, then switch to doing something else like texting or calling or watching TV or playing a video game, then come back to write another paragraph. In other words, people tend to work in bursts rather than at length. This often results in a lack of organization and coherence in writing, and a lack of polish in everything that is done. It's an attitude of "close enough."

Today people seem to have a much lower threshold of boredom. Let's take an example from the past. Abraham Lincoln and Stephen Douglas often debated, and audiences flocked to hear them. On one occasion, Douglas gave a three-hour speech, Lincoln delivered his rebuttal with another three-hour speech, and the audience hung on every word (they did take an hour for dinner between speeches). (Postman) In today's political debates, speeches are limited to three minutes or less, lest the audience get bored. Remote controls get a workout as people channel surf, looking for something to hold their attention. And then I consider my lectures. They're only 75 minutes long twice a week, and yet every day I see a handful of students get up and walk out, I presume because they're bored (I'd rather not believe they're just rude). I wonder how they would have survived lectures in the past that ran two to three hours. A personal anecdote illustrates the point. I once was given a class to teach that the previous professor met with once a week for three hours, and so it was scheduled that way for me. There were thirty students in the class. When I taught the same class the next semester, changing its schedule to three times a week for an hour a day, 175 people enrolled.

We've entered an era of instant gratification. Inundated with ads that say you can have it all, and have it now, with TV shows that solve problems in thirty or sixty minutes, with instant connection with anyone by phone or text or tweet, with whatever we want to know at our fingertips just by Googling or wikiing, we've lost that sense that things take time, that good things come to him who waits, that haste makes waste, and other assorted clichés.

This idea of "get it instantly" has even influenced the news and how it's gathered. TV news now relies on people shooting cell phone videos to illustrate stories, and ask for people to twitter. It's almost as though people's instant opinions are the same as facts. And they aren't.

But perhaps the greatest effect on society has been the invention that led the way to the modern age—the computer. Computers now run everything: our energy systems, our roads, our cars, every other form of communication—our lives. It used to be that people made the decisions; now they usually do what the computers tell them. After all, the computers have more information, so they should know better, right? Many decisions are turned over entirely to computers, without bothering with people. The first big stock market crash after the Great Depression, the one in 1987, was caused by the computers deciding to sell stock based on market conditions the computers' algorithms said should be responded to by selling. The more stock the computers sold, the lower the market dipped, which the computers interpreted as a reason to sell, which lowered the market, which led to more computer selling, etc., etc., etc. The market dropped more than 22 percent before it was stopped. It apparently hadn't occurred to anyone that computers only do what they're told to do, and if they're told to sell stock when the market goes down, that's what they'll do. In 2010, the Dow Jones Average suddenly dropped 1,000 points in a matter of minutes, then rebounded. The apparent explanation was a computer glitch set off by a human trader typing the wrong letter on his keyboard, telling his computer to sell a billion shares of a stock instead of a million. That triggered computers throughout the investment industry to sell stock. The computers don't think or even notice what's happening. They just follow orders, and millions of dollars were lost because there weren't any people involved in the decision making that would have prevented the event.

And, of course, everybody keeps their records on computers now, instead of on paper. Computer databanks are filled with information, just about anything anybody can think of to put in there. This includes everything they can find about **you**. And this information is used to make decisions—about you. Should you be given credit? Should you be able to buy a car or a house? Should you get health care, and if so what kind? Should you get hired for a job? People used to make those decisions. Now they look at what computers say about you, and they follow their recommendations. What if the information is wrong? Once it's in the computer, it's almost impossible to change.

What have modern communication media done to society? First of all, we're at the beck and call of our supposed servants, the phone and the computer. We answer the phone when it rings, interrupting conversations and ignoring the people we're with in favor of the person who's called. Where we are or what we're doing or who we're with is irrelevant. The phone rings and we talk—on the bus, in the restaurant, during the movie. We've actually become quite discourteous, annoying people with our one-sided conversations. When it came up for a vote to allow people to use their cell phones on planes, it was voted down, not because the phones might be dangerous by disrupting the plane's electronics, the excuse used for years, but because of how annoying it would be to be trapped on a plane with people yakking away in disjointed conversation. It would come in second only to the screaming baby.

Think about our other media. Books, newspapers and magazines can't demand to be read. We're not forced to go to movies or watch TV. In each of these cases **we** decide to use them. But that ringing phone or "you've got mail" ding compels our attention, shrilling that "do something about me, and do it now" demand. Personally, my favorite line from the movie ***First Monday in October***, set at the US Supreme Court, was delivered when a character refused to answer a ringing phone: "There's nothing in the Constitution that says you have to answer the phone."

Second, our threshold of boredom has dropped to a new low. Modern communication means always having something to do, if only to call somebody to tell them how bored you are. We've become so used to rapid change, especially in electronics, that we expect things to change, and we feel like something is wrong if no new product or device or application or whatever doesn't come out. Look at your cell phone. It works perfectly well, but I bet you're feeling vaguely dissatisfied with it and are looking forward to getting the next new thing in cell phones. What else it could do I have no idea. Maybe clean your room. Or fetch you a beer. Or talk to your mother so you don't have to. But whatever the new thing is, you're going to want it, right? And in the meantime you'll play solitaire on your computer.

Third, we've lost our privacy. Not the personal kind, like someone walking in while we're taking a shower. It's the privacy that means strangers don't know things about us we would rather they didn't. That kind of privacy is gone. Just think of the GPS, the global positioning system. There's a GPS chip in your phone, and as long as your phone is turned on, so is the GPS. There is a good reason for it: if you get lost or in an accident, your phone will tell people where you are so they can come and get you. But it also means that people know where you are, whether you want them to or not. The computer databanks know things about you that you probably don't want others to know. People know things, like that embarrassing thing you did in high school (*everybody* did something embarrassing in high school), and it'll appear on somebody's Facebook or MySpace page, in text and often with pictures. And once something is on the web, it's there forever. If you go to a party, don't post the pictures of you drunk out of your mind and dropping your pants on your page. Employers ten years from now will see those pictures, make a decision about your behavior and judgment on the basis of those pictures, and you won't get the job. That's happened.

Fourth, anything anybody wants to say they can say to everybody. Anyone can be a columnist—just start up a blog and spout any nonsense you want, which is what a lot of people do. Note I don't say that anyone can be a journalist, although that's what many bloggers call themselves. There's a difference. Journalists are, or at least should be, required to stick to facts and what those facts can mean. If they just make stuff up, they can lose their jobs and even get sued. Columnists, which is what bloggers who call themselves journalists usually are, can say anything they want—they aren't restricted to facts and logic and a desire to inform. Columnists are more driven by a desire to convince, to express their own points of view and try to get people to agree with them—even if it means distortions, special pleading (which is presenting only one side of an argument as though it contains all the evidence and thus is completely biased), and even outright lies. Before the computer, these people had no outlet but their friends (assuming they had any) and unwilling bartenders. Now they have the world.

Everyone can be an author. It used to be that a publisher had to agree to print your book, and it was tough to get published because it was expensive and there was no guarantee the publisher would get the money back through the sales of that book. Today, a person can write a book and put it on a website for almost no financial outlay. There's still no guarantee anyone will read it, but you can write it and put it out there.

But perhaps there's a greater effect of the new media on society. Remember how printing destroyed the village by opening up the world to everybody, leading to trade and knowledge, and the growth of cities and nations? No longer was knowledge limited to people's personal experience that covered only the seven miles around them, as far as they could travel and still get back before dark. Nor was knowledge limited to what was in old people's heads. Myths and legends and rumors no longer ruled people's belief of what the world outside their village was like. Communication before printing was one-on-one, one person talking to another.

Now we're in a new village, an electronic one that's global. Today we can travel anywhere in world just by logging on to the Internet. Knowledge is in computer databanks, not in people's heads. But myths and legends and rumors are back—with a vengeance. What we know is what we get from our choices of websites, and, as I mentioned long ago, what people read and watch is what they already agree with.

For example, I know you all use Wikipedia as the ultimate source of information — books and journals and anything else that may require some effort to get are the choice of last, not first, resort. But did you know that there's also a Conservapedia, a Wikipedia for conservatives? Resembling Wikipedia, it has articles that spin facts to reflect the conservative socio-political viewpoint. For instance, that there's no evidence for global warming, or that Obama is a foreign-born socialist in his biography, or that evolution is a hoax. Depending on which 'pedia' you go to, you'll have completely different "facts." And don't forget that Wikipedia is user edited, which is how Stephen Colbert of the satirical TV show

The Colbert Report tripled the number of elephants in Africa—simply by changing the number in the wiki article.

So we're back in a village. We've never been closer—and we've never been farther apart. As you walk around your campus or town, take a look around. Just about everybody is either talking or texting on the phone or have their ears plugged with earphones, locked in their own private little worlds and shutting out the rest. We connect with people everywhere—and rarely, if ever, see them. We ignore the people we're standing next to in favor of people far away, have friends we've never met, make romantic attachments while hundreds and thousands of miles apart, even go to school and never set foot in a classroom.

Modern communication, which is more about the technology than about the content, has changed the purpose of communication. For hundreds of thousands of years, communication was about survival or information or telling the social stories to bind a group, be it two people or two hundred million, together. But the ease of communication provided by modern technology has turned much of communication into the electronic version of small talk at a party, putting out words for the sake of putting out words. Think about that the next time you text, or tweet, or twerp, on whatever the next gadget is.

16

ADVERTISING

One of the major message types that appear in the media is advertising. So we'll start with a definition.

Advertising is the nonpersonal communication of information usually paid for and usually persuasive in nature about products, services or ideas by identified sponsors through the various media. (Bovee, 7)

Another nice piece of academese. So let's see what all that means.

■ NONPERSONAL

First, what is "nonpersonal"? There are two basic ways to sell anything: personally and nonpersonally. Personal selling requires the seller and the buyer to get together. There are advantages and disadvantages to this. The first advantage is time. The seller has time to discuss everything about the product in detail. The buyer has time to ask questions, get answers, examine evidence for or against purchase.

A second advantage of personal selling is that the seller can see you, the person rhe's selling to. Rhe can see your face and see how the sales message is getting across. If you yawn or your eyes shift away, you're obviously bored, and the seller can change rhis approach. Rhe can also see if you're hooked, see what features or benefits have your attention and emphasize them to close the sale.

Finally, the seller can easily locate potential buyers. If you enter a store, you probably have an interest in something that store sells. Street vendors and door-to-door sellers can simply shout at possibilities, like the Hyde Park (London) vendors who call out, "I say there, Guv'nor, can you use a set of these dishes?" Or they knock at the door and start their spiel with an attention grabber. From there on, they fit their message to the individual customer, taking all the time a customer is willing to give them.

Disadvantages do exist. Personal selling is, naturally enough, expensive, since it is labor intensive and deals with only one buyer at a time. Just imagine trying to sell chewing gum or guitar picks or popsicles one on one; it would cost a dollar a stick, pick or lick.

In addition, its advantage of time is also a disadvantage. Personal selling is time-consuming. Selling a stereo or a car can take days, and major computer and airplane sales can take years.

Nonetheless, although personal selling results in more rejections than sales, and they can be nerve-racking, frustrating and ego destroying for the salesperson, when the person is good at it, it is more directed and successful than advertising.

From the above, it appears that personal selling is much better than advertising, which is nonpersonal. This is true. Advertising has none of the advantages of personal selling: there is very little time in which to present the sales message; there is no way to know just who the customer is or how rhe is responding to the message, the message cannot be changed in mid-course to suit the customer's reactions.

Then why bother with advertising? Because its advantages exactly replace the disadvantages of personal selling, and it can emulate some of the advantages. Let's begin by looking at the latter.

First, advertising has, comparatively speaking, all the time in the world. Unlike personal selling, the sales message and its presentation do not have to be created on the spot with the customer watching. It can be created in as many ways as the writer can conceive; it can be rewritten, tested, modified, injected with every trick and appeal known to affect consumers. (Some of that is coming up later.)

Second, although advertisers may not see the individual customer, nor be able to modify the sales message according to that individual's reactions at the time, it does have research about customers. The research can identify potential customers, find what message elements might influence them, and figure out how best to get that message to them. Although the research is meaningless when applied to any particular **individual**, it is effective when applied to large groups of customers.

Third, and perhaps of most importance, advertising can be far cheaper per potential customer than personal selling. Personal selling is extremely labor intensive, dealing with one customer at a time. Advertising deals with hundreds, thousands, or millions of customers at a time, thus reducing the cost per customer to mere pennies. In fact, advertisers arrive at their costs in part by using a formula to determine, not cost per potential customer, but cost per thousand potential customers.

So, it appears that advertising is a good idea as a sales tool. For small ticket items, such as chewing gum and guitar picks, advertising is cost effective to do the entire selling job. For large ticket items, such as cars and computers, advertising can do a large part of the selling job, and personal selling is used to complete and close the sale.

Advertising is nonpersonal, but effective.

■ COMMUNICATION

Now for communication. Communication means not only speech or pictures but also any way one person can pass information, ideas or feelings to another. Thus communication uses all of the senses: smell, touch, taste, sound and sight. Of the five, only two are really useful in advertising—sound and sight.

Smell

Let's start with smell. Smell is an extremely strong form of communication. Research has shown that the smell receptors in the nose are wired straight into the emotion centers of the brain. However, when it comes to advertising, smell isn't very useful. A smell can immediately evoke memories. Remember times when you've smelled something and what memories came to your mind. The smell could be a perfume or an aftershave that reminds you of Megan or Jason. It could be popcorn, newly mown grass, charbroiled steak, or roses. Any smell can conjure up a memory for you.

However, that is smell's greatest problem for advertising. Although a smell can evoke a memory, everyone's memories are different. For example, the smell of hay in a cow barn always reminds me of my grandfather's farm in Indiana and the fun I had there as a child. To others, however, that same smell makes them think a cow had an accident in the living room, which is not at all the same response as mine. If an advertiser wanted to make **me** nostalgic about farms and grandparents, that smell would be perfect. To others, the smell might evoke ideas of cow accidents or the pain of having to buck bales on a hot summer day; neither image is of much use in making a product appealing.

The point is, the advertiser cannot control the **effect** of using smell in advertising. Although many people smell the same things, what they associate with those smells varies with each person. For instance, my reaction to those perfume smell strips in magazines is, "My god, what a stink!" An unlikely reaction to make me want to buy. So since smell lacks any control over a customer's reaction, smell is a very weak form of communication for advertising.

Touch

So how about touch? Touch has a limitation that makes it of little use to advertising—the customer has to come in actual contact with the item to be touched. Thus, the item must actually exist and be in a medium that can carry it. This puts touch more in the realm of personal selling than of advertising.

It is possible to use touch for a limited number of products. For example, samples of cloth or paper can be bound into magazines. The potential customer can thus feel percale or the texture of corduroy, tell through touch the difference between slick magazine stock, embossing, Classic Laid or 100% rag paper. However, for the majority of products, touch is useless for advertising.

Taste

As for taste, it's probably the least useful communication channel available to advertising. Like touch, taste requires the potential customer to come in actual physical contact with the product. However, taste is even more limited than touch. There are few products other than food for which taste is a major selling point, and there is virtually no medium in which an ad can be placed that people are likely to lick. I'm sure few people are going to lick a magazine page or the TV screen, nor get much sense of what the product tastes like from them. It **is** possible to use direct mail, sending samples to homes, but that is an expensive way to advertise.

Thus, taste is much more effective in personal selling, such as sampling foods in supermarkets or in door-to-door sales.

The remaining two senses, sound and sight, are the most effective and easily used channels of communication available to advertising. For these reasons virtually all advertising relies on them.

Sound

Let's start with sound. Sound is extremely useful for advertising. It can be used in a variety of media, from radio and television to the new technology of binding micro-sound chips in magazines to present 20-second sales messages. It is also capable of presenting words and "theatre of the mind."

Words, the method by which humans communicate their ideas and feelings, are presented by sound, by speaking aloud. Through the use of words, it is possible to deliver logical arguments, discuss pros and cons, and evoke emotions.

Even more, through the use of sound it is possible to create what is called "the theatre of the mind." What this means is that sound can conjure in the listener's mind images and actions that don't necessarily exist. For example, if you want to create before the mind's eye the image of a party, you need merely use the sound effects of people talking and laughing, the tinkle of glasses and ice, perhaps music in the background. Even easier, tape record a party and play it back. To evoke images of a soft spring day, it is sufficient to hear the sounds of a breeze rustling leaves, the chirrup of insects, the soft call of birds. The listener's mind will take those sounds, combine them, make sense of them, and create an image suited to their individual taste. For example, a beer commercial may play the sounds of a bar in the background, and the listeners may imagine themselves in their own favorite bar, and perhaps ordering that brand of beer.

So sound, in the forms of words and sound effects, are quite useful to the advertiser in affecting a listener.

Sight

Now for sight. Sight is arguably the most useful of the communication channels available to the advertiser. Through sight, it is possible to use both words and images effectively.

Words don't have to be spoken to be understood. They can be printed, as well. Although it's difficult to put in written words the emotional impact possible in spoken words, with their inflections and subtle sound cues, written words nevertheless are unsurpassed for getting across and explaining complex ideas or arguments.

There is an additional factor in sight that makes sight excellent for advertising. The old cliché, "A picture is worth a thousand words," is correct. Think how long it takes to describe something as opposed to showing a picture of it. No matter how many words you use, some details will be left out that are visible at a glance. So sight can quickly and concisely show a customer what the advertiser wants rher to see, be it a product or how buying the product can benefit rher.

In addition, the mind does not have to consciously recognize what the eye sees for it to have an effect on the subconscious. An advertiser can put many inconspicuous details into a picture that will affect a customer on the subconscious level. For example, a drop of water on a rose petal may not consciously register ("I see there's a drop of water on this rose"), but it will unconsciously leave an impression of freshness and delicacy. A small child looking upward into the camera, unsmiling with eyes wide, gives an impression of sadness and vulnerability, not shortness.

The five forms of human communication can be used to send any message to potential customers. However, not all five are equal. Smell, touch and taste are of little use, but sound and sight are of great value and effectiveness.

■ INFORMATION

Okay, let's go to information. Information is defined as knowledge, facts or news. However, you should bear in mind that one person's information is another person's scam, particularly when advertisers talk about their products.

Information comes in many forms. It can be complete or incomplete. It can be biased or deceptive. Complete information is telling someone everything there is to know about something: what it is, what it looks like, how it works, what its benefits and drawbacks are. However, to provide complete information about anything is time consuming and difficult. For example, to tell all about a car would require explaining its appearance, manufacture and manufacturer; what percentage of parts are made in which countries; cost of upkeep, mileage (city and highway), cost (basic and with any and all combinations of options), sales and excise taxes per state, preparation costs, insurance costs per state and locale; ride characteristics (noise by db interior and exterior, ergs required for steering and braking, relative comfort of seats, length of reach required to use controls, degrees of lean when cornering) acceleration; braking distance at many different speeds, etc. All of this would require a documentary, not a commercial. Complete information is impossible to provide in an ad.

Thus, for advertising, information must of necessity be incomplete; it cannot discuss everything there is to know about the subject. In advertising, what appears is everything the writer thinks the customer **needs** to know about the product in order to make a decision about whether or not to buy. That information will generally be about how the product can benefit the customer.

There is, of course, the concept of affirmative disclosure. This concept requires an advertiser to provide customers with any information that could materially affect their purchase decision. Lewis A. Engman, FTC Chair in 1974, said:

> "Sometimes the consumer is provided not with information he wants but only with the information the seller wants him to have. Sellers, for instance, are not inclined to advertise negative aspects of their products even though those aspects may be of primary concern to the consumer, particularly if they involve considerations of health or safety . . ."

The Federal Trade Commission, or FTC, deals with such omissions by demanding affirmative disclosure of such information, and it backs up its demands with the force of law.

Bias is being partial towards something, feeling that something is better or worse than other things. Biased information about a product emphasizes what is good and ignores what is bad about it. In advertising, this is not only normal, but also necessary. Of course, an advertiser is biased toward rhis own product and against the competition. Selling rhis product is the way rhe makes rhis money, and rhis competition's sales reduce that income. So any advertising will use words and images that show how good rher product is and/or how **poor** rhis competition's is. This is biased information, but it is recognized and accepted by industry, regulators and consumers—it's called puffery, the legitimate exaggeration of advertising claims to overcome natural consumer skepticism.

However, sometimes the biased information goes beyond legitimate puffery and slips into deception, which is the deliberate use of misleading words and images. In other words, deceptive information is lying to the customer about the qualities of a product. Such deception is illegal, and the FTC requires the advertiser to cease and desist and, in some instance, to do corrective advertising to repair any damage. For example, Listerine mouthwash advertised for years that their product was good for colds and sore throats. This was a lie— Listerine had no effect on colds or sore throats. So the FTC required that every Listerine ad, either print or broadcast, contain the disclaimer, "Listerine has no effect on colds or sore throats," and to run those ads for a year to correct the wrong impression they had made.

■ PAID FOR

". . . paid for . . ." is pretty straightforward. If an ad is created and placed in a medium, the costs of creation and the time or space in that medium must be paid for. This is a major area in which advertising departs from public relations.

PR seeks to place information about companies and/or products in the media without having to pay for the time or space. PR creates news releases and sends them to news media in hopes they will be run. Often PR departments produce events that will be covered by news media and thus receive space or time. There is no guarantee that the media will run any of the PR material.

Advertising doesn't have that problem. If time or space is bought in the media, the ads will appear (as long as they follow the guidelines set down for good taste, legal products and services, etc.). The drawback is that ads are clearly designed to extol the virtues of products and companies, and consumers perceive any ad as at least partly puffery. PR pieces are usually not so perceived.

■ PERSUASIVE

"Persuasive" stands to reason as part of the definition of advertising. The basic purpose of advertising is to identify and differentiate one product from another in order to persuade the consumer to buy that product in preference to another. Later I'm going to discuss some basic elements of persuasion.

■ PRODUCTS, SERVICES OR IDEAS

Products, services or ideas are the things that advertisers want consumers to buy. (In the case of ideas, "buy" means to accept or agree with, as well as to lay out hard, cold cash.)

However, there is more involved in products or services than simply offering items for purchase.

(During the following discussion, "products" will mean products, services and ideas, unless otherwise noted.)

A product is **not** merely its function. It's actually a bundle of values, what the product means to the consumer. That bundle may contain the product's function, but it also contains the social, psychological, economic or whatever other values are important to the consumer.

For example, let's look at a car. If the function of a car—transportation—is all that's important, then manufacturers would only need to build motorized boxes on wheels, and consumers would be happy with them. Such is obviously not the case. The number of models and types of cars is huge, and if consumers didn't demand the variety, it wouldn't exist. Consumers must find factors other than mere transportation just as, if not more, important.

Perhaps the value is social. The type of car a person drives is often indicative of that person's social status. A clunker shows a lower status than a Rolls Royce. A sports car shows that a person is (or wishes to be perceived as) more socially active and fun loving than a person in a sedan or a minivan. The type of car can even indicate which social grouping a person wants to be considered part of. In the 1980s, Volvos and BMWs were the cars for Yuppies. Today, green cars like the Prius are for the ecologically minded—and occasionally the pretentious.

Perhaps the value is psychological. Some cars may make people feel safer, or sexier, or give them self-esteem or enjoyment. I'll go further into this later.

Perhaps the value is economic. Some cars may be cheaper to run, give better mileage, carry more people or cargo, cause less damage to the environment.

The above four values—functional, social, psychological and economic—can stand alone. However, for most consumers, the values are bundled together in varying proportions. How closely a product approximates an individual's proportion of values will often determine whether rhe will buy that product or not.

Companies try to determine through research what values consumers want in their products, and then they advertise to show how their product satisfies the customers' bundle of values better than competitors' products. To do this, the company must differentiate its product from those of competitors. There are three basic differentiations: perceptible, imperceptible, and induced.

Perceptible

Perceptible differences are those that actually exist that make one product obviously different from others of the same kind. The difference may be in color or size or shape or brand name or some other way. In any case, the consumer can easily see that this car or couch or camera is different from other cars or couches or cameras. Perceptible differences allow a person to make an instant identification of one product as opposed to another.

Imperceptible

Imperceptible differences are those that actually exist between one product and others, but are not obvious. For example, there are imperceptible but profound differences between PC and Mac computers. You can't simply look at a computer and tell which it is. The machines themselves can and usually do look alike except for possible minor cosmetic differences such as logos. And yet buying one precludes being able to use software designed for the other.

The same applies to TVs. Although you can't see the difference between a regular 720p TV and a high-def 1080i TV by looking at the exterior case and screen, the difference in the picture you get is vast.

Induced

For many products, there is no actual substantive difference between one and another. For many brands of cigarettes, beer, cleansers and soaps, rice, over-the-counter health products, etc., etc., ad nauseam, there is essentially no difference between one brand and another. These products are called **parity** products.

The only way to differentiate one from another of these products is to induce that difference, to persuade people that there actually is some difference, and that the difference is important to them. These differences are created through advertising, not through any inherent difference in the products, and that creation often uses the appeals and methods discussed later in this lecture.

Heidelberg, the workingman's beer. Michelob, the sophisticated nightlife beer. Bud, the athletic beer. Bud Light, the sexy party beer. Miller Lite, the fun and funny beer. Coors, the environmental beer. Coors Light, the fast beer. All of these are images projected onto products that have virtually no difference between them. (Taste tests show that few people can tell one from the other, particularly after having a few of any.) This approach depicts the product in association with a lifestyle. For example, soft drinks show people having fun, usually athletic fun. (A root beer company countered this approach by calling itself "the sit down soft drink.") Beer ads show people having fun. Airline ads show people having fun. (Notice a trend here?) They want you to think that if you use their product, you will enjoy the lifestyle depicted, and if you don't, you won't. Of course, the fact that the product is not necessary to the lifestyle is ignored.

Another approach is to project an image on a parity product. Marlboro is rugged male, Virginia Slims is independent female, Benson & Hedges is intellectual, Camel is cool and sophisticated. That there is no real difference between one brand of cigarette and another is beside the point. The point is, if you want the image you must use the product. This image approach is so successful that a manly man wouldn't be caught dead (no pun intended) smoking Virginia Slims or Benson & Hedges—he'd feel like a sissy wimp (or rather, that is what he thinks his friends would think he was).

There is great difficulty in differentiating parity products from another. They must rely on creating a trivial or even nonexistent difference in the bundle of values their target audience might find important to their purchase decision. However, if and once that difference is firmly established in the target audience's perception, a company can often rely on habit, brand loyalty and/or cognitive dissonance to get repeat business.

■ IDENTIFIED SPONSORS

Identified sponsors means whoever is putting out the ad tells the audience who they are. There are two reasons for this. First, it's a legal requirement, and, second, it makes good sense.

Legally, a sponsor must identify itself as the sponsor of an ad. This prevents the audience from getting a misleading idea about the ad or its contents. For example, many ads that appear in newspapers look like news articles: same typeface, appearance, use of columns, etc. If the ad is not identified as such, the audience could perceive it as news about a product, rather than an attempt to persuade the audience to buy it. Case in point: what looks like a news article discusses a weight-loss plan. In journalistic style, it talks about the safety, efficacy, and reasonable price of the product. A reasonable person might perceive the "article" as having been written by a reporter who had investigated weight-loss programs and decided to objectively discuss this particular one. Such a perception is misleading and illegal. Since it is an ad, somewhere on it there must appear the word "advertisement" to ensure that the audience does not think it is an objective reporting of news.

Second, it makes good sense for a sponsor to identify itself in the ad. If the sponsor doesn't, it's possible for the audience to believe the ad is for a competitor's product, thus wasting all the time, creativity and money that went into making and placing the ad.

■ VARIOUS MEDIA

The various media are the nonpersonal (remember that?) channels of communication that people have invented and used and continue to use. These include newspapers, magazines, radio, television, billboards, transit cards, sandwich boards, skywriting, posters, anything that aids communicating in a nonpersonal way ideas from one person or group to another person or group. They do not include people talking to each other. First, talking is personal and advertising is nonpersonal; and, second, there is no way to use people talking to each other for advertising—word of mouth is not an advertising medium, since you can't control what is said. (The best you could do is start a rumor, which will undoubtedly distort the message in the telling; that is more the province of the PR department.)

So, to repeat (in case you've forgotten by now), "Advertising is the nonpersonal communication of information usually paid for and usually persuasive in nature about products, services or ideas by identified sponsors through the various media."

Advertising's not a new idea. It's been around for thousands of years. One way of looking at the cave paintings of Lascaux, which are about 17,000 years old, is as advertising. They could be selling to the spirits of animals the idea of showing up for the hunt. Or not.

Nonetheless, advertising recognizable as advertising has been around for millennia.

For the first few thousand years, people used advertising to promote three things: locations, services, and "want ads."

Daniel Mannix, in his book on the Roman games, ***Those About to Die***, quotes an ad found on a tombstone:

"Weather permitting, 30 pairs of gladiators, furnished by A. Clodius Flaccus, together with substitutes in case any get killed too quickly, will fight May 1st, 2nd and 3rd at the Circus Maximus. The fights will be followed by a big wild beast hunt. The famous gladiator Paris will fight. Hurrah for Paris! Hurrah for the generous Flaccus, who is running for Duumvirate!"

Below this is an ad for the copywriter: "Marcus wrote this sign by the light of the moon. If you hire Marcus, he'll work day and night to do a good job." (Mannix, 28)

That's an example of a location ad. So were the signs that hung outside the doors of taverns and inns.

Handbills and posters were also a popular form of advertising. They were passed out to promote such events as plays, or recruiting for the military. For example, in 1798 the captain of the U.S. frigate *USS Constitution* advertised for a crew:

"To all able-bodied and patriotic Seamen, who are willing to serve their Country, and Support its Cause:

"The President of the United States, having ordered the Captain and Commander of the good Frigate CONSTITUTION, of 44 guns, now riding in the harbor of Boston, to employ the most vigorous exertions to put said ship, as speedily as possible, in a situation to sail at the shortest command.

"Notice is hereby given, That a HOUSE OF RENDEZVOUS is opened at the sign of the Federal Eagle, kept by Mrs. BROADERS, in Fore-street;—where ONE HUNDRED and FIFTY able Seamen, and NINETY-FIVE ordinary Seamen, will have an opportunity of entering into the service of their country for One Year, unless sooner discharged by the President of the United States. —To all able bodied Seamen, the sum of SEVENTEEN DOLLARS; and to all ORDINARY SEAMEN the sum of TEN DOLLARS per month, will be given; and two month s advance will be paid by the Recruiting Officer, if necessary.

"None will be allowed to enter this honorable service, but such as are well organized, healthy and robust; and free from scorbutic and consumptive affections.

"A glorious opportunity now presents to the brave and hardy Seamen of New England, to enter the service of their country—to avenge its wrongs—and to protect its rights on the ocean.

"Those brave Lads, are now invited to repair to the FLAGG of the CONSTITU-TION now flying at the above rendezvous; where they shall be kindly received, handsomely entertained, and may enter into immediate pay." (Gruppe, 27)

Newspapers carried ads to help defray the cost of publication. The ads were often want ads, and a common type during the American colonial period was ads about runaway slaves, either trying to get them back or informing that one had been found.

What weren't advertised were products. Most products were one of a kind and handmade to order. So other kinds of advertising signs, hanging outside shops, promoted services. For example, boot makers would hang a boot-shaped sign outside their shops to let consumers know where to go to get their footwear. However, this was not product advertising so much as service advertising. Yes, the product was boots. But the sign was to tell people where they could get boots made. The boot maker didn't have a large stock of merchandise that the consumer could buy on the spot. Instead, he had samples of his work. The customer would choose the desired style, and the cobbler would take measurements and make the footwear. The customer would come back later to get it.

In both of these cases, what were being advertised weren't products. The purpose of the advertising was to gather people, as audience, as recruits, as customers.

It wasn't until the Industrial Revolution at the beginning of the nineteenth century that true product advertising began. This was because, for the first time, products were being mass-produced rather than made to order. This led to three eras in marketing.

The first era was production-oriented. When mass production began, it was still limited. Demand for off-the-shelf products exceeded supply. There was no need to promote products when they sold as soon as they were made. So if a company made cars, and people wanted cars, then all the company had to do was to tell people where to get them.

However, as time went on, production expanded and created a surplus of goods. Supply exceeded demand. This led to the sales-oriented era. Companies would promote their products to convince consumers to buy their products rather than those of their competitors. Nonetheless, manufacturers still produced what they wanted to, counting on their ability to convince consumer to buy whatever products they made.

Eventually, though, the supply so far exceeded the demand that consumers had more choices than any promotion could overcome. In addition, they developed a resistance to "hard-sell" advertising. Producers began to realize that it made more sense to find out what the consumers wanted before making them, rather than trying to talk them into buying afterward. We are, to a large extent, in this marketing-oriented era today.

An example of this progression is the American auto industry. When Henry Ford invented the production-line method of manufacturing cars, there was no need to promote them—Model-Ts were sold before they were built. This was production-oriented marketing of cars.

As time went on, more manufacturers started building cars, and the supply of cars went up. Advertising likewise went up, as producers tried to convince consumers that their cars were better than competitors' cars. Nonetheless, the manufacturers made their cars as they wished. For example, car companies would alter the appearance of their cars, apparently at random, then try to convince consumers that what they really wanted was tailfins so big you couldn't get the car in the garage. For example, Cadillac introduced a car with huge fins and loads of chrome, and it was a two-door car that was too long to fit in a parking space. Car makers counted on the advertising to convince people that whatever feature they put in the car was what people wanted, whether it was two-tone paint jobs, three tons of chrome, or fins like the tail on a 747.

However, when non-American manufacturers entered the American market, they first tried to find out what Americans wanted in their cars. The first and greatest example was the Volkswagen bug. American cars were big, long, wide, flashy, gas guzzling, and changed in appearance every year. The bug was small, ugly, and gas-efficient. It was also easy to park, cheap to run, ran forever and never changed appearance just to go out of style. What changed was what consumers said they wanted (like a gas gauge!). As other non-American manufacturers entered the market, they also found out what consumers wanted, then built their cars that way. This was marketing orientation.

Of course, marketing orientation doesn't mean "no advertising." Advertising is just as important in marketing orientation as in sales. It's the approach that changes.

Early consumer advertising during the sales-oriented era was basically caveat emptor ("Let the buyer beware"). Producers said just about anything they wanted in their ads. For example, a product of the 1880s was the "Health Jolting Chair," a chair festooned with springs and levers. The copy extolled its virtues to the skies:

"The most important Health Mechanism ever produced . . .

"It affords a PERFECT means of giving EFFICIENT exercise to the ESSENTIALLY IMPORTANT NUTRITIVE ORGANS OF THE BODY in the most DIRECT, CONVENIENT, COMFORTABLE, and INEXPENSIVE manner.

"Suitable for all ages and for most physical conditions.

"INDISPENSABLE TO THE HEALTH AND HAP-PINESS OF MILLIONS OF HUMAN BEINGS WHO MAY BE LIVING SEDENTARY LIVES through choice or necessity.

"It preserves Health, turns Disease, and prolongs Life.

"An ingenious, rational, scientific, mechanical means of overcoming those impediments

to the taking of proper exercise, erected by the artificial methods of modern society.

"For certain classes of invalids a veritable Treasure-Trove.

"A CONSERVATOR of NERVOUS ENERGY.

"No dwelling-house is completely furnished without The Health Jolting Chair." (Bovee, 19)

Quite a chair, wasn't it? Actually, it wasn't, and such extravagant claims, especially for patent medicines and health devices, led to consumer anger as they realized they were being deceived. It also led to legislation that required advertisers to substantiate their claims. In 1938, the Federal Trade Commission received the power to protect consumers and competitors from deceptive and unfair advertising. Since then, advertising has gone through several schools of thought.

In the 1940s and '50s, ads stressed the upward mobility provided by products. It was also the era of Rosser Reeves' irritation school of advertising, a hard-sell approach. Ads, particularly television commercials, relied on brain-numbing repetition and treated the consumer as an idiot. The basis of Reeves' approach was the Unique Selling Proposition—the USP. The USP was one unique feature of the product that was emphasized in the ad. Reeves believed that the consumer couldn't handle more than one point at a time, and he limited each ad to one point, repeated over and over. In one ad for Pepto-Bismol the word "coatability" is said four times and shown in text an additional three.

However, the 1960s shifted into a new approach: positioning. Instead of promoting a USP, advertising showed how a product compared with other products, where the product fit into the market. The most famous example of this was Doyle, Dane, Bernbach's Volkswagen campaign. In ads that used headlines such as "Think Small" and "Lemon," Volkswagen was positioned in the auto market as an intelligent alternative for intelligent people.

This was the beginning of the soft-sell approach. Soft-sell depends less on product description or function, and more on how the product will make the consumer feel emotionally. It is in this approach that psychological appeals become important, since they aim at a person's emotions rather than the intellect.

The way advertising goes about carrying out its job is many and varied. What follows is a discussion of many of the types and styles of ads that are used.

Before doing that, however, some general comments about ads are germane. First, advertising is limited in both time and space. Broadcast commercials are generally 10 to, rarely, 60 seconds in length. Print ads are generally no larger than two pages, and often much smaller. Advertising therefore must do its job quickly: It must get the consumer's attention, identify itself as being aimed at that consumer, identify the product, and deliver the selling message, all within that small time or space. To accomplish this, advertising often breaks the rules of grammar, syntax, image, and even society. For example, it relies on stereotypes to help the consumer identify the target market and the product.

The definition of stereotype is "a fixed form or convention," "something lacking in originality or individuality." It is a model for other things like it. What this means is that people use a set of characteristics, sensory impressions to identify and thus recognize a group of individual items as fitting within a certain category. It is creating a series of templates against which we can compare anything encountered to aid in identifying it. We categorize a large woody plant with branches and leaves within the stereotype of "tree." Thus, we can identify any large woody plant with branches or leaves, no matter what shape or configuration, as a tree.

The human mind gathers information and stores that information in the memory. However, there is so much information coming in that the mind must sort and categorize it. Random storage of masses of information would result in total confusion.

For example, you see a tree. You observe its size, the limb configuration, the leaf shape, the color and texture of its bark. You see another tree, and another, and another. They are all different. If you have to think about each tree as a distinct individual with no relationship to any other, your mind would soon become overloaded with all the sensory impressions. Thus, you sort the trees into categories by characteristics they have in common. It might be leaf shape: maple, oak, pine, willow. It might be by limb configuration: spreading, symmetrical. Overall they fit into the category of "tree."

This categorizing I call pigeonholing. A pigeonhole contains all the information you have gathered about any particular item or subject. This information is not only the direct impressions, such as might be gathered by any animal, from a slug to a dog, it also includes anything you've learned that is applicable to the item or subject. Your mind sorts all the information that comes in and puts it in an appropriate pigeonhole. Every time you perceive the characteristics of something, you place those characteristics in a pigeonhole. When you identify something else that has the same, or what you perceive as the same characteristics, it goes in that pigeonhole. Therefore, the pigeonhole "tree" contains the general features of all trees. Thus, the next time you see a tree it opens the appropriate pigeonhole. You can identify it as a tree without having to devote much, if any, thought to it.

The above example of a tree is very simple. Most stereotypes are not. They consist of a gestalt of impressions, many of which are stereotypes in and of themselves. Not only are there the sensory impressions, there are also the emotions, the collateral impressions, what other people have told you the impressions are and mean, and all the learned information about the subject. All go into the pigeonhole.

Once the input is stored as a stereotype, the information in the pigeonhole is recalled by the triggering effect of perceiving that stereotype. There are two triggers for each stereotype. The first is a direct sensory stimulus. The second is a word or a phrase. These are both labels on the pigeonhole.

Let me give you a brief description, and see what images and concepts the description calls up in your mind:

A woman, wearing a simple dress and carrying a purse, enters a small country store. She stops at a bushel basket of corn on the cob and starts looking for ones to buy. Up comes the grocer, a kindly, grey-haired man in a white apron, wearing wire-rimmed glasses. He identifies the woman by name and suggests that she buy a certain brand of canned corn since it is "just as good as fresh cooked corn." She smiles and agrees to buy the product.

What sorts of things came into your mind? Later we'll look at this description again and see how stereotyping influences people's perceptions and ideas.

The use of stereotypes to trigger pigeonholes full of information is important to advertising. It saves much time that would otherwise have to be spent in explanations and/or exposition. For instance, the ad above doesn't need to explain why the woman is in the store; her mere presence and attire tell the audience instantly that she is shopping. Going to the corn immediately shows what she is shopping for. Because it is a woman, she is shopping for her family.[1]

Words can and do trigger stereotypes. Since a word is a symbol for an input, the contents of a pigeonhole are as easily recalled with words as with sensory cues.

Stereotypes are common in advertising and therefore a good place to find examples of them and how they work. (To many the stereotyping in advertising is a flaw. However, to advertisers they are a godsend.)

There are some stereotypes that many people hold in common. A country's flag is such a stereotype, triggering a pigeonhole that contains patriotism, love of country, or whatever else is in there. A kindly father figure, a loving mother, a baby, a puppy or a kitten, or a Rolls Royce are also stereotypes. Whenever a group of people reacts the same to the same stereotype, then they are useful to advertising.

The criticism arises when the stereotype triggers pigeonholes that contain different information or information ranked in a different way from that of the critics. Let's take another look at that description from above and see what the stereotypes may contain.

A woman, wearing a simple dress and carrying a purse, enters a small country store. She stops at a bushel basket of corn on the cob and starts looking for ones to buy. Up comes the grocer, a kindly, grey-haired man in a white apron, wearing wire-rimmed glasses. He identifies the woman by name and suggests that she buy a certain brand of canned corn since it is "just as good as fresh cooked corn." She smiles and agrees to buy the product.

■ IMAGE

- Woman is grocery shopping
- Woman checks corn on the cob
- Male grocer appears
- Grocer suggests canned corn
- Woman buys canned corn

Positive Stereotypes

- Women are better shoppers
- Friendly, neighborhood atmosphere
- Women are selective

- Men are friendly
- Men are helpful
- Women make good decisions

Negative Stereotypes
- Women must do the shopping
- Supermarkets are impersonal
- Women are indecisive
- Only men are employed
- Women need male help to make decisions
- Women are easily led by men

As you can see by the above example, people can take the same commercial different ways according to the information in pigeonholes triggered by different stereotypes.

1. *Women, who are better shoppers, go to friendly, neighborhood stores. They are very selective in their purchases of food for their families. The nice thing about these stores is the friendly people who work there; they know you and wish to help you in your purchases. Once the advantages of a product are known, women know to choose the best product.*
2. *Women, who have to do the shopping because nobody else will, avoid the savings possible at supermarkets and go to small, overpriced neighborhood stores because they don't want to go all the way to the supermarket. Here they must deal with men because only men can get jobs. Men feel that women need help making even simple decisions and condescend to explain things to them in simple terms. Women are easily led by men and agree to do what men tell them.*

Obviously, there are contradictions in the above descriptions. Just as obviously, the contradictions are in the stereotypes people use when presented with sounds and images, stimuli that trigger the stereotypes. In advertising, advertisers count on the first set of stereotypes above rather than the second. Criticisms arise when people perceive some or all the second.

In any case, we filter whatever we perceive through our stereotypes. This influences our decisions about what to do and how to behave. This is how politicians, demagogues and advertisers try to influence what people actually do in response to stimuli. It may be to vote, riot or buy, but behavior is the final goal.

The second general comment about advertising is that ads usually contain two elements: copy and illustrations. Copy is the words, either printed or spoken, that deliver a sales message. Illustrations are the pictures, either drawn or painted, or photographs.

A point to bear in mind about copy and illustrations is the difference between the intellectual and the emotional processing of information in the human mind. Copy relies on intellectual processing. It has to, since converting the squiggles on a page (which is, after all, what printing is), or the random noises issuing from someone's mouth (which is, after all, what speaking is) must be translated into meaning in the reader's or listener's mind. Just think about reading or hearing a language you don't know. For you, it's just so much waste of ink or noise as far as content is concerned. Such a translation is an intellectual process. Words, particularly if spoken, can carry great emotion—they can create images before the mind's eye or call up events that can make you laugh or cry. Spoken words have the advantage over printed words of extra nuances, such as inflection, rate, volume and timbre that help the listener translate the noises into meaning. Nonetheless, words are always one step away—the step of translation—from "reality."

Although at first glance it may not seem so, drawings and paintings also rely on intellectual processing. Drawings and paintings, like words, are not the things themselves, but artists' conceptions of them. The lines, shapes and colors must be translated into meaning in the mind of the viewer. Again, illustrations can carry great emotional impact, particularly paintings with their greater verisimilitude, but, again, they are one step away from "reality."

Photographs, either still or moving, rely on emotional processing. To the mind, a photograph is the thing itself, and therefore it needs no translation to determine what it means. Of course, any photograph is, like a drawing or a painting, the product of an artist's conception. The artist selects, frames and composes, determines exposure, angle, distances, depth, etc., to present whatever emotional message desired. Nonetheless, a photograph has an immediate impact on the viewer, with no intervening step between perception and reaction.

Most ads contain a combination of copy and illustration, in proportions ranging from all one to all the other, depending on how the advertiser wants to present the sales message.

There are two basic ways of presenting a sales message: intellectually and emotionally. An intellectual presentation depends on logical, rational argument to convince a consumer to buy the product or service. For example, buying for many computer purchasers doesn't depend on what the case looks like or what effect the machine might have on their social life. What they're looking for is technical information: How fast does it process information? How much RAM does it have? How big and fast is the hard disk drive? How many drives are there, and of what type? How big is the power supply? What is the resolution of the monitor? Other products that are sold more for their functions than for other possible aspects in the consumer's "bundle of values" include some business and financial services, computer programs and accessories, construction materials and tools, and other complex but less "romantic" products.

Such ads are "copy heavy," since the sheer amount of information to explain the functions and benefits of the product or service requires many words. In addition, such ads usually appear in print media since it takes time and concentration on the consumer's part to absorb and understand the information. Such characteristics of time and concentration are lacking in broadcast media.

Illustrations are often sparse in intellectually aimed ads, and those will usually be drawings or paintings, thus keeping both elements aimed the same way. If photographs are used, they will usually be stark and simple, with little emotional content, merely showing what the product looks like.

The second basic way to present a sales message is emotionally. In an emotional presentation, the actual function of the product is often not its main selling point. Instead, there is a concentration on other aspects of the consumer's bundle of values: social, psychological, economic. For example, the presentation may show how the product or service enhances the audience's social life by improving their sex appeal or self-esteem, or how it will increase their earning power.

And now we're going to start looking at how advertising pushes people's buttons by appealing, not to their conscious minds, but to their subconscious minds.

Over millions of years, evolution has been at work, and one of the things it worked on was how an organism should respond to the world around it. That organism had to stay alive and get food and reproduce, and it developed various strategies to do that better than other organisms. These strategies are instincts, automatic responses to stimuli, like getting away from pain or moving toward pleasure, and, given the possibility, gathering resources or having sex. These instincts have been passed down through the generations and are built into the brains of every organism on Earth. Including humans.

Now, how and why this happened is an entire other book. But for now I'm going to give you an overview of how advertising works on people's subconscious minds.

First of all, advertising aims at people's subconscious minds much more than at their conscious minds. It tries to get people to react at an instinctive level rather than in a rational, logical way. In fact, advertising works better if the audience doesn't think at all.

Advertising wants you to act on your desires, and act now, not later, and to think only of yourself. This is because, on the whole, advertising works best by getting people to be selfish, self-centered, and anti-social. It does this by aiming below the psychological belt, and by using one or more psychological appeals.

A psychological appeal is a visual or aural influence on your subconscious mind and emotions. It works by implying that doing what is suggested (in the case of advertising, buying the product or service) will satisfy a subconscious desire. It is not subliminal, which involves elements in a visual or aural presentation that you can't consciously perceive but that influence your behavior. If a psychological appeal couldn't be perceived, it would have no effect at all. In fact, it is blatantly obvious the moment you know such an appeal exists. It doesn't aim at your intellect. In fact, your intellect can often get in the way of the effect of an appeal.

There are ten psychological appeals: self-preservation, sex, greed, self-esteem, personal enjoyment, constructiveness, destructiveness, curiosity, imitation and altruism.

Let's look at these one at a time, starting with self-preservation.

Self Preservation

An ad using self-preservation as an appeal is essentially saying, "Listen to me, I'll keep you alive." Of course, that could be keeping the target personally alive, like an ad promoting how your car will tell you if there's someone in the back seat so you can avoid him, or an ad promoting aspirin as a way to avoid having a heart attack and dying.

But, again, humans are the most social animals on earth, so we have a tendency to extend the idea of self-preservation beyond the self to those near and dear to us, like our families. The most common approach when using self-preservation as an advertising appeal is to create a fear in the mind of the audience: fear of death, fear of illness, fear of crime. The product being sold is usually shown as preventing what is feared: tires to prevent a fatal car accident; aspirin to prevent a fatal heart attack; a battery in a child locater to prevent an abduction. Creating fear is the basis of a self-preservation appeal.

Sex

Okay, now comes the common, but difficult, appeal: sex. An ad using sex appeal essentially says: "Listen to me, I'll get you laid."

The big problem with using sex as an appeal is that the appeal differs depending upon whether you're male or female. For males the appeal is to have sex with no strings, just have sex with as many females as possible; in other words, promiscuity. For females, the goal is to have sex with the best possible male, not the nearest; in other words, be picky.

Sexual Strategies

The difference in how the appeal works is because males and females have completely different reasons for and strategies to get sex, based on the biological imperative of passing on one's own genes to the next generation.

It's pretty much based on the cost of sex. For males, the cost is very low: a little time, a little energy, then move on. So the criteria for an acceptable mate are minimal: Basically, she has to be young enough to be impregnable and be healthy, alive and breathing.

For females the opposite is true. Since she's the one who has to carry any offspring to term, and then care for it until it's able to fend for itself, the cost to her can be enormous in terms of time and energy. So she doesn't have the option of being promiscuous. She needs to pick the male that will give herself and her offspring the best chance to live long enough and well enough for her offspring to become adults. Thus her criteria for an acceptable mate are far more extensive.

So, for virtually all male animals, the byword is: Spread it around. In other words, have sex with as many females as possible. That will spread their genes as widely as possible, greatly increasing the chance that their genes will continue into the next generation. For virtually all female animals, the approach is to pick the best male out of those who apply.

This is how it works with a non-human animal. A male competes with other males to demonstrate that he's the superior male and thus the one the female should choose. In much of the animal kingdom, this competition between males is a physical one—either intimidation through a show of superiority, like being the biggest, or having the most impressive antlers, or delivering the most food. If intimidation doesn't drive off other males, then it's time to fight and demonstrate superiority. Either way, the female chooses the winner since he has shown himself to be the best male around.

Once she has selected the best male, they mate, and then she usually wants little to do with him since for most animals the male has no role in raising offspring—she'll even drive him away. A major exception is birds and, of course, humans.

So, is that how it works with humans? Well, yes and no. Remember that humans are the most social creatures on Earth. So, subconsciously, on an instinctive level, men and women react the way other animals do: A man's instinctive criterion for an acceptable mate is essentially—she's there.

But women's criteria are far more extensive than for any other creature on Earth because she must take into account social as well as physical attributes in order to select the best man. Especially, he must be a good father and a good provider. This means he must bring more to the relationship than a good body and the ability to beat up other men. He must bring other things, like money and status and power, things that will help her and give her offspring a better chance in the social world of people.

So what does advertising do with this kind of information? Well, advertisers construct the ads to appeal to those instinctive reactions, which are quite different for men and women.

For example, an ad aimed at men basically says: Buy the product, get the woman. No strings, no hassles, no examination of her mind or political affiliations or fitness as a mother—she's just there, and she wants you because you have the product. The ad merely has to have a woman that will attract his attention and with whom he would like to have sex—in other words, that fits his instinctive physical desires. For example, an ad for beer will have a beautiful woman who suddenly shows an interest in the man when he buys the right beer. That's all that's necessary. An ad for body sprays shows the man using the product and immediately women are all over him, just what a male animal wants on an instinctive level.

So how is sex appeal used to appeal to women? Obviously, the approach used to attract men isn't going to work. So a different approach is used.

Ads aimed at women rarely use sheer physicality; they are far more likely to use romance and courtship. Such ads show that if she buys the product she will attract more men, increasing the pool of possibilities to choose from, and increasing the chance that she'll be able to choose someone who cares about her as a person, and be a good mate and a good provider.

Jewelry ads often illustrate the perfect mate for a woman: a good father, romantic and of course a good provider. (He clearly has money if he can afford to buy her jewelry, which shows he cares for her.) The ad implies: "Ladies, this is what you want in a man, and he can prove he's that kind of man if he spends a fortune on something that has no biological value—you can't eat a diamond."[2]

So, isn't the use of sex appeal sexist? Well, yes, because it is—on a social level. But advertising's job is to sell a product, not to promote a social agenda, which is conscious, not subconscious.

So here is the problem that arises. The use of sex in advertising often appeals to one gender at the social expense of the other. Those aimed at men treat women as objects, because a male's subconscious instinct is to *regard* her as a sex object, someone to have sex with, and that's it. This can be, and is, detrimental to the self-esteem and social position of women. But that's how instinct works. Ads aimed at women treat men as servants, lap dogs and gold mines, there only to give women what they need and want, putting the women before themselves in all things. This is detrimental to men's self-esteem and social position. But, again, that's how instinct works.

So why is sex used in advertising? Because it works and sells products—and that's what's important to advertising.

Greed

Okay. So let's go on to the third appeal—greed. An ad using greed basically says, "Listen to me, I'll make you rich." Human society requires that people have resources, usually represented by money. It's not like we can go out in the woods and pluck fruit from the trees to survive. So instinctively, greed is good. Any individual wants the most resources he or she can get, the more more the better. With money you can get anything you want, without money you can't get anything. There's the old saying: Money isn't everything. This is usually said by those who have money. To those who don't have money, money **is** everything. Ads using greed as an appeal get customers by implying that buying the product will increase their income, or at least require less money to buy the product than other products like it, and that the product will let you do more with the money you have.

The first three appeals are powerful because they're biological, based in instinct and not social. In fact, as you've seen, they're pretty much antisocial. They require no intelligence and no connections with others—in fact, the dumber you are, the more likely they are to work. But the other seven appeals require a society to work, or even to exist. So let's talk about them.

Self-esteem

The first of these social appeals is self-esteem. Self-esteem is social because it's a comparison of oneself to others, and if there are no others, there's nothing to compare to. Of course, this requires one other trait that doesn't exist in most creatures on Earth—a sense of self, a sense that you are an individual separate and distinct from other individuals. Experiments using mirrors show that most creatures will react the same as, say, a monkey will. A monkey, seeing a reflection of itself, thinks it's seeing another monkey and **not** itself. It'll look behind the mirror, wondering what happened to that other monkey. It may even attack the mirror, thinking the reflection is a rival. These experiments show that the great apes—that is, chimps, gorillas, orangutans—dolphins, orcas, and some birds, recognize themselves. Almost no other animals do. Except, of course, people.

So once you realize you're a separate individual, you can compare yourself to others in whatever way you deem appropriate, from height and weight to intelligence, wit, fund of jokes, amount of money, moral rectitude, or anything else. High self-esteem comes from feeling that you compare positively with others, and low self-esteem comes from feeling you compare poorly with others.

Again as with sex, there is a gender link for self-esteem. For men, self-esteem is a competitive sport. Men compete to establish their position in a hierarchy from inferior to superior. This can be linked back to sex appeal. Females choose to mate with the best male, and males know this. So a male must show he's superior to the other males to be chosen. How a man demonstrates that superiority varies from culture to culture, or even situation to situation. It could be through physical combat, although that doesn't impress women the way it does females like deer and cows and mountain goats. Usually it's done in a form of one-upmanship like verbal sparring or beating someone at a game or displaying the most wealth. Either way, high male self-esteem comes from a sense of superiority compared to other people, and low male self-esteem comes from a sense of inferiority compared to other people.

For women, it's less about competition and more about cooperation and connection. Throughout the animal kingdom, from elephants to baboons to chimpanzees, females band together in mutual support groups, often excluding males for being too competitive and disruptive. Females have a better chance for personal survival and for the welfare of their young if they work together. This also applies to women on an instinctive level.

Look at a print ad that appeals to men. Often there is an icon of superiority, such as a major sports figure that the target audience considers a superior male. But another man who, under ordinary circumstances, would be considered inferior to the icon, defeats him because that man uses the product. The males in the audience look at this ad and think if they use that product, they too can be superior men, and they go out and get the product.

In a slice of life TV commercial, the man is shown a loser because he doesn't use the product. For example, when a man's credit rating is poor, he not only gets a heap for a car, women laugh at him. These are both things that will lower a man's self-esteem. So men will buy the product with the intent of improving their poor credit, not only to avoid being like the man, but to be superior to him.

In ads aimed at women, there are often several women together enjoying each other's company while using the product. Note how the product increases the number and quality of connections a woman could get if she uses the product. Other ads show her bonding with a mate or her children, which implies that her wise choice of the product caused these people to gather around her and get closer.

Personal Enjoyment

The next appeal is personal enjoyment. Personal enjoyment is when a person feels happy or satisfied or elated or pleased or content, but in any case doesn't feel depressed or nothing at all.

The means of arriving at enjoyment are as varied as people are. What makes one person happy may make another depressed. Nonetheless, there are a few actions or events that most people find enjoyable. These include eating or drinking, sex, work, leisure, and play.

Many of the things that people do are actually biological necessities. For example, eating is necessary to stay alive; courtship is necessary to find a sexual partner; sex is necessary to pass on genes; the gathering of resources is necessary to ensure or enhance personal and offspring survival.

That these things are necessary does not automatically mean they are enjoyable. And even if something is enjoyable, it does not mean it enhances self-preservation or opportunities for sex or greed, or that it boosts self-esteem. In fact, there seems to be little biological necessity for personal enjoyment.

However, people do find many of the aspects of being alive enjoyable. There seems to be something inherently enjoyable in doing the actions dictated by biological necessities. For instance, people on liquid diets often comment how pleasant it is to chew again when they go back to solid foods. Certainly, most people find sex pleasurable, and many people like their jobs.

Personal enjoyment usually comes about through stimulating the senses in a positive way, like beautiful sights and sounds, good tastes and smells, and touches. Who doesn't like a hug?

One thing that is apparent about enjoyment is the idea of variety. People can live by eating a vitamin-laced protein and carbohydrate mush (this is called dieting). That it will keep you nourished doesn't mean that you would look forward to it three times a day. Even your favorite food, whether cheeseburgers, salads or pizza, will pall after a few straight meals of it. When variety is lacking, so, apparently, is enjoyment. Koalas and pandas, which live only on eucalyptus leaves or bamboo (respectively), don't seem to get much thrill out of eating. They look like they're simply stoking a furnace, if they pay any attention to their food at all beyond locating the next leaf or shoot. However, when Figan (one of the chimpanzees Jane Goodall observed in the wild for more than twenty years) received bananas for the first time, his excited hooting brought the band racing.

Because of the necessities of human life, life can often become boring. The ability of humans to remember the past, relate it to the present, and project it into the future gives them a totally different sense of personal enjoyment than other creatures. For example, think of going to work. You remember doing the same work in the past, you're doing it now, and you can imagine doing it into the future. Unless you have a really interesting job with lots of variety, it's like eating the same thing for every meal—it gets really old really fast.

Fortunately, people have provided for this; they have invented things to do that allow a person to get away from work, if only for a short time, and to do something else. These include vacations, sports, entertainment, and intellectual activities. These all provide a break from the routine, add a little variety to life, and give people enjoyment.

Advertising promotes products by implying that buying the product will provide the variety and stimulation of senses that we call personal enjoyment. When advertising uses personal enjoyment, the ad shows how the product or service will not only aid, but apparently cause, the enjoyment. It stimulates the senses, or it provides the variety that people crave, or both. For example, a soft drink ad showed Pepsi and Coca Cola delivered to the wrong places. The Coke turned a fraternity party into a lethargic bingo game, while the Pepsi turned a retirement home into a wild celebration of life. Obviously, the Pepsi provided the stimulation and variety that brought enjoyment to these elderly people.

The ads may also imply that the product brings or increases those things that people enjoy, including sexual or romantic encounters, greater wealth, or higher esteem. However, the ad will often show how the product will provide stimulation or variety, not for the purchaser, but for someone else, to the benefit of the purchaser. The ads are less appealing to sex, greed, or self-esteem than they are about showing how much more enjoyment there will be in sex, in gaining wealth, or by a rise in self-esteem.

Constructiveness

Next up is constructiveness. Constructiveness means building things, whether it's a set of bookcases, a house or a worldview. Many animals build things, like bowerbirds, but we go beyond building for self-preservation or sex. Humans build stories (remember that?) and then proceed to build what they imagine, and not just the physical things. We build our societies on those stories, and we construct entire concepts about what things are and how they work—including people.

Constructiveness is very useful when it comes to selling those products that are used to actually build or work on things. Such products include tools, building materials, and improvement and repair products. Constructiveness also includes how things are built for future purchase.

Although such products are useful in and of themselves, advertising usually links the constructiveness with other appeals to make the products even more attractive on a subconscious level.

One appeal that is linked with constructiveness is self-preservation. What is implied is that the product, while helping the consumer to build or repair something, is actually improving rher chances at survival. For example, oil or antifreeze or additives or an improved braking system or engine or building material will make the buyer safer. The ad may also tout the need for clean air or water or heat or cooling, and thus make getting a new water filter or different plumbing or safer paint or more insulation more imperative and thus more attractive.

When applied to products for purchase, manufacturers advertise how well they build their products. For example, car manufacturers emphasize how well they build their cars, and they list the safety features they've installed, all to ensure the safety of the purchaser.

Reproduction is rarely linked to constructiveness other than in building a physical appearance that may be attractive to the opposite sex. Such products include cosmetics and fashion in order to alter a person's facade before the world.

Greed is commonly linked to constructiveness. Many products are promoted as not only helping to build, but to save and earn money at the same time. For example, using the right paint or stain will save you hundreds or thousands of dollars in repairs, the proper insulation will save on heating and cooling costs.

Greed is also commonly used in ads for products for future purchase. In these instances, the manufacturer emphasizes how much money the purchaser can save by buying the product because of how the product is made. The ad may emphasize improved gas mileage, lower insurance rates, no need to buy extras or peripherals or anything else that implies spending money now means not having to spend money later. For example, a computer ad may say that when you buy the competition's computer, you also have to buy all the stuff you need to make the computer work, like a printer and a modem and memory and ports and software, but if you buy the sponsor's computer, everything is included. The manufacturer is saying that it's already built the computer the way you want it.

Advertising relies on constructiveness to sell products by building a worldview and fitting the consumer into that worldview. As you may remember, advertising rarely makes absolute claims about a product, especially when the product is a parity one. However, if the ad can either make the product a part of the consumer's worldview or link with it, then the product may be more attractive to that consumer.

Destructiveness

So if we have an instinct to build, we also have an instinct to destroy. There does seem to be a gender link to destructiveness—men are more likely to enjoy blowing things up or tearing them down than women. Nonetheless, there is an excitement to destruction. Everybody—but especially males—likes watching things blow up.

Since destructiveness can be damaging to the social fabric, it rarely appears overtly in advertising because it could cause a backlash in the form of protest and negative publicity. However, since it is also a part of most people's subconscious motivations, it can be effective in making a product or service seem more attractive. Thus, it will be used, but in subtle fashions.

Destructiveness is rarely used alone as an appeal. More often, it is linked with another appeal. Sex isn't used, but self-preservation, personal enjoyment, self-esteem and constructiveness are typical links.

A common use of destructiveness as an appeal appears for products and activities that are inherently destructive, and it is usually linked with personal enjoyment. For example, commercials for toys such as the Crash Dummies or for video games center on how much fun the players have fulfilling the toys' purpose—destroying things. The fact that nothing is actually destroyed is irrelevant; what's important is the feeling that using these products will allow you to demolish things.

Destruction is used to promote services or events more often than products. Scenes promoting the enjoyment of sports, such as football and hockey, almost invariably center on violent actions, for instance, fights, bone-crunching tackles and smashing bodies in general. Other events using destructiveness as the main appeal include monster truck rallies, demolition derbies and car races.

Occasionally, destructiveness is linked with self-preservation. This approach, which usually uses the slice-of-life ad, appears for crime-fighting products, such as mace. For example, one ad shows a woman approaching her car in a dark garage. As the camera zooms in on her, she turns and sprays mace, leaving an impression that she has destroyed her attacker and saved her life. A more subtle use of destructiveness and self-preservation, using either the slice-of-life or the testimonial types of ads, is for over-the-counter painkillers. As the product description implies, the product "kills" pain and destroys it.

More often, destructiveness is a subtle component in the appeals used in an ad, appearing more as an undercurrent than as a direct statement. Occasionally, ads will focus on self-esteem as a link with destruction, but they emphasize psychological rather than physical destruction. For example, an ad for business services or machines may show one man being more successful because he uses the service or machine than another with whom he is competing. This destroys the self-esteem of the latter and boosts the self-esteem of the former.[3]

Curiosity

The appeal to curiosity basically says, "Listen to me and I'll answer your questions." Of course, getting answers is a survival characteristic—finding out what's poisonous and what's good to eat would definitely improve longevity.

The problem with curiosity as an appeal is that it depends on the audience wanting to get the answer. If they don't care what the answer is, they won't care about what the advertiser is trying to sell either. And, even worse, what if they come up with their own answer—and it's not the one that makes the product look good? Still, as in one ad, curiosity might make a reader wonder just what the most dangerous place in the universe is, and buy the product to find out.

Curiosity is a difficult appeal to use in advertising, which is why it ranks only eighth in effectiveness. The basic problems are arousing curiosity in the first place, and not having the consumer come up with rher own answer in the second.

The first problem relates to how a particular consumer relates to the product. The consumer may have a high involvement, that is, a personal interest in the product rather than one induced by the ad. High involvement automatically creates curiosity about a product in the mind of a consumer interested in that product. For example, someone who is interested in computers may read the articles in computer magazines, but rhe will also look at most of the ads, searching for products that rhe might want, and concentrate on those that look like they might fulfill rher desires. Someone who wants a new car (cell phone, stereo, toothpaste, etc.) starts looking for one and has a high involvement in ads for it.

However, most products are low involvement. In other words, they are for products the average consumer isn't deeply interested in unless a need arises. And even if the consumer is interested in the product type, rhe might not care about the brand, although the brand is of vital importance in an ad. For example, a consumer may discover rhe's out of toilet paper. Although rhe will go get some, rhe may not care which brand rhe gets. Rhe may buy what's cheapest or what's available in the closest store. Or the brand that rhe remembers from an ad. Nonetheless, involvement in a product has a major impact on the interest a consumer will have in an ad, and the person's curiosity about the message in the ad. The fact that most products are low involvement is a major problem in using curiosity as an appeal—if the consumer doesn't care, rhe isn't curious.

The second basic problem is that, once an ad has aroused a consumer's curiosity, rhe has an irritating habit of searching for rher own answer. At least, it's irritating to the advertiser, because more often than not, the answer is not the one the advertiser wants—a desire for the advertised product. Remember that humans are the most insatiably curious creatures on Earth, constantly searching for answers even when no one has asked a question. For example, suppose an ad's headline asks, "Why aren't you buying an American [Japanese, German, etc.] car?" Assuming the headline stopped the reader long enough to make rher curious, rhe may also immediately come up with a series of answers: because American [Japanese, German, etc.] cars aren't any good, because I already have a car, because I prefer foreign [American] cars, because American [Japanese, German, etc.] cars are too expensive, because . . . because . . . because . . . The reader may even look to see if the ad is for an American or a foreign car and start formulating answers from there. In any case, the answer is unlikely to be the one the advertiser wants the consumer to have.

Imitation

Imitation says, "do what I tell you and I'll make you just like someone or something else." This can be a pretty weak appeal. It's based entirely on the audience **wanting** to be like someone else. Most people want to be themselves, not someone else. So what such an ad does is imply that if the audience buys the product, they will be like someone they admire in some way. For example, in a beauty product ad the person to imitate may be Nicole Kidman or Eva Longoria, and the audience can be as rich and beautiful and well known if they just buy and use the product. The same approach can be used to appeal to a male audience by implying the product will make them superior men like David Beckham or Michael Jordan.

Of course, in both cases the audience has to believe that Kidman or Longoria or Beckman or Jordan are models they want to imitate.

Altruism

Finally, there's altruism. Altruism is giving of yourself with no hope or expectation of a return. This is a wonderful idea—except it doesn't exist. Everyone expects some kind of return, if only a tax deduction or a better chance at heaven.

What does exist is reciprocal altruism. This is the old "I'll scratch your back, you scratch mine." Because humans are so social, can remember the past and project so far in the future, subconsciously we can believe that if I do something for you today, you'll do something for me tomorrow—even if that tomorrow is years away. And we apply this view not just to ourselves, but to our families, to our friends (as in "sure, I'll help you move"), to our neighbors ("you help put out my house fire, I'll help put out yours"), and even to our nation—"I'll go to war and protect our country and all it stands for; you, our country, protect my family, friends and neighbors."

Altruism in advertising is always linked to one or more of the other appeals, especially the top three, self-preservation, sex and greed. Now, granted, sex isn't used a lot, but self-preservation, especially things like donating to charity, implies that the charity will be there when the audience needs it. And the ad will often subtly remind the audience of that tax deduction, which of course is greed.

Self-esteem, when linked with altruism, is a very subtle appeal. If you recall, most men's self-esteem is directly related to where they believe they fit in a hierarchy—the higher the relative position, the higher the self-esteem. Ads could say that helping others demonstrates a man's superiority to those others, but such an approach would run counter to most men's social sensibilities, which believe that overt displays of superiority, better known as arrogance, are improper. To work, an altruistic appeal to men linked to self-esteem must make it appear that he is simply helping those less fortunate, rather than appearing that he is deigning to help. Deep down inside, he may feel a sense of superiority, but he can assuage his social conscience by telling himself that he's doing it out of a sense of fellowship.

Altruism is easier to link to self-esteem for women, since for many women self-esteem is related to a sense of connectedness rather than to competition. Ads asking women to be altruistic can easily show how her actions can benefit others, gaining their appreciation and even love. For example, ads asking for donations to help children in Third World countries emphasize how grateful the children will be, and how the children will write to express their appreciation. Pictures and ad copy personalize the children so they appear as individuals in need of her individual help. This gives her a personal connection with a child and implies a closeness akin to that she has with her own children.

So those are the ten psychological appeals used in advertising. All but altruism are selfish and self-centered, but they are all based on either biological or cultural instincts, and they do as little as possible to trigger any actual thinking in the audience. The moment someone starts thinking about the appeal in the ad, the appeal no longer works—and the ad doesn't sell.

But what if the audience does start thinking? Well, the trick is to get them to start thinking the right way, by which I mean not thinking about how they're being manipulated. So let's take a look at some of the most popular tricks of trade in advertising—all of which wouldn't work if the audience consciously noted what was being said and thought about it for a moment.

■ TRICKS OF THE TRADE

A trick of the trade replaces logic and reason with logical fallacies. The consumer thinks the ad is saying one thing when in fact it's saying something else, or saying nothing at all.

Black/White

The first of the tricks of the trade is the black\white, either\or fallacy. The black/white, either/or, trick is making a statement that provides insufficient options to your argument. "Love it or leave it" was a big slogan of the 1960s, and it sounds logical. Nevertheless, it provides no other possible options, such as "Love it, or don't love it, stay or not, you don't have to agree with me if you don't want to."

The reason this fallacy is often called the black/white fallacy is that it denies any shades of grey on an issue or an idea. Using it gives the impression that everything can be seen in terms of yes or no, true or false, on or off, with no maybes or both true and false, depending on circumstances allowed. This fallacy is particularly popular and effective in jingoism, where slogans replace thinking: "Love it or leave it," "If you're not for me, you're against me," "My country, right or wrong." Note that all of the above actually have other options, but the statements do not allow for them.

A common way in which this trick is used in advertising is by presenting two situations, one with the product and the other without. The one with the product shows circumstances that the advertiser presumes the target audience would like to be in, and vice versa for the situation without the product. For example, you have two groups of people. The first is young, beautiful, fit, happy, fun-loving and active; the second is old, ugly, out of shape, miserable and apathetic. The first group uses the product; the second doesn't. The underlying premise is that the product is an integral part of making you a member of the first group and that the absence of the product makes you a member of the second. Since most people would rather be in the first group, and it's implied that the product is a necessary part of being in the first group, then people should buy the product. And they do.

Buzzwords

Buzzwords are words that seem to say something, but what? They are extremely popular in advertising. For example, a major word is "crisp" when applied to soft drinks or wine. What does this word mean? That the drink crackles like broken glass when you drink it? You chew it like potato chips?

"Natural" is a big buzzword, particularly applied to food and drink. However, what exactly is "natural"? Definitions of the word include "produced by nature," "not artificial" or "not cultivated or civilized." Thus, what does the word mean when applied to, say, beer? If a beer is natural, is it produced by nature? That somewhere in the forest there exists a beer tree that need merely be tapped and bottled? Unlikely; beer is produced in breweries and does not exist in nature. Is natural beer not artificial? Artificial means "made by humans." Since humans make the beer in breweries, then beer is definitely artificial. Is natural beer not cultivated or civilized? The behavior of beer drinkers is occasionally not cultivated or civilized, but beer is one of, if not the first, achievement of civilization. Then what exactly does it mean for beer to be natural? That it's not made of polyester? In effect, the word natural applied to any product that doesn't exist in a finished state in nature is a buzzword.

Of course, there are products that exist in nature and can be called natural. What does it mean in those cases? For example, what is the difference between natural and refined honey? Basically, the difference is dirt. Refining honey does not change the honey, it just removes extra non-honey items like dirt, bees' wax, and perhaps bees.

And, of course, there's organic.[4] What does that mean? We think we know, but organic means "containing carbon in the molecules." Think of organic and inorganic chemistry. So if something contains carbon in the molecules, it's organic. So if you can digest it, it's organic. You might want to avoid certain fast foods and snacks, but everything else is okay.

There is a print ad for a product from Lancome cosmetics that touts its ability to fight wrinkles with a kind of serum. This product contains, well, something that has no meaning to the audience: Collaser 5-X. Just what is Collaser 5-X? Why 5-X? Because it sounds scientific? And what about serum? Serum is a medicine injected to fight a disease. So you inject this stuff? And when did wrinkles become a disease?

A TV commercial sells a sun blocker containing Avoplex technology. What is Avoplex technology? It's a word without meaning, but it seems to be saying something. That's a buzzword.

Weasel Words

Weasel words are words tossed into a sentence that change the actual meaning of the sentence while leaving a different impression. Let's look at some examples.

"Our canned corn is as good as fresh cooked corn."© The impression given is that the canned corn is as good (whatever that means) as corn on the cob right off the stalk. However, the phrase contains a weasel word: "cooked." Thus, the sentence actually says that the canned corn is as good as corn that has been cooked; now, you need to reheat it, that is, cook it again, to serve it. Note the sentence does not say that the canned corn is as good as fresh corn; it's as good as fresh *cooked* corn.

"Our dog food contains as much meat protein as 10 pounds of sirloin steak."© The sentence gives the impression that the dog food contains sirloin steak. In fact, it contains the *equivalent* of 10 pounds of steak in the form of meat *protein*. This protein can be anything made of meat: lips, cheeks, snouts, entrails, etc. It is doubtful that the dog food actually contains 10 pounds of steak. If it did, the sentence would read, "Our dog food contains 10 pounds of sirloin steak."

One of my favorites is the three out of four," like "three out of four doctors recommend the major *ingredient* in Excedrin." Wow, Excedrin must be good if three out of four doctors recommend it. Right? Right? Well, wait a minute. The doctors don't recommend Excedrin, they recommend the major ingredient in Excedrin. And what's that? It's aspirin. So they recommend aspirin, not Excedrin. So why would you buy Excedrin at 35 cents a pill instead of aspirin at 5 cents a pill? You wouldn't, would you?

It's the equivalent of saying, "three out of four doctors recommend the major ingredient in poisoned orange juice." The major ingredient is orange juice, which doctors do recommend, and we can ignore that minor ingredient of rat poison!

And how do they get that three out four? Companies ask doctors if they will accept a free sample, and if a doctor accepts the free sample, it is assumed the doctor will recommend it. I want to talk to that fourth doctor who won't take the product even if it's free.

Another example: "Some studies seem to suggest that eating the major ingredient in our cereal may have an effect on certain kinds of cancer." Wow. Is that loaded with weasels: some, seem, suggest, major ingredient, may, an, certain. You might as well say: Our cereal doesn't do a damn thing, but eat it anyway.

And then there's IF, the ultimate weasel. Just toss it in and you can imply anything. For example, the slogan for Nescafe coffee: "If the whole wide world can enjoy Nescafe, so can you." The impression given is that the whole wide world does indeed enjoy Nescafe. But they never said that. They said, *if* they did. But there's no evidence at all that anyone anywhere enjoys the coffee. The French have a saying: "With enough ifs you can put Paris in a bottle." This statement is true.

Begging The Question

Begging the question is making a statement that includes an unproven premise; basically it is saying that something is simply because it is. For example, the statement, "Why are so many mothers of cavity prone children switching to Aim [toothpaste]?" is begging the question. It contains the unproven premise that mothers of cavity-prone children are doing anything at all, much less switching to Aim. It looks like evidence that Aim is better for cavity-prone children, when it fact it provides no evidence whatsoever. They simply say it in the expectation that the statement will be accepted as proof in and of itself.

Genetic Fallacy

The genetic fallacy makes a prediction about something based on where it came from or on its origins. For example, saying, "He wouldn't do that—he's from a good family" is making a genetic fallacy. "You can't expect any better from her—she's from the slums" is also using a genetic fallacy. Note that in neither case is there any reference to the individual's personal abilities or lack thereof, only to their origins. Advertising uses this fallacy often. "If it's made by [company], it must be good" is an example. Such statements may indeed be true, but they need evidence as proof, not merely a statement of origin.

Self-Definition

Humpty Dumpty was very good at self-definition: "When I use a word it means just what I choose it to mean—neither more nor less" (Carroll 1960) This fallacy is very popular with people who wish to mislead, and is particularly effective using those slippery words that have no concrete referent. Such words as truth, beauty, justice, democracy, patriotism, love, and defense mean just what the person using them says they mean, assuming rhe actually says what they mean. It is in this way that self-definition works best: Use a word that you expect your audience to define one way, but mean another way when you use it.

Let's look at an example. A prime word is "justice." Most people will agree that justice is a consummation devoutly to be wished. However, when you use the word and you get your audience to agree with your desire for justice, you may mean vigilantism. Demagogues use this technique with great effect.

In advertising, self-definition is very effective. For example, if the product is a beauty aid such as mascara or eyeliner or lipstick, the ad will show a model wearing the make-up, labeling her as beautiful. Thus, her appearance is the definition of "beauty." To be "beautiful" the consumer must look like the model, and she's using the make-up to be beautiful, and therefore the consumer must use the advertised product to fit the definition of beauty.

Argumentum ad Populum

"Argument to the people." This is an appeal to emotion and/or prejudice to convince people to accept what you say, and it is particularly popular in political speeches. Basically, it is telling people how wonderful they are and how what they think (no matter what they think) is right and proper, and that anyone who thinks otherwise is an idiot and a fool. Since most people prefer to be considered right and proper, rather than idiots and fools, they will agree with those who tell them they are right and proper.

Naturally, nobody is right about everything all the time. But if a political candidate tells a crowd, "You people have been telling Washington to stop [whatever], and they don't listen. Yet you know, as I know, that you have a true view of the world; those [left-wing; right-wing; liberal; conservative; pinko; wishy washy; any adjective of your choice] politicians haven't listened to us. When we speak, they should listen!" Note what happens in the above: (1) The people in the crowd are right; (2) the politician making the speech has included himself in their number; (3) those who disagree are negatively labeled; and (4) there is no evidence given whatsoever that what the "people" say is right, no matter what they say.

It is popular in advertising to use the slogan "Made in America." This is an appeal to the patriotism of Americans (the "people") in an attempt to show that if a product is made anywhere else, it must be inferior. There is no proof given that the product is any better or worse than one made in another country—only that you should buy it because it was "made in America." Logically, the slogan is saying that it doesn't matter about quality, construction, price or anything else that most people consider important when making a purchase decision—ignore all those factors and buy only because of origin.

Argumentum ad populum can be dangerous. It can be used to get crowds to lynch blacks, beat up homosexuals or persecute Jews. As a matter of fact, it was—Hitler used the argumentum ad populum in the 1930s to build up the Germans' attitude that they were the master race and that blacks, homosexuals, Jews and handicapped people were inferior and should not be allowed to live because they were not like the master race. (There go 14,000,000 people in the death camps.)

Argumentum ad Vercundium

The argumentum ad vercundium is an appeal to tradition or authority in support of some contention. "If it was good enough for grandpa, it's good enough for me" is a capsule example of the argument. "As it was in the beginning, is now, and ever shall be" is another.

Advertising often uses the argumentum ad vercundium. Advertising often uses famous actors, sports figures and even politicians to endorse products and services. They are presented as authorities on the products as though they are experts. In fact, they usually have no expertise, knowledge or even regard for the quality or appropriate use of the product for the consumer—they simply say they use it. That is enough.

Appeal to Ignorance (argumentum ad ignorantiam)

The appeal to ignorance bases an argument on the idea that a claim or theory must be correct because no one can prove that the claim or theory is wrong. Note that last word; the argument does not attempt to prove the claim is right, but that it must be because it can't be proven wrong.

Often this argument uses a false or at least an unprovable cause-and-effect relationship and defies a challenger to show that the relationship is impossible.

For example, there are companies that claim that wearing copper bracelets will bring about an improvement in those people who suffer from arthritis, and they dare medical researchers to prove they don't. The researchers constantly state that such an effect cannot be supported by any medical or scientific evidence, but the promoters of the bracelets say since nobody has proved they don't work, and they have a right to say they do.

Dangling Comparative (Cross 1979)

One of my favorite tricks is the dangling comparative. A dangling comparative is a statement that seems to be comparing one thing to another, but in actuality it never actually says what the thing being compared is being compared to. What generally happens is that the comparison is left up to the audience to complete. For example, "Our tires stop 25 percent faster." Note that the statement never says what the tires stop faster than. The audience would naturally expect it to be other tires, and they would mentally finish the statement "Our tires stop 25 percent faster *than other tires.*" However, that is not what was said. The comparison is left open, and it could be other tires (in which case, it would be stronger to actually say so), but it probably isn't other tires. It could just as easily be doughnuts.

"Our toothpaste tastes better." Better than what? Day-old bacon fat, banana slugs, gasoline? The comparison is never finished except in the minds of the audience.

"Our dog food tastes better." Better than what? And considering what a dog will lick, is taste really high on its agenda? And who did this test, anyway?

"There is nothing just like [whatever the product is]." This is undoubtedly true. However, what is being compared? It could simply be the name of the product. Thus, if the sentence is, "There is nothing just like Armorall,"™ this is absolutely true; there is nothing else named Armorall.™ Other products may have exactly the same formula and do exactly the same thing, but "Nothing else is named Armorall."™ In fact, nothing else can be named that; the name is trademarked, and if anyone tried to use the name, they would end up in court being sued for trademark infringement.

So why are dangling comparatives used? Because advertisers must provide evidence to support anything they state as facts about products. But sometimes that evidence is stupid. One of my favorites was a car ad in which the major claim was that it was "600 percent quieter." I'm sure you now spot the dangling comparative—quieter than what? The audience would be expected to fill in the blank with "quieter than other cars." Well, that's not what they said, only what they implied. They did have evidence in support of this statement, but the evidence was stupid. The car was 600 percent quieter inside the car with the windows closed than riding on the hood at 60 miles an hour. So the ad's statement was correct, but if the advertisers finished it, people would think the car company was run by morons. So they leave out that little detail.

Another commercial, this time for an automatic dishwashing detergent: A crystal chandelier is dipped in pancake batter, then put inside a standard home dishwasher with a standard amount of the detergent, and the washer is turned on. Text was superimposed on the screen, saying the dishwasher was run for one regular cycle; it also said that the test was run with egg and oatmeal. The dishwasher was then opened and the chandelier was pulled out, sparkling clean.

It certainly appeared that the detergent did a good job of getting the pancake batter off the chandelier. The ad made several definitive statements, and therefore they had to be true: The chandelier was dipped in pancake batter, it was put in a normal home dishwasher with a standard amount of detergent, and it went through one regular washing cycle. Those must be true statements or the ad would be guilty of deceptive advertising, which is illegal.

So what's the dangling comparative? The ad made one further definitive statement, which was that the test was also run with egg and oatmeal. The dangling comparative is that the results of those tests weren't given. It was *implied* that the outcome was the same as for the batter, but it wasn't actually said. It could be that the detergent actually permanently bonded the egg and oatmeal to the chandelier; there's no way to tell.

What we can get from all this is that advertising is designed specifically to affect people in ways they usually aren't aware of, and, in fact, advertising tries to prevent people from becoming aware of how they're being manipulated.

Remember I said that advertising is limited in time and space—it has to accomplish its job, to sell, in a hurry. So it uses shortcuts like stereotypes. A common complaint about advertising is that it perpetuates stereotypes. This is absolutely true. If an ad needs to sell dishwashing soap, of course it'll be a woman in the ad, not a man. Research shows that men don't buy soap by brand name—they buy what's on sale. But women do buy soap by brand name, and that's why brand names advertise. Does it perpetuate the stereotype of the woman as the housekeeper? Absolutely. But that's what the ad has to do. It doesn't have the time or space to explain why it's a man using the soap, and a man is unlikely to be persuaded by the ad.

It is not advertising's job to fix social problems. Its job is to sell products. It's also not advertising's job to make social problems worse, and advertising doesn't go out of its way to make things worse. But if there is a conflict between selling and society—selling wins. Otherwise advertising is a total waste of time and money for the sponsor.

Having said that, there are things that advertising does that can have negative effects on the audience. For example, most of the women in ads have bodies that are not typical. The average woman in an ad is a size 2 to 4, 5 foot 7, 120 pounds. The average woman in America is a size 14, 5 foot 4, 145 pounds. So why those women in the ads? Because they **aren't** average. The ads are designed to make the audience want the product, and one reason they want it is to not be average. They already are, so if they ad implies no change from what they already are, why would they need the product? Yes, these images absolutely can have a negative effect on the audience's self-esteem or self-image. But, once again, selling tops society. What the audience needs to do is to understand that advertising is **trying** to make them feel inadequate in order to sell the product. Then they can fight off the effect.

Another complaint about advertising is that it makes people buy things they don't need. Well, this isn't true. Advertising can't make anybody do anything. It can influence, it can promote, it can persuade, it can create desire, but it can't force. Only the person can decide to buy something. Only the person can decide if it's necessary or not, or if it's wanted or not. Don't give advertising a power it doesn't have.

■ ENDNOTES

1. Research shows that women tend to buy the food products for their families by brand name, while men tend to buy only for themselves. Also, women tend to buy products like food and cleaning products by brand name while men tend to buy what's on sale. Thus, the ads use women since they're the target audience.
2. I often wonder, would diamonds be as expensive if they looked like raisins?
3. http://www.wsu.edu/~taflinge/destruc.html
4. There is a legal requirement that food has to meet to be able to use the term "organic." However, this discussion is what the word "organic" actually means, not what the FDA allows food producers to use.

17

PUBLIC RELATIONS

*P*ublic relations people use the mass media to deliver the messages of their clients to a mass audience in the same way advertisers do. But what those messages are and how they get into the media are really what separate PR from advertising.

Let's start with a definition of public relations. It is the practice of managing the communication between an organization and its publics. That practice focuses on two-way communication and fosters mutually beneficial relationships between an organization and its publics.

Of course, that's how PR companies would define PR. They say that PR's job is to make their clients, whether companies or individuals, look good to the public through getting positive publicity and reducing negative publicity. But, in fact, PR goes way beyond that.

Before we get into that, though, let's look at the history of PR.

Public relations has been with us for thousands of years. The Greeks had a word for it, *semantikos*: to signify, to mean. In English, semantikos has become semantics, the science of the meanings of words. Another way of looking at it is spin: choosing exactly the right word to have exactly the right effect on people in order to get them to believe what you want them to believe and to do what you want them to do. That is not a bad definition of public relations.

The illustration on the next page is of Ramses II's attempt to burnish his image as a war leader by telling his people that he won the battle of Kadesh against the Hittites in 1274 BCE. He covered the walls of temples with bas reliefs and hieroglyphics extolling his abilities as a general and a warrior, grinding the Hittites beneath his chariot wheels. Too bad he lost that battle. Or at least didn't win it. The war was to take the city of Kadesh, but when he left the field the Hittites still owned the city. Still, what Egyptian was going to travel to Kadesh to check out the facts? This is positive publicity, also known as spin.

In 50 BCE, Julius Caesar wrote the first campaign biography, *Caesar's Gallic Wars.* The Romans believed that military success was the most vital thing for anyone who wanted political success—you want to run for office and run the country, be a great general. Caesar did exactly that, disobeying the Roman senate and attacking the Gauls in what is now France. It's a good thing he won, adding huge new territories to the empire, because it provided him with just the kind of military reputation he needed. Naturally, he publicized his military exploits to convince the Roman people that he would make the best head of the Roman state. This approach to gaining a good reputation is still in play. Candidates for political office continue to publicize themselves with campaign biographies and accounts of military exploits to this day. Think of John McCain when he ran for President. His campaign ads and speeches continually played on his war record, especially the time he spent as a prisoner of war in Vietnam.

Caligula, the fourth emperor of Rome, tried to gain the same sort of military reputation. He went north to finish the job that Julius Caesar didn't—the conquest of the island of Britain. Too bad Caligula was a complete and total loon. He brought back loot from his expedition to demonstrate his generalship, but it only consisted of hundreds of thousands of seashells his soldiers had collected from the beach. This was a PR ploy that really backfired. Caligula didn't live much longer because his bodyguards stabbed him in the back just to rid Rome of a mad emperor.

Claudius followed Caligula as emperor and tried the same stunt —to conquer Britain. This time, though, Claudius succeeded. Well, his generals did. After they took southern Britain, Claudius dropped in for a few days, had himself declared a god, founded a few temples dedicated to himself, added the name Britannicus to his Tiberius Claudius Caesar Augustus Germanicus, and essentially told everyone, "what a good boy am I." Again, a lot of spin. His wife poisoned him so her son Nero could become the next emperor.

In 394 A.D., St. Augustine was a professor of rhetoric in Milan, the capitol of the Western Roman Empire. He delivered the regular eulogies to the emperor and was the closest thing to a minister of propaganda for the imperial court. Thus, St. Augustine was one of the first people to be *employed* by others to run their public relations. The modern equivalent would be the US President's press secretary or communication director.

When Christianity emerged at the height of Roman influence, the teachings of Jesus and his apostles took center stage in the battle for religious dominance in the public mind. Once the Christian church took shape, it relied on eloquent speeches and letters, such as Paul's epistle to the Romans, to win converts and guide the faithful.

Even the word "propaganda" originated in the Catholic Church. In the seventeenth century, it set up its Congregatio de Propaganda Fide, the "congregation for propagating the faith," in an attempt to counter the Protestant Reformation (remember that from the chapter on the rise of printing). In doing so, the Church explicitly acknowledged the need for a third party to facilitate communication between government (which the Church could be considered at the time) and the people. Along with the spread of new knowledge in new forms—such as translations in the fifteenth century of the Bible from Latin into everyday languages, mass printed books and newspapers—there was an explosion of public communications.

In 1776, Thomas Paine, who wrote "Common Sense" (which I believe I've mentioned a time or two), wrote a series of collected articles known as "The American Crisis." Their famous opening line is, "These are the times that try men's souls." At the time things were not going well for the American revolutionary forces. They were losing battles and soldiers, who had signed up for ninety days duty and wanted to go home. George Washington had the pamphlet read to the soldiers at Valley Forge in 1777. It was so powerful and persuasive that it convinced the soldiers of Washington's army to stay and fight. This was a time when many were prepared to desert so they could escape the cold and the hardships of a winter campaign. Paine was a master of political propaganda whose writing could get people to believe things and do things.

Benjamin Franklin was also a master of promotion. He made it a rule to forbear all contradiction to others, and all positive assertions of his own. He would say, "I conceive" or "I apprehend" or "I imagine" a thing to be so, or it appears to be so. Franklin pioneered the rules for "personal relations" in an era before mass media had made possible a profession called "public relations."

Franklin understood that image could be everything when he was the American envoy to France and trying to get French support for the American Revolution. Although diplomats dressed up in brocade and lace and ribbons to present a cultured image, Franklin dressed **down** in plain unadorned brown cloth to reflect the French stereotype of Americans: rough-hewn, independent, more concerned with substance than with style. He even avoided the norm of wearing a powdered wig and took to wearing a fur hat—how appropriately American! The French loved him—some of them literally—he was very popular with the ladies and often conducted business in ladies' bedrooms. His co-envoy, the strait-laced, uptight John Adams, deplored Franklin's methods, but he couldn't argue with the fact that Adams himself annoyed the French, while Franklin got everything the Americans needed through his public (and private) relations.

Of course, not all promotional antics had a positive outcome. For example, in 1720, in an attempt to raise their stock price, England's South Seas Company circulated false claims about how successful it was and how rich its holdings were in the South Seas. Their stock shot up more than 800 percent and spawned a slew of other stock offerings that had nothing behind them. (Sound familiar? The dot com boom of the 1990s was exactly the same thing.) When the lies were discovered and the bubble burst (just like the housing bubble burst in 2008), thousands of companies, banks, institutions, and individuals were wiped out (just like during the housing bubble of 2008).

The 1720s were not good years for PR. John Law tried the same thing as the South Seas Company did, promoting the French territory of Louisiana as the source of astounding wealth, and selling stock in his Mississippi Company. As it turned out, all of his claims were false, again thousands of investors lost all their money, and it almost brought down the French banking system.

In the middle of the nineteenth century a man appeared who was to become one of the leading publicists of all time, P. T. Barnum. His accomplishments include the founding of the American Museum and the establishment of the Barnum and Bailey Circus (now Ringling Bros., Barnum and Bailey Circus). Barnum was a master of promotion who could fill his enterprises with customers by using what we today would call sleazy methods of publicity. For example, he announced that his museum would exhibit a 161-year-old woman who had been Washington's nurse. He produced an elderly woman and a forged birth certificate to make his case. Barnum was really into hyperbole: Jumbo, the world's largest elephant; General Tom Thumb (a rank Barnum gave him), the world's smallest man; and The Giant, the world's tallest man.

William Seward, Abraham Lincoln's secretary of state in 1861, gained a large American audience through his understanding of how to use the press. He told his friend Jefferson Davis (they were friends before the Civil War): "I speak to the newspapers—they have a large audience and can repeat a thousand times what I want to impress on the public." After the Civil War, Seward used his knowledge of promotion to convince the people to go along with one of his biggest ideas, often called by his opponents Seward's Folly. He pushed for, and succeeded, in buying from Russia a huge chunk of useless land for two cents an acre: Alaska. Imagine how his opponents felt when that useless land turned out to be a treasure trove of natural resources such as gold and oil.

■ PUBLIC RELATIONS AS A PROFESSION

The history of public relations as a profession is mostly confined to the early half of the twentieth century; however, there is evidence of its practices scattered through history. A number of American precursors to public relations existed in the form of publicists who specialized in promoting circuses, theatrical performances and other public spectacles. In the United States, where public relations has its origins, many early public relations practices were developed in support of railroads. In fact, many scholars believe that the first appearance of the **term** "public relations" appeared in the 1897 *Year Book of Railway Literature.*

Public relations became a profession in 1903 as Ivy Lee agreed to advise John D. Rockefeller on how to conduct his public relations. Rockefeller was one of the group of people known as "robber barons," men who owned and built up huge companies that created virtual monopolies of many areas of commerce, including railroads, oil, and banking. These men were ruthless, driving out of business any potential rivals and treating their workers like the serfs of old. Rockefeller owned coal mines and the Pennsylvania Railroad.

As Lee took on his duties, miners were on strike, and the railroad hushed up the facts when its trains were involved with accidents. Public opinion turned against Rockefeller, and Lee began the first real example of "crisis management," using the media to convince the public through managed news releases and feature stories that Rockefeller wasn't the bad guy every one thought he was. He also advised Rockefeller on how to make himself and his companies look better through public works and philanthropy—in other words, use all of that money he'd gotten through ruthless means to pay for things the public would see as good.

After a railroad accident, Lee invited reporters to inspect the wreck and get the facts. The Pennsylvania Railroad then obtained its first favorable press coverage.

Other so-called robber barons picked up on the idea of looking better to the public. Just think about all the libraries and colleges and performance halls named Carnegie after Andrew Carnegie, the steel baron, whose wealth endowed them.

Lee professionalized public relations by following three basic principles:

1. Tell the truth
2. Provide accurate facts
3. The public relations director must have access to top management and must be able to influence decisions.

Lee defined public relations when he said, public relations means the actual relationship of the company to the people and that relationship involves more than talk. The company must act by performing good deeds—such as endowing universities and libraries.

Public relations took the next step toward professionalism in 1918 when Edward Bernays advised the president of the new country of Czechoslovakia to announce independence on a Monday, rather than on a Sunday, in order to get maximum press coverage. In 1923, Bernays published "Crystallizing Public Opinion," in which he established several public relations principles. He said that public relations have these functions:

- To interpret the client to the public, which means promoting the client
- To interpret the public to the client, which means operating the company in such a way as to gain the approval of the public

Bernays and Lee were stressing the idea that the corporation should accept social responsibility. Bernays' ideas about social responsibility led to his refusal to accept unethical clients.

Other Bernays concepts include:

a. Public relations is a public service.
b. Public relations should promote new ideas and progress.
c. Public relations should build a public conscience.

Bernays put his ideas into practice when he took on Proctor and Gamble and the Columbian Rope Company as clients. Proctor and Gamble had produced a radio commercial that was offensive to African-Americans. Bernays took these steps:

a. He changed the commercial.
b. He got the company to offer African-Americans significant jobs.
c. He invited them to tour the plant.
d. He featured African-Americans in the company newsletter.

The Columbian Rope Company had an anti-union image, so Bernays took these steps:

a. He produced a radio program featuring union and management panelists.
b. He induced the company to bargain with the union.
c. He offered tours of the plant.
d. He convinced the company to sponsor a vocational program.

Ivy Lee could be called the first public relations counselor, but Edward Bernays may truly be called the father of public relations. In describing the origin of the term Public Relations, Bernays commented,

> When I came back to the United States [after World War I], I decided that if you could use propaganda for war, you could certainly use it for peace. And propaganda got to be a bad word because of the Germans . . . using it. So what I did was to try to find some other words, so we found the words Counsel on Public Relations.

Bernays was the profession's first theorist. Bernays drew many of his ideas from Sigmund Freud's theories about the irrational, unconscious motives that shape human behavior. Bernays authored several books, including *Crystallizing Public Opinion* (1923), *Propaganda* (1928) and *The Engineering of Consent* (1947). He saw public relations as an "applied social science" that uses insights from psychology, sociology and other disciplines to scientifically manage and manipulate the thinking and behavior of an irrational and "herd like" public. He wrote in his book *Propaganda,*

> The conscious and intelligent manipulation of the organized habits and opinions of the masses is an important element in democratic society. Those who manipulate this unseen mechanism of society constitute an invisible government which is the true ruling power of our country.

Doesn't that make you feel all warm and runny inside? He's freely admitting that public relations isn't about logic, or reason or information, but about the manipulation of people's feelings, people for which he clearly has nothing but disdain. He also wrote, "The three main elements of public relations are practically as old as society:

informing people, persuading people, or integrating people with people. Of course, the means and methods of accomplishing these ends have changed as society has changed."

At this point we should examine how PR differs from advertising. Remember the definition of advertising: **Advertising is the nonpersonal communication of information usually paid for and usually persuasive in nature about products, services or ideas by identified sponsors through the various media.**

Let's see this in terms of PR.

PR is usually a nonpersonal communication of information. That information, just like advertising, is slanted to make the client look good, emphasizing the good stuff and soft-pedaling, or even leaving out, the bad. However, unlike advertising, there's no real requirement to **substantiate** the claims. In other words, you don't need evidence in support of any claims made—you can even lie.

Then there's "**. . . usually paid for . . .**" Advertising has to pay for the ads to run in the media, buying space in print media and time in broadcast media. Once the space or time is bought, as long as the ad obeys the dictates of decency and substantiation, the ad runs and appears before the public.

PR, on the other hand, does its best **not** to pay for placement in the media. PR firms spend a lot of time, effort and money creating and placing promotional material for their clients. They write "news" articles and feature stories extolling their clients and send them out to media outlets in hopes that they'll be published as news. Of course, since such news releases are not objective coverage of the client, it means they're **not** really news, and most such releases never appear. (Remember that advertising, having paid for the space to run, must run—PR, not paying for the space, doesn't have to run.) Nonetheless, when a news outlet needs some kind of filler, either because it needs something to fill a blank space or empty airtime, the outlet may run the release—often after rewriting or reediting it. However, since a PR piece isn't technically advertising, it doesn't have to be labeled as advertising, and thus it avoids the consumer's automatic distrust of what's being said. The consumer may indeed think it is news, not promotion, and be less skeptical of the claims in a PR story.

Another thing PR firms do is to create publicity stunts for their clients, including everything from sponsoring events like sports, movie openings or concerts, to putting on open houses, celebrations or contests, to press conferences, in the hope that media outlets will cover them as news and thus get out the clients' slant.

How about "**. . . about products, services or ideas . . .**"? Well, PR can indeed promote products, services or ideas, but more often the promotion is about companies or people. Companies need to look good in front of their publics in order to increase sales. And people need to look good in front of their publics to increase whatever they happen to want from those publics. Entertainers want to get bigger audiences, politicians want to get more votes, wannabe's wanna—be. Just look at Nadya Suleman, the Octomom, and Kate Gosselin, the reality show star and mother of eight. Following their PR advisors, they do interviews, appear in newspapers and magazines, do promotions, and even appear on "Dancing with the Stars." These activities keep their names before the public and give them possibilities of gaining fame—and money.

A major difference between advertising and PR lies in the next phrase in the definition—**"by identified sponsors."** Advertising needs to identify the sponsor of the ad—otherwise, how would the audience know? But PR often disguises the sponsor or even hides it. News releases put out by PR firms to promote a company or person often hide the fact that the articles are paid for by that company or person. This is because identifying who paid for a release will tell the audience that it is slanted in favor of a company or person and is not an actual, objective, balanced examination. If the audience thinks it's slanted, they'll discount any claims made in it, just as they do with advertising. After all, how accurate will you think a news article about the value of drinking milk is if you find out it was paid for by the American Dairy Association? Or an article about health and smoking paid for by the American Tobacco Council? So PR sponsors leave out that detail, or they come up with a name that disguises the actual source, like People for the American Way (after all, what Americans wouldn't like to consider themselves being for the American Way?), which promotes liberal causes, or the Heritage Foundation (whatever that means), which promotes conservatism. Just think of the neoconservative group Swiftboat Veterans for Truth that attacked presidential candidate John Kerry by telling lies. But of course, they couldn't be telling lies—it's in their name: "for Truth."

One of the biggest uses for public relations today is crisis management. Remember that's what Ivy Lee did for John D. Rockefeller. Today more people and more companies are in dire need of crisis management because today's media uncover and publish everything about everyone. An early example from the 1980s was the Tylenol scare, when some psycho was putting poison in bottles of Tylenol on store shelves. This did nothing for sales. Tylenol immediately started a PR campaign, telling the public about the problem and what they were doing about it, like pulling their product from the shelves and inventing new packaging that would prevent tampering. The public soon regained confidence in the company.

Sometimes a company doesn't think it needs crisis management. In 1989, an oil tanker belonging to Exxon Oil, the *Exxon Valdez,* went aground in Alaska, spilling millions of gallons of crude oil. Exxon decided to downplay the event. The public read this as arrogance, especially when pictures of the effects of the spill started coming out—and especially the pictures of wildlife covered in oil. It appeared as though Exxon considered itself too big and powerful to have to care, basically saying to the public, "You don't like it? Too bad." This did not go over well. Exxon became so hated that they decided they had to do something, and they turned to their PR people for some "crisis management." Exxon immediately started sending cleanup crews to the site, spent millions on technology, promised reparations to the fishermen around Prudoe Bay, and had executives appear in media interviews to express their regret about the events and what they'd do about it. It worked—until the price tag of the cleanup came in and Exxon refused to pay for it. All of a sudden they were the bad guys again. Sometimes you need to listen to your PR people.

British Petroleum also did a poor job of crisis management when one of its oil rigs in the Gulf of Mexico exploded and gushed millions of barrels into the water. They put their president in the media often, but he came across as arrogant and wealthy, especially when he was compared to the fishermen whose livelihoods were being destroyed. BP has still not managed to get a handle on its PR.

Of course, it's not just companies that need crisis management. For example, there's Mel Gibson and his drunken anti-Semitic rants. Or Governor Mark Sanford of South Carolina, who said he was "walking the Appalachian Trail" when he was actually in Brazil with his mistress. Or Lindsay Lohan going wild. And of course, there's Tiger Woods. Because everything becomes known about everyone, public figures especially, whose behavior might reflect badly on them, require the rehabilitation of their images. And it's public relations that takes on the job.

CHAPTER

18

NEWS

*P*eople have always been curious. They always want to know things—What's going on? Who's doing what? How will it affect me?

The stories that provide our worldviews, our sense of reality, often revolve around these questions, and the answers we receive can and do alter that reality. However, the people who provide us with those stories also live in that reality. Thus, what they tell us reflects what the journalists believe the world is like rather than what the world actually is like. The death of the pharaoh or the king altered people's worlds. For example, Ramses the Great ruled Egypt for sixty-six years in an era when life expectancy was forty-five years. This meant that the majority of Egyptians never knew any pharaoh but Ramses. Imagine how their world was overturned when he died. Ramses was a living god. Have the gods deserted us? Has the world come to an end? The uncertainty of the future after a lifetime of stability must have had people really on edge. The news of Ramses' death over-threw the Egyptians' entire worldview. The story of their society, with Ramses at its center as the hero who solves the problems, was over.

News has always driven the plots of our social stories. Events would occur that would add another crisis or complication, and those events would be put in the context of the story. For millennia, religion drove that narrative—conflicts between the gods, or the gods and people, drove the events. The priests would deliver the news. For example, when the kingdom of Uruk suffered a seven year famine, the priests told the people that it was because Ishtar, the goddess of love, had fallen in love with King Gilgamesh, but he had spurned her. So she asked her father, the god Anu, to punish him. This explained a famine when people's worldview didn't include factual reality, such as weather patterns. If anything unexplainable happened, it was because the gods were fighting or the people had sinned. Just think of Sodom and Gomorrah in Genesis 18 and 19. The cities were destroyed by God because people had violated the rules of their society, not because of earthquakes or meteor showers or whatever might actually have happened. And the news of what happened and why were delivered by the priests, along with the moral: Obey the rules. This maintained the story of the society.

Later, more events were explainable as people discovered that many things had natural rather than supernatural causes, that nature would do what it did without regard for anything that gods or people might or might not do. This created a whole new worldview, and the news would reflect that new view, although the old view was often difficult to shed entirely. For example, if there was a war, it was because the villainous king of another country attacked ours (sometimes ascribed a supernatural motivation like "the devil made him do it"), and our heroic king fought him off (usually because "God's on our side"). Both sides would use the same motivations, and the news of what happened in the war would back each society's worldview.

Think of World War II. Hitler, Mussolini and Tojo were evil villains leading the Axis powers, and Allied leaders Roosevelt, Churchill and Stalin were the heroes in the story; the news of battles would reflect this. Of course, the Axis powers of Germany, Italy and Japan reversed who the heroes and villains were, and news of battles reflected that. Thus, the Germans believed their hero Hitler's story that Poland attacked Germany; the rest of the world, listening to their heroes, believed the story that Germany attacked Poland. Newspapers and magazines would disparage the opposition, ascribing evil motivations and actions to them, and they would lionize the home team, ascribing to them noble motivations and actions. That both sides did this was seen by both sides as proof of the perfidy and unwillingness of the other to face reality, when in fact both sides distorted reality to reflect their own worldviews. This has been a constant throughout history.

How we hear the news has changed over time. At first it was in the temples because virtually all the news had a supernatural basis. In the Middle Ages, life was reduced to seven miles in any direction, so news was what other people told you was happening in the village, and everything else was either rumors or irrelevant. The occasional troubadour would relate what had happened in the outside world, like who was king at the moment and what new war was being fought, but in general people didn't care about the outside world unless it was getting close. In that case, they just wanted to hear the news in time to hide the crops and the cows and find a good place in the woods to wait for the outside world to pass them by.

As societies grew more secular, at least some of the news moved out of the temples and the troubadours' memories and into the streets—literally. Town criers would walk around the villages or towns and shout the news. Again, it was mostly local information, with occasional broader news announced if a rider arrived from the outside with messages.

Then printing was invented. News sheets were published, but they weren't for average people, but for the movers and shakers of society; in other words, people with money. They mostly contained shipping and financial news, along with information about war and politics, since those things affected shipping and finance. The average people still relied on town criers and rumor to inform their world.

However, in the early nineteenth century, newspapers and magazines began to be published that average people could afford. For the first time, people were hearing about events that were not only local, but also big, and outside their area. Their world expanded and their worldview had to expand with it. Their social story had to adapt to new problems, crises and complications, and climaxes. News became an integral part of that worldview, and it has remained so ever since. The media have changed, and the scope and speed with which we get that news has increased incredibly, but it's still a major part of our lives.

So we have the news, every day and in every medium. However, we run right up against a difficulty—just what is news? We all recognize the word when we hear it. But what do we mean by it?

There are all sorts of possibilities: "reports of recent events" appears in the dictionary. How about information or an examination of issues? Do any of these satisfy the definition? Not really.

So let's look at the criteria for newsworthiness that most journalists use, to see if those help.

The first of those is **timeliness**. The idea of timeliness seems to fit with the idea of recent, but what is recent? Five minutes ago? Five hours? Five days? How recent is recent? How quickly does something turn from recent to old?

Perhaps timeliness refers to hearing about something in time to do something about it. For example, hearing in a timely manner about how Wall Street banks were losing people's money left and right in risky investment schemes would have allowed people to do something about it. However, people didn't hear about it until it was too late, or rather they didn't believe it until it was too late. Those few people who saw what was happening and tried to issue warnings were effectively ignored since what they were saying didn't fit the prevailing social story. Of course, what we did hear we heard about in the news. So, was it news, then? It certainly filled the newspapers and the airwaves for months after the event, but not before or during the event. So perhaps timeliness has nothing to do with helping people to take action.

Maybe it just refers to finding out about things you haven't heard of before. But wouldn't that make this book news? Then timeliness would have nothing to do with the clock or the calendar, but with the individual. But news organizations can't be concerned with the individual—they're concerned with the mass audience. So it's more likely that timeliness refers to how close to publication or airtime an event occurs, and that the news organization hasn't been talking about it before. Thus, it's a matter of putting out today's news to replace yesterday's. And if something new occurs concerning yesterday's news, it becomes timely again and the new information is added—after all, it's now today's news.

How about the next criterion for newsworthiness: **proximity**. Proximity means how close or far away something is from the observer. But, again, what does that mean in terms of news? If it happens next door, is that news? How about in the next town? The next state? The next country? The other side of the world? What makes something proximate?

Maybe it has to do with impact on the audience. If something happens next door, it's certainly proximate to you, but is it news? Well, it is—to you. So will it appear in news media? It depends on what it is. If your neighbor chopped limbs off your tree, probably not. But if your neighbor murdered her husband, it probably would. Why the difference? The former would only impact you; the latter would impact the entire community— there's a murderer in their midst. The economic meltdown had an impact on the whole country, so it's news for the whole country. Iran, Iraq, Israel, Russia, North Korea, Egypt, all have an impact on the whole world.

So it could be that proximity refers to where the people are that could be affected by the event reported, and the more widely-spread the affected people are, the more likely it is that the event will be widely reported.

How about **prominence**? Something that is prominent is notable or distinctive. We can apply this to events, like elections or Supreme Court confirmations or hurricanes or wars. We can also apply it to people, such as politicians or criminals or celebrities. All of these events or people are out of the ordinary and attract attention.

But what makes them prominent enough to be news? A lot of events are clearly prominent—they can have a major effect on a lot of people, things like wars and hurricanes. But what about people? Barack Obama is clearly prominent. So are Bill Clinton and Hillary Clinton and Kim Jung-Il and Vladimir Putin. But what makes someone like Paris Hilton or Lindsay Lohan or Paula Abdul prominent? What they do or say has little or no effect on the lives of people who hear about them. So maybe what makes them prominent is the fact that they're reported on—that they're famous for being famous.

So even prominence is problematical.

Then there's **consequence**. For something to be news, it should have some consequence for people; it should affect their lives in some way. People make decisions about just about everything based on what they know, and what they know often comes from the news. So news should give them the information they need to make an informed decision about something. But does it? What kind of decisions do we make based on ten days of twenty-four hours a day coverage of the death of Michael Jackson? Don't die? How about the octomom, Nadya Suleman? Don't have eight babies at a time? How about Paris Hilton? Get a life?

If the news concentrates on trivialities, does that make the consequences of what's reported on trivial? Does it reduce all news to the same level of triviality? Are Afghanistan or Darfur on the same level of importance as Brittany Spears shaving her head or forgetting her underwear? And considering that the space and time in newspapers, magazines and television news are limited, can the trivial push out the significant if it's given equal prominence and thus has an implied equal consequence with the non-trivial?

How we answer these questions determines just how significant the news is to us. When news organizations give as much time to the non-consequential as to the information that could have an effect on people's lives, people come to believe that the non-consequential *does* have an effect on their lives, that the love lives (or lack thereof) or the self-control (or lack thereof) or the triumphs (or lack thereof) of celebrities have as much impact on news consumers as the economy or politics or war. Again, it comes down to the social stories that the news informs and reinforces in the audience's belief about what the world is and how it works. Thus, the news often lacks consequence.

Then there's **rarity**. Rarity refers to the event being out of the ordinary—in other words, odd. Things that are normal aren't news. You don't see a lot of news reports on planes not crashing or crimes not being committed or houses not burning down. It's normal for planes to land safely, for people to avoid being robbed or burgled or raped or murdered or abducted, and for houses to remain standing without so much as a single scorch mark.

It's the very fact that something is unusual that could make it newsworthy. For example, the octomom Nadya Suleman is unusual. It's normal for dogs, cats and rabbits to have eight babies at a time—people just don't do that. And we hear about child abductions because they're so rare, only 150 in 2008 in a population of 75 million children in America. The same goes for school shootings and Somali pirate attacks—they are extremely rare and thus attract a great deal of media, and therefore audience, attention.

How about **human interest**? What does that mean? It's usually applied to stories about rescuing a kitten from a pipe or ducklings from a sewer or a daredevil climbing the side of a building. What makes them human? For that matter, what makes them interesting? They seem to be stories that make us go "wow," or make us feel all warm and runny inside. They **are** out of the ordinary, but are they news?

According to news organizations, they are. Virtually all newscasts end with what's called a puff piece, some occurrence that has no consequence for anyone in the audience, but that makes them feel good. Newspapers have the comics, and they devote entire sections to things that many people are interested in but that have no real consequence to the world—the sports section and the food section and the travel section and the car section. The readers may make a decision about which team to support or what to eat or where to go or what car to buy, but are any of those of any great consequence? Well, maybe to those who read or watch those stories.

So how many of these criteria—timeliness, proximity, prominence, consequence, rarity and human interest—have to apply to an event to consider it newsworthy? All of them? Most of them? Just one?

Another dictionary definition of news is "a matter of interest to newspaper readers and newscast viewers." So maybe what everything I've been talking about comes down to is: News is whatever the individual thinks is news. Remember all those questions about consequence being a criterion for newsworthiness? Well, the answers to all of them are— what do you think? There **is** no hard and fast answer to what is news. If you think Michael Jackson or Paula Abdul or Nadya Suleman is important to you, then news **about** them is important to you. And if there are enough other people like you to buy the newspapers and magazines and watch the TV news and look for them online, then the media will feed you information about them; after all, that's how the media make money. And, of course, if there are enough people who avoid such stories and complain that they're not worth reporting, the media will stop running them.

So news fits into people's stories about what the world is and how it works. If that sense of reality includes what many people consider trivial and worthless, but is part of other people's reality because they consider it important and worthwhile, then it's appropriate to report it.

And if they want to include the horoscope, the comics page and the crossword puzzle, why not?

So let's look at who decides what's newsworthy, who applies those criteria to determine what people will be told about the world around them.

First there are the **gatekeepers**. A gatekeeper is a person or an organization that decides what news will appear in a news medium and thus what people should know. There are several people involved in this process.

First, there are **reporters**. Reporters are those people who go out into the world, whether it's the local flower show or the war on the other side of world, gather information about the event and the people involved, and then write up the story. They're gatekeepers because they decide how they'll gather the information: where they will go, what they'll look at, what they'll photograph, who they'll talk to. There's no way they can possibly get everything there is to know about an event—that would take forever. In addition, a great deal can depend on the personal predilections of the individual reporter. Rhe could decide to go into the field, experience events firsthand and talk to people actually involved, or rhe could decide to sit in an office and get information from handouts and phone calls; rhe could decide to examine every aspect and look at everything involved, or rhe could decide to look only at those things that fit a preconceived notion; rhe could decide to talk to everyone involved, or only to those people in authority; rhe could decide to take pictures of everything, or only point the camera in a direction that supports a point of view.

Once they've gathered the information, reporters have to decide how to tell the story—what angle to take, how to organize the information, what words and pictures to use. Note that I deliberately use the word "story." The reporter finds the angle, the problem that is at the base of the event; rhe organizes the information to create a rising sense of action through crises and complications, selecting those words, pictures, and interviews as though they were dialogue; and rhe ends the story with a climax, an apparent solution to the problem selected for the story. The fact that most stories are linear as they unfold, but that most events are non-linear as they occur, is subordinated to the structure imposed by the art of storytelling. This rearrangement of reality to turn it into a story could completely change the audience's perception of the event.

For example, I once saw a CBS news report on the crisis in Bosnia. It was about how people were suffering under the constant warfare and ethnic cleansing. As the camera panned across a refugee camp containing 10,000 women and children under absolutely miserable conditions, it stopped on an image of a circle of women talking. The reporter said, "And the women sit, and gossip, and wonder what will happen next." Note what just happened. The reporter used the word "gossip," which means idle chatter, reducing what these women were doing to the level of, "Oh, did you hear what Svetlana did?" He completely trivialized the entire story. Why did he use that word? Couldn't he have picked a word, like "discuss" or "confer"? It leaves the audience thinking things can't be that bad if the women are gossiping, as opposed to trying to figure out how to keep their kids alive one more day.

Even choosing where to put and where to point a camera can have a major influence on the audience's understanding of a news story. A camera placed into the middle of a group of people can make it appear that the event is well-attended and crowded; a camera set some distance away from that same group could show that there are actually very few people in it; and if the camera is turned away from the group that there aren't any people there at all. Each decision is deliberate, and each decision completely alters what the audience believes in the end.

So reporters must pick and choose what they'll do. Those choices influence the final outcome of a story. For example, if the reporter chooses to interview five people who are on one side of a story and only one on the other, this weights the story in favor of one side, the side that **appears** to have a majority. Or if rhe interviews all the people on one side as a group, which implies they're all the same, and all the people on the other side one on one, which implies they're important and have diverse views on the topic, this influences the final effect of the story on the audience. It implies that the opinions of the one on one people are the ones that should receive greater credence.

Many times a reporter's decisions are unconscious and automatic—that's the best way to tell the story. That's probably what happened in the Bosnia story. But occasionally a reporter will deliberately slant a story to give a certain point of view. After all, reporters are just as human, and they are just as susceptible to their own biases and prejudices as anyone.

Once the reporter is done, the story goes to the **editor**. Here a story may be approved as is, or rearranged, or even rewritten, to reflect how the **editor** thinks the story should be told.

Then the **publisher** may get involved. The publisher is the owner of the news organization and sets the tone. Everything must reflect the publisher's ideas and ideals. Some publishers are essentially hands off, leaving everything up to the managing editor, and setting a tone of "If it's true, run it." An example was Katherine Graham, the publisher of the

Washington Post during Watergate, the event that brought down President Nixon. She let Ben Bradlee, the executive editor, guide the story. She just insisted that the reporters, Bob Woodward and Carl Bernstein, get independent corroboration of anything they wanted to write. But once something was supported, she let it run. The effect was that the audience got verified facts to make a decision.

Other publishers are more hands on. An example is Rupert Murdoch, owner of News Corp., which owns such news organizations as Fox News Network on cable TV and the *Wall Street Journal* newspaper. Murdoch has set the tone of being politically conservative, and has hired Roger Ailes, the spinmeister of the Republican Party, as executive editor. If something is liberal or liberals support it, it's attacked, and if something is conservative or conservatives support it, it's extolled. Facts are less important than the slant that one can put on those facts. The effect is that the audience gets told how to regard the facts.

Another gatekeeper group is the **advertisers**. Because news organizations have to pay their way, and there's no possibility that newspaper subscriptions or cable fees can support a paper or a network on their own, news organizations are supported by advertisers who buy space or time. As can be expected, advertisers sometimes can tell a news organization, "We pay your bills, so do what's good for us and don't do what's bad for us." For example, a big advertiser might not like a story that's going to be done because it might reflect badly on that advertiser, the advertiser's products or the advertiser's business in general (e.g., the tobacco or oil industries), and that advertiser may threaten to pull its advertising if the story appears. This puts the news organization in a bind. It can either run the story in the public good and lose the money, or it can cut the story and keep getting the money. Publishers and editors end up weighing the factors, like how much money is involved and how badly they need it, and then they decide which way to go. Sometimes the story runs—and sometimes it doesn't.

In any case, what news consumers get is what these people, reporters, editors, publishers and advertisers, decide they will get. And consumers will probably never hear about what they decide not to cover. In this way, the gatekeepers may not tell us what to think, but they certainly tell us what to think about.

A final group that decides what's newsworthy is the **news consumers** themselves. They can control what appears in the news by deciding what to consume in the first place. Consumers are what news organizations need because that's what the organizations sell to advertisers—their audiences. So if a story type, like hard science, doesn't sell papers or get good ratings, then that type of story doesn't get much space or airtime. If, on the other hand, a story type like celebrity scandals sells a lot of papers or gets good ratings, then that's what news organizations devote large amounts of space and airtime to.

Until the 1980s, consumers didn't have as much power as they do now, especially with TV news. Prior to the 1980s, news divisions were considered loss leaders, something a network had because it was the right thing to do. The news wasn't supposed to turn a profit—that would be provided by the regular programming of sports, dramas, comedies, and game shows. However, with all the mergers of networks with regular business companies, like NBC with GE, the profit motivation of regular business, the requirement that everything turn a profit or get cut, became part of the business model for TV networks. This meant that the news divisions now had to turn a profit, and that meant keeping the audience happy and tuning in, in large numbers, to satisfy advertisers. Thus, there was less news in the public interest and more in what interested the public. And what interested the public seemed to be material that was more lightweight and ephemeral, or shocking and sensational.

Forms of News Writing

So how do audiences get the news? Let's start with print media. Print has two basic ways of writing their stories: inverted pyramid and feature. The inverted pyramid style puts all the basics of the story in the first paragraph. The paragraph gives the five Ws: who, what, where, when and why. Every paragraph of the story thereafter provides more and more detail about each of the Ws.

Feature writing, on the other hand, delivers the information as though it were a short story, with exposition, problem, a rising series of crises and complications, and a climax to deliver the what, where, when and why. The who, the people in the story, are presented as though they are characters rather than people, and they are usually presented as hero, villain and victims. This is the same format you find in fiction.

The inverted pyramid style is used for most hard news stories in newspapers and for news shorts (one to three paragraphs about an event or person) in magazines. This style allows the readers to get the basics of the event very quickly and decide if they want more details. If they want more details, they can continue reading and get more and more information. If not, they can simply go on to the next story. The style also has an advantage for the newspaper. If it runs out of room for any reason, such as needing space for an advertisement, it can simply cut paragraphs off the end of the story until it fits the available space without removing anything but the least important details.

Feature writing is used for magazine articles, television news, and newspaper columns. Because the format is that of a short story, feature writing is particularly good at building suspense and evoking emotion in the reader and viewer. Of course, that means that feature stories are less about information than they are about how the audience should feel about the information, and it is useful to get the audience to accept a point of view or to spur them to some kind of action. Issues such as the environment, spousal abuse, homelessness, disease, education, poverty and the like are often reported on using feature writing.

■ NEWS ORGANIZATIONS

Now let's look at **news organizations**. Different news organizations concentrate on different things.

Print Media

Newspapers are generally local or regional. Local papers are those for a small locale, like a single city and the area around it. They concentrate on stories of local interest, like local celebrities, schools, police and court reports, and other items that will be of interest in a small area. They also print editorials by local writers. They support themselves with subscriptions, advertising from local businesses such as supermarkets, car dealerships and restaurants, and the classified or want ads.

Regional papers have a larger circulation than local papers. They may cover the city of publication and the counties or even the neighboring states around it. Examples are the *Spokesman Review* out of Spokane, Washington, *The Seattle Times* and *The Oregonian* out of Portland, Oregon. These larger papers cover stories in their circulation area, and they often carry national news, but they do it with a regional slant, emphasizing how a national story could affect the local region. They also are more likely to carry nationally syndicated comic strips, advice columns, games like crosswords and Sudoku, and nationally known editorial columnists. They're supported by subscriptions and local, regional and national advertising.

There are also a few newspapers that are considered national, with circulation across the country. The most famous of these are *The New York Times, The Wall Street Journal* and *USA Today.*

Newspapers of this last type concentrate on stories of national interest like national, as opposed to regional or local, politics. They cover Washington, DC, rather than Olympia, Washington, or Pierre, South Dakota. They look at the national economy more than state or local economies, and they discuss national figures, people who are prominent in the minds of most of the country.

The New York Times is considered the "newspaper of record" for the country. If it appears in *The Times,* it's something that's important for the entire country to hear about. *The Wall Street Journal* is considered the same in the area of finance and the economy. And *USA Today* is simply the most popular newspaper in the country.

There are **news magazines**, but few are devoted to general news in the same way newspapers are. Examples are *Time, Newsweek* and *US News and World Report.*

Unlike newspapers, magazines don't come out every day, and therefore they're useless for breaking news (that is, happening while it's being reported). But they're great for in depth analysis and understanding events because the reporters have the time to dig for more information. Magazines have another advantage over newspapers. Unlike newspapers, which have to cover everything regardless of a reporter's personal knowledge, magazines tend to hire reporters with educational expertise and experience in certain areas, such as national and international politics, medicine, the environment, and business. Because of this expertise, they understand what they're reporting on better than newspaper reporters do.

Of course, just like newspapers, news magazines reflect the social or political slant of their publishers. For example, *Time Magazine* is generally considered more conservative on social and political stories than other magazines, and that slant appears in their reporting.

But as I said, there aren't many general news magazines. Most news magazines specialize in a certain category of story. For example, **Sports Illustrated** concentrates on sports, **Rolling Stone** on music and **People** on—well, people, especially celebrities. Again, magazines of this type have in depth stories written by experts in the field.

Broadcast Media

Television news comes in two types, local and national. **Local news** comes out of, naturally enough, local television stations, wherever they happen to be. They tend to cover local and regional news for the most part, with a short segment devoted to national stories.

There's a standard format that local TV news tends to follow. First they give the big local and regional stories, generally dealing with crime, fires (which doesn't have to be local; they occasionally will find a fire someplace else in the country, but they'll have a fire) and car accidents. This may end with a feel good, human interest story, like someone being rescued from a fire or helping the less fortunate. A short segment on national news follows. Then they present what a lot people tune in to see in the first place: the weather. Sports will follow, with a concentration on local, and if there are any, regional teams. Finally, there's a feel good, human interest puff piece.

In addition, local news programs tend to have what is called "happy talk" delivery. This approach has the news anchors and sports and weather anchors acting as though they are friends (whether they can stand each other or not) and chatting between news stories. During these unscripted chats, the anchors will often give a personal, emotional instant reaction to the story just completed or relate it in some way to their own lives. This can have two effects. First, it tells the audience that they should respond emotionally rather than intellectually to the story just reported. Second, it gives the audience a sense of personal connection with the anchors, as though the anchors were the audience's friends and neighbors who just happen to know things the audience doesn't and are sharing it. However, it could also have the effect of putting the news on the same level of importance to the audience as idle conversation (which happy talk is), and it does subtract valuable time from the coverage of news.

The alternative to local news is national and international news. There are two ways television audiences receive such news. The first, and oldest form, is **network news**. The Big Three networks, ABC, CBS and NBC, have had a nightly newscast almost from the beginning. In the beginning, it was just a talking head, a news presenter who read the news to a camera, essentially radio news with a camera. At first it was only fifteen minutes long, but in the late 1950s and early 1960s all three networks expanded their newscasts to thirty minutes during which they began adding the ways their audiences got news from other places: radio and movie theatre newsreels. The networks started sending out film cameras, not just reporters, to cover news events, and adding those visuals to their nightly news. They also started adding graphics, both text and animations, although at first they were quite amateurish looking and often didn't work. However, at least they were trying.

Then, in 1980, something new was added: **cable news**. That was the year that Ted Turner started CNN (Cable News Network), and twenty-four-hour a day news hit the nation. At first, Turner wanted to avoid the "cult of personality" that surrounded networks anchors like Chet Huntley, David Brinkley, and Walter Cronkite (for whom the term anchor was first coined). CNN didn't even identify its news anchors.

Many people wondered if there was enough news for a twenty-four-hour newscast. After all, didn't the networks cover everything important enough to know in their half-hour broadcasts? However, they didn't have to worry—like work, news (or what is perceived as news) expands to fill the amount of time available to present it.

National news, as the name implies, concentrates on national and international news. This usually consists of major disasters, like hurricanes, tornadoes, earthquakes, volcanic eruptions, national and international politics, war, famine and the like. Occasionally, there's a story that could be considered local, but it's put in the context that it could have national significance—say, as an example of things that are happening across the nation.

Since CNN began in 1980, other twenty-four-hour news networks have started up, like Fox News, MSNBC and ESPN, which concentrates on sports; CNBC, which concentrates on financial news; and the Weather Channel, which is all weather (of course).

Then there's **radio** news. There isn't as much radio news as there was in the past. Up until 1950, when TV took over the task, radio news was where people went when they didn't read newspapers. Anchors would read the stories they wrote over the air, and reporters went out in the field to do on the scene reports. There were also commentators who would put the news in context.

However, when TV came along, with its ability to actually show events, not just describe them, radio news hit a big decline. Today radio news, in the main, consists of a five-minute headline service at the top and bottom of each hour. There are few all-news radio networks, like National Public Radio, which isn't advertiser supported but supported by listeners and government grants.

Finally, there's probably the fastest growing source of news, the Internet. Even as newspapers shut down, they start up web sites containing their news stories. Virtually every news organization has a web site running its stories, often with video, and they even stream their newscasts live to consumers' computers and Smart phones. The sites usually have an archive of past stories, and invariably they have links to past stories, related stories, web sites with more information—much like newspapers use sidebars—and photos and videos.

Perhaps what makes Internet news so popular is its accessibility. You can get it on your computer anywhere you can get a Wi-Fi signal, and you can even get it on your cell phone. Any time you want to know what's happening, just log on.

Of course, another reason for the popularity of Internet news could be because a lot of it consists of blogs (blog is short for web log). Staffs of writers write some blogs, like the Drudge Report and Huffingtonpost.com, much like regular news organizations. But many are the personal blogs of individuals, and these express only the opinions of the authors. Anyone can start a blog, so anyone can consider oneself a reporter, writing about whatever rhe sees or experiences—or thinks. Thus, they aren't news, they're commentary. And yet readers regard them as news, not commentary.

Of course, Internet news does have a drawback. In the main it doesn't have reporters, people who go out and gather the information to turn into stories. Internet news is very dependent on other media, especially newspapers, for the news it reports. It gathers not the information, but the news stories that are already written, and then it either rewrites them or just copies them to a website. So as newspapers disappear, mostly because the Internet draws their readership away, it leaves one to wonder where the Internet will get its news.

Characteristics of Each Medium

Each medium has its own characteristics, and it can also have different effects on its audience than the other media. So let's take a look at that aspect.

First, **newspapers** are, of course, a print medium. For this reason, their coverage of any event is long form, in depth, and aimed at the audience's intellect. Long form simply means a newspaper story can be as long as it takes to cover the event to the satisfaction of the reporter, editor and publisher. This allows the reader to get a much more in depth understanding of the event because print can provide many more details than any other medium. And because it's in print, the approach is much more intellectual than in any other medium. It has all the rules of spelling, punctuation, grammar and syntax, and the organization of information is in linear fashion as sentences and paragraphs.

Television news, on the other hand, is short form, shallow, emotional. TV, especially network TV with only a half hour window, is limited in time. A common statement about TV versus newspapers is that there are more words on the front page of a newspaper than in an entire newscast, that TV is a headline service and thus has no choice but to be shallow. Many details have to be omitted, and analysis and context are missing, simply because there isn't enough time. You might think cable news would be able to avoid these problems, but in general they don't—their newscasts are just as short-form and shallow as the networks; they just present the same stories more often.

However, TV can do something because it uses video that newspapers can't—it can add an emotional component that print, because of its appeal to intellect, can't. There are times when that appeal to emotion has the greatest effect. For example, the 1960s was a turbulent time, and television's emotional coverage of it could bind the nation together or tear it apart. One example was the fight for civil rights. Newspapers could provide an intellectual appreciation for the arguments, but TV could show them. The assassination of President Kennedy shocked the nation, affecting even the newscasters who delivered the news, and the nation came together for four days of mourning. The Vietnam War tore the nation apart. It was called the living room war, because every night on the news people saw the war in all its horror on TV during dinner, as network newscasts played video of what the correspondents reported on. This came to a head when Walter Cronkite, CBS anchor and the most trusted man in America because he never let his own feelings influence how he reported the news, delivered one of the only editorials in his career as he spoke about Vietnam after being there. In this editorial, Cronkite said the U.S. should not be in Vietnam. The mood of the nation, divided and depressed, was reflected on TV and in the news. But then came the moon landing, seen live on TV by hundreds of millions of people. And many people said the landing and Cronkite's elated reaction saved the decade from being a complete disaster.

The thing is, not everything can, or should be emotional. We don't think in emotions. Emotions aren't logical or reasonable—they just are. And the fact that TV can so easily affect our emotions takes away our ability to think about problems and come up with reasonable solutions to the problems news reports present.

You may wonder why I place so much emphasis on Walter Cronkite. Well, it's because he was the last newsman to wield so much power over the national social story, and wield it so well. As the most trusted man in America, he could have let his own opinions affect most of the country, leading people to one side or the other of political or social debates. But he felt it was neither his job nor his place to use his power to promote his own agenda, and that's why people trusted him so much. His commentary on Vietnam was so powerful for that very reason—people knew it would take something monumental for him to break his hard and fast rule of objectivity. In fact, when Lyndon Johnson, President at that time, heard Cronkite's commentary, he thought to himself, *"If I've lost Cronkite, I've lost middle America,"* and he decided not to run for reelection. No broadcast journalist since has had, or earned, that kind of respect, especially as TV news has turned more and more away from the important and toward the trivial, letting the network bean counters instead of journalists decide what should go on the air.

Then there's **radio** news. Radio news is long or short, in depth or shallow, intellectual or extremely emotional, all depending on the station's format. For most stations that have music or talk as their formats, news reports are usually short, a minute or less in length, essentially providing headlines during the five minute news break. On the other hand, news radio can provide reports of great length and go into great depth, devoting ten or twenty or more minutes to covering a single story.

Radio news has a characteristic that doesn't plague the other media—it consists entirely of people talking. There are no images to affect our emotions, but there are also no images to hold our attention. Radio demands that the audience concentrate on listening to disembodied voices, which is often difficult since people are more used to being able to see who's talking to them, if it's to deliver the news. And many people simply aren't able or willing to concentrate.

And finally, there's news on the **Internet**. Although it's easily accessible, it's also fragmentary. As you read an article, which more often than not has come from a newspaper since Internet sites generally don't have reporters, you're always coming across links to other pages. And when you go to them, they also have links to other pages, which also have links to other pages, and if you follow those links you can't logically follow the original story—if you ever get back to the original story in the first place. To understand the news, you have to be able to follow the train of information and thoughts logically, and it's so easy to be distracted by these multiple layers of links to information that are only peripherally related to the original story. Thus, you may never get a clear idea of the reported event.

General Characteristics of News

There are some general characteristics of news that we should consider. The first of these is that news, especially television news, is **personalized**.

Most news stories revolve around people. For example, if a news organization wants to do a report on homelessness or a natural disaster or a war, it will typically locate and focus on one person or family involved in the event as the center of its story. This makes for interesting journalism that can increase ratings or circulation by putting a face, preferably an emotional one, on the story. Discussions of the impersonal forces of nature or society can't provide the same impact on the audience as a tear-stained face. However, it turns out that these real people are used to personify news stories by turning them into characters (and often caricatures) in a story—heroes, villains and victims—and presenting them with all the shallowness of emotion and thought that's the norm for characters. These people cannot be given any depth or individuality that are the hallmarks of persons because they aren't individuals in a news story—they're exemplars of the tens or hundreds or thousands of people also affected by the event. Personalizing an event reduces the important social, political and/or scientific problems that are in the background, and that perhaps are the cause, of the reported event to the level of a soap opera—all crisis and tears with no resolution. The two likely outcomes of personalization are that the audience dismisses the problems as only applicable for the characters in the story, and the audience doesn't see the social, political and/or scientific contexts of the problems that might suggest avenues of public action.

This approach could be based on the idea that one death is a tragedy and a million is a statistic, but the statistics may be more important than the tragedy, which is only a simplistic representation of the problem of the deaths. An example of this is the trials in which women who had received breast implants complained of health problems that they blamed on the implants. News coverage of the trials focused on the women and their suffering, often with one on one interviews with individual women that brought out their emotional reactions.

What were left out of virtually all the news reports were those aspects of the cases for which there was no face and no emotion—the science. Scientific explanations are confusing, hard to understand and boring for most of the news audience, certainly compared to a crying woman in pain. News organizations must avoid all three of those difficulties with science reporting if they want to hang onto their audiences. So the science got little coverage, even though the scientific evidence contradicted the women's anecdotal evidence, which is that they got the implants and then got sick. This could be a good example of false cause and effect—post hoc, ergo propter hoc, also known as "after this, therefore because of this." By the end of the trials, not only was Dow Chemical, the implant manufacturer, bankrupt, but everyone in country also knew how dangerous breast implants were—even though there was no scientific evidence for the danger.

Another characteristic of news is that it's **fragmented**. The daily time and cost demands of journalism, as well as the rapid rate of change that occurs in modern life, result in newspapers and broadcasts that are composed of a large number of brief, encapsulated stories, maybe three or four paragraphs or as little as twenty seconds long, which usually have little or no connection to each other. I saw a report on *NBC Nightly News* about flooding in Italy that consisted of a single video of a car being washed down a street along with the simple statement that there's flooding in Italy. It was a grand total of fifteen seconds long. So what do I know? There was a flood in Italy. I don't know why there was a flood, or how there was a flood, or how many people were affected in what way, only that there was a flood.

There's little room in a given report for perspective or to put it into the context of the rest of what's going on in the world. For example, reports on Somali pirates give no context of why or how such events could happen, such as the economic or political situation in Somalia, so we react to the event as though the pirates were straight out of *Pirates of the Caribbean* and are surprised to see the pirates attacking in speedboats instead of galleons.

Another contributor to the fragmentation of news is journalists' obsession with objectivity. Objectivity means the journalists don't inject their own opinions into the coverage of the stories they report. Instead, they just give the facts. But putting any given day's story in context—connecting it to other events going on at that time or in the past—requires a reporter to make decisions about which links are most important since it would be impossible to give all such links. Of course, such choices are subjective, based entirely on the reporter's opinions, and so they're avoided. Reporters typically get one comment from one side of the issue and a second comment from the other side. They put them together as if they were equally valid, and then they move on to the next assignment.

Judgment calls are the banes of objectivity. The thing is, not every point of view **is** valid. When all the evidence supports one point of view, and there's no evidence for the other, then even **saying** that would be considered subjective and a commentary on the issue, and thus it wouldn't be news, but an editorial.

For example, a news story that covers the birth status of President Barack Obama that gives equal time to each side implies that both points of view are valid, when one is clearly not. By implication, the story is giving equal status to both the so-called "birthers," who deny Obama is an American citizen with no evidence whatsoever, and those who accept the mountains of evidence that say he is a citizen,.

However, when there **is** evidence for multiple views, ignoring all but one would again be telling the audience what to believe instead of giving them the information they need to make their own decisions. But, again, leaving out context in an attempt to be "fair and balanced" can leave the audience with a distorted view. For example, several years ago there was a controversy over the use of alar, a chemical spray used on apples to help them stay fresh longer. Given equal weight were the contentions that alar causes cancer and that alar was virtually harmless. Left out of most reports was, once again, the science—that alar could indeed cause cancer in lab rats—if they ate several million times the amount the average person would get in twenty years of eating an apple a day. To include this fact in the stories would have been a judgment call that knocked down one point of view in favor of the other, and thus the story would have lacked "objectivity."

News is now also put in niches. That is, different news organizations aim their news at specific audiences: social and political conservatives, social and political liberals, sports fans, ecological promoters, science aficionados, etc. The delivery of news is also put in niches:

blogs, the Internet, tweets, cable, satellite radio, etc. Because of this, different audiences get different information, and thus they end up with different worldviews. When Walter Cronkite was "the most trusted man in America," he defined what he did as: "Journalism is telling people what they need to know." What he reported was what everybody knew, but today there is no one like him—no one voice for all.

Another aspect of the news is that it's **conventionalized**. This means that, over the years, news organizations have developed what might be called standard scenarios for various story subjects. Each scenario lays out the angle of the story, the kinds of facts and interviews the reporter should gather and the format of how the story should be delivered. All the reporter and/or editor need do is fill in the details of the scenario with the particulars of the event. For example, the typical scenario for reporting on natural or human-made disasters is to look for and report the opinions and perspectives of figures in authority. Those authorities are then asked a standard set of questions for which they often have a standard set of answers, and that comprises the report. For example, blanks to fill in when an airplane crashes include the FAA's level of involvement (e.g., "The FAA was quickly on the scene."); the status of the cockpit recorder (e.g., "the cockpit recorder [has been retrieved / has yet to be found (pick one)]"; and a feel-good ending (e.g., "the reason for this tragedy will be determined soon."). In other words, what happened is bad, but the authorities will sort it out. Reporters often unconsciously limit their thinking about the story to those conventions that allow for fill-in-the-blank journalism and give little attention to investigating any of a number of angles that a plane crash or a flood or a war might suggest, angles that might produce information different from that provided by officials. This leaves the audience comfortable that everything is in hand and there's nothing they need to do.

This may be why, when the authorities fail, the disaster seems so much worse. The government response to Hurricane Katrina is an example. The news filled in the blanks on the scenario labeled "Hurricane Story" and reported the hurricane hit, things are bad, X number of people have lost their homes, but the Federal Emergency Management Agency, FEMA, is on the way so everything is in hand. The scenario also caused reporters subconsciously to fall prey to stereotypes upon which such scenarios are often based. For example, when white refugees took food from flooded markets, it was "searching for food"; when black refugees took food from flooded markets, it was "looting." That element of the scenario comes from the race riots of the 1960s and later, in such places as Detroit and Watts in Los Angeles, where protests against racial injustice disintegrated into smashing storefronts and looting.

It was a few days before reality caught up with the convention and the news really started reporting that FEMA was screwing up **big** time, and the victims of Katrina were in big trouble. Even news organizations seemed surprised, except for a few reporters on the scene whose reports didn't fit the story and were discounted, and Internet stories and blogs, some of which were accurate but many of which were just plain wrong and sensationalized. However, as soon as news organizations realized that events weren't going the way they were supposed to according to the scenario, they jumped all over it. That news got out, causing people all over the country to mobilize on their own to help the victims, but days were wasted as the news conventionalized the situation, following the standard scenario for a disaster. A result of the poor reporting on Katrina has created a new scenario about reporting on such disasters, one in which the former automatic assumption of competence on the part of authorities such as FEMA has been replaced with an automatic assumption of **in**competence that FEMA must counter, an assumption just as unfair as the former.

The cultural effect of news produced according to these conventions is daily reassurance by the media that the system works if those in power are allowed to do their jobs. Any suggestions about opportunities for people to get involved are suppressed as reporters serve those in authority as "stenographers with amnesia." This really became evident as the United States rushed into the war in Iraq. Reporters simply parroted the line from the White House about weapons of mass destruction, about Saddam Hussein being involved in the 9/11 attacks on New York's World Trade Towers and trying to buy the materials to make atomic bombs, and about Iraq having biological weapons. They didn't ask the questions they should have. In the following years, these same reporters admitted as much, berating themselves for failing in their purpose—to investigate the facts and report them, to find out if the "facts" the White House was feeding them were indeed facts, and to give the public the information they needed to make good decisions.

■ SUMMARY

We have a tradition in this country of being blessed with a free press. But what does that mean? It's not free in the sense of money because we have to pay for it in one way or another. We pay for a subscription or we pay higher prices for what we buy from advertisers. So maybe what's free is that journalists are free to print what they like. And why are they free to print what they like? Because it's in the public interest. In Terry Pratchett's brilliant satire *The Truth* about the creation of the first journalist and his newspaper on Discworld (a flat world riding on the backs of four elephants that stand on a giant space-ranging turtle), he points out the quandaries that journalists and news consumers face every day: What's in the public interest doesn't seem to be what the public's interested in, which mainly seem to be human interest stories. So there's what the people are interested in, and human interest stories, which is what humans are interested in, and the public interest, which no one is interested in. Except, of course, the public. Which apparently isn't the same as people and humans.

Getting complicated, isn't it? Does that mean that the public is a different thing from the people you just see walking around? That the public thinks big, sensible measured thoughts while **people** run around being silly? It's interesting to note though that intelligent people are capable of really stupid ideas.

What it comes down to is that people like to be told what they already know. They get uncomfortable when you tell them new things, because new things aren't what they expect. The old saw about news—that a dog biting a man isn't news, but a man biting a dog is—isn't true. People like to know that a dog will bite a man. That's what dogs **do**; it's expected and doesn't upset their worldview. "They don't want to know that a man bites a dog because the world isn't supposed to happen like that. In short, what people think they want is news, but what they really crave is olds." (Pratchett, *The Truth*, 79)

Something **really** new changes the stories by which we live our lives. We already know that hurricanes cause great destruction and flooding, that wars cause casualties, that tornadoes tear houses apart. There's nothing new there. But if a tornado put a house back together? That would be **real** news—and it would really upset people because it violates the rules—that's not how the world works. The stories tell us so.

CONCLUSION

So we have completed our journey through the millennia, examining the ways humans communicate, from talking to tweeting, and how, as the way humans communicate change, so do the societies in which they live. Every time a new medium of communication arose, from the printing press to the smartphone, it altered the society possessing it: it changed the way that society told its stories, the stories through which it understood the world and people's place within it, and thus changed the stories themselves.

Talking was personal and face to face, society comprised of the local village of people living together and sharing their stories. Writing removed the need for personal contact to communicate, and society became stratified. Printing allowed communication with hundreds and thousands of people that the author would never see or know, separated from them by miles and by years, and as knowledge spread, society turned away from superstition and myth and created new stories to explain the world. Radio instantly carried voices around the world, and the world shared its stories. Movies made a society's stories real, and created new stories woven into the fabric of people's realities. Television brought all other media together and brought the world into people's living rooms. And modern media, especially the internet, have turned society inward on itself, with people once again living in villages, but virtual villages in cyberspace, face to face contact replaced with surrogate contact through devices.

So where do we go from here? As is obvious from our exploration of the creation of the media, it's impossible to predict what apparently random and unrelated bits and pieces someone will bring together to create the next new thing. Who could have guessed that water-powered pipe organs would lead to computers, or that a desire to make gas lighting brighter would lead to lasers? Maybe someday someone will put together a fishbowl, a bathmat and a powerful laxative and create a new revolution in communication. Until then, people will continue to communicate through every means available, because that's what people do: they are *pans narrans*—the storytelling chimps.

BIBLIOGRAPHY

Aberth, John. 2005. *The Black Death: The great mortality of 1348–1350: A brief history with documents.* Boston, MA: Bedford/St. Martin's.

Americanrhetoric.com/speeches/newtonminow.htm

Baran, S. 2010. *Introduction to mass communication.* Boston: McGraw-Hill.

Bovee, C. L., and W. F. Arens. 1992. *Contemporary advertising.* Boston: Richard D. Irwin, Inc.

Brooks, T., and E. Marsh, 1999. *The complete directory to prime time network and cable TV shows.* New York: Ballantine.

Burke, J. 1995. *Connections.* Boston: Little, Brown and Company.

Burke, J. 1985. *The day the universe changed.* Boston: Little, Brown and Company.

Byerly, C. M. 1993. Toward a Comprehensive History of Public Relations. Paper presented to Public Relation Division at the Annual meeting of the Association for Education in Journalism and Mass Communication.

Carroll, L. 1960. *Alice in Wonderland.* New York: New American Library.

Cross, D. W. 1983. *Media speak: How television makes up your mind.* New York: New American Library.

Cross, D. W. 1979. *Word abuse.* New Castle, DE: Coward, McCann & Geoghegan, Inc.

de Tocqueville, A. 1956. *Democracy in America.* Trans. By Richard D. Heffner. New York: New American Library.

Edwards, B. 2004. *Edward R. Murrow and the birth of broadcast journalism.* Hoboken, NJ: John Wiley & Sons.

Folkerts, J. et al. 2009. *Voices of a nation: A history of mass media in the United States.* Boston: Allyn and Bacon.

Gruppe, H. E. 1979. *The frigates.* Alexandria, VA: Time-Life Books.

Hazard, T. R. 1915. *The Jonny-cake Papers of "Shepherd Tom,": Together with reminiscences of Narragansett schools of former days.* Boston: Printed for the subscribers.

Holy Bible, King James Version. 1964. Grand Rapids, MI: Zondervan Publishing.

Kemp, Barry J. 2003. *Ancient Egypt: Anatomy of a civilization.* London; New York: Routledge.

Koscielniak, Bruce. 2003. *Johann Gutenberg and the amazing printing press.* Boston: Houghton Mifflin Co.

Leakey, R., and R. Lewin. 1978. *People of the lake.* New York: Avon Books.

Lewis, Tom. 1991. *Empire of the air: The men who made radio.* New York: Edward Burlingame Books.

MacLeod, R. ed. 2004. *The Library of Alexandria: Centre of learning in the ancient world.* London; New York: I.B. Tauris.

Mannix, D. P. 1958. *Those about to die.* New York: Random House.

Meyer, H. 1971. *A history of electricity and magnetism.* Cambridge, MS: MIT Press.

Movie Times, The. 2011. www.the-movie-times.com/thrsdir/alltime.mv?domestic+ByDG, retrieved 21 Jan 2011.

Museum of Broadcast Communication. www.museum.tv

Museum of Learning. www.museumstuff.com/learn/topics/illuminated_manuscript

Postman, N. 1985. *Amusing ourselves to death.* New York: Penguin Group.

Pratchett, T., I. Stewart, and J. Cohen. 1999. *The science of Diskworld.* London: Edbury.

Pratchett, T., I. Stewart, and J. Cohen. 2002. *The science of Diskworld II.* London: Edbury.

Pratchett, T. 2001. *Thief of time.* New York: HarperCollins Books.

Pratchett, T. 2000. *The truth.* New York: HarperCollins Books.

Remini, R. V. 1966. *Andrew Jackson.* New York: Twayne.

Remini, R. V. 1981. *Andrew Jackson and the course of American freedom.* Vol. II. New York: Harper and Row.

Rowan University Communication Institute. 2000. *A brief history of public relations.*

Sagan, C., and A. Druyan. 1992. *Shadows of forgotten ancestors.* New York: Century Books.

Shulman, A., and R. Youman. 1964. *The golden age of television.* New York: Bonanza Books.

Stampp, K. M. 1956. *The peculiar institution: Slavery in the Ante-Bellum South.* New York: Vintage Books.

Tannen, D. 1990. *You just don't understand.* New York: Ballantine Books.

Wasson, J. 1977. Graduate class in Elizabethan Theatre. Washington State University.

Whitman, W. 1940. *Jefferson's letters.* Eau Claire, WI: E. M. Hale & Co.